Handbook of Japanese Popular Culture

Handbook of Japanese Popular Culture

EDITED BY

RICHARD GID POWERS

AND

HIDETOSHI KATO

ASSOCIATE EDITOR
BRUCE STRONACH

GREENWOOD PRESS

New York

Westport, Connecticut

London

Library of Congress Cataloging-in-Publication Data

Handbook of Japanese popular culture.

Bibliography: p.
Includes index.
1. Japan—Popular culture.   2. Japan—Civilization—
1945– . I. Powers, Richard Gid, 1944– .
II. Katō, Hidetoshi, 1930– . III. Stronach, Bruce.
DS822.5.H347   1989   952.04′8   87–7586
ISBN 0–313–23922–3 (lib. bdg. : alk. paper)

British Library Cataloguing in Publication Data is available.

Library of Congress Catalog Card Number: 87–7586
ISBN: 0–313–23922–3

First published in 1989

Greenwood Press, Inc.
88 Post Road West, Westport, Connecticut 06881

Printed in the United States of America

The paper used in this book complies with the
Permanent Paper Standard issued by the National
Information Standards Organization (Z39.48–1984).

10 9 8 7 6 5 4 3 2 1

Contents

Introduction

RICHARD GID POWERS

This *Handbook of Japanese Popular Culture* provides a convenient and efficient guide to the prevalent ways of life, recreations, and artistic creations of contemporary Japan. It is designed to be useful to the general reader as well as the specialist in Japanese culture. The fields covered are those that have been of relatively durable interest to the Japanese, such as sports, science fiction, and popular music, but they do not neglect those passing fads and fancies that provide variety and surprise to what otherwise would be a dreary succession of work and days. Each essay follows the same format: a survey of the historical development of the topic under discussion, with special attention to the most useful published works in the field, followed by a guide to the research collections and reference works that should be consulted for deeper knowledge of the subject. All sources mentioned are listed in bibliographies following each chapter.

While all the essays in this volume are the work of specialists in the field, the impulse that led to this *Handbook* was decidedly that of an amateur in the study of Japan, namely, myself. The project originated in the difficulty I had preparing myself for a year teaching American popular culture at the University of Hiroshima. I could find no practical way of quickly acquiring the information that would have made my stay more profitable (or at any rate less perplexing). Thus, when Greenwood Press decided to publish selected volumes on national popular cultures modeled on the three-volume *Handbook of American Popular Culture* edited by M. Thomas Inge, and contacted me regarding a Japanese volume, I thought a book like this one would satisfy a need felt by others besides myself.

By that time I had acquired some experience in the study of international popular culture. I was editor of the *Journal of International Popular Culture*, for which I supervised studies of the popular cultures of India, Poland, and the

Philippines. It was clear to me that the preoccupations of American students of popular culture—the relationship between the high and popular arts, the impact of the media of communications on the artist and the audience, and the problematic existence of a popular aesthetic—were not necessarily relevant once the study of popular culture passed beyond the national borders. Thus, I chose to collaborate in this venture with the leading Japanese expert on Japanese popular culture, Hidetoshi Kato, as coeditor, and to see that the subjects, structure, and methods of the volume would reflect the experience of scholars who had made the study of Japan their life work. I saw my role as that of a common reader, making sure that the work of the specialists would be interesting to the wider audience, as well as that of a mediator between them and the requirements of American publishing. (I confess, however, to having been less successful than I had hoped in such mediation, and I take responsibility for delays that stretched to four years between the completion of the essays and publication. But now I can add one more item to Cyril Connolly's list of the three delusions that tempt all men: falling in love, editing a magazine, and trying to earn a living by raising chickens.)

And yet, the reactions of a non-specialist to the results of this enterprise also seem to me to be of more than personal interest, because the nature of Japanese popular culture, as revealed in these studies, is a comment on American popular culture too significant to be gainsaid or ignored. In fact, the experience of editing this *Handbook* suggests that, far from serving as a model for the study of international popular culture, American popular culture studies should rather be regarded as a special case, even an aberration.

A knowledge of international popular culture also raises the possibility that the American study of popular culture, as a separate discipline with its own unique subject matter and methodology, has been largely a response to peculiar conditions in American intellectual life and intellectual politics. Those conditions seem to belong to the past, as probably, a special phase of American cultural development, one characterized by the struggle of an entrenched intellectual elite, largely academic, to hold onto a concept of culture that was outmoded, irrelevant, and, most important, without any organic relationship to the realities of American life. This notion of culture was the selective tradition, "the best that has been thought and said," in Matthew Arnold's somewhat hackneyed formulation. This was an idealized house of intellect furnished, for the most part, with European imports, and, most of all, insistently respectable, aloof from the vulgarities and crudities of life as suffered and enjoyed.

The revolt against the selective tradition can be seen as early as the rebellion of Jonathan Edwards's congregation against his authoritarian rule, in the popular support for Andrew Jackson in his teapot tempest with Harvard University, in Van Wyck Brooks's early writings, Constance Rourke's and Henry Nash Smith's research, and in other outbreaks of popular resentment against the hegemony of the entrenched American intellectual aristocracy.

It was in these circumstances that there emerged first an American studies movement in the 1950s and then a popular studies movement as a discrete discipline in the 1970s, with the organization of the Popular Culture Association as an offshoot of the American Studies Association. Both were, in reality, protests against unrealistically restrictive boundaries on the subject matter and methodology held appropriate for the study of culture in America. Thus, at the outset, there was understandably great interest in defining these fields and marking the boundaries that set them off from the parent disciplines of American history and literature.

Readers wishing to follow the course of this dispute, some of it interesting, much of it not, are referred to the back volumes of the *Journal of Popular Culture* and to the many volumes published by the Popular Press at Bowling Green. Much of this effort seems less worthwhile now than it did at the time, because the element linking the materials embraced by the popular studies movement was their exclusion by the guardians of a "great tradition." As the mainstream disciplines became less exclusive (or more promiscuous), the raison d'être for a defiantly separatist study of popular culture came to seem less compelling.

Perhaps the example and pressure of the popular studies movement helped force American historians and literary scholars to broaden their perspective to include popular arts and entertainment. But a more compelling motive was surely the realization that it was self-defeating for scholars to deny themselves access to any type of information or experience if the goal were, in the words of Sinclair Lewis's ever-ardent Carol Kennicott, "a more conscious life."

The expertise of the Japanologists in this volume (and of others in the discipline) suggests that whatever justification there once may have been for the study of popular culture as a special discipline, it no longer applies. Scholars trained in Japanese literature and history are at ease using social scientific perspectives to explore and analyze the significance of popular materials. Whatever remains of the vestigial barrier between the serious and the popular has been brushed aside within the field of Japanese studies, as it should be by anyone attracted to the fascinating variety and unity of that nation, its culture, and history.

A knowledge of popular culture limited to the American variety will make the international quality of Japanese popular culture seem remarkable. The Japanese strategy for integrating the native and the imported aspects of their popular culture, while retaining the "foreign" label on the imports, is remarkably precise and well developed. An acquaintance with worldwide popular culture, however, suggests it is not Japanese popular culture that is unusual for its large proportion of imported components or the strategies it has evolved for dealing with them. Most countries find their popular cultures largely, even overwhelmingly, composed of materials developed abroad and, though altered for local consumption, still identifiably non-native. The great exception is the United States.

American popular culture is largely, almost exclusively, home grown. What popular culture *is* imported has usually been formulated in the American style (British rock) or tailored to suit American tastes. This means that while the impact of popular culture around the globe has been to "internationalize" the popular consciousness, at least to the extent of reminding the public that there is a world outside the national boundaries, popular culture has had the opposite effect on the American public. Popular culture has insulated the American public from any sense of belonging to an international community. What observers such as Sanford J. Ungar have called America's "estrangement" from the world can thus be observed on the most basic level in the American popular arts and entertainments. Nothing reveals the difference between America and most other nations more than popular culture, and perhaps this difference is symptomatic of much greater and deeper differences. In other nations popular culture fosters a consciousness of being part of the world; in the United States it creates a feeling of being apart from, and perhaps above, the international community.

Theodore C. Bestor's essay on "Lifestyles and Popular Culture in Urban Japan" demonstrates the extent to which the study of Japanese popular culture has been integrated within a unified approach to Japanese history and society. He gives a panorama of research on "the stuff and texture of the everyday lives of the common people in urban Japan" and guides the reader through the development of urban life in Japan from the Heian period to the present, surveying the scholarship on a broad range of aspects of contemporary urban life: the traditional arts and popular culture in the lives of today's Japanese; youth culture and education; lifestyles, life stages, and careers; community life and interpersonal relations; and mass society and the search for national and personal identity.

The Japanese fascination with their own national identity has produced a literature of self-reflexive studies (*Nihonjinron*) so extensive as to constitute a branch of popular culture in itself. This includes the travel guides to Japan, produced by this nation for whom internal tourism is another popular obsession. In his essay Bestor provides a guide to such attempts by the Japanese to explain themselves to themselves, a revealing monologue for the foreign eavesdropper.

Japan is as subject as any country to the inexorable laws of supply and demand, particularly with respect to urban space. ("They aren't making any more land," as the saying goes.) The characteristic talent of the Japanese to extract an aesthetic order out of the environment has to war with the brutal dictates of the economic imperative to utilize space in the most profitable manner and the need to cope with the demands of communication and transportation in the ensuing crush. Since modern urban development has been so destructive to traditional ideas of proper form in landscape and architectural design, resistance movements have appeared dedicated to restoring architectural traditions in the uncongenial modern setting.

The architectural kaleidoscope that pummels the retina in the contemporary Japanese city is Renato A. Pirotta's subject. He discusses Japanese environmental design as an adaptation of foreign ideas to the Japanese aesthetic, from the early Chinese ideas of the Heian period through the English influences of the Meiji period and the impact of America's version of the International Style after World War II. This clash has provoked an interesting tradition of manifestos, in which

Japanese architects in cyclic fashion affirm and reject their architectural heritage, producing a continuing debate on the nature of Japanese architectural design.

As religion loses its juridical, political, scientific, and metaphysical significance, and to a great extent its ethical impact as well, a decline in its influence is observable in every modern society. The result is a search for ways to restore religion's lost cultural role. This can take the form of fundamentalism or of "New Religion." It is this latter phenomenon that is explored by H. Byron Earhart.

Japanese culture is so fecund in spawning new religions that its religiosity, like that of America, can be considered a part of popular culture. Earhart firmly locates the "Japanese New Religions" of the last century and a half within Japan's ancient religious traditions of Shinto, Buddhism, and folk religions. He demonstrates how such New Religions as Tenrikyo and Shinkyo arose as "revitalizing" forces in Japanese culture and, as is customary in Japanese society, soon became permanent "socioreligious organizations."

The prototypical popular Japanese performing arts are the comic dialogues (*manzai*) and comic storytelling (*rakugo*) of Japanese vaudeville (*yose*). Muneo Jay Yoshikawa traces the history and literature of these classic forms of popular Japanese theater and discusses their survival, in altered form, on radio and television and their revival as "urban folk" entertainment in forms that sometimes involve a return to their ancient roots.

The performing arts emerge out of prayer and ritual and eventually develop into a symbolic representation of the community. The storehouse of stock characters, situations, and modes of presentation contained within the popular theater is grist for the mill of the entertainment industry. Folk theater is interesting, indeed intelligible, only to the community that gives it birth. The professional entertainers who exist even in folk communities are part of that community, so the communication in folk art, so to speak, is "of, by, and for" the people. The modern entertainment industry, on the other hand, must deal with a public that is no longer a community in the original sense of the word, but seeks diversion and, often, a vicarious and artificial sense of community. Popular entertainment, particularly on television, is truly a wasteland in T. S. Eliot's sense of the term as well as Newton Minow's: a junk heap populated with fragments of once-vigorous cultural forms, now detached from their communities and belief systems and turned into mindless diversions, sometimes narcotic, other times stimulant.

Japanese film has achieved worldwide renown through the achievements of such directors as Akira Kurosawa. It is also well known for its children's cartoons. Keiko I. McDonald's essay surveys the less familiar but more popular film entertainments of Japan.

The popular film industry, which produces movies for the home market, faces the same uncertain future, due to cable and video cassette competition, as the American industry. It is fighting back in much the same way: big-budget special effects extravaganzas and also, owing to the peculiarities of Japanese censorship, soft core pornography. The Japanese film industry followed much the same development as the American industry, influenced in some degree by the international industry, but even more by the intrinsic difficulty of solving the technical problems of film production and distribution and of mastering the transition from stage to film drama. One contrast between Western films and the Japanese movie industry is in the romantic stereotype of the film heroine. Japanese movies have seen her status shift from "wife" to the "object of man's affections"—in other words, a sex object. The place of women in Japanese (or any other) society is far from ideal, but the ideal from which women's status diverges and the way it diverges are startlingly different from the situation in the West. The popular film, which is in large part a vehicle for the dreams and fantasies of the feminine audience, is thus a valuable window into this disturbed and disturbing situation.

Japanese electronics now dominate the world market, and Bruce Stronach shows how they have had a powerful impact on Japanese culture as well. Japan's culture today is very thoroughly permeated with the influence of the tube. For much of the public, the high culture of old Japan is most often encountered as carefully staged television entertainment; many traditional festivals and performances are kept alive for the purpose of television spectaculars in which the entire nation participates in the modern mode: by passively watching as performers enact "being Japanese" for the edification of the nation. Besides the enormous mass of Japanese-created programing (which forms the preponderance of television entertainment), the Japanese also watch many American programs, mainly hit shows with expensive production values. Japan's acceptance of foreign programing conforms more to the international norm than to American practice. Japanese television also provides the internationally minded Japanese with a large amount of programing about foreign nations and foreigners, although Stronach points out that this is often entertainment masquerading as education, with the approach tailored to suit Japanese stereotypes of themselves and the rest of the world. His essay surveys the research on the history and development of Japanese telecasting and guides the reader through scholarship that uses the nation's viewing habits to analyze the popular consciousness.

William R. May discusses sports as an aspect of the modernization of Japanese society. He surveys the history of play and of the physical disciplines in historical Japan and outlines the research on this aspect of contemporary Japanese culture.

The Japanese martial arts are one of the few facets of Japanese popular culture to attain international popularity, although one might distinguish between the impact of the Hong Kong kung-fu movies (and their influence on show business dance) and the somewhat more cultic popularity of Japanese-style judo, kendo, and karate, since the Japanese martial arts' more recherché and inaccessible aspects almost disqualify them from being considered popular culture. The sustained popularity of such foreign sports as soccer, baseball, and volleyball, as well as the perhaps more faddish vogue of bowling and golf, reveals the Japanese fascination with the deliberately *unassimilated* varieties of foreign cultures.

Sometimes, as in the case of ''Japanese'' tennis, this goes so far as to preserve the purity of foreign imports after they have disappeared or been radically modified in their homelands. (In Japanese schools, children are taught a form of tennis with a soft ball and a carpet-beater-shaped racquet that is closer to the nineteenth-century game than to today's.) Similarly, Japanese university students participate in riding, yachting, and *wandervogel* (mountain climbing) clubs, all with scrupulous regard to authenticity in costume, etiquette, and (somewhat Japanized) jargon.

Linda Fujie evaluates the competing definitions of ''popular music'' before settling on a notion of ''popular musics'' as a workable solution, since among the Japanese so many different styles of music are popular, ranging from *gunka* and *enka* to ''Japanese Pops'' and ''New Music.'' She analyzes the specific musical characteristics and performance styles that are common to most popular music in Japan and discusses some of the ways in which this music is presented to the public: the Red-White song competition on television on New Year's Eve, the barroom *karaoke* (sing-along) machines, and the emergence of *kawaiko-chan* (cute) girl singers.

If music is the most universal language, it is also the one most intimately connected to the characteristic emotions and feelings of a people. What is not universal is the particular rapport that the sound evokes in a nation: All popular music is in some degree ''soul'' music, though this is more or less cynically manipulated by the entertainment industry.

But if popular music by definition touches on the feelings of the masses, also by definition it is a commercial product. While Japan both borrows and adapts much Western music, Fujie explores popular music produced in its original form by the Japanese record industry. She describes the peculiar vocal style beloved of the Japanese, redolent of falsetto and vibrato to the point of visibly quivering throats as a sine qua non for popular vocalists. She shows the historical sources of current-day popular music in Japan and its modernization today by use of the traditional Japanese scales performed on Western instruments. The roots of *enka* in the political movement of the early Meiji also reveal an interesting parallel between Japanese music and the populist tradition of modern folk music in the United States.

Fujie's essay explores other fascinating aspects of the contemporary Japanese character: the special relationship between the visual and oral elements of contemporary popular music in Japan that is quite different from the American presentation of popular songs on music video; the rise of the *karaoke* as an ingenious adaptation of popular music that caters to the urge to perform that is so much a part of the Japanese personality; the demand of Japanese tourists in the United States for Japanese performers in such places as Las Vegas, where some Japanese singers specialize in performing before audiences of their compatriots.

Though popular around the world, there is no country where comics are as popular as in Japan, where some comic periodicals have circulations in the millions and cartoonists earn some of the highest salaries in the nation. Here is an aspect of Japanese culture that deserves—and has received, as John Lent's essay shows—serious attention.

Comics are a form of modern popular culture with long antecedents in Japanese history. Japan may, in fact, have produced the world's first comic book, perhaps as early as 1702, in the form of the popular woodblock prints known as *ukiyoe*. The introduction of Western cartoons to Japan early in the Meiji period released a burst of creativity by alerting Japanese cartoon artists to hitherto unsuspected possibilities in their native cartoon tradition. In fact, today's comics are so idiosyncratically Japanese that it is probably a mistake to make too much of the diffusion of Western influences. More important than American correspondences are those with other cultures—Latin American and Philippine, for example— that use the comic form to retell folk legends in a manner closer to the oral tradition (due, perhaps, to the atmosphere created by balloons and hand lettering) than pure print texts. Nonetheless, there is a long history of interaction between British and American comics and the Japanese, and Lent traces this history and discusses the research that has been done in this field, presenting evidence that Japanese comics *do* draw on important cultural forces. One instance is the censorship that the comics had to endure during World War II, when censors forced the magazines to restrict themselves to patriotic themes. Likewise, both Japanese and American propagandists tried to capitalize on comics' wide readership among the troops, as both used them in efforts to win over the hearts and minds of Japanese soldiers. The obvious failure of American efforts, despite wide readership among Japanese troops, again should caution against simplistic "conveyer belt" theories of media influence.

Science fiction has rallied fans into fandom organizations around the world. With their bent for group dynamics, the Japanese have carried this tendency to extremes, as Elizabeth Anne Hull and Mark Siegel demonstrate in their guide to Japanese science fiction and its fans.

At its best, science fiction communicates a strong sense of human possibility and potential, an enlargement of life, that separates it from other popular formulas that diminish life by resolving "problems" by means of trite "secrets" that explain everything. (Popular entertainment depends on suspense and its resolution to sustain interest, since formulas repel the personal involvement that engages the audience in serious art.) Japan's writers remain drawn to Western science fiction and its forms, but, as Japanese critics themselves note, they less frequently use science fiction to explore the social forms and mores of their own culture. Perhaps this reflects Japanese culture's characteristic distinction between *wants* and *needs*. A playful attitude toward superficial wants is tolerated, but a more respectful attitude is required toward the traditional ways Japan has dealt with more basic and universal human needs.

It is not surprising that a country like the United States should turn crime into popular entertainment. America's high crime rate is unsettling to the public, which has been conditioned by both national history and national culture to see crime as a test of strength between the forces of law and lawlessness. Conditions make it inevitable that crime in America should be politicized, since lawlessness forces Americans to evaluate the strength of the bonds that hold them within the community. After all, American public officials swear allegiance to the Constitution, and the original text of that legal document is one of the attractions drawing tourists to official Washington. (Another is the headquarters of the Federal Bureau of Investigation.) It is therefore taken for granted by American students of popular culture that crime entertainment touches on important American attitudes and values; thus, Rambo, Dirty Harry, and their ever-recurring clones are made to provide support for whatever point is being made about the defects bedeviling American civilization.

The hardly less avid interest in crime entertainment in law-abiding nations like Japan and England might cast doubt on any assumed connection between a readiness to break the law in real life and a fascination with fictional crime entertainment. One explanation is that crime entertainment may exploit one society's readiness to commit real crimes, while in another culture, crime entertainment may be entirely an escape, wholly unrelated to the values that govern behavior. It is perhaps relevant that a noted Japanese criminologist politely informed me that Durkheim's theories about the role of punishment in producing social solidarity were very good explanations of *French* crime and punishment; he intended thus to express his skepticism that the great French savant had provided a *universal* explanation of crime and punishment.

There are perhaps two main forms of crime entertainment: the mystery, which features a rational attempt to unravel a puzzle, and the action detective story, which is essentially a prolonged chase, with the identity of the criminal usually no secret from the very beginning. (Of course, there are all manner of permutations within these two basic types.) The police procedural is one example that, in its classic form, can be pure characterization and setting, with hardly any element of plot suspense. As Kazuo Yoshida demonstrates in his essay on Japanese detective stories, all of these forms have appeared in Japan, but to the Japanese the essence of the detective story is the solving of the logical puzzle. One suspects that the emotional fuel of punishing the transgressor is a minor factor in the popularity of the Japanese formula, although violence that is extreme by Western standards is certainly common in Japanese crime entertainment. The continuing influence of Western detective writing on authors and audiences in such a law-abiding nation also suggests that crime entertainment's hold on the Japanese is different from its attraction to Westerners, and that its emotional roots in Japan are more shallow than in the West.

Handbook of Japanese Popular Culture concludes with Hidetoshi Kato's survey of the history of Japanese popular culture studies, a field that he himself did much to define and develop. He points out the unique features of Japanese popular culture, among them Japan's success in achieving the world's highest literacy rate by the nineteenth century, thus creating the world's earliest "mass audience." He discusses the wide dissemination of popular culture throughout Japan as an aspect of the country's social democracy, another area in which Japan has advanced beyond the rest of the world. He also raises the provocative possibility that Japan's isolation created a surplus of energy that found its release in cultural rather than economic development.

Kato surveys and evaluates the classic studies of Japanese popular culture by such figures as Yanagita, Kon, Gonda, and Ohya, and demonstrates that a knowledge of the intellectual tradition of popular culture studies is essential for any further work in the field. He discusses some of the more recent movements in popular culture studies, such as Tsurumi's "Science of Thought" and new advances in sociological and anthropological methodologies. His conclusion is that "Japanaese popular culture is unique, and its research methodology requires that special consideration be given to this singularity." His essay provides a solid grounding for any serious investigation of scholarship on Japanese popular culture.

This *Handbook** of Japanese popular culture studies should serve as a touchstone for specialists, and can be an important step up the Oriental Parnassus for novices who might also wish to consult such works as Oliver Statler's *All-Japan Catalog* or the all-inclusive nine-volume *Kodansha Encyclopedia of Japan*. For a non-Japanese this *Handbook* should be more proof that nothing alien can be excluded from a vision that is truly humane. While the book is intended, of course, as a window into Japanese culture, it can also serve, depending on the angle of vision, as a looking glass in which the observer can glimpse a reflected image of himself against a setting strange in its differences, yet nevertheless familiar enough to function as a conceivable alternative to the environs in which the accident of birth has cast him, for better—or for worse.

* Editor's note: Due to delays in the publication of this *Handbook*, for which this editor takes full responsibility, and over which the authors had no control, these bibliographies, with minor updatings, cover only works published before 1985. (RGP)

Some Thoughts on Japanese Popular Culture

HIDETOSHI KATO

The term "popular" is not popular in Japan. To be more precise, there is no proper Japanese word that corresponds to "popular" in English, especially in its American usage and, more particularly, in the context of "popular culture."

Of course, a Japanese scholar, if he or she is given the English term "popular culture" to translate into Japanese, would, generally speaking, supply *taishu bunka*[1] without hesitation; but, strangely enough, if *taishu bunka* had to be translated into English, there is no doubt it would then find its equivalent as "mass culture."

Very close to this cluster of meanings, Japanese scholars often use such words as *minshu bunka*[2] and *minzoku bunka*[3] but the former means "public culture" and the latter means "folk culture." But these terminologies, on the contrary, cannot be equated with the American usage of "popular culture." Not only in the study of "popular culture" in general, but also in particular areas of "popular culture," the Japanese find it rather difficult to communicate what Americans mean by "popular" in the Japanese language. For example, what Americans call "popular songs" can be translated only as *ryukoka*,[4] of which the reverse literary translation is "temporarily widespread songs" or "updated but soon obsolete songs." Needless to say, such a reverse translation will clearly cause semantic difficulties. Therefore, it was a natural trend among contemporary Japanese artists to refer to what Americans labelled "pop art" simply as *poppu ato*, instead of attempting the desperate task of translation.

As a common-sense matter of ethnomethodology, each culture has its own cluster of meanings denoting or connoting its own references, and "popular culture" in its American usage is no exception. In this volume, the authors were well aware of such basic cultural differences, and so when they discuss "Japanese popular culture,'' they more or less mean *taishu bunka,* whose implications were mentioned above.

Why the American sense of ''popular culture'' is not applicable in the Japanese context is an interesting intellectual and cultural question. In the first place, the term *taishu,* which originates in the Buddhist tradition, has an egalitarian meaning where there is no distinction between ''elite'' and ''mass,'' ''literate'' and ''non-literate,'' and so on. People may say that today's *taishu bunka* tends to be vulgar, with lots of violence and sex on the television screen, but they will not agree that ''popular culture'' by itself is vulgar or second-rate by nature. In the second place, Japanese scholars engaged in sociological, anthropological, and literary disciplines have been much less defensive in conducting research than their American counterparts. A study of detective fiction, for instance, could be regarded as an ordinary research subject, and if such a study were done well, it could receive a high evaluation. Second-rate research on sophisticated ''pure literature'' would be rated lower than a first-rate study of ''popular fiction.'' In other words, in the Japanese academic tradition, the subject matter of research in the humanities and social sciences has nothing to do with research methodology. A study of street life, baseball, bars, or *bonsai* would be evaluated highly if its basic methodology were well established and persuasive. In this context, there are no specialists in ''popular culture'' per se in Japan. The names cited in the bibliographies of the essays compiled in this volume are mostly eminent scholars in the humanities and social sciences and not ''popular culturists,'' since there are really no scholars in Japan who specialize exclusively in ''popular culture.'' It may thus be worthwhile to point out that ''popular culture'' or *taishu bunka* has never been taught as an independent discipline in Japanese academic institutions, simply because the material is already interwoven into the various appropriate areas of the humanities.

With these points in mind, we sincerely hope that the readers of this volume are generous enough and curious enough to understand the cultural and semantic differences between the Japanese and American concepts of popular culture and *taishu bunka.*

NOTES

1. 大衆文化
2. 民衆文化
3. 民族文化
4. 流行

Lifestyles and Popular Culture in Urban Japan

THEODORE C. BESTOR

I do not intend to address in this essay the full range of popular culture genres that are found in Japanese city life, for many of these—such as theater, television, popular religion, and sports—are fully covered by other chapters in this *Handbook*. Instead, this chapter will focus on the historical development of urban life as something distinctly different from what was found in rural society, and on contemporary urban lifestyles and those aspects of popular culture that are wrapped up in the daily lives of city dwellers in Japan.

By "urban life" and "urban lifestyles," I mean the popular customs and habits that appear in the patterns of urbanites' daily interactions, the rites and rituals that surround their passages through the stages of life, and the differences in lifestyle that set one segment of the urban population off from another. In a sense I include as part of this the urban manifestations of what the anthropologist Robert Redfield called a society's "little tradition"—the unsystematic or un-codified beliefs, values, lore, religion, arts, recreations, and entertainments of the common people—which Redfield contrasted with an elite "great tradition" of sophisticated fine arts, reflective philosophy, orthodox theology, and scholarly knowledge. Beyond beliefs and tangible cultural products such as arts and lit-erature, I include in my definition of urban popular culture those aspects of ordinary daily life—relations with family, friends, coworkers, and neighbors; the effects of class divisions on consumption patterns; the role of educational institutions in the lives of the young—that give form and meaning to the lives of city dwellers. In short, I am examining here the stuff and texture of the everyday lives of the common people in urban Japan—plebeian life (in the non-pejorative sense of the word).

Although this may be a somewhat idiosyncratic definition of "popular cul-ture," urban culture and urban lifestyles differ from other forms of popular culture in several important ways. First, many aspects of urban life and popular culture, as I use the terms, are intangible and transitory; popular beliefs about religion, for example, or participation in briefly fashionable lifestyles, are not only elusive as they are happening, but are even more difficult to retrieve from the past. Second, lifestyles and the rhythms of city life are not as readily identified with particular creators, producers, or distributors as are other genres of popular culture—such as music, drama, or illustration—nor do they necessarily leave as many tangible products whose styles and provenance can be compared with one another. Finally, most forms of popular culture are associated with commercialized mass production and consumption, but lifestyles (although they may be defined by the sorts of commercialized consumption they promote) are not themselves direct products of commercial cultural production in quite the same sense.

For these and other reasons, there are neither systematic collections of primary sources for the study of city life as a form of popular culture nor bodies of secondary material that examine everyday urban life and its cultural expressions in any comprehensive fashion. What published resources exist for the study of urban daily life are generally monographs and journal articles that happen to touch on aspects of urban culture while examining something else—the rise of class stratification in medieval cities, for example, or the social effects of mass consumption after the Second World War. This essay, therefore, will review those historical, anthropological, and sociological articles, monographs, and reference works—as well as a few primary sources—from which one can garner insights and information about urban lifestyles and popular culture in Japanese cities both past and present. Because Tokyo has been the premier Japanese city since at least the seventeenth century (when it was known as Edo and was the capital of the Tokugawa shogunate), much of the literature on urban lifestyles and urban popular culture is devoted to examining Tokyo and Edo, a bias this essay will share.

HISTORICAL SURVEY

This discussion of urban popular culture will take two approaches. In the first three sections, I will address the historical development of urban life in Japan from the origins of cities, through their flowering during the feudal period, to nineteenth- and twentieth-century urbanization and the creation of a mass society. Following these historical sections, under the general heading of ''Contemporary Urban Culture and Lifestyles,'' are five sections that each consider a particular feature of present-day urban life, such as youth culture or community life.

The Origins of Japanese Urban Culture

There have been cities in Japan since the seventh and eighth centuries. The first permanent Imperial capital, Nara, was founded in A.D. 710, but the court remained there for only about eighty years. In 794 a new capital was established a short distance away, and this city—Heian-kyo (now known as Kyoto)—remained the Imperial capital until 1868.

Both Nara and Kyoto were modeled on Ch'ang-an, the capital of T'ang China. They were laid out in a rectangular grid pattern that still marks the cities with a symmetry seldom found in other Japanese cities. Despite the use of a Chinese model of city planning appropriate to much larger urban populations, the early Imperial capitals were not centers of bourgeois urban life; they were aristocratic settlements with highly refined artistic, literary, and cultural resources for the elite.[1] At that time, and for several centuries to come, Japanese towns and cities lacked the concentration of transportation, commercial, or military functions that lead to the development of large commoner populations of urban dwellers who create and participate in a distinctly urban, non-aristocratic way of life. However, by late medieval times—the Muromachi period (1336–1573)—Kyoto and a few other cities had begun to develop as commercial centers; trade flourished, regional and national markets were developing, merchant guilds were formed, and townspeople were beginning to create an urban lifestyle neither aristocratic nor rural.

As yet, there has been little research on the early history of Japanese urbanization, and even less on the lives of common town and city dwellers. What works there are only tangentially discuss the emergence of urban, non-aristocratic culture. Instead they focus on the economic, social, and political forces that led to the development of Japanese cities during the late medieval Muromachi period. These factors, however, were inextricably linked to the rise of urban commoner classes, among whom a distinctively urban popular culture first emerged. Therefore, historical consideration of the origins of urban popular culture must begin here.

Haruko Wakita and Susan B. Hanley's essay—"Dimensions of Development: Cities in Fifteenth- and Sixteenth-Century Japan"—focuses on the economic emergence of cities and the gradual development of urban dwellers' political and cultural autonomy. Barbara Ruch's article on "Medieval Jongleurs and the Making of a National Literature" discusses popular urban oral literature during the Muromachi era.

More general historical coverage of urban life throughout the preindustrial period is provided in Takeo Yazaki's book, *Social Change and the City in Japan*, a compendium of facts about urbanization and city life, and his essay, "The History of Urbanization in Japan," which summarizes the main trends in the development of urban life.

Works that deal with the late medieval period, and that in part discuss the development of urban life, include *Japan in the Muromachi Age*, edited by John W. Hall and Takeshi Toyoda; *Warlords, Artists, and Commoners*, edited by George Elison and Bardwell L. Smith; and *Japan Before Tokugawa*, edited by John W. Hall, Keiji Nagahara, and Kozo Yamamura. All contain essays that deal with the development of cities and the early creations of urban popular culture during the late medieval period. Louis Frederic's *Daily Life in Japan at the Time of the Samurai, 1185–1603*, although not focused on urban life, provides general information about the period. George B. Sansom's *Japan: A Short Cultural History,* first published in 1931, remains an authoritative overview of premodern cultural life; a much more recent cultural history is H. Paul Varley's *Japanese Culture.* Both discuss plebeian as well as aristocratic culture.

Urban Culture During the Tokugawa Period

The developments of the Muromachi period laid the groundwork for a vibrant, truly sophisticated urban culture created and sustained by the mercantile townspeople, or *chonin,* during the following Tokugawa period (1603–1868).

The century or more of civil wars that brought the Muromachi period to a close shaped the development of urban life by stimulating the creation of fortified military towns and cities. These castle towns, or *jokamachi,* were the most significant type of urban place throughout the Tokugawa period, and it is within them that the major patterns of preindustrial urban life took shape. *Jokamachi* were not, however, simply military encampments; each *daimyo* (feudal lord) gathered within the walls of his castle town the outfitters, artisans, and merchants whose trades were essential to the defense and economic strength of the domain. As the Tokugawa regime succeeded in restoring peace, internal trade gradually flourished and the urban mercantile classes began to achieve economic prosperity beyond that enjoyed by the ruling warrior caste—the *samurai. Samurai* had become in effect an urban bureaucracy based in *jokamachi;* divorced from landholdings or any other sources of economic power other than their fixed feudal stipends, the *samurai* class gradually fell in debt to the urban merchants and artisans—the *chonin.*

During the Tokugawa period, society was rigidly stratified and segregated into castes or estates, which separated classes that had mixed and intermingled during the civil wars of the fifteenth and sixteenth centuries. Under the Tokugawa regime, society was divided into four major groups—*samurai,* peasants, artisans, and merchants[2]—ranked according to Neo-Confucian criteria of social usefulness. The warrior caste stood first as society's rulers and defenders; followed (in principle) by society's most productive members, the peasants; then by the also productive artisan classes; and finally by what were seen as the parasitic, unproductive merchant classes. Each estate was hereditary; in theory, individuals had no possibility of moving from one to another.

The lifestyles of each estate were carefully legislated. Sumptuary regulations were issued again and again to force people to conform to the standards deemed appropriate for their stations in life and to prevent members of one estate from emulating the mores of another. In their manners of dress, styles of architecture, forms of speech, and types of pastimes and diversions, members of each estate were rigidly distinguished from members of others. Within this strict caste system, the politically impotent, socially immobile, but economically powerful *chonin* of the castle towns developed a distinctive culture, cultivating arts, leisure activities, and a style of life that was usually only a step or two ahead of a new round of regulations aimed at curtailing the townspeople's flamboyance. Charles J. Dunn's *Everyday Life in Traditional Japan* summarizes the lifestyles each estate was assigned. William H. Coaldrake's essay, "Edo Architecture and Tokugawa Law," examines the social context of architecture, including the impact of sumptuary regulations on the lives of the *chonin*.

Accounts by early European travellers and traders provide a great deal of information on Japanese customs and lifestyles during the Tokugawa period. One of the most famous of these works is Engelbert Kaempfer's *The History of Japan,* first published in 1727 and republished in 1971. Kaempfer was a doctor attached to the Dutch trading post in Nagasaki who accompanied the official delegations that travelled from Nagasaki to Kyoto and Edo. Michael Cooper's *They Came to Japan* is a collection of reports on Japan by Europeans during the sixteenth and seventeenth centuries. The popularity of the novel and television series *Shogun* has stimulated interest in this period of Japanese history recently, and Henry D. Smith has edited a volume entitled *Learning from Shogun: Japanese History and Western Fantasy,* which includes chapters on many aspects of Japanese life during this time.

An article by John W. Hall, "The Castle Town and Japan's Modern Urbanization," provides an overview of the political, economic, social, and cultural significance of the Tokugawa era's *jokamachi;* Takeo Yazaki's book and article, cited earlier, sketch more broadly the nature of urban development during the preindustrial era. There is as yet only one major English-language study of life in a Tokugawa castle town, James L. McClain's *Kanazawa: A Seventeenth-Century Japanese Castle Town.* His study focuses on the role played by commoners in the development of urban social and cultural life in one of the largest and wealthiest provincial *jokamachi.*

Surprisingly, there is little work in English on ordinary life in the largest *jokamachi*—the Tokugawa capital, Edo (which was renamed Tokyo in the nineteenth century); there are only scattered works on Osaka and Kyoto, the major commercial center of Western Japan and the Imperial capital, respectively.

A chapter in Dunn's book cited above specifically deals with Edo, and Robert J. Smith's article, "Pre-Industrial Urbanism in Japan," examines the development of distinctly urban lifestyles in Edo. Smith discusses the varying social and cultural patterns of *shitamachi* (the merchant quarters) and *yamanote* (the *samurai* districts) in both premodern and present times, and sketches the *Edokko* or "children of Edo"—the prototypical *chonin* denizens of Edo, carefree spendthrift sophisticates whose lives were governed by canons of *iki* (style or taste) and *tsu* (connoisseurship). Andrew J. Markus has written an article, "The Carnival of Edo," that catalogues the public spectacles and entertainments of the city. Several articles in a collection edited by W. G. Beasley, *Edo Culture and Its Modern Legacy,* address the popular culture of the Edo period and the images of Edo that are now embodied in popular culture.

Osaka also has received little attention. Smith's article, mentioned above, contrasts life in Edo and Osaka, and his "Town and City in Pre-Modern Japan" is a study of urban commoner households in the Osaka vicinity, shedding light on the nature of neighborhood social organization during the feudal period. William B. Hauser has written a general overview entitled "Osaka: A Commercial City in Tokugawa Japan."

Japanese-language materials on preindustrial urban life, particularly in Edo, are, of course, many and varied. The *Edogaku Jiten,* edited by Matsunosuke Nishiyama, is an encyclopedic reference work on the city of Edo and all aspects of its social and cultural patterns during the Tokugawa period. Volume 1 of the seven-volume *Tokyo Hyakunen-shi* [One hundred year history of Tokyo], compiled by Tokyo-to (the Tokyo Metropolitan Government), is an account of the political, social, and cultural history of Edo up to the Meiji Restoration in 1868, which brought the Tokugawa period to an end. The daily life and popular culture of Edo's townspeople are examined in a three-volume series entitled *Edo Sanbyakunen* [Three hundred years of Edo], authored by Matsunosuke Nishiyama with several collaborators—Shinzo Ogi, Noboru Haga, and Makoto Takeuchi. One volume in this series—*Edokko no Seitai* [The ecology of the *Edokko*] by Nishiyama and Takeuchi—focuses on the lifestyles and popular culture of Edoites of the Tokugawa period. *Edokko* by Koji Kata examines the life of these prototypical Edoites—somewhat analogous to London's Cockneys—in both the preindustrial and the contemporary periods.

Compared with what is available on lifestyles and the texture of everyday life in Tokugawa cities, the arts and refinements of *chonin* popular culture are well documented. *Chonin* developed many artistic and literary forms that are today regarded as part of the legacy of traditional cultural achievements that make up the "high culture" of the Japanese "great tradition." During the Tokugawa period, however, the arts and leisure activities patronized by *chonin* were parts of an urban popular culture that was officially scorned and occasionally proscribed. A vast range of art forms and cultural activities—*ukiyoe* woodblock prints, *sumo* wrestling, *kabuki* drama, *bunraku* puppet theater, *rakugo* storytellers, *geisha,* and pleasure quarters such as the famous Yoshiwara of Edo or Gion in Kyoto—were all products of the urban popular culture of the common townspeople.

The many studies that focus on specific arts and cultural products of the premodern urban world are in most cases dealt with more appropriately in other chapters of this *Handbook;* a few should be mentioned here for the general perspectives they provide on urban life in addition to information on a particular art form or cultural activity. Howard Hibbett's *The Floating World in Japanese Fiction* examines the literature and the demimonde of the Genroku period (1688–1705), generally considered the most sophisticated era of *chonin* culture during the Tokugawa period (1603–1868).[3] Donald H. Shively's article, "*Bakufu* Versus *Kabuki,*" discusses the restrictions placed on *kabuki* drama by the Tokugawa government (the *bakufu*), as part of its effort to control *chonin* society. Liza C. Dalby's *Geisha,* although largely focused on the contemporary *karyukai,* or "world of flowers and willows" as *geisha* society is often called, includes extensive historical information on *geisha,* especially in Kyoto. J. E. de Becker's *The Nightless City, or the History of the Yoshiwara Yukwaku,* first published in 1899, recounts the history of Tokyo's most famous pleasure quarter. Patricia L. Cuyler's *Sumo: From Rite to Sport* includes extensive historical information on *sumo*'s development as part of the urban popular cultural milieu of premodern *chonin* life.

Another aspect of premodern popular culture—linked to urban life, yet not confined to cities—was travel. With the development of the great highways linking Edo with major provincial cities, travel became a favorite pastime for all classes. The most famous of these roads was the *Tokaido* between Edo and Kyoto, the subject of Hiroshige's famous series of *ukiyoe* prints, "The Fifty-three Stations of the *Tokaido.*" Sometimes to make religious pilgrimages, sometimes simply to see the sights, and sometimes as part of mass crazes that swept the country, the Japanese took to the roads. James H. Foard's essay, "The Boundaries of Compassion: Buddhism and National Tradition in Japanese Pilgrimage," examines Tokugawa travel and popular Buddhism and their role in creating a sense of national identity. Oliver Statler's *Japanese Pilgrimage* is an account, both historical and contemporary, of one of Japan's most popular pilgrimage circuits around the island of Shikoku. McClain's book, *Kanazawa,* and his article, "Castle Towns and Daimyo Authority," mention the effects of mass travel crazes on urban life. A popular novel of the Tokugawa period—*Hizakurige* by Jippensha Ikku (1766–1831), translated by Thomas Satchell under the title *Shank's Mare*—is a lively account of life on the road.

General surveys of the period include two works mentioned earlier—Sansom's *Japan: A Short Cultural History* and Varley's *Japanese Culture*—which have excellent discussions of *chonin* artistic and cultural attainments. The nine-volume *Kodansha Encyclopedia of Japan* has entries ranging from brief capsule sketches to lengthy articles on almost all facets of the traditional arts and popular culture of Tokugawa urban life.

Urbanization and Urbanism from the Meiji Restoration Through the Second World War

During the Tokugawa period Japan developed a sophisticated urban culture and a large urban population—by the late Tokugawa period, Edo's population exceeded 1 million—but Japan remained a fundamentally agrarian society until after the Meiji Restoration in 1868. This event, which overthrew the Tokugawa shogunate and restored the emperor as the head of state, led to the opening of Japan to Western influences and set the country on a course of industrialization and social change that within a few decades would radically alter all aspects of life. The Meiji (1868–1912), the Taisho (1912–1926), and the early Showa (1926–1945) periods span the development of industrialized urban life in Japan, the adoption and adaptation of many facets of Western life, the ultranationalistic

reaction against foreign influences during the 1930s, and the almost total destruction of city life during the Second World War.

The development of urban life from the Meiji Restoration through the Second
World War can be examined both in terms of urbanization—the physical growth
of cities and the cityward migration of people—and from the perspective of
urbanism—the cultural and social patterns created by and reflected in the lives
of urban dwellers.

Japanese urbanization per se is the subject of few works. General surveys of
Japanese urban development during the Meiji period include the previously
mentioned book and article by Takeo Yazaki. Two articles by Gary D. Allinson,
"Japanese Cities in the Industrial Era" and "Japanese Urban Society and Its
Cultural Context," are bibliographic essays that discuss the historical development of urban life from the mid-nineteenth century onward. John W. Hall's
essay, "The Castle Town and Japan's Modern Urbanization," and Susumu
Kurasawa's article, "The Structure of Urban Society," examine the transfor-
mations of feudal towns—such as *jokamachi* and post towns—into new and more
diverse types of cities during the period of industrialization. Taking one particular
urban type—the provincial industrial city—Gary D. Allinson's book, *Japanese
Urbanism,* is a historical study of Kariya (a manufacturing city, home to the
Toyota automobile company) from the 1870s to the present.

There is a richer variety of sources from which to study urbanism—the cultural
and social patterns that are internal features of urban life—during the Meiji
period and the early twentieth century.

Kunio Yanagida, the founder of Japanese folklore studies, supervised the
compilation of a volume entitled *Japanese Manners and Customs in the Meiji
Era,* one of a series issued to commemorate the centennial of the Meiji Restoration. Although the book does not focus exclusively on urban life, Yanagida
was concerned with the effects of urbanization and of Western influence on
traditional ways of life. The volume, therefore, carefully documents both rural
and urban lifestyles, ranging from food and clothing to holiday observances and
religious rituals.

Useful sources of information on life in early Meiji cities are the writings of
foreign residents and visitors during the period. Such accounts, of course, often
have very ethnocentric biases, but nevertheless they provide glimpses of otherwise unrecorded urban life. Although primarily known for his romantic accounts of Japanese life and his exotic renderings of traditional Japanese tales,
Lafcadio Hearn was a perceptive observer of Japanese society during the late
Meiji period, and a recently republished selection of his essays, *Writings from
Japan*, contains many pieces that carefully describe life in nineteenth-century
urban Japan and Western influences on daily life and customs. *Unbeaten Tracks
in Japan,* first published in 1880 (reissued in 1973), is an account of Japanese
customs by Isabella L. Bird, an Englishwoman who traveled throughout Japan
in the 1870s. In a related vein, *Clara's Diary* by Clara Whitney, an American
girl who arrived in Japan in 1875 at age fourteen, recounts her observations of

daily life in Tokyo, of the traditional pastimes of the city, and of popular crazes surrounding such Western novelties as hot-air balloons and ballroom dancing.[4] Housing and domestic architecture are treated by Edward S. Morse, an American naturalist who taught at Tokyo Imperial University between 1877 and 1883. In 1886 he published *Japanese Homes and Their Surroundings* (reissued in 1961), a detailed outline of Japanese domestic architecture and a useful glimpse at varying styles of life in late nineteenth-century urban Japan. His diary, *Japan Day by Day*, published in 1917, also provides observations of everyday life. *Home Life in Tokyo*, originally published in 1910, was written by a Japanese diplomat, Jukichi Inouye, to describe (in somewhat idealized fashion) the customs and habits of middle- and upper-class Japanese.

Other accounts from the period focus much more on the unrest of the times. A British journalist, John R. Black, wrote *Young Japan: Yokohama and Yedo 1858–79* from his vantage point as the editor-in-chief of the *Japan Herald* (which started publication in 1861) and several other newspapers and journals. Sir Ernest Satow, in his memoirs, *A Diplomat in Japan*, also portrays the political and social turmoil of Edo, Yokohama, and other cities just before and after the Meiji Restoration.

Not surprisingly, Tokyo is the focus of most material on Japanese urbanism during this period. Shinzo Ogi's book, *Tokei Jidai: Edo to Tokyo no Aida de* [The Tokei era: Between Edo and Tokyo], examines Tokyo during the first years of the Meiji period, as the old shogunal capital of Edo was being transformed into Tokyo, the Imperial capital of a new Japan dedicated to "Civilization and Enlightenment." He looks at the society, culture, and patterns of everyday life that he considers to have been indigenous to late Tokugawa Edo, tracing them through the first several decades of the Meiji period when the city was known briefly as Tokei, a transitional period during which the society of the old regime had not entirely disappeared and the innovations of the new order had not yet penetrated into the lives of Tokyo's ordinary residents.

Henry D. Smith's essay, "The Edo-Tokyo Transition," particularly focuses on the shifting relationship between the culture of *shitamachi*—the old merchant quarters, the territory of the ordinary townspeople—and that of *yamanote*, the residential districts historically associated with the *samurai* that gradually were to become the home of new bureaucratic and commercial elites. The previously mentioned article by R. J. Smith, "Pre-Industrial Urbanism in Japan," also provides insights into the interaction of the *shitamachi* and *yamanote* traditions during this period and the ways in which *shitamachi* and *yamanote* represented alternative styles of urban living for new migrants to the city.

James W. White's article, "Internal Migration in Prewar Japan," and his monograph, *Migration in Metropolitan Japan*, examine migration to Tokyo, particularly before the Second World War. The development of social institutions that incorporated migrants into urban life, governed neighborhood life, sponsored festivals, and maintained the prevailing social order is discussed by Hachiro Nakamura in a booklet, *Town Organizations in Prewar Tokyo*, and by Theodore

C. Bestor in his article, "Tradition and Japanese Social Organization." The social and cultural changes that took place during the Meiji, Taisho, and Showa periods in one section of what came to be *shitamachi* are outlined in an essay by Hiroshi Wagatsuma and George A. DeVos, "Arakawa Ward: Urban Growth and Modernization."

Hiromichi Ishizuka's *Tokyo no Shakai-Keizai-Shi* [The socioeconomic history of Tokyo] examines industrialization and the growth of Tokyo from the Meiji Restoration to the Kanto earthquake. Tokyo's changing cityscape during this and later periods is the subject of *Tokyo no Seikatsu Chizu* [An atlas of life in Tokyo], a book by Yasuo Masai, an urban geographer interested in the interplay of architectural environments with cultural and social life. Masai has also produced an interesting map, *Edo no Toshiteki Tochi Riyo-zu: 1860-Nen Goro* [Urban land use map of Edo: circa 1860], which illustrates the patterns of land use and the distribution of social and cultural activities in Edo on the eve of the Meiji Restoration.

Shitamachi, the low-lying merchant quarters of Edo that survived the Meiji Restoration as the center of plebeian culture, is the subject of the most elegant account of Japanese urban culture of this period: Edward Seidensticker's *Low City, High City*. Seidensticker's elegiac history traces *shitamachi* from the Meiji Restoration to the Kanto earthquake of 1923—which destroyed most of central Tokyo and which Seidensticker regards as the deathknell of *shitamachi*. A specialist on literature, Seidensticker examines the influence that *shitamachi*'s cultural ethos exerted over the arts and letters of the period, and meanders through the diversions and entertainments that occupied Tokyo during the last decades of the nineteenth century and the first decades of the twentieth. In an earlier work, *Kafu the Scribbler*, Seidensticker presents both a biography and an anthology of the works of Kafu Nagai, an author Seidensticker considers to have been a quintessential voice for and chronicler of *shitamachi*.

Other books on the cultural ethos of *shitamachi* include Koji Kata's *Edokko*, which examines the prototypical townsperson of Edo-Tokyo, and Kata's *Shitamachi no Minzokugaku* [The ethnology of *shitamachi*], a collection of essays on various cultural traits, products, and values that were (or are) typical of *shitamachi*. A periodical entitled *Edokko* includes articles on the history of *shitamachi*, traditional crafts, and contemporary survivals of the old *shitamachi* way of life.

Henry D. Smith's article, "Tokyo as an Idea," traces the developing attitudes toward urban life held by government officials, scholars, planners, and ordinary citizens from the late Meiji period through the Second World War. He focuses on ways in which attitudes toward urban life reflected and shaped changing social and cultural patterns within Tokyo; he leads the reader from the early Meiji view of Tokyo as a showcase for Japan's successful acquisition of the architectural, economic, and political wherewithal to emulate European society, down to the late 1930s view of Tokyo as a cesspool of decadence and class struggle that undermined the vitality of traditional Japanese values. From a comparative perspective, H. D. Smith's "Tokyo and London" is also useful for its discussion of nineteenth-century development in the two cities. Shun-ichi J. Watanabe's article, "Metropolitanism as a Way of Life: The Case of Tokyo, 1868–1930," covers some of the same ground from the perspective of urban planning and suburbanization.

Valley of Darkness, by Thomas R. H. Havens, is a study of life in Japan, primarily Tokyo, during the Second World War. Havens's work is a unique portrayal of this turbulent period, from the crackdown on "decadent" popular culture and the gradual prohibition of almost everything "Western" that began in the late 1930s, through wartime efforts to reshape the Japanese spirit, to the chaotic breakdown of urban life during the American bombing raids in the closing months of the war.

The seven-volume *Tokyo Hyakunen-shi* [A hundred year history of Tokyo]— completed in the 1970s by Tokyo-to (Tokyo Metropolitan Government) to commemorate the centennial of the modern administration of Tokyo—is a detailed source of information on Tokyo's social and cultural history, as well as its political and economic development, from the Meiji Restoration (1868) through the present, but particularly through the end of World War II. Each of the twenty-three wards, or *ku,* that make up Tokyo and almost every town or city of any size has published a similar multivolume local history; these are essential sources for anyone interested in the historical roots of urban lifestyles and popular culture in particular locales.

The dramatically changing styles of urban life during the early twentieth century are documented in many popular Japanese-language publications. The *Mainichi Shimbun,* one of Japan's major newspapers, publishes a series entitled *Ichiokunin no Showa-shi* [One hundred million people's history of the Showa period], which now includes several dozen volumes that chronicle many aspects of Japanese life during the last six decades. A series of books compiled by Kawade Shobo Shinsha, titled *Waga Sedai* [Our generation], traces the experiences of people born in various years; the series includes volumes for 1921, 1926, 1929, 1931, 1936, 1938, 1941, 1947, and 1956. Each volume traces the popular culture and events of the Showa period as they intersect with the lives of people born in a particular year. In the 1921 volume, for example, the late 1920s and 1930s are described from the perspective of schooling and children's games and pastimes, while the sections on the 1940s focus on how the war affected people who were then in their early twenties.

CONTEMPORARY URBAN CULTURE AND LIFESTYLES

The preceding, chronologically organized sections of this chapter have focused as much on the urbanization of Japanese society—the growth and spread of cities—as on the lifestyles and popular customs that develop within cities. In this section I will concentrate more closely on the inner workings of urban culture in several domains of everyday life, rather than on the life of cities as a whole.

As I noted at the outset of this chapter, my working definitions of "urban life" and "urban lifestyles" are necessarily selective, to avoid overlap with topics covered more fully in other chapters of this *Handbook*. In discussing contemporary urban life, I will concentrate on the following domains: traditional arts and popular culture in contemporary life; youth culture and education; lifestyles, life stages, and careers; community life; gender and mass society and identity.

Although the focus of this section is contemporary urban life, it is important to keep in mind that social customs and cultural patterns do not exist in a timeless ethnographic present. The postwar period is now entering its fifth decade and spans the total physical devastation and cultural reorientation of the immediate postwar years, the years of frantic economic growth during the 1960s, and the pervasive middle-class affluence of the 1980s. Each period has spawned very different patterns of life. Unfortunately, many of the features of urban lifestyles I will discuss below have been the subject of so little description or analysis that their historical development within the postwar period is almost impossible to trace through the existing literature. My discussions, therefore, cover secondary sources from throughout the period along with a few primary sources from the 1970s and 1980s.

Traditional Arts and Popular Culture in Contemporary Life

Popular culture is a transitory thing, yet fads and fancies in popular culture that persist soon take on the status of high culture. Thus, many aspects of the popular culture of preindustrial cities, the popular culture of the *chonin*—the townspeople of the Tokugawa period (1603–1868)—are now high art, or have acquired a durable patina of respectability that befits venerable tradition. Although performing arts such as *kabuki* and *bunraku* and fine arts like *ukiyoe* are firmly established as serious genre, other products of *chonin* life stand today at the intersection of popular and high culture

Three examples of *chonin* popular culture that continue to thrive are *geisha, sumo*, and *rakugo* storytelling. Historical studies of *geisha* have been mentioned previously, and of these Liza C. Dalby's book provides an insider's view of Kyoto's contemporary *geisha*. Contemporary *sumo* is the subject of several books, including Doug Kenrick's *The Book of Sumo*, Patricia L. Cuyler's *Sumo: From Rite to Sport* and *Takamiyama: The World of Sumo* by Jesse Kuhaulua with John Wheeler. Kuhaulua, better known by his *sumo* name Takamiyama, is the Hawaiian-American who became the first foreign *sumo* star. This autobiographical account of his early career provides an unparalleled inner view of the contemporary *sumo* world. *Rakugo*, a tradition of comic storytelling, retains its plebeian flavor more than many historical genres of popular culture. Although the old *yose* (vaudeville halls) in which *rakugo* was performed are almost a thing of the past, it is still popular on television. Studies of contemporary *rakugo* include Robert J. Adams's "Folktale Telling and Storytellers in Japan" and Mary Sanches's "Falling Words."

There are several studies that shed light on traditional arts and crafts from the perspective of the sociology of art. Francis L. K. Hsu's book, *Iemoto*, although not exclusively about the art world, analyzes the familistic structure around which most traditionalistic arts and crafts "schools" are organized. Thomas R. H. Havens's book, *Artist and Patron in Postwar Japan,* examines the system of support for the arts—both traditional and Western—and the forms of patronage that shape them. Brian Moeran's ethnography of a pottery village in Kyushu, *Lost Innocence,* discusses the marketing of folk art as popular culture, as does his two-part article, "Exhibiting in Japan." A special issue of *Craft International,* entitled *The Sociology of Craft: Japan,* edited by John Mock, includes several articles on crafts as an element of contemporary popular culture.

Rather than as professional performances or commercial entertainments, traditional arts and accomplishments are much more commonly found in contemporary life as personal hobbies and pastimes or as forms of self-cultivation. Suzanne H. Vogel's essay, "Professional Housewife," briefly discusses the arts and accomplishments—known as *okeiko, keikogoto,* or *hanayome shugyo* (bridal training)—that women study to prepare for marriage and to attain status as well-rounded, cultured ladies. Bestor's article, "Craft Life in a Tokyo Neighborhood," describes the practice of such arts as tea ceremony, doll making, traditional dance, and *ikebana* (flower arranging) and the social networks that surround teachers and practitioners in an ordinary Tokyo neighborhood. An article by Robert Frager and Thomas P. Rohlen, "The Future of a Tradition," examines the meaning traditional arts hold for their practitioners and students, pointing out their popularity as social and psychological devices to attain spiritual maturity, a particularly important goal among middle-aged Japanese.[5]

Other, very different forms of traditional belief and practice—medical therapies and folk remedies—also continue to be vital parts of the urban scene. Margaret M. Lock's book, *East Asian Medicine in Urban Japan,* is a perceptive study of the popular use of traditional medical techniques such as acupuncture, moxibustion, and *kanpoyaku* (Chinese herbal medicine), which remain an important element in the methods of treatment used by Japanese physicians who practice "Western" medicine. Emiko Ohnuki-Tierney's *Illness and Culture in Contemporary Japan* examines the cultural beliefs underlying Japanese medical practices, including the persistence of traditional folk cures and religious practices. *Furo: The Japanese Bath,* by Peter Grilli and Dana Levy, is a profusely illustrated account of Japanese bathing in all its forms—private, public, and at hot springs—for purposes both therapeutic and recreational.

Youth Culture and Education

Among the most obvious features of popular culture in industrialized, urban societies is the existence of distinctive, generationally differentiated cultures and

lifestyles. The creation of these separate lifestyles is related in part to the seg-
regation of youth from society as a whole that is imposed by a system of mass
education.

Youth culture and its links to the educational system have been the focus of
several studies. Donald T. Roden's *Schooldays in Imperial Japan* examines the
daily lives and culture of male students in prewar elite high schools; although
these students were only a tiny minority of prewar youth, Roden's book illu-
minates general cultural values and the attitudes of youth during the prewar
period. Many of the values and attitudes that ran through the lives of prewar
students are still symbolically important in postwar youth culture, and one can
draw striking parallels between Roden's study and the sections of Ian Buruma's
Behind the Mask that describe Japanese machismo as expressed in postwar
popular culture.

For the contemporary period, Thomas P. Rohlen's book, *Japan's High
Schools,* gives a detailed picture of mass secondary education in the postwar
years and provides insights into the interaction between the educational system
and adolescent life. Ezra F. Vogel's essay, "Entrance Examinations and Emotional Disturbances in Japan's 'New Middle Class,' " and Christie Kiefer's
article, "The Psychological Interdependence of Family, School, and Bureaucracy
in Japan," both address a crucial rite of passage faced by contemporary Japanese
adolescents: the so-called "examination hell" or *nyugaku shiken jigoku*. These
articles link the examination system to family dynamics and the so-called *kyoiku
mama* (education mama) syndrome, demonstrating one among the many ways
that the educational system drastically affects the contours of contemporary
adolescent culture. More recent developments are the now extremely common
juku (cram schools)—private academies that specialize in preparing students for
entrance examinations—which are described in Rohlen's "*Juku* Phenomenon"
and in a brief essay on "*Ranjuku Jidai*" [The cram school era] by Lynne E.
Riggs.

Recently, as foreign interest in Japanese educational achievements has grown,
several studies have been published that examine the early years of schooling
and the interaction of childhood socialization, family life, and the formal educational system. These include: Joy Hendry's *Becoming Japanese: The World
of the Pre-School Child; Child Development and Education in Japan,* edited by
Harold Stevenson, Hiroshi Azuma, and Kenji Hakuta; Merry I. White's *The
Japanese Educational Challenge: A Commitment to Children;* and a study prepared by the U.S. Department of Education entitled *Japanese Education Today*.

Although the educational system plays a major role in the lives of the young,
it is not the sole influence on the formation of youth subcultures. The mass
media—through books, comics, movies, and songs—provide varied role models
for the young. Ian Buruma's *Behind the Mask* focuses on gender roles and sexual
identities as portrayed in a wide variety of popular media. He distinguishes
between the "*koha*" (the macho "hard school") and the "*nanpa*" (the sensitive
"soft school") as stereotypical characters in popular culture, and argues the

koha hero—the stoic, unflinching, combative gangster, or *samurai,* or baseball star—is a central popular culture idol to be emulated by Japanese boys. Another aspect of popular culture and adolescent sexual identity is the focus of Mamoru Mochizuki's "Cultural Aspects of Japanese 'Girls' Opera,' " which examines the all-female Takarazuka dance troupe with its wildly popular "leading men" as part of girls' popular culture.

Throughout the last several decades, popular fads and fashions pursued by urban Japanese youth have been the basis for informally identified subcultural groups (generally known as *zoku* or tribes), distinguished by their tastes in clothing, music, pastimes, hangouts, and demeanor. Contemporary *zoku* include the *kurisutaruzoku,* the *takenokozoku,* and the *bosozoku.*

Kurisutaruzoku or the crystal tribe comprises the affluent youth of Tokyo whose lifestyles revolve around imported fashions, expensive cars, elaborate stereos, and the fashionable "foreign" areas of Tokyo; a recent novel, *Nantonaku, Kurisutaru* by Yasuo Tanaka, documents (and satirizes) the lives of the crystal tribe. *Takenokozoku,* the bamboo shoot tribe—so named for a shop in the Harajuku section of Tokyo that sells clothing popular with this group—are younger teenagers who dress in elaborate, gaudy costumes vaguely reminiscent of Chinese silk gowns and who gather in parks on weekends to dance to rock-and-roll music.[6] C. Scott Littleton's "Tokyo Rock and Role" is a brief, well-illustrated study of the *takenokozoku* and the *bosozoku. Bosozoku,* the hot rodder tribe, are young men who affect the haircuts and clothes of James Dean and Marlon Brando. Like the *takenokozoku* they pose and dance in public parks. However, they have a darker image as well; racing their cars or motorcycles in packs in the middle of the night, they have frequent confrontations with the police and are seen as a social menace. Ronald P. Loftus's brief essay, "*Bosozoku,*" describes and analyzes this group.

As with the *bosozoku,* youth subcultures at times verge toward juvenile delinquency, which in recent years has re-emerged as a social problem. Youth crime, especially in schools and directed toward teachers, is now the subject of serious concern in Japan; Rohlen's article on "Violence at Yoka High School" addresses student violence in a school wracked with sensitive charges and countercharges of discrimination against minority youth, but the growing problem of school vandalism and crime committed by mainstream students has yet to be carefully examined. George A. DeVos and Hiroshi Wagatsuma have written extensively on Japanese juvenile delinquency and deviance; several chapters in DeVos's *Socialization for Achievement* and sections of *Heritage of Endurance,* by Wagatsuma and DeVos, report the findings of their research on the sociological background of Japanese delinquency, particularly in the 1950s and 1960s.[7]

From a historical perspective, there is little material available that traces the rapid evolution of youth culture throughout the postwar years. For the early postwar period up through the late 1960s, some aspects of its changing character are documented in popular Japanese-language publications. Two that I have mentioned earlier are the *Mainichi Shimbun*'s series *Ichiokunin no Showa-shi*

[One hundred million people's history of the Showa period], which now includes several dozen volumes, and the series *Waga Sedai* [Our generation], compiled by Kawade Shobo Shinsha, which traces the popular culture and events of the last fifty years as they intersect with the lives of people born in particular years.

Lifestyles, Life Stages, Gender, and Careers

Although youth create what are probably the most readily apparent generational subcultures, patterns of everyday life vary across occupational, age, and gender lines, forming a variety of lifestyles equally as distinctive (even if not as attention getting) as those of the young.

In contemporary Japan, the ubiquitous *sarariiman* or "salary man"—the white-collar organization man (only rarely woman)—is generally seen both by Japanese and foreign observers as the stereotypical urbanite. Thomas P. Rohlen's study, *For Harmony and Strength,* is an ethnography of a Japanese bank and its organizational culture, examining life in the office as well as the impact of the bank on the lives of its employees outside the office. Rohlen's book is the most comprehensive available work on middle-class lifestyles in the workplace, and complements Ezra Vogel's study, *Japan's New Middle Class,* which focuses on the family life of *sarariiman* households. Rodney Clark's *The Japanese Company* examines life in the workplace as well as the general environment of Japanese business.

Other facets of *sarariiman* lifestyles are best seen through literature. The humorous short stories by Keita Genji, collected in English-language editions entitled *The Guardian God of Golf* and *The Ogre,* take as their subject matter the office politics and the family troubles of *sarariiman* life. Genji's stories can be read both as examples of a particular genre of popular culture and for the insights they provide into the *sarariiman* way of life. Kenneth Skinner's essay, "*Sarariiman Manga,*" deals with a related genre, the "salaryman comic."

Sarariiman are among the major patrons of the world of *mizushobai*—the so-called "water trades"—the bars, cabarets, and other diversions of urban night-life. David W. Plath's book, *The After Hours* in part deals with after-work drinking and group recreations that are so stereotypically a part of the Japanese male world, and Reiko Atsumi's study, "*Tsukiai*—Obligatory Personal Relationships of Japanese White-Collar Company Employees," also examines the relationship between organizational culture and after-hours drinking. Other studies that explore various aspects of *mizushobai* include David H. Bayley's *Forces of Order,* which portrays urban pleasure quarters from a police perspective; Liza C. Dalby's *Geisha,* which focuses on traditional female entertainers; and Laura Jackson's "Bar Hostesses," which discusses the commercialized female companionship available in so many bars and nightspots. Other features of urban entertainment districts such as *pachinko* (pinball) or *karaoke*—the currently popular electronic sing-alongs—have not yet been subjects of published work.

The salaryman way of life is generally thought to revolve around permanent employment in the same organization, but recently attention has been paid to the limited scope of "lifetime" employment and to the shifts and variations that mark most individuals' working and family careers. Several volumes written or edited by Plath—*Long Engagements, Adult Episodes in Japan,* and *Work and Lifecourse in Japan*—examine the progression of life stages and lifestyles individuals pass through from young adulthood to old age.

Plath and his collaborators also make the point that urban life cycles—and lifestyles—are heterogeneous, and that the *sarariiman* way of life is not the only, or the preferred, lifestyle for many urbanites. A quite different way of life is led by the small merchants and craftspeople who continue to be a major sector in contemporary urban life. Despite the significance of the mercantile classes in the historical development of urban life, there are few studies of their present-day lifestyles. Howard W. Wimberley's "On Living with Your Past" focuses on traditional patterns of consumption and living arrangements among merchant families in the city of Kanazawa. Plath's *The After Hours* compares the recreational activities of merchant households in Matsumoto with those of *sarariiman* and farming families. Bestor's *Neighborhood Tokyo* is an ethnography of the social life maintained by local merchants and craftspeople in a Tokyo neighborhood.

Some of the differences between the lives of the urban self-employed and those of white-collar company employees reflect the distinctions drawn between *shitamachi* and *yamanote* areas of Tokyo. The historical dimensions of these divisions have been discussed previously, but as features of postwar Tokyo life they are described and analyzed in R. P. Dore's *City Life in Japan* and Robert J. Smith's "Pre-Industrial Urbanism in Japan."

The lives of members of another occupational group, industrial workers, are the subjects of Robert E. Cole's *Japanese Blue Collar* and Satoshi Kamata's *Japan in the Passing Lane.* These accounts—the former by a sociologist and the latter by a journalist—focus on the working lives of blue-collar assembly-line workers, but also provide some information on their non-work lifestyles as well.

The lower strata of urban society are portrayed in passing in two studies. Winston Davis's *Dojo* is an ethnographic study of an urban religious movement. His book not only is a detailed account of the worldview of a syncretistic popular religion, but also discusses the lifestyles of blue-collar and self-employed Japanese. *Heritage of Endurance* by Hiroshi Wagatsuma and George A. DeVos is primarily a study of juvenile delinquency, but by analyzing delinquency in the context of a lower-class area of Tokyo, it presents much general information on urban lower-class life.

Many studies of occupational groups and their lives on and off the job are focused primarily on male workers. The careers—both domestic and vocational—of women differ greatly from those of Japanese men and create or contribute to lifestyles different from but equally as varied as those of men. The most wide-ranging source of information is *Women in Changing Japan,* edited by Joyce

C. Lebra and others, which includes fourteen essays on women in small business, politics, the media, sports, and other domains of society. Takie S. Lebra's *Japanese Women* traces women's lives through typical progressions of events from adolescence through marriage, motherhood, and careers to old age. Dorothy Robins-Mowry's *The Hidden Sun: Women of Modern Japan* traces the status of women throughout Japanese history as background for examining postwar changes in women's roles. Susan J. Pharr's *Political Women in Japan* focuses on females in the political arena and on the cultural politics of women's status in the workplace.

Suzanne H. Vogel's essay, "Professional Housewife," considers the majority of urban women who define themselves primarily as wives and mothers. Her essay examines the role of *keikogoto*—training in womanly accomplishments such as flower arrangement, tea ceremony, and music—in preparing a woman for marriage, and her analysis of the dynamics of urban middle-class family life touches on contemporary dating and romance, patterns of women's recreation, and the *kyoiku mama* (education mama) phenomenon.[8] A recent study, *Urban Japanese Housewives: At Home and in the Community* by Anne E. Imamura, examines in detail the lives of women in a middle-class Tokyo suburb. Another study of housewives is Sonya Salamon's article on women's friendships and patterns of socializing, entitled "The Varied Groups of Japanese and German Housewives."

A much more exotic lifestyle is that of the *geisha*. Liza C. Dalby's book on the *geisha* world not only provides a detailed look at the inner workings of a venerable form of traditional urban popular culture that has survived into the present, it also portrays what Dalby argues is an alternative lifestyle for independent woman. Dalby's study, therefore, provides interesting insights into male and female roles—and the relationship between them—in contemporary Japanese culture. Laura Jackson's article, "Bar Hostesses," provides contrast by focusing on contemporary quasi-counterparts to the *geisha*.

Gender roles and their definition through popular culture are dealt with in several of the previously mentioned works. In particular, Ian Buruma's book, *Behind the Mask,* examines a wide array of popular culture genres—from pornography to gangster movies, from comic books to the all-female Takarazuka revue—for their images of masculinity and femininity in Japanese culture.[9]

Community Life

Urban community life—the patterns of social interaction and the kinds of institutional frameworks within which local social life is played out—reflects something of the occupationally distinctive lifestyles that were discussed in the previous section. But because Japanese cities are not as residentially segregated along class or occupational lines as are American cities, neighborhoods are heterogeneous and community life overarches occupational subcultures to incorporate residents of socially diverse backgrounds.

The classic study of an urban Japanese community is R. P. Dore's book, *City Life in Japan*, based on research in a Tokyo neighborhood in the early 1950s. Dore's volume presents the neighborhood he studied as representing a cross-section of urban life; Bestor's more recent study, *Neighborhood Tokyo*, focuses on the social life of a neighborhood in a lower-middle-class, mercantile district of Tokyo. Several community studies that center on political attitudes and behavior also illustrate diverse styles of life within contemporary urban settings. Gary D. Allinson's *Surburban Tokyo* is a history of Tokyo's affluent Western suburbs, providing insights into the attitudes and lifestyle of the new middle class. Gerald Curtis's *Election Campaigning Japanese Style* is an ethnography of political culture and of the interaction of campaigns with community life in an urban setting. James W. White's *Migration in Metropolitan Japan* studies social and political attitudes of residents in three Tokyo neighborhoods—one in the suburbs, one in the old *shitamachi* district, and one in the *yamanote* section of Western Tokyo. White's book includes detailed comparisons of subculturally distinctive areas of Tokyo and examines the assimilation of migrants into differing urban lifestyles, a point also taken up in Robert J. Smith's article, "Pre-Industrial Urbanism in Japan."

Central to life in many urban neighborhoods are interlocking local institutions that offer services to residents and establish frameworks within which informal relations among neighbors may be maintained or elaborated. Bestor's article, "Tradition and Japanese Social Organization: Institutional Development in a Tokyo Neighborhood," examines the sets of organizations that center around a single *chonaikai* or neighborhood association. Hachiro Nakamura's essay, "Urban Ward Associations in Japan," analyzes the same sets of institutions as more general phenomena of urban Japanese life.

Neighborhoods are arenas of mutual aid and social control, which can take many forms and can affect a wide range of social phenomena. Walter L. Ames's *Police and Community in Japan* and David H. Bayley's *Forces of Order* discuss the role played by community sentiments and institutions in combating crime and social disorder. Ezra F. Vogel's article, "The Go-Between in a Developing Society: The Case of the Japanese Marriage Arranger," describes the role of matchmakers and their reliance on neighborhood gossip in making suitable pairings. Masao Fujii's article on "Maintenance and Change in Japanese Traditional Funerals and Death-Related Behavior" discusses the role of neighbors in assisting at funerals, through such customs as *koden* or "incense money," sums of money offered to a bereaved family by each mourner attending a funeral.

The social ties that are maintained among neighbors reflect many of the fundamental principles of Japanese social organization and involve careful considerations of reciprocal obligations.[10] The complicated etiquette involved in funeral offerings as well as in all sorts of other exchanges, such as those accompanying births, weddings, seasonal greetings, departures for trips, house raisings, and other events, forces many urban Japanese to depend on detailed encyclopedias of etiquette that explain the proper terminologies to be used, quantities and commodities to be given, and types of behavior to be followed on all occasions. Etiquette guides for these purposes are widely available in bookstores and news-stands; a typical example is the *Kankonsosai to O-Tsukiai no Subete* [All about interaction at ceremonial occasions] published in 1980 as a special issue of a housewives' magazine entitled *Shoppingu* [Shopping]. On a more general level, Harumi Befu has analyzed the patterns of social exchange seen in these reciprocal gift exchanges in his articles on "Gift-Giving in a Modernizing Japan," "Gift-Giving and Social Reciprocity in Japan," and "An Ethnography of Dinner Entertainment in Japan."

In addition to the sorts of interpersonal ties that neighborhoods promote, communities sponsor vivid, popular events that celebrate the importance of local life. Festivals or *matsuri*—a quintessential part of Japanese community life—are among the most popular of popular cultural traditions. These festivals come in a wide variety: from venerably aged to almost new creations; from observances important only to local residents to nationally advertised events; from festivals peculiar to a particular locality to those observed in the same fashion throughout the nation.

An extensive series of articles by A. W. Sadler presents a comprehensive picture of ordinary urban festivals in ordinary communities, and Bestor's *Neighborhood Tokyo* and "Tradition and Japanese Social Organization" also discuss the significance of a local festival in the life of the community that stages it. Noriaki Akaike's essay on "Festival and Neighborhood Association" analyzes in detail the interaction of local patterns of social structure in the staging of a festival in a Japanese town as does C. Scott Littleton's essay, "The Organization and Management of a Tokyo Shinto Shrine Festival." In recent years, urban festivals have become the focus of a great deal of attention by Japanese anthropologists and sociologists. Studies include Kiyotaka Aoyagi's "Viable Traditions in Urban Japan: *Matsuri* and *Chonaikai*," Shoji Kurahayashi's *Matsuri no Kozo* [The structure of the festival], Minoru Sonoda's "The Traditional Festival in Urban Society," and Chizuko Ueno's "Matsuri to Kyodotai" [Festival and communal organization].

One of the most famous annual celebrations in Japan is Kyoto's Gion festival, which has been the subject of many studies. Toshinao Yoneyama has written two anthropological studies of urban festivals—one, *Gion Matsuri*. about this event and the other, *Tenjin Matsuri,* about another famous Kyoto festival. An essay by Hiroshi Soeda, entitled "Festivity and the City," examines the Gion festival's floats and stages as a form of popular rebellion against society by the townspeople who put on the festival. Soeda uses the term "anarchitecture" (combining "anarchy" and "architecture") to describe his conception of the festival's structures. A more traditional view of the Gion festival is presented in Geoffrey Bownas's *Japanese Rainmaking and Other Folk Practices,* which includes essays on traditional holidays and festivals observed throughout Japan.

Another conception of festivity is portrayed in "A Festival with Anonymous *Kami*," by Nobutaka Inoue and others, which examines a non-traditional festival created by a municipal government as a means of promoting a sense of local identity among the city's residents. Although the vast majority of community festivals continue to be of the traditional variety, the type of event Inoue, et al. discuss is not unusual; whether for political or for commercial purposes, newly created festivals are common throughout Japan. Robert J. Smith's essay, "The Eclipse of Communal Ritual in Japan"—although primarily concerned with the decline of traditional community festivals—makes important observations on the changing role of festivals and holidays in a society where mass media play an important role and opportunities for leisure and recreation are increasingly widespread.

Mass Society and Identity

In a highly urbanized, well-educated society with well-developed media, mass marketing and mass consumption are important elements of popular culture, not only because advertising and the products it touts have a major impact on daily life, but also because in a consumer society, patterns of consumption are closely related to beliefs and attitudes about self and identity.

Studies of Japanese consumer behavior are useful sources of information on current trends in urban life. *The Japanese as Consumers* by Boye De Mente and Fred Thomas Perry was published in 1967, shortly after Japan's postwar economic recovery had led to a major boom in consumerism. George Fields's *From Bonsai to Levi's* gives a view of Japanese consumers in the 1980s. Written from the perspective of market research and advertising, Fields's book is particularly valuable for the insights it provides on the role mass markets and mass media play in shaping the tastes and desires of Japanese consumers.[11]

The media and mass marketing organizations such as department stores play a major role as arbiters of taste. They not only shape popular demand for new fashions, imported goods, and high-technology gadgetry, but also promote cultural activities. Department stores, newspapers, railroad companies, and travel agencies all actively sponsor cultural events not just for their publicity or public service values but also as products to be consumed or appreciated. Department stores and newspapers stage art exhibitions, concerts, dance recitals, and plays. Railways build cultural and historical attractions: Meiji Mura, a historical park near Nagoya, preserves Meiji-era buildings moved there from all over Japan; Takarazuka, an amusement park near Osaka, is the headquarters of the all-female Takarazuka dance troupe, which also has a theater in Tokyo. Newspapers own major league sports teams, and the *Asahi* newspaper sponsors the national high school baseball championships each summer.

Although the activities of commercial cultural impresarios range across the entire spectrum of arts and cultural activities, there has been only scattered attention paid to the phenomenon. Thomas R. H. Havens's book, *Artist and Patron in Postwar Japan*, discusses the role of department stores and other commercial institutions as patrons and promoters of the arts. Brian Moeran has written a two-part article, "Exhibiting in Japan," that humorously recounts his experiences in putting on a pottery exhibit and points up the role played by the media and by department stores in sponsoring artistic exhibits.

One form of cultural consumption that has become particularly important in recent decades is travel. Nelson H. H. Graburn's study of Japanese tourism, *To Pray, Pay and Play*, analyzes the cultural symbolism surrounding much contemporary Japanese travel and the ways in which customs surrounding travel fit with Japanese patterns of interpersonal relations. Brian Moeran's article, "The Language of Japanese Tourism," examines the images evoked in travel advertising and their appeal to the Japanese consumer. Fields's *From Bonsai to Levi's* includes a chapter on travel; the works by Foard and Statler discussed earlier address travel as a form of cultural self-expression. *Furo,* by Grilli and Levy, lavishly describes *onsen*—the hot springs resorts that are so frequently the destination of Japanese travellers.

Harumi Befu's essay, "Internationalization of Japan and *Nihon Bunkaron*," examines many features of contemporary Japanese society—including travel— to consider how these are linked to Japanese views of their cultural identity. Theories, musings, and speculations about Japanese cultural identity—a category of thought that Befu calls *Nihon Bunkaron* (theories of Japanese culture) and others call *Nihonjinron* (theories about the Japanese)—are themselves a major genre of popular culture. Japanese bookstores are crowded with works that purport to explain (to a Japanese audience, of course) the uniqueness of Japanese culture. Travel as a means of self-discovery is only one part of this general quest for cultural identity reflected in the *Nihonjinron* phenomenon; the present renewed interest in all aspects of Japanese traditions, including the popular culture of the urban past, also reflects the same tendency.[12] Robert J. Smith's *Japanese Society* examines the ways in which beliefs about the past shape contemporary Japanese attitudes toward their own culture.

Considering consumption as an expression of identity, two Japanese intellectuals recently have addressed the philosophical, sociological, and political meanings of mass culture. Masakazu Yamazaki's *Yawarakai Kojinshugi no Tanjo* [The birth of soft individualism] analyzes consumption as the source of identity and social values in postindustrial societies.[13] Another theoretical piece that interprets Japan as a consumer-oriented mass society is an essay by Yasusuke Murakami, "The Age of New Middle Mass Politics." Although Murakami is not directly concerned with popular culture as such, he examines the homogenization of urban lifestyles and patterns of consumption to understand the nature of contemporary Japanese society and the political consequences of mass society's emergence.

REFERENCE WORKS

Because the study of urban Japanese lifestyles and the popular customs and traditions of city life has not yet become a distinguishable field of inquiry, and because the subject matter does not lend itself to the systematic collection and classification of cultural artifacts, reference works that specifically focus on urban popular culture are almost non-existent. However, more general reference series contain a great deal of material on these topics.

The most comprehensive and up-to-date reference work on Japan in English is the *Kodansha Encyclopedia of Japan,* compiled by Kodansha. The nine-volume *Encyclopedia* contains several thousand articles by Japanese and foreign experts on all aspects of Japanese history, society, and culture. Most longer entries conclude with a brief bibliography, and the *Encyclopedia's* entire ninth volume is an extensively cross-referenced index. A one-volume encyclopedia of Japanese customs—*All-Japan: The Catalogue of Everything Japanese,* by Oliver Statler and others—contains useful essays on a variety of traditional and contemporary genres of popular culture. Two other general reference works are specifically historical in focus: The *Encyclopedia of Asian History,* published in four volumes under the auspices of the Asia Society, and the *Cambridge History of Japan* to be published in six volumes by the Cambridge University Press. An encyclopedia exclusively devoted to Edo's history, society, and culture is *Edo-gaku Jiten* edited by Matsunosuke Nishiyama.

The *Bibliography of Asian Studies,* published annually by the Association for Asian Studies, contains the most comprehensive listings of scholarly publications on Japan in Western languages. The several dozen categories into which this bibliography classifies citations of works on Japan do not specifically include popular culture, but sources on the subject can be found under headings such as "Social Customs," "Recreational Arts," and "Radio and Television." The Japan Foundation annually publishes *An Introductory Bibliography for Japanese Studies,* a collection of overviews of recent Japanese-language scholarship in disciplines such as history, anthropology, sociology, and literature. An essay on each of the dozen or so disciplines that are covered by this publication appears in every other year's volume.

English-language journals and periodicals that regularly publish articles and reviews of books on Japanese society and popular culture include *Asian Folklore Studies, Japan Echo, Japan Interpreter, Japan Quarterly, Journal of Asian Studies, Journal of Japanese Studies, Look Japan, Modern Asian Studies, Monumenta Nipponica, Pacific Affairs,* and *PHP Intersect.* The major English-language newspapers published in Japan—the *Japan Times* (and its weekly international airmail edition), the *Asahi Evening News,* and the *Mainichi Daily News*—all include essays and columns that comment on urban lifestyles, current fads, and popular culture.

The last decade or so has seen the publication of several Japanese-language series that present overviews of popular trends throughout this century. One I have mentioned previously is the ambitious *Ichiokunin no Showa-shi* [One hundred million people's history of the Showa period], a large-format, illustrated, paperback series published by one of Japan's largest newspaper chains, the *Mainichi Shimbun.* The series now includes several dozen volumes, each of which is devoted to a particular span of years within the Showa period (1926 to the present) or to a specific series of events, activities, or aspects of popular culture, such as *sumo,* popular songs, professional baseball, or Japanese weaponry of the Second World War. Drawing on the extensive *Mainichi* files of photographs, these profusely illustrated volumes also include many firsthand accounts. One supplementary volume in the series is the *Showa-shi Jiten*—a historical dictionary of the Showa period—which includes capsule biographies of prominent personalities including writers, critics, artists, singers, actors and actresses, as well as political figures. It also includes brief entries on social and cultural events, fads, and trends throughout the period.

During the late 1960s and the 1970s, Japan went through what some Japanese commentators have called an "age of regionalism." Among the many results of this trend was a renewed interest in preserving local traditions and creating local histories. In cities and towns throughout the country, extremely detailed local histories were compiled. Although these histories tend to concentrate on administrative, political, and economic history, they are invaluable sources of information on local cultural events and activities, and often give documentary accounts of the fads and fancies of urban popular culture and daily life from the Tokugawa period through the Second World War. Such histories have been published for most municipalities in Japan, as well as for each of the twenty-three wards or boroughs (*ku*) that make up Tokyo.[14] A massive example of the genre is the seven-volume *Tokyo Hyakunen-shi* [One hundred year history of Tokyo] completed in 1979 by Tokyo-to, the Tokyo Metropolitan Government.

Another resource for students of urban popular culture, particularly if they are in Japan, is a variety of urban guidebooks. An excellent guide to Tokyo, which emphasizes its past and the survival of traditional elements of urban life, is Paul Waley's *Tokyo Now and Then: An Explorer's Guide.* A smaller, more specialized guidebook, devoted to traditional popular crafts in Tokyo, is *Kites, Crackers and Craftsmen* by Camy Condon and Kimiko Nagasawa. An informative introduction to aristocratic Kyoto is *Kyoto: A Contemplative Guide* by Gouverneur Mosher. Although Mosher's book focuses on a handful of major temples, shrines, and palaces, it successfully places these in their appropriate historical, social, and cultural contexts, meanwhile providing much information on preindustrial urban culture in Kyoto.

Extremely detailed Japanese-language guides to every city and province are widely available in Japan in several series, and these guides are useful for locating capsule histories and descriptions of landmarks, temples, and festivities in particular locations. One authoritative series is published by the Japan Travel Bureau (Nihon Kotsu Kosha), and another is the *Blue Guide* series published by Jitsugyo no Nihonsha.

A comprehensive English-language guide that covers the entire country is *The New Official Guide: Japan,* compiled by the Japan National Tourist Organization; it is a useful, although somewhat dry, source of background information on cities, their histories, and their traditional festivals, handicrafts, and local specialties. Recently, English-language guides have been written to introduce particular areas of the country that are not commonly on tourist itineraries, including the city of Kanazawa, the Tohoku region, and the *shitamachi* district of Tokyo.[15]

Other urban guidebooks take an aggressively modern approach to city life and can provide the reader with a good sense of the differentiation of the lives of city dwellers by age groups, interests, socioeconomic class, and so forth. *Tokyo Access*, compiled by Richard S. Wurman, for example, is a bilingual guide that captures the hectic rhythm of contemporary Tokyo's cultural life, from the bars of Kabuki-cho to the department stores of the Ginza, from the pandas at the Ueno Zoo to the bustling shopping areas around Tokyo's many railway stations.[16]

Several magazines published in Tokyo give up-to-date information on the city's attractions and popular culture. Although they are aimed primarily at college students and people in their early twenties, *City Road*, *Angle*, and *Pia* provide comprehensive pictures of what is going on in Tokyo in a wide range of cultural domains. The magazines often include special sections on particular neighborhoods in Tokyo, providing maps and detailed information on shops, restaurants, bars, and cabarets, as well as commenting on local habitués and the kinds of social and cultural scenes that dominate particular subcenters of Tokyo. *Angle*'s December 1982 special issue, *Tokyo Seikatsu Zenjoho* [Complete report on life in Tokyo], is a good example of these popular guides to Tokyo's culture.

RESEARCH COLLECTIONS

The major resources for research outside of Japan on Japanese urban lifestyles and popular culture are library collections rather than museum collections. None of the major American libraries that have major holdings on Japan, however, has a special emphasis on popular culture per se. The following institutions with strong Japanese collections are the starting points for any serious investigation of Japanese urban life, either historical or contemporary: Columbia University, Cornell University, Harvard University and the Harvard-Yenching Library, the Library of Congress, Princeton University, Stanford University and its Hoover Institution, the University of California at Berkeley, the University of Chicago, the University of Hawaii, the University of Michigan, the University of Washington, and Yale University.

In Tokyo English-language libraries with extensive materials on Japanese society and culture include the library of the International House of Japan (open to members and their guests) and the library of the Japan Foundation's Japanese Studies Center. The National Diet Library is open to the public, but it is noncirculating and, like most Japanese libraries, it has closed stacks. A private organization, the Tokyo Shisei Chosakai (Tokyo Municipal Administration Research Institute), maintains a library on urban affairs and urban history in its headquarters in Tokyo's Hibiya Park. The Tokyo Metropolitan Government's

Chuo Toshokan (Central Library) in Minami Azabu has a special section housing an extensive open-stack non-circulating collection of material on Tokyo's history, society, and culture.

Public libraries and collections maintained by municipal governments are essential resources for any research on a particular location. The same revival of interest in local traditions and historical preservation that led to the compiling of extensive city and town histories also led to the creation of historical museums and archives sponsored by municipal libraries, governments, and boards of education. Most municipal libraries have *chiiki shiryo-shitsu* (collections of historical materials), and many municipalities maintain local archives. *Kyoiku iinkai*, or boards of education, throughout Japan are responsible for collecting and disseminating materials on local history and customs; they publish wide ranges of pamphlets and booklets on local cultural monuments, folklore, and the development of local social patterns and customs. Community centers often include local historical museums that display the material artifacts of local culture. A local museum particularly relevant to the study of urban culture is the Shitamachi Fuzoku Shiryokan (Shitamachi Museum), established by the ward government in Taito-ku, Tokyo, to preserve and display the local history and culture of Tokyo's *shitamachi* districts.

Traditional culture can be studied through the facilities of several nationally sponsored research institutions: the National Ethnology Museum in Osaka, the National History Museum in Chiba, and the International Research Center for Japanese Studies to be established in Kyoto. The Kokuritsu Minzokugaku Hakubutsukan (National Ethnology Museum), built on the site of the 1970 Osaka Exposition, has elaborate and striking displays of Japanese cultural artifacts, as well as an extensive automated collection of video tapes on all aspects of Japanese culture that may be viewed on request.

Films and video tapes portray many aspects of Japanese urban life—both past and present. *Japan in Film,* edited by Peter Grilli and published by the Japan Society of New York, is a comprehensive, well-indexed catalogue of theatrical and documentary films on Japan that are available in the United States.[17] Some recent documentary films that deal with urban life include *Full Moon Lunch,* which shows something of the lives of household members and workers in a family-run business in Tokyo's *shitamachi*; *Japanese Fighting Festival,* a video documentary on an annual festival staged by several rival neighborhoods in the city of Himeji; and *The World's Safest City,* a film that discusses the Japanese police as well as historical, social, and cultural reasons for urban calm.[18] The Asia Society has produced a series entitled *Video Letter from Japan,* which portrays Japan through the eyes of children. Three segments that particularly deal with urban life include *Tokyo Sunday,* which shows shopping and amusement districts in contemporary Tokyo; *My Day,* about a Tokyo child's school and recreational activities; and *My Town,* about life in the provincial city of Matsumoto.[19]

NOTES

I am grateful to Gary Allinson, Victoria Lyon-Bestor, and James L. McClain for their substantive suggestions, and to Dorothy and Arthur Bestor for their extensive editorial comments. Marilyn Oldham provided meticulous assistance with the bibliography.

1. Ivan Morris's *The World of the Shining Prince* sketches an evocative and entertaining portrait of the lives of Kyoto's aristocracy during the flowering of the Heian period (794–1185).

2. These rankings are sometimes called the *shi-no-ko-sho* (warrior-agriculturalist-artisan-merchant) system. Two other groups are not generally considered in discussions of Tokugawa period stratification. One group is the nobles of the Imperial house and its court, who never numbered more than a few hundred households. The other is the outcaste population, who may have numbered in the hundreds of thousands and whose occupations were considered by Buddhist precepts to be polluting or defiling; for example, outcastes were butchers and leather workers, and they served as executioners during the Tokugawa period. *Japan's Invisible Race*, edited by George A. DeVos and Hiroshi Wagatsuma, provides historical and contemporary information on Japan's outcastes; Thomas P. Rohlen's article, "Violence at Yoka High School," is a more recent portrayal of the current political struggles that surround the outcaste issue and continuing discrimination. In contemporary Japan, Koreans form another major urban minority group. *Koreans in Japan*, edited by Changsoo Lee and George A. DeVos, is a collection of articles on the history and present-day status of Japan's Korean population.

3. The literature of the period is not only a product of *chonin* culture but also a source of insight into the lives of commoners. The novelist Saikaku Ihara (1623–1693) and the playwright Monzaemon Chikamatsu (1653–1725) are among the most prominent writers whose works reflect *chonin* culture; their works are widely available in translation (e.g., Ivan Morris's translation of Saikaku Ihara's *The Life of an Amorous Woman*).

4. An extremely interesting analysis of the introduction of one form of Western popular culture into Japan is Donald T. Roden's "Baseball and the Quest for National Dignity in Meiji Japan." For a contemporary view of baseball, see Robert Whiting's *The Chrysanthemum and the Bat*.

5. See David W. Plath's "Bourbon in the Tea: Dilemmas of an Aging *Senzenha*" and *Long Engagements* for perspectives on Japanese born and raised before the war and their attitudes toward Japanese traditions and postwar culture. Thomas P. Rohlen's article, " 'Spiritual Education' in a Japanese Bank," illustrates the popular use of tradition-laden activities to inculcate a spirit of loyalty and group identity among young white-collar workers. Winston Davis's book, *Dojo*, portrays the interweaving of traditional prewar ideologies and beliefs into a postwar, lower-middle-class religious movement.

6. Members of the crystal tribe—like American yuppies—are noted for jaded and expensive tastes in food, drink, foreign clothes, sports equipment, stereos, cars, and all the other symbols of an affluent consumer-oriented culture. An unusual feature of Tanaka's novel—which he wrote when he was a college senior—is that it includes 442 footnotes that identify the accessories of the crystal tribe's lifestyle for the benefit of Japanese readers unfamiliar with au courant slang, fashions, shops, cuisine, hangouts, and pastimes of Tokyo's fast set.

The *takenokozoku* take their name from a shop in Harajuku, a section of Tokyo that has long been the scene of new youth fads. The shop originated as a place that sold old clothes, and the shop's name itself is a reference to the *takenoko seikatsu*, or "bamboo shoot life," of the immediate postwar years when people had to keep shedding and selling garments (just as a bamboo stalk sheds leaves) to survive.

7. *Heritage of Endurance* also discusses the ways in which community concern is mobilized to combat delinquency and to resolve juvenile problems. Two other studies— David Bayley's *Forces of Order* and Walter Ames's *Police and Community in Japan*— focus on the police, including their role in stemming juvenile delinquency by working through community-based institutions of social control.

8. Suzanne H. Vogel's study of housewives parallels and expands upon Ezra F. Vogel's book on urban family life, *Japan's New Middle Class*.

9. Sheila K. Johnson's review article, "Japanese Women: Three Approaches," perceptively examines the portrayal of gender roles in the scholarly literature, specifically focusing on Buruma's book, Dorothy Robins-Mowry's *The Hidden Sun: Women of Modern Japan*, and *Women in Changing Japan*, edited by Joyce Lebra and others.

10. General patterns of Japanese social relationships are analyzed in several works: Ruth Benedict's *The Chrysanthemum and the Sword*, Harumi Befu's *Japan: An Anthropological Introduction*, Takie Lebra's *Japanese Patterns of Behavior*, and Chie Nakane's *Japanese Society*. Other, less harmonious views of Japanese social relations are presented in *Conflict in Japan*, a collection of essays edited by Ellis S. Krauss and others.

11. Practitioners of an old-fashioned form of advertising, still popular in urban Japan, are *chindonya* (wandering musicians carrying signboards), described in Adam Woog's article, "*Chindonya*: Street Artists of Advertising."

12. From the perspective of the sociology of knowledge, Nozomu Kawamura has examined the origins and characteristics of these so-called theories of cultural distinctiveness in his book, *Nihon Bunkaron no Shuhen*, and in an essay, "The Historical Background of Arguments Emphasizing the Uniqueness of Japanese Society."

13. An English translation of Yamazaki's book is being prepared for publication.

14. Carol Gluck's essay, "The People in History: Recent Trends in Japanese Historiography," pays special attention to the recent popularity of local history and of *seikatsushi* (the history of everyday life), both of which are valuable genres of scholarship for the study of urban popular culture.

15. See, for example, *Discover Shitamachi* by Sumiko Enbutsu, a walking guide to Tokyo's *shitamachi* districts. Another example is Ruth P. Stevens's *Kanazawa: The Other Side of Japan*.

16. Street life and the local social scene in Shibuya—one of Tokyo's major entertainment and shopping subcenters—are the subjects of one essay in Hidetoshi Kato's *A Comparative Study of Street Life: Tokyo, Manila, New York*. Peter Popham's *Tokyo: The City at the End of the World* also portrays the chaotic energy of contemporary Tokyo life, as expressed both through the architectural environment and through the overlapping and interacting social worlds that form tiny enclaves in the metropolis. Other postmodernist views of the energy of Tokyo are presented in the lavishly illustrated catalogue for the exhibition *Tokyo: Form and Spirit*. The catalogue, edited by Mildred Freedman, includes two dozen essays by leading authorities on Tokyo's history, architecture, and culture both past and present.

17. The catalogue, *Japan in Film*, can be ordered from the Japan Society, 333 East 47 Street, New York, New York 10017.

18. *Full Moon Lunch* was written and directed by John Nathan and is distributed by

Japan Society, 333 East 47 Street, New York, New York 10017. *Japanese Fighting Festival* by Keiko Ikeda is distributed by University of California Extension Media Center, 2223 Fulton Street, Berkeley, California 94720. *The World's Safest City* is distributed through Japanese consulates and offices of the Japan Foundation.

19. Information on the *Video Letter from Japan* series can be obtained from The Asia Society, 725 Park Avenue, New York, New York 10021. Teachers' guides for each of the twelve segments are available.

BIBLIOGRAPHY

Adams, Robert J. "Folktale Telling and Storytellers in Japan." *Asian Folklore Studies* 26 (1967), 99–118.

Akaike, Noriaki. "Festival and Neighborhood Association." *Japanese Journal of Religious Studies* 3 (1976), 127–74.

Allinson, Gary D. "Japanese Cities in the Industrial Era." *Journal of Urban History* 4 (1978), 443–76.

———. *Japanese Urbanism*. Berkeley: University of California Press, 1975.

———. "Japanese Urban Society and Its Cultural Context." In *The City in Cultural Context*. Ed. J. A. Agnew, et al. Boston: Allen and Unwin, 1984.

———. *Suburban Tokyo*. Berkeley: University of California Press, 1979.

Ames, Walter L. *Police and Community in Japan*. Berkeley: University of California Press, 1981.

Angle, comp. *Tokyo Seikatsu Zenjoho*. Special issue of *Angle*, December 1982.

Aoyagi, Kiyotaka. "Viable Traditions in Urban Japan: *Matsuri* and *Chonaikai*." In *Town Talk*. Ed. G. Ansari and P. Nas. Leiden: E. J. Brill, 1983, 96–111.

The Asia Society. *Encyclopedia of Asian History*. Ed. Ainslee T. Embree. 4 vols. New York: Scribners, 1987.

Association for Asian Studies, comp. *Bibliography of Asian Studies*. Ann Arbor, Mich.: Association for Asian Studies. Annual publication.

Atsumi, Reiko. "*Tsukiai*—Obligatory Personal Relationships of Japanese White-Collar Company Employees." *Human Organization* 38 (1979), 63–70.

Bayley, David H. *Forces of Order: Police Behavior in Japan and the United States*. Berkeley: University of California Press, 1976.

Beasley, W. G., ed. *Edo Culture and Its Modern Legacy*. Special issue of *Modern Asian Studies* 18, no. 4 (1984).

Befu, Harumi. "An Ethnography of Dinner Entertainment in Japan." *Arctic Anthropology* 11 (1974), Supplement, 196–203.

———. "Gift-Giving and Social Reciprocity in Japan." *France-Asie/Asia* 21 (1966/67), 161–77.

———. "Gift-Giving in a Modernizing Japan." *Monumenta Nipponica* 23 (1968), 445–56.

———. "Internationalization of Japan and *Nihon Bunkaron*." In *The Challenge of Japan's Internationalization: Organization and Culture*. Ed. H. Mannari and H. Befu. Tokyo and New York: Kodansha International, 1983, 232–66.

———. *Japan: An Anthropological Introduction*. San Francisco: Chandler, 1971.

Benedict, Ruth. *The Chrysanthemum and the Sword*. Boston: Houghton Mifflin, 1946.

Bestor, Theodore C. "Craft Life in a Tokyo Neighborhood." In *The Sociology of Craft:*

Japan, special issue of *Craft International*. Ed. J. Mock. January-March 1984, 10–12.

———. "Life in a Tokyo Neighborhood: An Anthropologist's Journal." *Japan Society Newsletter* (December 1984), 3–6.

———. *Neighborhood Tokyo*. Stanford: Stanford University Press, 1988.

———. "Tradition and Japanese Social Organization: Institutional Development in a Tokyo Neighborhood." *Ethnology* 24 (1985), 121–35.

Bird, Isabella L. *Unbeaten Tracks in Japan*. 1880; rpt. Rutland, Vt., and Tokyo: Charles E. Tuttle, 1973.

Black, John R. *Young Japan: Yokohama and Yedo 1858–79*. 1883; rpt. Tokyo, London, New York: Oxford University Press, 1968.

Bownas, Geoffrey. *Japanese Rainmaking and Other Folk Practices*. London: George Allen and Unwin, 1963.

Buruma, Ian. *Behind the Mask: On Sexual Demons, Sacred Mothers, Transvestites, Gangsters, Drifters, and Other Japanese Cultural Heroes*. New York: Pantheon Books, 1984.

Cambridge University Press. *Cambridge History of Japan*. Cambridge University Press, forthcoming.

Clark, Rodney. *The Japanese Company*. New Haven: Yale University Press, 1979.

Coaldrake, William H. "Edo Architecture and Tokugawa Law." *Monumenta Nipponica* 36 (1981), 235–84.

Cole, Robert E. *Japanese Blue Collar*. Berkeley: University of California Press, 1971.

Condon, Camy, and Kimiko Nagasawa. *Kites, Crackers and Craftsmen*. Tokyo: Shufunotomo, 1974.

Cooper, Michael, ed. *They Came to Japan: An Anthology of European Reports on Japan, 1543–1640*. Berkeley: University of California Press, 1965.

Curtis, Gerald L. *Election Campaigning Japanese Style*. New York: Columbia University Press, 1971.

Cuyler, Patricia L. *Sumo: From Rite to Sport*. New York and Tokyo: John Weatherhill, 1979.

Dalby, Liza C. *Geisha*. Berkeley: University of California Press, 1983.

Davis, Winston. *Dojo: Magic and Exorcism in Modern Japan*. Stanford: Stanford University Press, 1980.

de Becker, J. E. *The Nightless City, or the History of the Yoshiwara Yukwaku*. 1899; rpt. Rutland, Vt., and Tokyo: Charles E. Tuttle, 1971.

De Mente, Boye, and Fred Thomas Perry. *The Japanese as Consumers*. New York and Tokyo: Walker/Weatherhill, 1967.

DeVos, George A. *Socialization for Achievement*. Berkeley: University of California Press, 1973.

DeVos, George A., and Hiroshi Wagatsuma, eds. *Japan's Invisible Race*. Berkeley: University of California Press, 1966.

Dore, R. P. *City Life in Japan*. Berkeley: University of California Press, 1958.

Dunn, Charles J. *Everyday Life in Traditional Japan*. 1969; rpt. Rutland, Vt., and Tokyo: Charles E. Tuttle, 1972.

Elison, George, and Bardwell L. Smith. *Warlords, Artists, and Commoners: Japan in the Sixteenth Century*. Honolulu: University Press of Hawaii, 1981.

Enbutsu, Sumiko. *Discover Shitamachi*. Tokyo: Shitamachi Times, 1984.

Fields, George. *From Bonsai to Levi's*. New York: Macmillan, 1983.

Foard, James H. "The Boundaries of Compassion: Buddhism and National Tradition in Japanese Pilgrimage." *Journal of Asian Studies* 41 (1982), 231–51.

Frager, Robert, and Thomas P. Rohlen. "The Future of a Tradition." In *Japan: The Paradox of Progress.* Ed. L. Austin. New Haven: Yale University Press, 1976, 255–78.

Freedman, Mildred, ed. *Tokyo: Form and Spirit.* Minneapolis and New York: Walker Art Center, and Harry N. Abrams, Inc., 1986.

Fujii, Masao. "Maintenance and Change in Japanese Traditional Funerals and Death-Related Behavior." *Japanese Journal of Religious Studies* 10 (1983), 39–64.

Genji, Keita. *The Guardian God of Golf, and Other Humorous Stories.* Trans. Hugh Cortazzi. Tokyo: Japan Times, 1972.

———. *The Ogre, and Other Stories of the Japanese Salaryman.* Trans. Hugh Cortazzi. Tokyo: Japan Times, 1972.

Gluck, Carol. "The People in History: Recent Trends in Japanese Historiography." *Journal of Asian Studies* 38 (1978), 25–50.

Graburn, Nelson H. H. *To Pray, Pay and Play: The Cultural Structure of Japanese Domestic Tourism.* Aix-en-Provence: Centre des Hautes Etudes Touristiques, 1983.

Grilli, Peter, ed. *Japan in Film.* New York: Japan Society, 1984.

Grilli, Peter, and Dana Levy. *Furo: The Japanese Bath.* Tokyo and New York: Kodansha International, 1985.

Hall, John W. "The Castle Town and Japan's Modern Urbanization." *Far Eastern Quarterly* 15 (1955), 37–56.

Hall, John W., Keiji Nagahara, and Kozo Yamamura, eds. *Japan Before Tokugawa.* Princeton: Princeton University Press, 1981.

Hall, John W., and Takeshi Toyoda, eds. *Japan in the Muromachi Age.* Berkeley: University of California Press, 1977.

Hauser, William B. "Osaka: A Commercial City in Tokugawa Japan." *Urbanism Past and Present* 5 (1977/78), 23–36.

Havens, Thomas R. H. *Artist and Patron in Postwar Japan.* Princeton: Princeton University Press, 1982.

———. *Valley of Darkness: The Japanese People and World War Two.* New York: W. W. Norton, 1978.

Hearn, Lafcadio. *Writings from Japan.* Ed. Francis King. Harmondsworth: Penguin Books, 1984.

Hendry, Joy. *Becoming Japanese: The World of the Pre-School Child.* Honolulu: University of Hawaii Press, 1986.

Hibbett, Howard. *The Floating World in Japanese Fiction.* London: Oxford University Press, 1959.

Hsu, Francis L. K. *Iemoto: The Heart of Japan.* Cambridge: Schenkman Publishers, 1975.

Ihara, Saikaku. *The Life of an Amorous Woman.* Trans. Ivan Morris. New York: New Directions, 1969.

Ikku, Jippensha. *Hizakurige.* Trans. Thomas Satchell as *Shank's Mare.* 1929; rpt. Rutland, Vt., and Tokyo: Charles E. Tuttle, 1960.

Imamura, Anne E. *Urban Japanese Housewives: At Home and in the Community.* Honolulu: University of Hawaii Press, 1987.

Inoue, Nobutaka, et al. "A Festival with Anonymous *Kami:* The Kobe *Matsuri.*" *Japanese Journal of Religious Studies* 6 (1979), 163–85.

Inouye, Jukichi. *Home Life in Tokyo*. 1910; rpt. London, Boston, Sydney and Henley: KPI Limited, 1985.

Ishizuka, Hiromichi. *Tokyo no Shakai-Keizai-Shi*. Tokyo: Kinokuniya Shoten, 1977.

石塚弘道 『東京の社会経済史』 紀ノ国屋書店 １９７７

Jackson, Laura. "Bar Hostesses." In *Women in Changing Japan*. Ed. J. Lebra, et al. Stanford: Stanford University Press, 1978, 133–56. Originally published by Boulder, Colo.: Westview Press, 1976.

Japan Foundation, comp. *An Introductory Bibliography for Japanese Studies*. Tokyo: University of Tokyo Press. Annual publication.

Japan National Tourist Organization, comps. *The New Official Guide: Japan*. Tokyo: Japan Travel Bureau, 1975.

Johnson, Sheila K. "Japanese Women: Three Approaches." *Journal of Japanese Studies* 11 (1985), 258–65.

Kaempfer, Engelbert. *The History of Japan*. 1727; 1906; rpt. New York: AMS Reprints, 1971.

Kamata, Satoshi. *Japan in the Passing Lane*. New York: Pantheon, 1982.

Kata, Koji. *Edokko.* Kyoto: Tankosha, 1972.

加太こうじ 『江戸っ子』 淡交社 １９７２

――――. *Shitamachi no Minzokugaku*. Kyoto: PHP Kenkyujo, 1980.

加太こうじ 『下町の民俗学』 ＰＨＰ研究所 １９８０

Kato, Hidetoshi, ed. *A Comparative Study of Street Life: Tokyo, Manila, New York*. Occasional Papers, No. 5. Research Institute for Oriental Cultures, Gakushuin University, Tokyo, 1978.

――――. *Japanese Popular Culture*. Rutland, Vt., and Tokyo: Charles E. Tuttle, 1959.

Kawade Shobo Shinsha, comp. *Waga Sedai: Taisho Junen Umare*. Tokyo: Kawade Shobo Shinsha, 1979.

河出書房新社編 『わが世代・大正10年生まれ』 河出書房新社 １９７９

Kawamura, Nozomu. "The Historical Background of Arguments Emphasizing the Uniqueness of Japanese Society." *Social Analysis* 5/6 (1980), 44–62.

――――. *Nihon Bunkaron no Shuhen*. Tokyo: Ningen no Kagaku-sha, 1982.

河村望 『日本文化論の周辺』 人間の科学社 １９８２

Kenrick, Doug. *The Book of Sumo*. New York and Tokyo: John Weatherhill, 1969.

Kiefer, Christie W. "The Psychological Interdependence of Family, School, and Bureaucracy in Japan." *American Anthropologist* 72 (1970), 66–75.

Kodansha, comp. *Kodansha Encyclopedia of Japan*. 9 vols. Tokyo: Kodansha International, 1983.

Krauss, Ellis S., Thomas P. Rohlen, and Patricia G. Steinhoff, eds. *Conflict in Japan*. Honolulu: University of Hawaii Press, 1984.

Kuhaulua, Jesse, with John Wheeler. *Takamiyama: The World of Sumo*. Tokyo and New York: Kodansha International, 1973.

Kurahayashi, Shoji. *Matsuri no Kozo*. Tokyo: Nihon Hoso Shuppan Kyokai, 1975.

倉林正次 『祭りの構造』 日本放送出版協会 １９７５

Kurasawa, Susumu. "The Structure of Urban Society." *Journal of Social and Political Ideas in Japan* 3 (1965), 21–31.

Lebra, Joyce C., Joy Paulson, and Elizabeth Powers, eds. *Women in Changing Japan*.

Stanford: Stanford University Press, 1978. Original publication, Boulder, Colo.: Westview Press, 1976.

Lebra, Takie S. *Japanese Patterns of Behavior*. Honolulu: University of Hawaii Press, 1976.

———. *Japanese Women*. Honolulu: University of Hawaii Press, 1984.

Lee, Changsoo, and George A. DeVos, eds. *Koreans in Japan*. Berkeley: University of California Press, 1981.

Littleton, C. Scott. "The Organization and Management of a Tokyo Shinto Shrine Festival." *Ethnology* 25 (1986), 195–202.

———. "Tokyo Rock and Role." *Natural History* (August 1985), 48–57.

Lock, Margaret M. *East Asian Medicine in Urban Japan*. Berkeley: University of California Press, 1980.

Loftus, Ronald P. *"Bosozoku." Japan Interpreter* 11 (1977), 384–94.

Louis Fredéric. *Daily Life in Japan at the Time of the Samurai, 1185–1603*. New York: Praeger, 1972.

Mainichi Shimbun, comp. *Ichiokunin no Showa-shi*. Tokyo: Mainichi Shimbun-sha.

———. *Showa-shi Jiten*. Tokyo: Mainichi Shimbun-sha, 1980.

毎日新聞社編 『昭和史事典』 毎日新聞社 1980

Markus, Andrew J. "The Carnival of Edo: *Misemono* Spectacles from Contemporary Accounts." *Harvard Journal of Asiatic Studies* 45 (1985), 499–541.

Masai, Yasuo. *Edo no Toshiteki Tochi Riyo-zu: 1860-Nen Goro*. Tokyo: (privately published), 1975.

正井泰夫 『江戸の都市的土地利用図・1860年頃』 自費出版 1975

———. *Tokyo no Seikatsu Chizu*. Tokyo: Jiji Tsushinsha, 1972.

正井泰夫 『東京の生活地図』 時事通信社 1972

McClain, James L. "Castle Towns and Daimyo Authority: Kanazawa in the Years 1583–1630." *Journal of Japanese Studies* 6 (1980), 267–99.

———. *Kanazawa: A Seventeenth-Century Japanese Castle Town*. New Haven: Yale University Press, 1982.

Mochizuki, Mamoru. "Cultural Aspects of Japanese 'Girls' Opera.' " In *Japanese Popular Culture*. Ed. H. Kato. Rutland, Vt., and Tokyo: Charles E. Tuttle, 1959, 165–74.

Mock, John, ed. *The Sociology of Craft: Japan*. Special Issue of *Craft International*, January-March 1984.

Moeran, Brian. "Exhibiting in Japan." *Ceramics Monthly*, March 1985, pp. 21, 23, 25, 27; April 1985, 19, 21, 55, 57.

———. "The Language of Japanese Tourism." *Annals of Tourism Research* 10 (1983), 93–108.

———. *Lost Innocence: Folk Craft Potters of Onta, Japan*. Berkeley: University of California Press, 1984.

Morris, Ivan. *The World of the Shining Prince*. London: Oxford University Press, 1964; republished Harmondsworth: Penguin Books, 1969.

Morse, Edward S. *Japan Day by Day*. Boston and New York: Houghton Mifflin, 1917.

———. *Japanese Homes and Their Surroundings*. 1886; rpt. New York: Dover Publications, 1961.

Mosher, Gouverneur. *Kyoto: A Contemplative Guide*. Rutland, Vt., and Tokyo: Charles E. Tuttle, 1964.

Murakami, Yasusuke. "The Age of New Middle Mass Politics." *Journal of Japanese Studies* 8 (1982), 29–72.

Nakamura, Hachiro. *Town Organizations in Prewar Tokyo*. Tokyo: United Nations University, Project on Technology Transfer, Transformation, and Development, 1980.

———. "Urban Ward Associations in Japan." In *Readings in Urban Sociology*. Ed. R. Pahl. Oxford: Pergamon, 1968, 186–208.

Nakane, Chie. *Japanese Society*. Berkeley: University of California Press, 1970.

Nishiyama, Matsunosuke, ed. *Edogaku Jiten*. Tokyo: Kobundo, 1984.

西山松之助編 『江戸学事典』 弘文堂 1 9 8 4

Nishiyama, Matsunosuke, and Noboru Haga. *Edo Sanbyakunen: Tenka no Chonin*. Tokyo: Kodansha, 1975.

西山松之助・芳賀登編 『江戸三百年 第1 ・天下の町人』 講談社 1 9 7 5

Nishiyama, Matsunosuke, and Shinzo Ogi. *Edo Sanbyakunen: Edo kara Tokyo e*. Tokyo: Kodansha, 1975.

西山松之助・小木新造編 『江戸三百年 第3 ・江戸から東京へ』 講談社 1 9 7 5

Nishiyama, Matsunosuke, and Makoto Takeuchi. *Edo Sanbyakunen: Edokko no Seitai*. Tokyo: Kodansha, 1975.

西山松之助・竹内誠編 『江戸三百年 第2 ・江戸ッ子の生態』 講談社 1 9 7 5

Ogi, Shinzo. *Tokei Jidai: Edo to Tokyo no Aida de*. Tokyo: Nihon Hoso Shuppan Kyokai, 1980.

小木新造 『東京時代』 日本放送出版協会 1 9 8 0

Ohnuki-Tierney, Emiko. *Illness and Culture in Contemporary Japan*. Cambridge: Cambridge University Press, 1984.

Pharr, Susan J. *Political Women in Japan*. Berkeley: University of California Press, 1981.

Plath, David W., ed. *Adult Episodes in Japan*. Leiden: E. J. Brill, 1975.

———. *The After Hours: Modern Japan and the Search for Enjoyment*. Berkeley: University of California Press, 1969.

———. "Bourbon in the Tea: Dilemmas of an Aging *Senzenha*." *Japan Interpreter* 11 (1977), 362–83.

———. *Long Engagements: Maturity in Modern Japan*. Stanford: Stanford University Press, 1980.

———, ed. *Work and Lifecourse in Japan*. Albany: State University of New York Press, 1983.

Popham, Peter. *Tokyo: The City at the End of the World*. Tokyo and New York: Kodansha International, 1985.

Riggs, Lynne E. *"Ranjuku Jidai."* *Japan Interpreter* 11 (1977), 541–49.

Robins-Mowry, Dorothy. *The Hidden Sun: Women of Modern Japan*. Boulder, Colo.: Westview Press, 1983.

Roden, Donald T. "Baseball and the Quest for National Dignity in Meiji Japan." *American Historical Review* 85 (1980), 511–34.

———. *Schooldays in Imperial Japan*. Berkeley: University of California Press, 1980.

Rohlen, Thomas P. *For Harmony and Strength*. Berkeley: University of California Press, 1974.

———. *Japan's High Schools*. Berkeley: University of California Press, 1983.

———. "The *Juku* Phenomenon." *Journal of Japanese Studies* 6 (1980), 207–42.

———. " 'Spiritual Education' in a Japanese Bank." *American Anthropologist* 75 (1973), 1542–62.

————. "Violence at Yoka High School." *Asian Survey* 16 (1976), 682–99.

Ruch, Barbara. "Medieval Jongleurs and the Making of a National Literature." In *Japan in the Muromachi Age*. Ed. J. W. Hall and T. Toyoda. Berkeley: University of California Press, 1977, 279–309.

Sadler, A. W. "At the Sanctuary: Further Field Notes on the Shrine Festival in Modern Tokyo." *Asian Folklore Studies* 33 (1974), 17–34.

————. "Carrying the *Mikoshi*: Further Field Notes on the Shrine Festival in Modern Tokyo." *Asian Folklore Studies* 31 (1982), 89–114.

————. "Folkdance and Fairgrounds: More Notes on Neighborhood Festivals in Tokyo." *Asian Folklore Studies* 34 (1975), 1–20.

————. "The Form and Meaning of the Festival." *Asian Folklore Studies* 28 (1969), 1–16.

————. "The Grammar of a Rite in Shinto." *Asian Folklore Studies* 35 (1976), 17–27.

————. "*O-Kagura*: Field Notes on the Festival Drama in Modern Tokyo." *Asian Folklore Studies* 29 (1970), 275–300.

————. "The Shrine: Notes Towards a Study of Neighborhood Festivals in Modern Tokyo." *Asian Folklore Studies* 34 (1975), 1–38.

————. "Of Talismans and Shadow Bodies: Annual Purification Rites at a Tokyo Shrine." *Contemporary Religions in Japan* 11 (1970), 181–222.

Salamon, Sonya. "The Varied Groups of Japanese and German Housewives." *Japan Interpreter* 10 (1975), 151–70.

Sanches, Mary. "Falling Words: An Analysis of a Japanese *Rakugo* Performance." In *Sociocultural Dimensions of Language Use*. Ed. M. Sanches and B. G. Blount. New York: Academic Press, 1975, 269–306.

Sansom, George B. *Japan: A Short Cultural History*. 1931; rev. ed. New York: Appleton-Century-Crofts, 1943.

Satow, Ernest. *A Diplomat in Japan*. 1921; rpt. Rutland, Vt., and Tokyo: Charles E. Tuttle Co., 1983.

Seidensticker, Edward. *Kafu the Scribbler*. Stanford: Stanford University Press, 1965.

————. *Low City, High City: Tokyo from Edo to the Earthquake*. New York: Alfred A. Knopf, 1983.

Shively, Donald H. "*Bakufu* Versus *Kabuki*." *Harvard Journal of Asiatic Studies* 18 (1955), 326–56.

Shoppingu, comp. *Kankonsosai to O-Tsukiai no Subete*. Special issue of *Shoppingu*, September 1980.
「冠婚葬祭とおつきあいのすべて」 「ショッピング」 1980・9

Skinner, Kenneth. "*Sarariiman Manga*." *Japan Interpreter* 12 (1979), 449–57.

Smith, Henry D. II. "The Edo-Tokyo Transition: In Search of Common Ground." In *Japan in Transition: From Tokugawa to Meiji*. Ed. Marius B. Jansen and Gilbert Rozman. Princeton: Princeton University Press, 1986, 347–74.

————. "Tokyo and London: Comparative Conceptions of the City." In *Japan: A Comparative View*. Ed. A. M. Craig. Princeton: Princeton University Press, 1979, 49–99.

————. "Tokyo as an Idea: An Exploration of Japanese Urban Thought Until 1945." *Journal of Japanese Studies* 4 (1978), 45–80.

————. *Learning from Shogun: Japanese History and Western Fantasy*. Santa Barbara: Program in Asian Studies, University of California, 1980.

Smith, Robert J. "The Eclipse of Communal Ritual in Japan." In Y. Yamamoto, *The*

Namahage: A Festival in the Northeast of Japan. Philadelphia: Institute for the Study of Human Issues, 1978, 1–8.

―――. *Japanese Society: Tradition, Self and the Social Order*. Cambridge: Cambridge University Press, 1983.

―――. "Pre-Industrial Urbanism in Japan: A Consideration of Multiple Traditions in a Feudal Society." *Economic Development and Cultural Change* 9, no. 1, pt. II. (1960), 241–57.

―――. "Town and City in Pre-Modern Japan." In *Urban Anthropology*. Ed. A. Southall. New York: Oxford University Press, 1973, 163–210.

Soeda, Hiroshi. "Festivity and the City: Mobile Stages of the Gion Festival." *Concerned Theatre Japan* 2 (1973), 190–207.

Sonoda, Minoru. "The Traditional Festival in Urban Society." *Japanese Journal of Religious Studies* 2 (1975), 103–36.

Statler, Oliver. *Japanese Pilgrimage*. New York: William Morrow, 1983.

Statler, Oliver, et al. *All-Japan: The Catalogue of Everything Japanese*. New York: Quill, 1984.

Stevens, Ruth P. *Kanazawa: The Other Side of Japan*. Kanazawa: Nakagawa Taisho Printing Co., 1979.

Stevenson, Harold, Hiroshi Azuma, and Kenji Hakuta, eds. *Child Development and Education in Japan*. New York: W. H. Freeman & Co., 1986.

Tanaka, Yasuo. *Nantonaku, Kurisutaru*. Tokyo: Kawade Shobo Shinsha, 1981.
田中康夫 『なんとなくクリスタル』 河出書房新社 １９８１

Tokyo-to [Tokyo Metropolitan Government]. *Tokyo Hyakunen-shi*. 7 vols. Tokyo: Gyosei, 1979.
『東京百年史』 ぎょうせい 　１９７９

Ueno, Chizuko. "Matsuri to Kyodotai." In *Chiiki Bunka no Shakaigaku*. Ed. S. Inoue. Kyoto: Sekaishisosha, 1983, 46–78.

U.S. Department of Education. *Japanese Education Today*. Washington, D.C.: U.S. Government Printing Office, 1987.

Varley, H. Paul. *Japanese Culture*. 3d ed. Honolulu: University of Hawaii Press, 1984.

Vogel, Ezra F. "Entrance Examinations and Emotional Disturbances in Japan's 'New Middle Class.' " In *Japanese Culture*. Ed. R. J. Smith and R. K. Beardsley. Chicago: Aldine, 1962, 140–52.

―――. "The Go-Between in a Developing Society: The Case of the Japanese Marriage Arranger." *Human Organization* 20 (1961), 112–20.

―――. *Japan's New Middle Class*. 2d ed. Berkeley: University of California Press, 1971.

Vogel, Suzanne H. "Professional Housewife: The Career of Urban Middle Class Japanese Women." *Japan Interpreter* 12 (1978), 16–43.

Wagatsuma, Hiroshi, and George A. DeVos. "Arakawa Ward: Urban Growth and Modernization." *Rice University Studies* 66 (1980), 201–24.

―――. *Heritage of Endurance*. Berkeley: University of California Press, 1984.

Wakita, Haruko, with Susan B. Hanley. "Dimensions of Development: Cities in Fifteenth- and Sixteenth-Century Japan." In *Japan Before Tokugawa*. Ed. J. W. Hall, et al. Princeton: Princeton University Press, 1981, 295–326.

Waley, Paul. *Tokyo Now and Then: An Explorer's Guide*. New York and Tokyo: John Weatherhill, 1984.

Watanabe, Shun-ichi J. "Metropolitanism as a Way of Life: The Case of Tokyo, 1868–

1930." In *Metropolis: 1890–1940*. Ed. A. Sutcliffe. Chicago and London: University of Chicago Press and Mansell, 1984, 403–29.

White, James W. "Internal Migration in Prewar Japan." *Journal of Japanese Studies* 4 (1978), 81–123.

———. *Migration in Metropolitan Japan*. Berkeley: Institute of East Asian Studies, University of California, 1982.

White, Merry I. *The Japanese Educational Challenge: A Commitment to Children*. New York: Free Press, 1987.

Whiting, Robert. *The Chrysanthemum and the Bat*. New York: Dodd, Mead, 1977.

Whitney, Clara. *Clara's Diary: An American Girl in Meiji Japan*. Tokyo and New York: Kodansha International, 1979.

Wimberley, Howard W. "On Living with Your Past: Style and Structure Among Contemporary Japanese Merchant Families." *Economic Development and Cultural Change* 21 (1973), 423–28.

Woog, Adam. "Chindonya: Street Artists of Advertising." *Japan Society Newsletter* (February 1986), 3–6.

Wurman, Richard S., comp. *Tokyo Access*. Los Angeles: Access Press, 1984.

Yamamura, Kozo, and Susan B. Hanley. "Ichi hime, ni Taro: Educational Aspirations and the Decline of Fertility in Postwar Japan." *Journal of Japanese Studies* 2 (1975), 83–125.

Yamazaki, Masakazu. *Yawarakai Kojinshugi no Tanjo*. Tokyo: Chuo Koronsha, 1984.

山崎正和　『やわらかい個人主義の誕生』　中央公論社　１９８４

Yanagida, Kunio, comp. and ed., and Charles Terry, trans. and adapter. *Japanese Manners and Customs in the Meiji Era*. Tokyo: Obunsha, 1957.

Yazaki, Takeo. *Social Change and the City in Japan*. Tokyo: Japan Publications, 1968.

———. "The History of Urbanization in Japan." In *Urban Anthropology*. Ed. A. Southall. New York: Oxford University Press, 1973, 139–61.

Yoneyama, Toshinao. *Gion Matsuri*. Tokyo: Chuo Koronsha, 1974.

米山俊直　『祇園祭』　中央公論社　１９７４

———. *Tenjin Matsuri*. Tokyo: Chuo Koronsha, 1979.

米山俊直　『天神祭』　中央公論社　１９７９

2

Popular Architecture

RENATO A. PIROTTA

In May 1984, the government of Japan appointed a commission to study the effects of advertising in public places and, based on its findings, to formulate legislation whereby advertising on billboards attached to building facades or as free-standing structures would in the future be controlled by legislation. Even in the land of the rising sun, some have come to recognize the visual chaos that gaudy advertisements can create. Assuming that the commission's work proceeds smoothly and that legislation is finally introduced, this may lead to the uncovering of Japan's architectural masterpieces in uncluttered splendor.

The thirty-six-year-old Hajime Yatsuka, a noted critic and scholar, was recently quoted by the *Japan Times Weekly* as having said that the future is more likely to bring to pass pessimistic truths than optimistic lies. Quality architecture, Yatsuka believes, died with the 1970 Osaka World Fair.

A walk down a street of any large Japanese city offers little more than a chain of visual insults. The problem is the result of the nation's building laws, which set the minimum permissible distance between buildings at fifty centimeters, dictate the building materials that can be used, and enforce the basic concepts that govern urban planning. The urban sprawl is spreading as if in a race to cover every square inch of remaining space with plastic products and fast-food outlets.

Man-made materials have replaced the traditional Japanese building materials of wood, paper, and bamboo. From the northern island of Hokkaido to Okinawa in the south, fast-food outlets represent an omnipresent ogre to the seeker of architectural beauty. Not only are there such overseas outlets as MacDonald's and Dunkin' Donuts, but numerous local imitators: the Love and Lotteria hamburger chains; Hoka Hoka Bento, a takeout hot-food chain; *pachinko* parlors;

game centers; and a myriad of vending machines. The environment does not reflect architectural quality, but rather imparts an atmosphere of inevitable doom.

Yatsuka has not been timid in voicing his opinion regarding these current trends, even suggesting that Japanese architects would be well advised to set aside their drawing boards and reassess their function within the framework of the needs of society. As he points out, it is becoming increasingly difficult to find examples of aesthetically pleasing Japanese architecture. The average city dwelling is characterized by the frenetic expansion of the last twenty years since the 1964 Tokyo Olympics.

Although housing for the average worker is of a relatively high standard, commuting distances to work are great, rents are exorbitant, and dwellings exceedingly compact. A survey released by the prime minister's office at the end of May 1984 revealed that 62.9 percent of the dwellings in Japan were owned by their occupants and that the average area of dwellings increased from 80.3 square meters in 1978 to 86.2 square meters in 1983. This does not, however, apply to the Tokyo metropolis, where the average size of a dwelling increased from 54.5 square meters in 1978 to 58.2 square meters in 1983.[1]

Another survey, conducted in April 1984 by the Japan Institute for Social and Economic Affairs, shows that, at the time of the survey, 120 million people were living in an area of 377,581 square kilometers. Other relevant statistics are as follows: 99 percent of Japanese households possess such durables as refrigerators and televisions, 63 percent own cars, and 17.4 percent own pianos; 54.8 percent of the population consider themselves to belong to the middle class, 27 percent to the lower middle class, 0.7 percent to the upper class, 7.2 percent to the upper middle class, and 6.9 percent to the lower class.[2]

Not least in importance as mirrors of popular culture are the more than 2,756 national weekly and periodical magazines (as of 1981). They cover the whole gamut of social interests, from *Brutus* for the slick city man to weeklies for children. A look at any of these reminds one of the versatility of Japanese architecture, no aspect of which can be overlooked.

HISTORICAL SURVEY

Japanese architecture, with its origins in the construction of shrines and temples, began with highly demanding standards. Architectural styles were continually undergoing stringent refinement as aesthetic dictates were developed by temple carpenters (*miya daiku*) and artisans. Aesthetic and practical considerations governed the choice of materials, usually wood, bamboo, and paper, most of which were produced in the vicinity of the construction site. These light materials were ideal for a nation intermittently jolted by earthquakes of varying intensity. Techniques were sophisticated; structures exuded artistic beauty and blended with the environment to give an appearance of overall unity. Those ideas that did filter through from overseas were adapted and applied, gradually over the years, until they had become part of the Japanese process.

Although Japan has long been known as an isolated nation, it has not been closed to foreign ideas and items, many of which have been adopted and subsequently adapted. The arrival of Commodore Perry in 1853 and the subsequent demand that Japan open its doors to foreign traders sparked a flurry of changes. This culminated, following the Meiji Restoration (1868), in the establishment of a new and modern governmental structure.

Among the many developments ushered in during this period was the adoption of the solar calendar in 1872. Architecture around that time was guided by Chinese philosophical principles of orientation, known as the *Kaso* in Japan. These came to be successfully integrated with Western precepts that were gradually increasing in academic importance. Heijokyo (Nara) and Heiankyo (Kyoto) are two examples of urban design based on Chinese theories of orientation. The modern interpretation of the *Kaso* style by Kiyoshi Seike (published in 1983 in Japanese) has given the style currency again; it is also the basis for most of the designs of modern houses.

This was also a time when instructors and technical experts were invited from abroad, including such men of note as the English architect Josiah Conder who, following his arrival in Japan in 1877, went on to gain great fame. His *Domestic Architecture in Japan*, written in 1887, and *Landscape Gardening in Japan*, written in 1893, are two volumes from that period. Conder became the first professor of architecture at Tokyo Technical College (today the Architectural Department of the University of Tokyo), and the graduation of his first student in this new academic field marked Japan's transition into the era of modern architecture. European technology witnessed a relative boom in Japan. Western buildings soared as stone and brick became the preferred building materials, replacing wood for structures other than dwellings.

Another great change came in the wake of the Great Kanto Earthquake of 1923, in which most European-style structures were destroyed. Structural engineering advanced, as did the application of ferroconcrete frame building techniques, which were to leave their mark on Japanese architecture until the end of World War II.

Following World War II, the legal requirement that architects be registered led to the establishment of two categories of architects, namely, those who had passed national examinations (first-level architects) and those who had passed prefectural examinations (second-level architects). Those with first-level qualifications are licensed to design multistory structures and factories, while second-level architects are limited to designing individual dwellings and other small structures. In January 1984 there were 629,783 professional architects in Japan; 182,515 belonged to the first category and 447,268 to the second. Fortunately, however, there remain many carpenters who have maintained the traditional techniques upon which the architecture for wooden structures is based; it is still possible to use relatively more wood than steel for structures in the country—though not in the cities.

In the early postwar period, small- and medium-sized construction companies and the carpenter-cum-architect were in great demand, but nowadays the large construction companies have come to monopolize the housing market, especially in metropolitan and outer-metropolitan areas.

It is interesting to note that the government did not avail itself of the opportunity to rebuild those areas around Tokyo and other big cities destroyed by either the Kanto earthquake or World War II according to any special plan, but merely allowed them to be rebuilt much as they had been before, using outdated codes. The outstanding layout of Kyoto, based on an ancient Chinese plan, is not at odds with modern Japanese architecture and could have been used as a guide in the rebuilding of those areas.

Postwar architecture has departed greatly from Japanese traditions, with city dwellings often resembling barracks in appearance. Innovative American concepts have, however, made their mark, and pleasing examples of planning can be found in the layout of Nagoya and Hiroshima, as well as in the designs used by some Japanese construction companies for apartment buildings until around 1975.

In 1951 the Japanese architect Kiyoshi Seike presented what he called the "Mori house," an attempt to use traditionally Japanese ideas in home design. Sliding doors, tatami matting, and other aspects of traditional design briefly regained acclaim, but, following a period in which old and new were blended, modern technology came to the fore, resulting in the architecture of today.

Design requirements of dwellings hurled architects from pillar to post as they tried to keep pace with fashion dictates. At the time of the Osaka World Fair in 1970, it was believed that the nuclear family home must be primarily Japanese, with only one Western room. By 1978 there was a brief period when it was thought that the ideal nuclear family home should be primarily Western in design, with only one Japanese room. Today's market requirements are dictated by technological concepts, emphasizing greater space in a computerized home.

The latest housing designs developed in Japan are based on high-tech and the most advanced architectural precepts. They have not yet reached the West, but this made-in-Japan architecture promises to be a major export commodity in the future. It is also distinctly possible that such construction giants as Mitsui Home and Toyota Home may, in the process of revolutionizing housing design, revive and popularize some traditional aspects of architecture.

Theory and Criticism

Architectural concepts and traditions have come a long way since Otto Wagner defined the basic precepts of the discipline and the ultimate role of the architect. Change in architecture is also reflected in Japan, where the need has now been recognized for a reassessment of the role of the interrelationships between building designers, landscape gardeners, and interior designers. However, while the need for systemization has been recognized, rapid postwar developments have prevented any really fruitful relationships from occurring between the different schools of architecture.

The lack of functional coordination and clearly defined goals is probably a result of the complex conglomeration of traditional ideas and philosophies, both Japanese and Western, combined in such a way as to compound the task of the researcher. There are no clear-cut trends or rules that have not been subject to exceptions. If the student attempts the gargantuan task of putting architectural developments into some kind of logical sequence, changes move apace, leaving him behind. Those who manage to catch up are soon frustrated by the realization that theory and practice reflected in every facet of popular architecture are poles apart. Current Japanese architecture is characterized by a previously unknown vitality that springs from the blending of diverse concepts. It is this diversity that frustrates any attempt at simple historical analysis.

Japanese Architecture (Volumes 1 and 2) presents a clear overview of the recent trends in Japanese architecture. A compendium of essays, it covers museums, religious and high-rise architecture, housing, and the incorporation of both reclaimed land and man-made islands into the fabric of urban planning.

This work is well supplemented by *Residential Architecture Japan Part II*, a lucid presentation of the latest designs in the form of an architect's biography. The reader is left to assess the strengths and weaknesses of the trends, however, since the authors give little criticism or historical comparison.

The explosion of rebuilding projects, in the wake of the devastation of the war, resulted in confusion and near paralysis in cities and metropolitan areas. The inconsistency and total lack of systematic town planning inspired a group of architects to propose a series of feasible designs in 1959; these are presented in the publication of Noforu Kawazoe's *New Urbanism: Metabolism 1960*. A subsequent work, Werner Frank's *Japanischen Metabolisten*, analyses the movement, tracing its historical development and explaining its origins. Of great value is the author's attempt to explain the relationship between what have come to be perceived by many as the good and bad aspects of architecture in Japan.

Still on the theme of the metabolic movement is Hajime Yatsuka's work, "Hiromi Fuji's Vision-Reversing Machine," in which Fuji criticizes the group that, in the writer's opinion, failed in its avowed attempt to overcome the final crisis in modern culture. While this group of architects set out to create symbolic works of art in the houses they designed, he accuses them of producing little more than second-rate shelters.

This reflects a tendency that is steadily gaining international currency. Urban planners are using the links between respect for the nature worship of the past and modern ecology to reassess the needs of urban design in Tokyo. Tokyo is a relatively old city, but its structures are mostly postwar. Minoru Takeyama and a group of graduate students set out to decode the confusing hodge-podge that is Tokyo planning, and their ideas make interesting reading in Takeyama's "Tokyo Urban Language."

The city of Kurashiki, Okayama prefecture (see Volume 31 of *Process Ar-*

chitecture, 1982), has come to attract much attention as a harmonious blend of ideas, Eastern and Western, old and new. The restoration of the old rice storehouses in the city was so successful that it set in motion trends in modern design that have come to influence the modern architecture of the city. It remains to be seen whether these reverberations will have any effect.

"Modernization, a Messy Form of Madness," by Dr. D. A. Rain, outlines the impact that modernity has had on society and the mixed blessings that have come in its wake. The price of modernization, with its fast, technology-oriented, materialistic way of life, has led to the destruction of traditional spiritual values. Nevertheless, vestiges of these values remain. The *noren*, a half-curtain traditionally hung at the top of the entrance to shops, can still be seen even in Tokyo. Serving not just as a shop sign, it is an integral part of the overall design of the structure, and this relationship is clearly presented in "Japanese Signs," edited by Yukio Ota, Osami Sakano, and Miwako Ito, which looks into relationships between signs and architecture in the urban environment.

"Shomei Suru Imi" [The significance of naming] is a critical essay on the responsibility of architects vis-à-vis their designs and suggests that, in the interest of attaining higher standards, architects should be required to sign their work, so that the public would know where to direct praise or anger.

Based on this concept, Peter Popham's article, "Mori Story," looks at Taikiichiro Mori who, since 1957, has been naming and numbering all his buildings, now up to Mori Building 43. Nevertheless, the author of the article, while respecting Mori's motives in seeking to beautify his native country, detects little more than banality in his vision.

Gardens have traditionally played an important role in Japanese design, but they have been sacrificed in both number and size as urban density has increased and large-scale projects for free-standing dwellings and high-rise apartment blocks have proliferated. Since recreational facilities and contact with nature remain major social needs, new garden and park concepts have evolved. Together with suggestions for future development, these are dealt with in Tsunekata Naito and Haruto Kobayashi's "Landscape Design in Japan."

"Architecture and Water Space" (edited by Kenji Horigome, Twn Chung Kuo, and Kazuji Watabe), traces the historical importance and use of water and related structures in Japanese architecture and their influences on contemporary design. An enormous amount of material is covered in this publication, which looks at all aspects of architecture from city planning to the design of buildings and plazas.

The reader will observe that almost all publications lament the decline and, in some cases, the total disappearance of traditional Japanese craftsmanship. As the carpenter, the architect of traditional values, has adapted his skills to the dictates of modern society, the techniques that had created the splendors of the past have been largely lost. The street stalls selling cooked food, still to be found throughout Japan albeit in decreasing numbers, are praiseworthy survivals of wooden structural design. In "A Culture of Wood," Kiyoshi Seike amply illustrates how the architecture of wooden structures is gradually being sacrificed at the altar of modernity; there will, it is hoped, be more research on this aspect of architecture before the last vestige disappears.

Even the institution of the public bath survives almost solely in the memory of older members of society. These wooden masterpieces have succumbed to the dictates of modern hygiene and a revolution in the design of dwellings— almost all of which now have a bath. But not all is lost, and scholarship has preserved the philosophy of the Japanese carpenter and some 250 traditional techniques in Moriya's *Toryo no Chiebukuro* [The wisdom of master carpenters].

REFERENCE WORKS

Since reference works covering the whole range of architectural developments throughout Japanese history are not available, it is necessary to approach any study on the basis of what has been written about each of the periods into which the nation's history is divided. Although a look at the history of Japan reveals the close interrelationship between historical and architectural developments, no major detailed work has entailed such a thesis.

For the professional architect, however, there is no lack of reference materials, from handbooks and guides that are updated annually to such publications as the *Kenchiku Daijiten* [Dictionary of modern architectural terminology], which stands out from the rest in that it deals with the philosophy behind certain techniques and movements in architecture and urban design.

For students of architecture, there is *Kapuseru for Architecture Students*, a handbook in three volumes; the first (1982) discusses architecture as a science, the second (1983) comprises a bibliography, and the third (1984) is a computer guide for architects, with a section devoted to advice regarding examinations and the job market.

Many consider the following reference works to be the most useful:

1. *Kenchiku Tosho Mokuroku* [Architecture book catalogue], published annually by Ko-gakusho Mokuroku Kankokai, is divided into thirteen sections, listing 3,700 books, each with brief descriptive comments.

2. Inoue Eiko's *Kenchiku Book Guide 1000* [Book guide for architects], published in 1984 by Inoue Shoin, is divided into one hundred sections dealing with architecture and related endeavors; it lists 1,000 books, each with a short descriptive comment; 157 architecture newsletters; 846 publications; and 174 public relations publications (with company names, addresses, and telephone numbers).

3. "Nihon no Kenchikuka" [The Japanese architects], a December 1981 special issue of *Shinkenchiku*, the monthly magazine, gives a bibliography of the top Japanese architects for 1920–1980. The layout is clear and may be of particular value to those seeking information on the development of architecture in Japan and the influence of various schools of thought.

4. Japan Travel Bureau's *A Look into Japan*, published in English by the Japan Travel Bureau with comic book–style illustrations, gives an insight into the culture, traditions, and lifestyles of Japan. Japan Travel Bureau's *Living Japanese Style* is similar to the above. *A Cultural Dictionary of Japan* published by the *Japan Times* (edited by Momo Yamaguchi and Setsuko Kojima) is a compendium of Japanese words covering traditional arts and an invaluable reference work for students.

5. *A Guide to Japanese Architecture* (1985) provides a comprehensive overview of modern architecture in Japan. Names and addresses of architects and buildings are included.

6. *Pia Map '83* and *Pia Map '85* are for those with an interest in the architecture connected with the pleasures of nightlife. These guidebooks list 121 places to go for galleries, entertainment, and traditional events and contain campus maps and special maps of Tokyo's twenty-three wards. In a similar vein is the English publication *Tokyo Access*, by Richard Saul Wurman. *Pia Map 2* is a guidebook listing such locations as theaters, cinemas, and athletic grounds in the Tokyo area. *Pia* itself is a weekly publication listing cultural events.

Some video films are worthy of mention because of their visual value to architecture students. The Japan Foundation's video library has the following films: *Ise: The Roots of Japanese Architecture, Japanese Carpenters, The Landscape of the Soul—Kiichi Sano, A Sense of Urban Space: Kisho Kurokawa,* and *Houses: Japan Today and Yesterday.*

NHK, Japan's semi-governmental broadcasting corporation, produced a series of five video cassette tapes in 1984, each forty-five minutes long, which deals with current problems such as the improper use of materials and mistakes in design.

RESEARCH COLLECTIONS

With the fast pace at which Japanese society is changing and the penchant of its people for collecting information, it is virtually impossible for a foreigner to easily ascertain certain items of information without some form of aid.

Broadly speaking, information on current architecture can be gleaned by following three approaches: field work, during which information and impressions are collected and collated; reference work, scouring libraries for plans, drawings, books, magazines, microfilms, slides, and videos; and research in the files kept by the public relations departments of local government bodies dealing with architecture and those of real estate agencies and architectural companies.

Some art lovers have even collected examples of architectural hardware, some of which are to be found in open-air museums that provide an almost natural environment for the displays. While such collections are few, they are of profound interest to the architecture student and researcher.

An exciting and vivid example of Edo period (1615–1867) architecture can be found surrounding Ivy Square in the city of Kurashiki, Okayama Prefecture. A red-brick factory, remodeled in 1974, and the square are in complete harmony with the surrounding white-walled restored warehouses along the river. Five museums that hold excellent displays are to be found in this area, perhaps the most famous of which being the Torajiro Kojima Memorial Museum, opened in 1981, also in a renovated red-brick warehouse.

Meijimura, or Meiji village, built on an area of 1 million square meters on a hillside facing Lake Ikura in Inuyama City, Aichi Prefecture, is an open-air museum displaying examples of Meiji period architecture. There are over fifty buildings that have been collected from around the nation and rebuilt at the site, which, opened in 1965, is of great historical significance. It is the only village made up entirely of buildings from that era that escaped the devastation of World War II, the ravaging fires that followed earthquakes, and the postwar rebuilding boom. The houses include original period furniture and household items.

The economic development of the nation sounded the deathknell of the traditional farmhouse. Fortunately, this situation has not gone entirely unnoticed, and some collectors have seen to it that examples of these fine structures remain intact for posterity. There are three open-air museums designed to preserve rural buildings. Each has some twenty structures completely intact. Of the three, the closest to Tokyo is the Kawasaki Shiritsu Nihon Minkaen (Kawasaki Municipal Park for Traditional Japanese Houses), in which the buildings are well presented. In Osaka City there is the Nihon Minka Shuraku Hakubutsukan (Museum of Japanese Village Farmhouses), which is also well designed. Then there is the Hida Minzoku Mura (Hida Folklore Village), near Takayama City, Gifu Prefecture, some six hours by train from Tokyo. On display in the houses are various tools that were the key to survival for rural mountain communities in times past. As of July 1985 all exhibits provide English-language pamphlets.

In 1869 the first Meiji pioneers came to Hokkaido, the northernmost island of Japan, and started to cultivate this area. The historical village of Hokkaido, Hokkaido Kitaku no Mura, is a new and very large open-air museum with twenty buildings dating from 1882 to 1919. Unfortunately, this place is remote from Tokyo and cannot be reached on a day trip.

Also of interest, not just to the consumer but also to researchers, are some 170 standing exhibits such as the Jutaku Tenjijo (Housing Exhibition Place), in which an average of ten to twenty family homes are displayed as advertisements for consumers, all containing the latest in design innovations. Such outdoor exhibits, which are open to the public at no charge, play an important role in setting trends in housing design. Continual fierce competition among the leading builders—Daiwa House, Mitsui Home, Sekisui Heim, National Jutaku—results in a seemingly unending flow of new ideas.

NOTES

1. *The Japan Times,* May 29, 1984, p. 12.
2. Ibid.

BIBLIOGRAPHY

Books and Articles

A Guide to Japanese Architecture. Tokyo: Japan Architect, 1985.

Alex, William. *Japanese Architecture*. New York: George Braziller, 1963.

A Look into Japan. Vols. 1–5. Tokyo: Japan Travel Bureau, 1984.

Blaser, Werner. *Structure and Form in Japan*. Zurich: Artemis, 1963.

Cleaver, Charles Grinnell. *Japanese and Americans: Cultural Parallels and Paradoxes*. Tokyo: Charles E. Tuttle, 1978.

Conder, Josiah. *Domestic Architecture in Japan*. London: Royal Institute of British Architects, 1887.

————. *Landscape Gardening in Japan*. Tokyo: Kelly and Walsh, 1893.

Critchlow, Keith. "The Siting of a Japanese Rural House." In *Shelter, Sign, and Symbol*. Ed. Paul Oliver. New York: Overlook Press, 1977.

Endes, Siegfried. *Japanische Wohnformen und ihre Veränderung* [Japanese forms of housing and their transformation]. Hamburg: Institut für Asienkunde, 1979.

Engel, Heinrich. *The Japanese House: A Tradition for Contemporary Architecture*. Tokyo: Charles E. Tuttle, 1977.

Fawcett, Chris. *The New Japanese House*. London: Granada, 1980.

Fluchter, Winfried. *Neulandgewinnung und Industrieansiedlung vor den japanischen Küsten: Funktionen, Strukturen und Auswirkungen dur Aufschüttungsgebiete "umetate-chi"* [Land reclamation and industrial development of near-shore coastal areas in Japan: functions, structures and effects of reclaimed areas: *"umetate-chi"*]. In German with an English summary. Schoningh: Paderborn, 1975.

Frank, Werner. *Die Japanischen Metabolisten*. In German, with a copy of *Metabolism 1960* in English. Graz: Technische Universität Graz, 1980.

Gale, Simon J. "Orientation." In *Japan: Climate, Space and Concept*. Tokyo: Process Architecture Publishing, 1981, pp. 36–50.

Ganjehlou, A. *Industrialized Architecture*. Tokyo: Prefabrication Division Ando Construction Co., 1980.

Hayakawa, Masao. *The Garden Art of Japan*. In *Heibonsha Survey of Japanese Art*. Vol. 28. New York: Weatherhill/Heibonsha, 1976.

Hayashi, Masako. *House Design in Today's Japan*. Tokyo: Shokokusha, 1969.

Hirai, Kiyoshi. *Feudal Architecture of Japan*. In *Heibonsha Survey of Japanese Art*. Vol. 13. New York: Weatherhill/Heibonsha. 1973.

————. *Nippon Jutakushi Toshu* [History of the Japanese house]. Tokyo: Nippon Hoso Shuppan Kyokai, 1974.

平井聖　「日本住宅史踏襲」　日本放送出版協会　東京　１９７４

————. *Nippon Jyutakuzusetsu* [Historical condensation of the development of the Japanese house]. Tokyo: Maikotosho Kabushiki Kaisha, 1976.

平井聖　「日本住宅図説」　まいこ図書株式会社　東京　１９７６

Horigome, Kenji, Twn Chung Kuo, and Kazuji Watabe, eds. "Architecture and Water Space." *Process Architecture*. Vol. 24. Tokyo: P. A. Publishing, 1981.

Horiike, Hideo. *Japanese-English Practical Terms of Architecture*. Tokyo: Inoue Shoin, 1980.

Hoshino, Kazuhiro. *Kenchiku Eigo Jiten* [Architecture's English dictionary]. 1978; rpt. Tokyo: Shokokusha, 1984.

星野和弘 『建築英語辞典』 初版１９７８ 新版１９８４ 彰国社 東京

Itoh, Teiji. *Space and Illusion in the Japanese Garden*. New York: Weatherhill/Heibonsha, 1973.

―――. *Traditional Domestic Architecture of Japan*. New York: Weatherhill/Heibonsha, 1972.

Iwamiya, Takeji. *The Japanese Garden*. Tokyo: Zokeisha Publication, 1987.

Japan 1983: An International Comparison. Tokyo: Keizai Koho Center, 1983.

"Japanese Architecture, Recent Trends." *Process Architecture*. Vol. 28. Tokyo: P. A. Publishing, 1982.

"Japanese Architecture, Two Recent Developments." *Process Architecture*. Vol. 36. Tokyo: P. A. Publishing, 1983.

"Japanese City and Architecture: Kurashiki." *Process Architecture*. Vol. 31. Tokyo: P. A. Publishing, 1982.

Jyutaku Hand Book 1984 [Housing handbook 1984]. Tokyo: Nihon Jyutaku Kyokai, 1984.

『住宅ハンドブック１９８４』 日本住宅協会 東京 １９８４

Kapuseru for Architecture Students. Tokyo: Inoue Shoin, 1982, 1983, 1984.

Kawazoe, Noboru, ed. *Contemporary Japanese Architecture*. Tokyo: Kokusai Koryu Kikin, 1973.

―――. *The New Urbanism: Metabolism 1960*. Tokyo: Bijitsu Shuppansha, 1960.

Kenchiku Book Guide 1000 [Book guide for architects]. Tokyo: Inoue Shoin, 1984.

『建築ブックガイド１０００』 井上書院 東京 １９８４

Kenchiku Tosho Mokuroku [Architecture book catalogue]. Tokyo: Kogakusho Mokuroku Kankokai, 1984.

『建築図書目録』 工学書目録刊行会 東京 １９８４

Kuck, Loraine E. *The Art of Japanese Gardens*. New York: John Day, 1940.

Living Japanese Style. Tokyo: Japan Travel Bureau, 1984.

Masuda, Tomoya, and Yukio Futagawa. *Japan*. Munchen: Hirmer Verlag, 1969.

Matsumura, Keizo, ed. *Japanese Houses Today*. Tokyo: Asahi Shimbun, 1958.

Meid, Michiko. *Der Einführungsprozess der europaischen und der nordamerikanischen Architektur in Japan seit 1542* [The introduction of European and North American architecture into Japan since 1542]. Köln: Abteilung Architektur des Kunsthistorischen Instituts der Universität Köln, 1977.

Miyawaki, Dan. *Zoku Gendai Kenchiku Yogoroku* [Modern architectural term dictionary II]. Tokyo: Shokokusha, 1975.

宮川壇 『続現代建築用語録』 彰国社 東京 １９７５

Moriya, Haru. *Toryo no Chiebukuro* [The wisdom of master carpenters]. Tokyo: Kodansha, 1979.

Morse, Edward S. *Japanese Homes and Their Surroundings*. 1886; rpt. Tokyo: Charles E. Tuttle, 1976.

Naito, Tsunekata, and Haruto Kobayashi, eds. "Landscape Design in Japan: Current Issues and Some Ideas." *Process Architecture*. Vol. 46. Tokyo: P. A. Publishing, 1984.

"Nihon no Kenchikuka" [The Japanese architects]. In *Shin Kenchiku*. Tokyo: Shin Kenchikusha, 1981.

『新建築』 日本の建築家特集 １９８１.１２ 新建築社 東京 １９８１

Okawa, Naomi. *Edo Architecture: Katsura and Nikko*. New York: Weatherhill/Heibonsha, 1975.

Ota, Yukio, Osami Sakano, and Miwako Ito, ed. "Japanese Signs."*Process Architecture*. Vol. 42. Tokyo: P. A. Publishing, 1983.

Paine, Robert Treat, and Alexander Soper. *The Art and Architecture of Japan*. Middlesex: Penguin, 1955.

Pia Map 2. Tokyo: Pia, 1984.

「ぴあマップ2」 ぴあ株式会社 東京 1 9 8 4

Pia Map '83. Tokyo: Pia, 1983.

「ぴあマップ' 8 3」 ぴあ株式会社 東京 1 9 8 3

Pia Map '85. Tokyo: Pia, 1985.

「ぴあマップ' 8 5」 ぴあ株式会社 東京 1 9 8 5 .

Popham, Peter. "The Mori Story: Up from the Ashes." *Tokyo Journal* (March 1984).

Rain, D. A. "Modernization, a Messy Form of Madness." *Japan Times* (September 1983).

Residential Architecture Japan Part II. Tokyo: A. D. A. EDITA, 1983.

Residential Architecture of 1970s in Japan. Tokyo: A. D. A. EDITA, 1970.

Roberts, Laurence P. *Roberts' Guide to Japanese Museums*. Tokyo: Kodansha International, 1978.

Sakamoto, Taro. *Japanese History*. Tokyo: Shobi Print Co., 1975.

Schaarschmidt-Richter. Irmtraud, and Osamu Mori. *Japanese Gardens*. New York: William Morrow, 1979.

Seike, Kiyoshi. *The Art of Japanese Joinery*. New York: Weatherhill/Tankosha, 1977.

———. "A Culture of Wood." In *Japan: Climate, Space, and Concept*. Tokyo: P. A. Publishing, 1981, pp. 17–24.

———. *A Japanese Touch for Your Garden*. Tokyo: Kodansha International, 1980.

———. *Kaso*. Tokyo: Sakei Shuppansha, 1983.

Takeyama, Minoru. "Tokyo Urban Language." *Process Architecture,* Vol. 49. Tokyo: P. A. Publishing, 1984.

Tange, Kenzo, and Noboru Kawazoe. *Ise, Prototype of Japanese Architecture*. Cambridge: M. I. T. Press, 1965.

Tanigawa, Masami. *Kindai Kenchiku Shojiten* [A modern architectural dictionary]. Tokyo: Omusha, 1975.

谷川正己 「近代建築小事典」 オーム社 東京 1 9 7 5

Taut, Bruno. *Fundamentals of Japanese Architecture*. Tokyo: Kokusai Bunka Shinkokai, 1936.

———. *Houses and People of Japan*. Tokyo: Sanseido, 1958.

Yamaguchi, Momo, and Setsuko Kojima. *A Cultural Dictionary of Japan*. Tokyo: The Japan Times Co., 1979.

Yatsuka, Hajime. *Architecture Without Quality*. Tokyo: Japan Foundation, 1984.

———. "Hirome Fuji's Vision-Reversing Machine." In *Oppositions*. Vol. 22. Cambridge: M. I. T. Press, 1980.

Yoshida, Tetsuro. *Gardens of Japan*. New York: Praeger, 1957.

———. *The Japanese House and Garden*. New York: Praeger, 1969.

White Paper on Construction. Tokyo: Ministry of Construction, Research Institute of Construction and Economy, 1982–1983.

Wurman, Richard Saul. *Tokyo Access*. Los Angeles: Access Press, 1984.

Periodicals

Box. Tokyo: Diamond, 1980.
ボックス　ダイヤモンド社　東京　1980
Brutus. Tokyo: Magazine House, 1980.
BRUTUS(ブルータス)　マガジンハウス株式会社　東京　1980
Detail. Tokyo: Shokokusha, 1964.
ディティール　彰国社　東京　1964
Housing Review. Tokyo: Wiseman System Board, 1981.
Nikkei Architecture. Tokyo: Nikkei, 1976.
SD. Tokyo: Kashima Suppankai, 1965.

SD　鹿島出版会　東京　1965

Shin Kenchiku. Tokyo: Shin Kenchikusha, 1925.
新建築　新建築社　東京　1925

Institutions

Japan Foundation. Park Building, 3–6 Kioi-cho, Chiyoda-ku, Tokyo 102.
国際交流基金　東京都千代田区紀尾井町3－6パークビル
Japan Society of Architecture. Shiba 5–26–20, Minato-ku, Tokyo.
日本建築協会　東京都港区芝5－26－20
Keizai Koho Center, Japan Institute for Social and Economic Affairs. 6–1–1- Otemachi,
　　Chiyoda-ku, Tokyo.
経済文報センタ　東京千代田区大手町6－1－1
National Library of Japan. Nagata-cho 1–10–1, Chiyoda-ku, Tokyo.
国会図書館　東京都千代田区永田町1－10－1
NHK Service Center. Shibuya-ku, Jin-nai 1, Tokyo.
NHKサービスセンター　東京都渋谷区神内1

3

Japanese New Religions

H. BYRON EARHART

Japan is a land of many individual religious traditions that exist at various levels. Throughout Japanese history, from prehistoric times more than 2,000 years ago to the present, these individual traditions either have emerged out of Japanese culture or have been transmitted to Japan from other cultures and eventually have interacted to form the Japanese religious heritage. During the last century and a half, many changes have occurred in Japanese society and religion, and these changes are evident in the formation of many new religious movements. These movements, usually known in English as "New Religions,"[1] are distinguished from the older established religious institutions of Shinto and Buddhism and from the unorganized popular and folk traditions.

Most of the New Religions were founded by charismatic individuals who had revelatory experiences or rediscovered the power of earlier teachings and practices and arranged (or rearranged) such experiences, teachings, and practices into separate religious groups when a sufficient number of people had been attracted to a founder and the founder's message. As can be seen from even this brief sketch, the "new" character of the New Religions is their novel arrangement of old elements from other traditions: They are new configurations of the most vital aspects of the living religious heritage in Japan. The New Religions have been very active in seeking members, and have been successful not only through individual initiative and small groups but also through use of publishing and other mass media. The many New Religions constitute the most conspicuous religious force in contemporary Japan by virtue of both their rapid growth and dynamic activities. In order to focus on our central topic of New Religions, we must first explore briefly the variety of individual traditions as well as the several levels of religious life found in Japan.

Of the many religious traditions in Japan, those easiest to recognize are the ones that appear as organized religious and philosophical systems: Shinto, Buddhism, Taoism, Confucianism, and Christianity. These traditions are characterized by either standard ecclesiastical forms (priesthood, specific buildings for worship, regular rituals, and teaching or doctrine) or at least bodies of writing (such as philosophical and ethical texts). Shinto is the most distinctively Japanese religious tradition, having emerged out of prehistoric Japanese beliefs and practices related to *kami* (spirits or "gods"), nature, fertility, and celebration of communal life in relation to these forces. Under the influence of Buddhism, the priesthood, doctrine, and rituals of Shinto came to be organized more elaborately. Shinto is characterized both by local festivals at small shrines that petition the gods for the protection and blessings of the local people and by the national tradition of the "way of the *kami*." The latter is a distinctively Japanese religious heritage that recognizes the founding of the nation, the line of emperors, and the livelihood of the Japanese people as due to the blessings of *kami*.

Buddhism originated in India around 500 B.C. and, after interaction with Chinese and Korean culture, entered Japan about A.D. 500. In contrast to Shinto, which emerged gradually out of many beliefs and practices, Buddhism is a "founded" religion as initiated by Siddhartha Gautama, a historical person later revered as the Buddha or enlightened one. The Buddha's teaching reflected Indian practices and doctrines, but also pioneered a new understanding of overcoming suffering through an enlightened way of life. In the 1,000 years between its foundation and its entrance into Japan, Buddhism became an elaborate ecclesiastical structure with numerous divinities and colorful rituals. In Japan the practice of Buddhism is closely associated with funeral and memorial rites, as well as techniques of healing, exorcism, and meditation.

Taoism and Confucianism are two Chinese traditions that entered Japan more as systems of teaching than as organized religions. Taoism, literally the religion of the "way" (*tao*), emphasized harmony with the basic principle of nature and with the spatial and temporal expressions of that basic principle (the *tao*), especially the cosmic cycles of the Chinese calendar. From about A.D. 675, the Japanese court adopted a bureau of divination based on the Chinese bureau of divination and Taoistic notions of cosmic cycles. The Japanese bureau was not maintained, but the influence of the Chinese calendar was a lasting contribution of popular Taoism to Japanese culture and religion. In Japan, Taoist influence continues to shape popular notions such as lucky and unlucky days for weddings and funerals.

Confucianism is the teaching of a Chinese teacher of the sixth and fifth centuries B.C., known in the West as Confucius. Where Taoism emphasized harmony with nature, Confucius founded his teaching on harmony with society. He advocated a "way" of society based on hierarchical social relations with benevolence expressed by people in higher positions (such as rulers and fathers) and loyalty expressed by people in lower positions (such as citizens and sons). The basic principles of this teaching were filial piety and humanity. After the death of Confucius, the Chinese government used these principles as the rationale of a unified state. When these teachings entered Japan, along with Buddhism and Taoism, they were utilized to support loyalty to the emperor and to strengthen family solidarity. Confucian influence in Japan continues as a pervasive rationale for social and ethical behavior, especially as the foundation of family and nation.

Christianity, when viewed within Japanese religious history, presents an interesting case of comparison and contrast. Generally, Christianity is more comparable with Shinto and Buddhism (as a highly organized religion) than with Taoism and Confucianism (which are essentially systems of teaching). But, on the whole, Christianity within Japan stands apart from the other four religious and philosophical traditions because it has not become part of the Japanese tradition. Christianity first entered Japan in the mid-sixteenth century through Roman Catholic missionaries and, after a brief century of some success with conversions, was banned by the government until the late nineteenth century when both Catholic and Protestant missionaries became active. Because Christianity entered Japan after Japan's distinctive cultural and religious heritage had been formed, and because its monotheistic system and emphasis on exclusive affiliation conflicted with Japanese customs, Christianity has remained a minority religion in Japan, with less than 1 percent of the population holding church membership. Although Christian influence in Bible reading and ethical issues is more considerable than might be expected from its low membership, Christianity has not become an integral part of Japanese culture and religion.

In addition to these five traditions of organized religions and systems of teaching, there are several aspects of informal and formal religious life that are more difficult to categorize but are very important for the religious lives of the Japanese people. The beliefs and practices of average laypersons (as opposed to priests and philosophers) are not limited to the boundaries of organized religions and systems of thought; in fact, much of what ordinary people do in their religious behavior occurs at the periphery or outside these boundaries. For example, some rituals related to the growing of rice, especially rice-transplanting festivals, may derive from prehistoric practices. Although usually associated with Shinto, they have been practiced by farmers and villages outside of or in loose association with Shinto shrines. Usually this kind of informal tradition of beliefs and practices handed down orally and maintained apart from organized religions has been called "folk religion." However, "folk religion" is a catchall term that is too ambiguous to define all religious behavior outside organized religions.

In general, Japanese religion can be seen as a combination of organized religions and folk religion (similar to the fashion in which Robert Redfield has juxtaposed "great tradition" and "little tradition,"[2] but there are many beliefs and practices that lie somewhere between the two categories. A good example is religious life in the home, a religious institution in its own right. A traditional Japanese home within the last few centuries might have both a Shinto-style altar (*kamidana*) and a Buddhist-style altar (*butsudan*) and would observe regular rituals at these altars for *kami* protecting the home and family ancestors blessing the household. From the viewpoint of organized religions, the home may appear as an extension of Shinto and Buddhism, but it would be equally appropriate to view religious practices in the home as an expression of the heritage handed down by the family. In fact, the family can be seen as a religious institution in its own right: It has its own altars, the male head of the house is a kind of priest (although often his wife makes the offerings), and each house has its own ritual calendar (observing annual memorials for its own family ancestors). In this sense, one could just as well talk about "family religion" as folk religion.

The relationship between formal religious traditions and folk religion is complicated not only by the complexity of the phenomena themselves but also by the competing intellectual frameworks for handling the phenomena. In general, Japanese scholars can be divided into two major avenues of interpretation: those viewing folk religion as an expression of organized religion, and those viewing organized religion as an expression of folk religion. The scholars who view folk religion as an expression of organized religion are the Buddhist and Shinto scholars who see their respective organized traditions as the watershed from which "folk" traditions have emerged. Just as there is a general category for folk religion (*minkan shinko*), so do some scholars refer to folk Shinto (*minkan shinto*) and folk Buddhism (*minkan bukkyo*). This scholarly position views the "great tradition" as the ultimate origin of all "little tradition": Shinto is the source of "folk Shinto," just as Buddhism is the source of "folk Buddhism."

The opposite view is held by scholars—especially folklorists—who claim that folk traditions are actually the original and ongoing implicit foundation of the organized traditions. For example, the ancient, distinctively Japanese attitude toward nature can be seen as the foundation of Shinto, but the authentic expression of this attitude is manifested more fully in folk traditions than in the more formal and bureaucratic Shinto shrine organization. Similarly, folklorists hold that the ancient, distinctively Japanese concern for family unity and spirits of family ancestors is the indigenous basis for the acceptance and maintenance of Buddhism in Japan.[3]

The above discussion of organized religions and folk religion may be oversimplified, but at least it demonstrates the difficulty of dealing with religious traditions in Japan. Unfortunately, there is no consensus on adequate categories for dealing with the whole of Japanese religion, and it is easier to criticize the current categories than to develop satisfactory new categories. For example, the terms "folk Shinto" and "folk Buddhism" are inappropriate because the customs covered by these terms did not actually emerge directly from their respective organized traditions. Even if these folk customs did derive from the organized traditions, it would be more appropriate to call them "popular Shinto" and "popular Buddhism" in the sense of a popularized form of the organized tradition. In some instances, such as the formation of a special group (*ko*) for veneration of a Buddhist divinity or recitation of a Buddhist prayer, a term such as "popular Buddhism" does have some legitimacy. However, these "folk" or "popular" practices are almost never purely Buddhist or Shinto; they are a mixture of these two traditions with possible additions of Confucian and Taoist notions (and even Chinese popular and folk practices).

There is an inevitable tension in the two ways of seeing the relationship between organized religions and folk religion. It may be safe to say that, consciously or unconsciously, most Buddhist and Shinto scholars tend to look down upon folk Buddhism and folk Shinto as not only derivative, but dilutions of or even corruptions of the major traditions. On the other hand, it may be fair to say that folklorists, consciously or unconsciously, see organized religions as superimpositions or false superstructures resting on the folk tradition that is the authentic spirit or life of the people.

Any attempt to understand Japanese New Religions must take into account the complexity of the religious situation itself as well as the ambiguity of intellectual categories for dealing with this situation. In the simplest sense, New Religions are the new religious movements that arose during the last century and a half. They stand apart from the older organized religions as competing religious bodies, and are distinguished from folk and popular traditions because they are formally constituted as voluntary organizations.

The term "New Religion" is a translation of the commonly used Japanese *shinko shukyo*, literally "newly arisen religion," which apparently was coined by journalists in the disparaging sense of "new rich." A more neutral term is favored by these groups, *shin shukyo*, which is literally "new religion," without the disparaging notion of an upstart religion. Throughout this essay the term "New Religion" is used as a translation of the commonly accepted *shinko shukyo*, but in the more neutral sense of *shin shukyo*, and as a general rubric for new religious movements in Japan. This category obviously has its weaknesses, especially the carryover of disparaging nuances, but unfortunately a less cumbersome scholarly category has yet to appear.

It is worth noting that New Religions cut across the entire spectrum of Japanese religion: They depend heavily on the organized religions of Shinto and Buddhism, incorporate aspects of Taoist and Confucian ideas, and revive and modify popular and folk practices. Usually the New Religions have been charged with diluting and corrupting organized religions, but there is less recognition of the fact that the New Religions have formulated many beliefs and practices out of the folk tradition. Although many of their critics may resist the notion, the New Religions are perhaps the clearest expression of the living religious heritage in contemporary Japan.

Few Japanese people are interested in the abstractions of Buddhism (such as the numerous scriptures, commentaries, and doctrinal writings), just as few Japanese people are concerned with the historical details of Shinto (such as the mythological writings and numerous *kami*). But the elements of Buddhism and Shinto that are still vital—such as beliefs in Buddhist techniques for purifying human life and honoring ancestors, beliefs in basic Shinto notions of the benevolent power of nature—live on in the New Religions. Similarly, elements from Confucianism such as emphasis on filial piety, and elements from Taoism such as harmony with cosmic patterns, are contained within the New Religions. Folk traditions like local festivals and village celebrations are not as prominent as they once were, but the deities that are still honored and the customs that are still observed (such as seasonal festivals) find their way into the practices of New Religions. There is no clear-cut category that applies to the New Religions. They are separate from the older established religions, but in turn have become highly organized institutions. They draw on popular aspects of the organized religions and systems of thought, but have adapted these aspects into new patterns. They selectively incorporate features of folk religion, but transform these informal customs into formal patterns. Although there is no single category that includes the New Religions, they constitute one of the most significant forces on the contemporary religious scene.

HISTORICAL SURVEY

The New Religions developed out of the background of Japanese society and religion and should be understood in this context, but in the present essay only the religious background is covered. Standard treatments of Japanese religion in English are Masaharu Anesaki's older but still useful *History of Japanese Religion* (1930), Joseph M. Kitagawa's more recent thematic approach in *Religion in Japanese History* (1966), and H. Byron Earhart's historical survey, *Japanese Religion: Unity and Diversity* (1982). Kitagawa's work includes extensive references to Japanese materials. Earhart's work has a comprehensive bibliography of English-language materials and is complemented by a source book, *Religion in the Japanese Experience: Sources and Interpretations* (1982), which includes some materials on New Religions. A good collection of essays on individual religious traditions edited by Ichiro Hori is *Japanese Religion: A Survey by the Agency for Cultural Affairs* (1972). An interesting overview of Japanese religiosity in comparison with other Asian cultures and religions is Hajime Nakamura's *Ways of Thinking of Eastern Peoples: India-China-Tibet-Japan* (1964). Kiyomi Morioka has provided a sociological analysis of the context of Japanese religion and the New Religions in his collection of essays, *Religion in Changing Japanese Society* (1975).

For a more detailed treatment of individual religious traditions, readers should consult specific works. Tsunetsugu Muraoka discusses the nature of Shinto (especially Shinto theorists) in his *Studies in Shinto Thought* (1964). Daniel C. Holtom's *The National Faith of Japan: A Study in Modern Shinto* (1938) is still the most useful survey of Shinto. For Buddhism, Sir Charles Eliot's older *Japanese Buddhism* (1935) is a convenient one-volume work, but the two-volume *Foundation of Japanese Buddhism* (1974) by Daigan Matsunaga and Alicia Matsunaga is more comprehensive. The only major Western-language treatment of Taoism in Japan is Bernard Frank's "Kata-imi et Kata-tagae: Etude sur les Interdits de direction à l'époque Heian" [Kata-imi and kata-tagae: a study of the taboos of direction in the Heian Period] (1958). A concise treatment of

Confucianism in Japan is *Confucianism in Modern Japan: A Study of Conservatism in Japanese Intellectual History* (1973) by Warren W. Smith, Jr. For folk religion, the essays by Ichiro Hori in his *Folk Religion in Japan: Continuity and Change* (1968) are quite useful. Richard H. Drummond has provided a survey of Christianity in Japan in his *A History of Christianity in Japan* (1971).

There is no single work that interprets the background and development of Japanese New Religions, but many scholars have sketched aspects of this story in articles and books. Two of the most valuable overall interpretations of the historical context out of which the New Religions developed are a volume edited by Hideo Kishimoto, *Japanese Religion in the Meiji Era* (1956), and an article by Yoshiya Abe, "Religious Freedom Under the Meiji Constitution" (1968–1970). An incisive article that deals generally with the conditions and customs out of which the New Religions arose is Hitoo Marukawa's "Religious Circumstances in the Late Tokugawa and the Early Meiji Periods: Religious Backgrounds in the Cradle Years of Tenrikyo" (1970). The most comprehensive interpretation of the social organization of Japanese religions, including New Religions, is Winston B. Davis's *Toward Modernity: A Developmental Typology of Popular Religious Affiliations in Japan* (1977). Ronald P. Dore provides a case study of declining interest in established religions and increasing interest in New Religions in urban Tokyo in his *City Life in Japan: A Study of a Tokyo Ward* (1963). For a rare view of New Religions within a village study, see Bernard Bernier's *Breaking the Cosmic Circle: Religion in a Japanese Village* (1975).

A number of scholars have offered analyses of the origin and nature of Japanese New Religions. Some of the early articles on the subject, and useful for first reading, are Wilhelm Schiffer, "New Religions in Postwar Japan" (1955); Baiyu Watanabe, "Modern Japanese Religions: Their Success Explained" (1957); Carmen Blacker, "New Religious Cults in Japan" (1962); and Hiroo Takagi, "The Rise of the New Religions" (1964).

Sociological interpretations of the rise of the New Religions as a reflection of changing social conditions are contained in Iichi Oguchi and Hiroo Takagi, "Religion and Social Development" (1956); Fujio Ikado, "Trend and Problems of New Religions: Religion in Urban Society" (1968); Ted J. Solomon, "The Response of Three New Religions to the Crisis in the Japanese Value System" (1977); and Bryan R. Wilson, "The New Religions: Some Preliminary Considerations" (1979). Eimi Watanabe Rajana criticizes sociological interpretations of the New Religions as "antidotes of anomie" in her "New Religions in Japan: An Appraisal of Two Theories" (1975). H. Byron Earhart also criticizes the "crisis" or "anomie" theory of the development of New Religions and presents an interpretive model in his "Toward a Theory of the Formation of the Japanese New Religions: A Case Study of Gedatsu-kai" (1980). The lively theoretical debate and lack of unanimity concerning the origin and nature of Japanese New Religions reflect generally the variety of approaches to the problem of the relationship between religion and social change.

Some scholars have helped us understand the rootedness of the New Religions in traditional Japanese religion by focusing on more concrete aspects of this relationship. For example, Ichiro Hori interprets the survival of shamanism within the lives of some founders of New Religions in his "The New Religions and the Survival of Shamanic Tendencies" (1968). Werner Kohler interprets the relationship of shamanism, ancestor worship, and veneration of the Lotus Sutra in *Die Lotus-Lehre und die modernen Religionen in Japan* (1962). Robert J. Smith, in his comprehensive work on ancestor worship, *Ancestor Worship in Contemporary Japan* (1974), demonstrates that "the New Religions have continued to foster the household ideal and concepts of filial piety" (p. 34). Shigeru Nishiyama, et al., construct a synthetic overview of "the common underlying structure to the teachings of the various New Religions"(p. 140) in "The Vitalistic Conception of Salvation in Japanese New Religions: An Aspect of Modern Religious Consciousness" (1979). Susumu Shimazono has a synthetic interpretation of founders of New Religions as living *kami* in "The Living Kami Idea in the New Religions of Japan" (1979). Kiyomi Morioka contributes an incisive analysis of institutionalized procedures in his "The Institutionalization of a New Religious Movement" (1979).

In addition to these analytical or "outside" views of New Religions, it is also important to view the subject more from the "inside." Two valuable autobiographical accounts are by the cofounder of Rissho Kosei-kai, Nikkyo Niwano, *Lifetime Beginner: An Autobiography* (1978); and by the founder of a utopian movement (who seceded from Tenrikyo), Yoshie Sugihara, who along with David W. Plath wrote *Sensei and His People: The Building of a Japanese Commune* (1969). These two autobiographies give insight into the dynamics of the founding of New Religions not found in analytical works. Another "inside" view on the level of the individual member of a New Religion is recorded by H. Byron Earhart in two works: "Gedatsu-kai: One Life History and Its Significance for Interpreting Japanese New Religions" (1980) and *Religions of Japan: Many Traditions Within One Sacred Way* (1984).

In this essay we are concerned with the Japanese New Religions within Japan, but it is worth noting that they have expanded and developed in both North and South America as well as in other countries. Robert S. Ellwood, Jr., in *The Eagle and the Rising Sun: Americans and the New Religions of Japan* (1974), has the only lengthy treatment of this subject, with case studies of five New Religions in the United States. Two briefer treatments of Japanese New Religions in South America are Takashi Maeyama, "Ancestor, Emperor, and Immigrant: Religion and Group Identification of the Japanese in Rural Brazil (1908–1950)" (1972), and Robert J. Smith, "The Ethnic Japanese in Brazil" (1979).

Individual New Religions: Denominational and Secondary Material

To this point we have discussed Japanese New Religions in general, but the remainder of this essay focuses on individual New Religions. Where possible, examples of denominational materials will be included. There is no consensus on the definition of these New Religions, the time of their emergence, or their exact nature. In another context I have argued that

there seem to be three major criteria for distinguishing new religious movements: (1) chronologically, those movements that appeared from late Tokugawa or early Meiji to the present; (2) in origin, those movements that arose as renewal or "revitalizing" forces; and (3) in formation, those movements that led to permanent socioreligious organizations."[4]

For convenience we will move historically from the earliest movements to the most recent, grouping some similar movements together.

Much of the secondary literature on Japanese New Religions has focused on post–World War II social conditions and movements, but if we follow the above three criteria, New Religions arose from the early 1800s. Perhaps the first datable New Religion is Nyorai-kyo, founded in 1825. Nyorai-kyo has not published in Western languages, but a glimpse of this movement can be found in two secondary works: Heinrich Dumoulin and Tomonobu Ishibashi, "Aus dem Kanon der Nyoraikyo" (1938), and Arthur Waley, "Kono Tabi: A Little-Known Japanese Religion" (1933–1935).

Thirteen of the New Religions that arose in the nineteenth century came to be officially recognized by the government as "Sect Shinto." The best single source for information on the branches of Sect Shinto is Daniel D. Holtom, *The National Faith of Japan: A Study in Modern Shinto* (1938). An interesting set of translated materials on the formation of Sect Shinto (called here "Sectarian Shintoism") is Tadaaki Yoshimura, *Commentary on Documents Regarding Establishment of Sectarian Shintoism* (1935). Another brief treatment of each of the thirteen branches of Sect Shinto (from the viewpoint of Shinto) is *Sectarian Shinto (The Way of the Gods)* (1937), edited by Shinto Shogakukai.

Within the movements eventually recognized as Sect Shinto, the first major movement to achieve extensive membership and elaborate organization—and thereby constituting an important model for the development of other New Religions—was Tenrikyo, founded in 1838. Tenrikyo has published many pamphlets, books, and magazines in various Western languages—more publications than any other New Religion except Soka Gakkai. An inside view of Tenrikyo can be found in such denominational publications as *A Short History of Tenrikyo* (1967), *Tenrikyo, Its History and Teachings* (1966), and Takahito Iwai, *The Outline of Tenrikyo* (1932). Tenrikyo has attracted the attention of many secondary publications, one of the first major works being Henry van Straelen's "The Religion of Divine Wisdom, Japan's Most Powerful Religious Movement" (1954). A more recent monograph (a revised doctoral dissertation) is Johannes Laube's *Oyagami: Die heutige Gottesvorstellung der Tenrikyo* (1978). The most recent general interpretation is Robert S. Ellwood, Jr., *Tenrikyo: A Pilgrimage Faith. The Structure and Meanings of a Modern Japanese Religion* (1982).

Two movements that separated from Tenrikyo are the New Religion called Hommichi and a utopian movement called Shinkyo. Hommichi has published a number of English-language materials on its history and doctrine, such as *Guideposts: An Introduction to "Hommiti" (A Religion in Japan)* (1952). A brief secondary account of Hommichi is given in Shigeyoshi Murakami, *Japanese Religion in the Modern Century* (1980). The formation of Shinkyo as a reaction to social ostracism invoked owing to families leaving Tenrikyo is detailed in Yoshie Sugihara and David W. Plath, *Sensei and His People: The Building of a Japanese Commune* (1969).

Of the former thirteen branches of Sect Shinto, Tenrikyo is the largest and most successful and features more publications by and about it. Materials on the other twelve groups can be found in the general works mentioned above; the single most helpful work is Daniel C. Holtom, *The National Faith of Japan: A Study in Modern Shinto* (1938). For Kurozumikyo we have a useful earlier study that has not been superceded, Charles William Hepner's *The Kurozumi Sect of Shinto* (1935). Konkokyo has published a number of pamphlets in English, one of the most useful being *The Founder of Konko Religion* (1966). One brief secondary treatment is provided by Delwin B. Schneider in his *Konkokyo, a Japanese Religion: A Study in the Continuities in Native Faiths* (1962). A recent doctoral dissertation interpreting Konkokyo is Michio Araki, "Konko Daijin and Konko-kyo: A Case-Study of Religious Mediation" (1982).

The gradual recognition of thirteen members of Sect Shinto was an uneasy compromise on the part of both the government and the religious groups. These new religious movements wanted to establish independent organizations, but it was almost impossible to escape government suppression as unrecognized movements. They had to accept official recognition and conform to Shinto practices and support of the state. The government had opposed the new religious movements, but eventually found it convenient to label them the "religious" aspect of Shinto in order to declare most Shinto shrines the civil and patriotic aspect of the Japanese tradition—hence "non-religious." Thus, the government could require all citizens (especially schoolchildren) to participate in services at local Shinto shrines as part of their civil duties, without violating the formal principle of freedom of belief.[5] Some scholars view the close alliance between nineteenth-century new religious movements and Sect Shinto—for whatever reasons—to be so close that they should be considered as extensions of Shinto rather than as "New Religions." Some scholars reserve the term "New Religion" for movements that arose in the late nineteenth and twentieth centuries and broke more sharply from previous traditions such as Shinto.

One of the most important of the twentieth-century movements is Omoto, founded in 1892; it was influenced by Tenrikyo and Konkokyo, and in turn was the training ground for the founders of a number of other movements. Omoto has published a number of works in English and also Esperanto (in an attempt to encourage peace and brotherhood). Two key works are *The Oomoto Movement:*

Its Origin, Aims and Objects and the Universal Love and Brotherhood Association (1950; 3d ed. 1955) and a volume edited by Iwao P. Hino, *The Outline of Omoto* (1970). The only Western-language monograph on Omoto is the thorough study by Ulrich Lins, *Die Omoto-Bewegung und der radikale Nationalismus in Japan* (1976). Brief accounts of Omoto in English can be found in general works on the Japanese New Religions—Murakami (1980), Offner and van Straelen (1963), and Thomsen (1963).

Three of the many New Religions that emerged out of Omoto are Seicho-no-Ie, founded in 1930; Sekai Kyuseikyo, founded in 1935; and Ananaikyo, founded in 1949. Masaharu Taniguchi, founder of Seicho-no-Ie, was a prolific writer in Japanese; seven volumes of his *Truth of Life* (1961–1977) have been published in English. Through his direct connection with Western spiritualism, he coauthored a work with Fenwicke L. Holmes, *The Science of Faith: How to Make Yourself Believe* (1953). Sekai Kyuseikyo, known in English as the Church of World Messianity, was founded in 1935 by Mokichi Okada, who is known as Meishu-Sama. Translated teachings of Okada are contained in two volumes titled *Teachings of Meishu-Sama* (1965, 1968). A short pamphlet introducing the group is *World Messianity and What It Means* (1979). Two works by the founder of Ananaikyo, Yonosuke Nakano, are *A Guide to Ananaikyo* (1955) and *The Universe Has Spirit* (1954). Secondary treatments of these movements can be found in one or more of the standard works on New Religions such as McFarland (1967), Offner and van Straelen (1963), and Thomsen (1963).

Reiyukai was founded in 1923 on the basis of popular belief in the Lotus Sutra and ancestors. It continues today as a strong movement, but has also been the source of a number of other movements. Reiyukai has published only a few pamphlets in English, but rare insight into it is afforded in Nikkyo Niwano's frank work, *Lifetime Beginner: An Autobiography* (1978). Niwano, cofounder of Rissho Koseikai, was previously a participant in Reiyukai. The only significant study of Reiyukai in Western languages is Helen Hardacre's *Lay Buddhism in Contemporary Japan: Reiyukai Kyodan* (1984).

Of the many New Religions that descended from the Reiyukai lineage, two notable movements are Kodo Kyodan, founded in 1935, and Rissho Koseikai, founded in 1938. The founder of Kodo Kyodan, Shodo Okano, has written *An Introduction to Kodo Kyodan Buddhism* (1967), but there are no secondary treatments. Rissho Koseikai has outgrown its parent religion, Reiyukai, to become one of the largest and most influential New Religions, especially in the area of international peace. Rissho Koseikai has published a number of works in Western languages. In addition to the founder Niwano's interesting autobiography, Kosei Publishing Company has released a number of books on peace and general treatments of the Lotus Sutra and Buddhism. One of the works by Niwano is *A Buddhist Approach to Peace* (1977). A useful introduction to the movement is the (English-language) *Rissho Kosei-kai* (1966). Brief secondary treatments of Rissho Koseikai are given in the general works on Japanese New

Religions. Especially helpful is Kiyomi Morioka's analysis of how Rissho Ko-seikai was formed, in "The Institutionalization of a New Religious Movement" (1979).

The fact that only a few New Religions have emerged from Christianity in Japan is probably due, in part, to the fact that Christianity has not yet become an integral part of Japanese culture. Two movements that may be considered New Religions of Christian derivation are Genshi Fukuin Undo (literally "Orig-inal Gospel Movement") and Iesu no Mitama Kyokai Kyodan (literally "The Spirit of Jesus Church Organization"). Ikuro Teshima, the founder of Genshi Fukuin Undo, has written *Introduction to the Original Gospel Faith* (1970), and a brief secondary account of Makuya ("Tabernacle of Christ," a popular name for Genshi Fukuin Undo) can be found in Carlo Caldarola, *Christianity; The Japanese Way* (1979). For Iesu no Mitama Kyokai Kyodan, a brief description is given by Hiroshi Yamada and Dayle M. Bethel in "The Spirit of Jesus Church" (1964).

All New Religions have drawn upon the rich and varied Japanese religious heritage, but some have not emerged so directly out of contact with previous New Religions such as Tenrikyo, Omoto, and Reiyukai. One such movement is PL Kyodan (PL is an abbreviation for Perfect Liberty), initiated shortly after World War II on the foundation of several previous organizations influenced by Shingon Buddhism and the mountain pilgrimage association, Ontakekyo. In its modern form, PL Kyodan emphasizes the unity of religion with art and sports. This teaching is reflected in denominational writings such as *PL: A Modern Religion for Modern Man* (1968) and *Perfect Liberty—How to Lead a Happy Life* (1951). The most complete treatment of PL Kyodan in Western languages is Maurice A. Bairy's *Japans neue Religionen in der Nachkriegszeit* (1959), but brief English interpretations are given in the general works on Japanese New Religions.

Another recent New Religion, Sukyo Mahikari, although small in size, is the subject of one of the most thorough studies of any New Religion: Winston B. Davis's *Dojo: Magic and Exorcism in Modern Japan* (1980). Another of the smaller New Religions, Gedatsukai, founded in 1929, is an interesting blend of Buddhism, Shinto, and belief in ancestors. The life of the founder and some practices of the movement are recorded by Eizan Kishida in the denominational publications, *The Character and Doctrine of Gedatsu Kongo* (1969) and *Dynamic Analysis of Illness Through Gedatsu* (1962). Minoru Kiyota has analyzed the Buddhist doctrine of the movement in *Gedatsukai: Its Theory and Practice (A Study of a Shinto-Buddhist Syncretic School in Contemporary Japan)* (1982). Takie Sugiyama Lebra has written a number of articles on the psychological aspects of members of Gedatsukai, such as "Self-Reconstruction in Japanese Religious Psychotherapy" (1982). H. Byron Earhart's articles on Gedatsukai have been cited earlier.

A number of utopian movements have appeared in Japan, and although they are not exactly the same as New Religions, they are similar in their origin and nature. Indeed, as was indicated in the section on Tenrikyo, one utopian movement arose when a number of families in a village left Tenrikyo. This is recounted in Sugihara and Plath, *Sensei and His People: The Building of a Japanese Commune* (1969). This utopian movement is called Shinkyo, and although it has released no materials in Western languages, Plath has written about this and other utopian movements in "The Fate of Utopia: Adaptive Tactics in Four Japanese Groups" (1966) and "Modernization and Its Discontents: Japan's Little Utopias" (1969). Two general works describing a number of utopian movements are the edited volumes by Richard Fairfield, *Communes, Japan* (1972), and Moshe Matsuba, *The Communes of Japan* (1977). The best-known utopian group, Ittoen, founded by Tenko Nishida, is discussed in some of these publications, but has also released its own Western-language materials. The writings of Tenko Nishida are translated in *A New Road to Ancient Truth* (1969). The most detailed secondary treatment is Winston B. Davis's "Ittoen: The Myths and Rituals of Liminality" (1975).

The largest and most controversial Japanese New Religion, Soka Gakkai, was founded shortly before World War II, but experienced its phenomenal growth from about 1950 on. Soka Gakkai promises hope for the country and solution of all individual problems through faith in the Lotus Sutra. Formally Soka Gakkai is a lay movement of the traditional Buddhist denomination Nichiren Shoshu, but its active recruitment and style of organization clearly mark it as a New Religion. It is the only religious movement in Japanese history to have initiated a successful political party (Komeito, the Clean Government party).

Soka Gakkai has published more Western-language materials (and more secondary accounts have been written about Soka Gakkai) than any other New Religion. Of the denominational materials, some of the most significant are by the first three leaders of the movement. Tsunesaburo Makiguchi, founder of Soka Gakkai, established its theoretical foundation in *The Philosophy of Value* (1964). The thinking of the second leader of Soka Gakkai, Josei Toda, is included in his *Essays on Buddhism* (1961). Daisaku Ikeda, the third leader, has authored or coauthored several dozen volumes; his life is mirrored in his three-volume work, *The Human Revolution* (1972–1976). One of the most useful introductions published by the group is *The Nichiren Shoshu Sokagakkai* (1966). A valuable view of Komeito from Soka Gakkai headquarters is *The 8th National Convention, June 15–17, 1970* (1972).

The secondary literature on Soka Gakkai, including many books, doctoral dissertations, and theses as well as countless articles, tends to be rather critical of its recruitment techniques and eventual goals. Two exceptions are the rather sympathetic treatments of Dayle Morgan Bethel, *Makiguchi, the Value Creator: Revolutionary Japanese Educator and Founder of Soka Gakkai* (1973), and Kiyoaki Murata, *Japan's New Buddhism: An Objective Account of Soka Gakkai* (1969). At the other extreme is the polemical work of Hirotatsu Fujiwara, *I Denounce Soka Gakkai* (1970). Among more scholarly works, James Allen Dator provides a balanced and useful account in *Soka Gakkai, Builders of the Third*

Civilization: American and Japanese Members (1969). Arthur A. Palmer's *Buddhist Politics: Japan's Clean Government Party* (1971) is a brief and useful introduction to Komeito. The most complete study of Soka Gakkai in a Western language is James W. White's *The Sokagakkai and Mass Society* (1970), which utilizes social science models to discuss Soka Gakkai as a "mass movement."

In the last century and a half, there have been hundreds, perhaps thousands of New Religions in Japan. Although not so many are appearing today as in some previous decades, it is likely that some of the present movements will disappear and others will arise.

REFERENCE WORKS

Research on Japanese New Religions is not sufficiently developed for there to be standard reference works such as exist in some other fields. There are a few works devoted just to this topic, especially a handbook in Japanese and a Western-language bibliography. The single most important work in Japanese is Nobutaka Inoue, et al., *Shinshukyo Kenkyu Chosa Handobukku* [Handbook for study and field research of the new religions] (1981). This book includes separate chapters on aspects of the New Religions, literature by and about the New Religions, and research methods for studying them; it also features a derivation chart for most groups, a vocabulary for major organizations, and a list of statistics for forty New Religions. The bibliography by H. Byron Earhart, *The New Religions of Japan: A Bibliography of Western-Language Materials* (1983), is the most comprehensive work on the subject in a Western language. It contains almost 1,500 items by and about Japanese New Religions, organized according to general items and by individual New Religion; it features both topical and author indexes and appendixes for comparative materials. (The present essay is based on this bibliography.) These two works are logical beginning points for further research, depending on the language capabilities of the reader.

A number of single-volume works have been written to introduce the New Religions to general readers. Some of the first general surveys to appear were Maurice A. Bairy, *Japans neue Religionen in der Nachkriegszeit* (1959); Harry Thomsen, *The New Religions of Japan* (1963); and Clark B. Offner and Henry van Straelen, *Modern Japanese Religions, with Special Emphasis upon Their Doctrines of Healing* (1963). A standard treatment that analyzes the "social crisis and the rise of the new religions" and describes five New Religions is H. Neill McFarland's *The Rush Hour of the Gods: A Study of New Religious Movements in Japan* (1967). Edward Norbeck provides considerable material on New Religions in his *Religion and Society in Modern Japan: Continuity and Change* (1970). A unique, sympathetic treatment of religious conditions after World War II from the viewpoint of the New Religions has been edited by the Union of the New Religious Organizations in Japan, Research Office, in "Reminiscences of Religion in Postwar Japan" (1965–1966). The most critical and comprehensive coverage of the development of Japanese New Religions as grassroots religious movements in spite of governmental suppression is Shigeyoshi Murakami, *Japanese Religion in the Modern Century* (1980). These are the basic reference works for studying Japanese New Religions.

RESEARCH COLLECTIONS

Unfortunately, there is no single repository in the world for materials by and about Japanese New Religions. Until 1980 the small library of the International Institute for the Study of Religions (Kokusai Shukyo Kenkyujo) in Tokyo was the best place for locating materials published by the New Religions, but the office of the institute closed and the library was scattered. (The institute, now at Nanzan University in Nagoya, still publishes the *Japanese Journal of Religious Studies*.) To the best of my knowledge, the only international repository for materials on New Religions or "new religious movements" is the Project for the Study of New Religious Movements in Primal Societies, headed by Dr. Harold W. Turner, Department of Religious Studies, King's College, University of Aberdeen, Aberdeen AB9 2UB, Scotland; however, this project focuses on the encounter of primal or tribal societies with more complex societies (as seen in African religious movements) and does not concentrate on Japanese movements. Turner himself has published two volumes of a planned four-volume series titled *Bibliography of New Religious Movements in Primal Societies*; Volume 1: *Black Africa* (1977) and Volume 2: *North America* (1978) have appeared, while the planned Volume 3 will cover Asia and Oceania and Volume 4 Latin America and the Caribbean.

Materials on the Japanese New Religions tend to fall into two distinct categories: publications by the New Religions themselves and secondary publications about the New Religions (by scholars and journalists). Secondary publications can be found at most larger libraries, although some of the monographs and periodicals mentioned in this essay can be found only in major university libraries specializing in Japanese studies and religious studies. It is the first category—which I have called "denominational"—that is the most difficult to locate. Even New Religions themselves do not always save copies of their publications, and libraries tend to consider such publications as ephemeral. Neither in Japan nor in the United States does any library systematically collect such materials. Perhaps the most complete collection in the United States is in the Library of Congress. Its counterpart in Japan, the Diet Library (in Tokyo), has considerably fewer such publications in Western languages. For materials released for and by Japanese New Religions in the United States, there is a good collection in the Program for the Study of New Religious Movements, Graduate Theological Union, 2465 LeConte Avenue, Berkeley, California 94709. This program focuses on all American new religious movements, of which Japanese (or Japanese-derived) groups are a minority. Another American center is the Institute for the Study of American Religion, P.O. Box 1311, Evanston, Illinois 60201. From the files of this institute, J. Gordon Melton and James V. Geisendorfer have published *A Directory of Religious Bodies in the United States* (1977), including information about and addresses of Japanese movements in the United States. Some of the larger New Religions in Japan have extensive publishing facilities and will send price lists of their publications; addresses of New Religions in Japan are included in Ichiro Hori, *Japanese Religion: A Survey by the Agency for Cultural Affairs* (1972).

Much to my regret, there is no simple solution to the task of acquiring materials by Japanese New Religions. My own experience has been that historical circumstances have resulted in these materials being received and catalogued in various libraries. Those persons having access to computerized searching facilities and interlibrary loan privileges may find these techniques to be more efficient and less expensive than travel to several library centers.

NOTES

1. In this essay the term "New Religions" is capitalized to indicate its use as a specific category referring to Japanese New Religions (and not to "new religions" or "new religious movements" as found in many cultures outside Japan).

2. For the categories "little tradition" and "great tradition," see Robert Redfield, *Peasant Society and Cultures* (Chicago: University of Chicago Press, 1956), p. 70. Ichiro Hori has applied Redfield's categories of "little tradition" and "great tradition" to Japanese religion in his *Folk Religion in Japan*, pp. 49–81. Redfield's notions have been criticized and modified by a number of scholars. George M. Foster in his work, "What is Folk Culture?" (*American Anthropologist* 55, no. 2, pt. 1 [April-June 1953], 159–73), has pointed out the overlap between these two categories, especially in the context of cities. See also Gananath Obeyesekere, "The Great Tradition and the Little in the Perspective of Sinhalese Buddhism," *Journal of Asian Studies* 23, no. 2 (February 1963), 139–53, whose re-evaluation of Redfield's notions insists upon the "common idiom" that "not only links the little tradition with the great, but also links the little traditions with one another."

3. A convenient volume featuring both an introductory chapter on Japanese folklore by the editor and individual articles by Japanese folklorists is Richard M. Dorson, ed., *Studies in Japanese Folklore*, trans. Yasuyo Ishiwara (Bloomington: Indiana University Press, 1963).

4. Earhart, *The New Religions of Japan: A Bibliography of Western-Language Materials* (1983), pp. 5–6.

5. The complicated scenario of freedom of religion (and lack thereof) is sketched in publications such as Abe, "Religious Freedom Under the Meiji Constitution" (1968); Kishimoto, *Japanese Religion in the Meiji Era* (1956); Kitagawa, *Religion in Japanese History* (1966); and Murakami, *Japanese Religion in the Modern Century* (1980).

BIBLIOGRAPHY

Abe, Yoshiya. "Religious Freedom Under the Meiji Constitution." *Contemporary Religions in Japan* 9, no. 4 (December 1968), 268–338 (continued in the four subsequent issues).

Anesaki, Masaharu. *History of Japanese Religion*. London: Kegan Paul, Trench, Trubner, 1930; rpt. Rutland, Vt.: Charles E. Tuttle, 1963.

Araki, Michio. "Konko Daijin and Konko-kyo: A Case-Study of Religious Mediation." Ph.D. dissertation, University of Chicago, 1982.

Bairy, Maurice A. *Japans neue Religionen in der Nachkriegszeit*. Bonn: Ludwig Rohrscheid Verlag, 1959.

Bernier, Bernard. *Breaking the Cosmic Circle: Religion in a Japanese Village*, Cornell University East Asia Papers, no. 5. Ithica: Cornell University, Cornell China-Japan Program, 1975.

Bethel, Dayle Morgan. *Makiguchi, the Value Creator: Revolutionary Japanese Educator and Founder of Soka Gakkai*. New York: John Weatherhill, 1973.

Blacker, Carmen. "New Religious Cults in Japan." *Hibbert Journal* 60 (July 1962), 305–13.

Caldarola, Carlo. *Christianity. The Japanese Way*. Leiden: E. J. Brill, 1979.

Dator, James Allen. *Soka Gakkai, Builders of the Third Civilization: American and Japanese Members*. Seattle: University of Washington Press, 1969.

Davis, Winston B. *Dojo: Magic and Exorcism in Modern Japan*. Stanford: Stanford University Press, 1980.

———. "Ittoen: The Myths and Rituals of Liminality." *History of Religion* 14, no. 4 (May 1975), 282–321; 15, no. 1 (August 1975), 1–33.

———. *Toward Modernity: A Developmental Typology of Popular Religious Affiliations in Japan*, Cornell East Asia Papers, no. 12. Ithaca: Cornell University, Cornell China-Japan Program, 1977.

Dore, Ronald P. *City Life in Japan: A Study of a Tokyo Ward*. Berkeley: University of California Press, 1963.

Drummond, Richard H. *A History of Christianity in Japan*. Grand Rapids, Mich.: William B. Eerdmans, 1971.

Dumoulin, Heinrich, and Tomonobu Ishibashi. "Aus dem Kanon der Nyoraikyo." *Monumenta Nipponica* 1, no. 1 (1938), 222–41.

Earhart, H. Byron. "Gedatsu-kai: One Life History and Its Significance for Interpreting Japanese New Religions." *Japanese Journal of Religious Studies* 7, nos. 2–3 (June-September 1980), 227–57.

———. *Japanese Religions: Unity and Diversity*. 3d ed. Belmont, Calif.: Wadsworth, 1982.

———. *The New Religions of Japan: A Bibliography of Western-Language Materials*, Michigan Papers in Japanese Studies, no. 9. Ann Arbor: Center for Japanese Studies, University of Michigan, 1983.

———. *Religion in the Japanese Experience: Sources and Interpretations*. Belmont, Calif.: Wadsworth, 1974.

———. *Religions of Japan: Many Traditions Within One Sacred Way*. San Francisco: Harper & Row, 1984.

———. "Toward a Theory of the Formation of the Japanese New Religions: A Case Study of Gedatsu-kai." *History of Religions* 10, nos. 1–2 (August-November 1980), 175–97.

The 8th National Convention, June 15–17, 1970. [Tokyo:] Komeito, [1972].

Eliot, Sir Charles. *Japanese Buddhism*. London: Edward Arnold, 1935; rpt. London: Routledge & Kegan Paul, 1959.

Ellwood, Robert S., Jr. *The Eagle and the Rising Sun: Americans and the New Religions of Japan.* Philadelphia: Westminster Press, 1974.

————. *Tenrikyo: A Pilgrimage Faith. The Structure and Meanings of a Modern Japanese Religion.* Tenri, Nara: Oyasato Research Institute, Tenri University, 1982.

Fairfield, Richard, ed. *Communes, Japan.* Special Issue of *The Modern Utopian.* San Francisco: Alternatives Foundation, 1972.

The Founder of Konko Religion. Konko: Konko Hombu Kyocho, 1966.

Frank, Bernard. "Kata-imi et Kata-tagae: Etude sur les Interdits de direction à l'époque Heian." *Bulletin de la Maison Franco-Japonaise* 5, nos. 1–4 (1958), 1–246.

Fujiwara, Hirotatsu. *I Denounce Soka Gakkai.* Trans. Worth C. Grant. Tokyo: Nishin Hodo, 1970.

Guide-posts: An Introduction to "Hommiti" (A Religion in Japan). Osaka: Hommichi, 1952.

Hardacre, Helen. *Lay Buddhism in Contemporary Japan: Reiyukai Kyodan.* Princeton: Princeton University Press, 1984.

Hepner, Charles William. *The Kurozumi Sect of Shinto.* Tokyo: Meiji Japan Society, 1935.

Hino, Iwao P. *The Outline of Oomoto.* 3d ed. Kameoka: Oomoto Headquarters, 1970.

Holtom, Daniel C. *Modern Japan and Shinto Nationalism. A Study of Present-Day Trends in Japanese Religions.* New York: Dutton, 1938; rpt. New York: Paragon, 1965.

————. *The National Faith of Japan: A Study in Modern Shinto.* London: Kegan Paul, Trench, Trubner & Co., 1938; rpt. New York: Paragon, 1965.

Hori, Ichiro. *Folk Religion in Japan: Continuity and Change.* Ed. Joseph M. Kitagawa and Alan L. Miller. Chicago: University of Chicago Press, 1968.

————, ed. *Japanese Religion.* Tokyo: Kodansha International, 1972.

————. *Japanese Religion: A Survey by the Agency for Cultural Affairs.* Trans. Yoshiya Abe and David Reid. Tokyo: Kodansha International, 1972.

————. "The New Religions and the Survival of Shamanic Tendencies." In Ichiro Hori, *Folk Religion in Japan: Continuity and Change.* Ed. Joseph M. Kitagawa and Alan L. Miller. Chicago: University of Chicago Press, 1968, 217–51.

Ikado, Fujio. "Trend and Problems of New Religions: Religion in Urban Society." In *The Sociology of Japanese Religion.* Ed. Kiyomi Morioka and William H. Newell. Leiden: E. J. Brill, 1968, 101–17.

Ikeda, Daisaku. *The Human Revolution.* 3 vols. New York: Weatherhill, 1972–1976. Vol. 1, 1972; Vol. 2, 1974; Vol. 3, 1976.

Inoue, Nobutaka, et al. *Shinshukyo Kenkyu Chosa Handobukku* [Handbook for study and field research of the new religions]. Tokyo: Yuzankaku, 1981.

井上順孝他 『新宗教研究調査ハンドブック』 東京 雄山閣出版 １９８１

Iwai, Takahito. *The Outline of Tenrikyo.* Nara: Tenrikyo Doyusha, 1932.

Kishida, Eizan. *The Character and Doctrine of Gedatsu Kongo.* Trans. Louis K. Ito. San Francisco: Gedatsu Church of America, 1969.

————. *Dynamic Analysis of Illness Through Gedatsu.* Trans. Louis K. Ito. N.p.: Gedatsu Church of America, 1962.

Kishimoto, Hideo, ed. *Japanese Religion in the Meiji Era.* Trans. John F. Howes. Tokyo: Obunsha, 1956.

Kitagawa, Joseph M. *Religion in Japanese History.* New York: Columbia University Press, 1966.

Kiyota, Minoru. *Gedatsukai: Its Theory and Practice (A Study of a Shinto-Buddhist*

Syncretic School in Contemporary Japan). Los Angeles: Buddhist Books International, 1982.

Kohler, Werner. *Die Lotus-Lehre und die modernen Religionen in Japan*. Zurich: Atlantis Verlag, 1962.

Laube, Johannes. *Oyagami: Die heutige Gottesvorstellung der Tenrikyo*, Studien zur Japonologie, Monographien zur Geschichte, Kultur und Sprache Japans 14. Wiesbaden: Otto Harrassowitz, 1978.

Lebra, Takie Sugiyama. "Self-Reconstruction in Japanese Religious Psychotherapy." In *Cultural Conceptions of Mental Health and Therapy*. Ed. A. J. Marsella and G. M. White. Dordrecht, The Netherlands: D. Reidel, 1982, 269–83.

Lins, Ulrich. *Die Oomoto-Bewegung und der radikale Nationalismus in Japan*, Studien zur Geschichte des neunzehnten Jahrhunderts 8. Munich: R. Oldenbourg Verlag, 1976.

Maeyama, Takashi. "Ancestor, Emperor, and Immigrant: Religion and Group Identification of the Japanese in Rural Brazil (1908–1950)." *Journal of Interamerican Studies and World Affairs* 14, no. 2 (May 1972), 151–82.

Makiguchi, Tsunesaburo. *The Philosophy of Value*. Trans. Translation Division, Overseas Bureau. Tokyo: Seikyo Press, 1964.

Marukawa, Hitoo. "Religious Circumstances in the Late Tokugawa and the Early Meiji Periods: Religious Backgrounds in the Cradle Years of Tenrikyo." *Tenri Journal of Religion* 11 (1970), 43–78.

Matsuba, Moshe, ed. *The Communes of Japan: The Kibbutz on the Other Side of the World*. Imaichi-shi, Tochigi-ken: Japanese Commune Movement, 1977.

Matsunaga, Daigan, and Alicia Matsunaga. *Foundation of Japanese Buddhism*. 2 vols. Los Angeles: Buddhist Books International, 1974.

McFarland, H. Neill. *The Rush Hour of the Gods: A Study of New Religious Movements in Japan*. New York: Macmillan, 1967.

Melton, J. Gordon, and James V. Geisendorfer. *A Directory of Religious Bodies in the United States*. New York: Garland, 1977.

Morioka, Kiyomi. *Religion in Changing Japanese Society*. Tokyo: University of Tokyo Press, 1975.

————. "The Institutionalization of a New Religious Movement." *Japanese Journal of Religious Studies* 6, nos. 1–2 (March-June 1979), 239–80.

Murakami, Shigeyoshi. *Japanese Religion in the Modern Century*. Trans. H. Byron Earhart. Tokyo: University of Tokyo Press, 1980.

Muraoka, Tsunetsugu. *Studies in Shinto Thought*. Trans. Delmer M. Brown and James T. Araki. Tokyo: Ministry of Education, 1964.

Murata, Kiyoaki. *Japan's New Buddhism: An Objective Account of Soka Gakkai*. New York: Walker/Weatherhill, 1969.

Nakamura, Hajime. *Ways of Thinking of Eastern Peoples: India-China-Tibet-Japan*. Rev. English translation ed. Philip P. Wiener. Honolulu: East-West Center Press, 1964.

Nakano, Yonosuke. *A Guide to Ananaikyo*. Shimizu: International General Headquarters of Ananaikyo, 1955.

————. *The Universe Has Spirit*. Shimizu: International General Headquarters of Ananaikyo, 1954.

The Nichiren Shoshu Sokagakkai. Tokyo: Seikyo Press, 1966.

Nishida, Tenko. *A New Road to Ancient Truth*. Trans. Makoto Ohashi in collaboration with Marie Beuzeville Byles. London: George Allen & Unwin, 1969.

Nishiyama, Shigeru, et al. "The Vitalistic Conception of Salvation in Japanese New Religions: An Aspect of Modern Religious Consciousness." *Japanese Journal of Religious Studies* 6, nos. 1–2 (March-June 1979), 139–61.

Niwano, Nikkyo. *A Buddhist Approach to Peace.* Trans. Masuo Nezu. Tokyo: Kosei, 1977.

———. *Lifetime Beginner: An Autobiography.* Trans. Richard L. Gage. Tokyo: Kosei, 1978.

Norbeck, Edward. *Religion and Society in Modern Japan: Continuity and Change.* Houston: Tourmalinie Press, 1970.

Offner, Clark B., and Henry van Straelen. *Modern Japanese Religions, with Special Emphasis upon Their Doctrines of Healing.* Tokyo: Rupert Enderle, 1963.

Oguchi, Iichi, and Hiroo Takagi. "Religion and Social Development." In *Japanese Religion in the Meiji Era.* Trans. John F. Howes. Ed. Hideo Kishimoto. Tokyo: Obunsha, 1956, 313–51.

Okada, Mokichi (Meishu-Sama). *Teachings of Meishu-Sama.* 2 vols. Trans. Kiyoko Higuchi. Atami: Sekai Kyusei-kyo Headquarters. Vol. 1, rev. ed., 1965; Vol. 2, 1968.

Okano, Shodo. *An Introduction to Kodo Kyodan Buddhism.* Trans. Taitetsu Unno. Yokohama: Kodo Kyodan, 1967.

The Oomoto Movement: Its Origin, Aims and Objects and the Universal Love and Brotherhood Association. 3d ed. Kameoka: Oomoto Headquarters, 1955.

Palmer, Arthur A. *Buddhist Politics: Japan's Clean Government Party.* The Hague: Martinus Nijhoff, 1971.

Perfect Liberty—How to Lead a Happy Life. Tondabayashi: Perfect Liberty Order, 1951.

PL: A Modern Religion for Modern Man. Tondabayashi: Perfect Liberty Order, 1968.

Plath, David W. "The Fate of Utopia: Adaptive Tactics in Four Japanese Groups." *American Anthropologist* 68, pt. 2 (1966), 1152–62.

———. "Modernization and Its Discontents: Japan's Little Utopias." *Journal of Asian and African Studies* 4, no. 1 (January 1969), 1–17.

Rajana, Eimi Watanabe. "New Religions in Japan: An Appraisal of Two Theories." In *Modern Japan: Aspects of History, Literature and Society.* Ed. W. G. Beasley. Berkeley: University of California Press, 1975, 187–97.

Rissho Kosei-kai. Tokyo: Rissho Kosei-kai, 1966.

Schiffer, Wilhelm. "New Religions in Postwar Japan." *Monumenta Nipponica* 11 (April 1955), 1–14.

Schneider, Delwin B. *Konkokyo, a Japanese Religion: A Study in the Continuities in Native Faiths.* Tokyo: International Institute for the Study of Religions, 1962.

Shimazono, Susumu. "The Living Kami Idea in the New Religions of Japan." *Japanese Journal of Religious Studies* 6, no. 3 (September 1979), 389–412.

Shinto Shogakukai (The Society for Promoting Shinto), ed. *Sectarian Shinto (The Way of the Gods).* Tokyo: Japan Times & Mail, 1937.

A Short History of Tenrikyo. 4th ed. Tenri: Tenrikyo Kyokai Honbu, 1967.

Smith, Robert J. *Ancestor Worship in Contemporary Japan.* Stanford: Stanford University Press, 1974.

———. "The Ethnic Japanese in Brazil." *Journal of Japanese Studies* 5, no. 1 (Winter 1979), 53–70.

Smith, Warren W., Jr. *Confucianism in Modern Japan: A Study of Conservatism in Japanese Intellectual History.* 2d ed. Tokyo: Hokuseido Press, 1973.

Solomon, Ted J. "The Response of Three New Religions to the Crisis in the Japanese Value System." *Journal for the Scientific Study of Religion* 16, no. 1 (March 1977), 1–14.

Straelen, Henry van. "The Religion of Divine Wisdom, Japan's Most Powerful Religious Movement." *Folklore Studies* 13 (1954), 1–165. Published in revised form as a book, Kyoto: Veritas Shoin, 1957.

Sugihara, Yoshie, and David W. Plath. *Sensei and His People: The Building of a Japanese Commune*. Berkeley: University of California Press, 1969.

Takagi, Hiroo. "The Rise of the New Religions." *Japan Quarterly* 11, no. 2 (April-June 1964), 283–92.

Taniguchi, Masaharu. *Truth of Life*. 7 vols. 1961–1977. Vol. 1, *Truth of Life*, Tokyo: Seicho-no-Ie Foundation, 1961; Vol. 2, *The Spiritual Essence of Man*. Playa Del Rey, Calif.: Seicho-no-Ie Truth of Life Publishing Department, 1979.

Taniguchi, Masaharu, and Fenwicke L. Holmes. *The Science of Faith: How to Make Yourself Believe*. New York: Dodd, Mead, 1953.

Tenrikyo, Its History and Teachings. Tenri: Tenrikyo Kyokai Honbu Kaigai Dendobu, 1966.

Teshima, Ikuro. *Introduction to the Original Gospel Faith*. Tokyo: Light of Life Press, 1970.

Thomsen, Harry. *The New Religions of Japan*. Rutland, Vt.: Charles E. Tuttle, 1963; rpt. Westport, Conn.: Greenwood Press, 1978.

Toda, Josei. *Essays on Buddhism*. Trans. Takeo Kamio. Tokyo: Seikyo Press, 1961.

Turner, Harold W. *Bibliography of New Religious Movements in Primal Societies*. 4 vols. Boston: G. K. Hall, 1977-. Vol. 1, *Black Africa*, 1977; Vol. 2, *North America*, 1978. (The planned Volume 3 will cover Asia and Oceania and Volume 4 Latin America and the Caribbean.)

Union of the New Religious Organizations in Japan, Research Office, ed. "Reminiscences of Religion in Postwar Japan." *Contemporary Religions in Japan* 6, no. 2 (June 1965), 111–203 (continued in the five subsequent issues).

Waley, Arthur. "Kono Tabi: A Little-Known Japanese Religion." *Bulletin of the School of Oriental Studies* 7 (1933–35), 105–9.

Watanabe, Baiyu. "Modern Japanese Religions: Their Success Explained." *Monumenta Nipponica* 13 (1957), 153–62.

White, James W. *The Sokagakkai and Mass Society*. Stanford: Stanford University Press, 1970.

Wilson, Bryan R. "The New Religions: Some Preliminary Considerations." *Japanese Journal of Religious Studies* 6, nos. 1–2 (March-June 1979), 193–216.

World Messianity and What It Means. Rev. ed. Atami: Sekai Kyusei-kyo Headquarters, 1979.

Yamada, Hiroshi, and Dayle M. Bethel. "The Spirit of Jesus Church." *Japanese Christian Quarterly* 30, no. 3 (July 1964), 220–24.

Yoshimura, Tadaaki. *Commentary on Documents Regarding Establishment of Sectarian Shintoism*. Tokyo: Shinshukyo Daijyocho Shuppanbu (also Kokusai Shuppan Insatsusha, International Publishing & Printing Co.), 1935.

Editor's note: Due to delays in the publication of this *Handbook*, for which the editor takes full responsibility, and over which the author had no control, this bibliography covers only works on Japanese religion published before 1984. (RGP)

4

Popular Performing Arts:
Manzai and *Rakugo*

MUNEO JAY YOSHIKAWA

There are prototypical examples of the performing arts in the many mythologies and folk tales contained in the *Kojiki* [Record of ancient matters] (A.D. 710) and the *Nihon Shoki* [Chronicle of Japan] (A.D. 710), which were completed by the beginning of the Nara period (710–794) and the Heian period (794–1185), respectively. Among them, for instance, is the story about the rock cave of heaven recorded in the *Kojiki*. In this story, the sun goddess, Amaterasu Omikami, was sequestered in a cave while numerous other gods and goddesses were assembled outside. They began a festival with the purpose of arousing the sun goddess's curiosity, causing her to emerge from the cave. Just then, in order to entice the sun goddess out of the cave, one of the other goddesses, Amenouzume no Mikoto, started to chant and perform a striptease on an inverted wooden tub. Those deities present were delighted with her performance, and their laughter rocked the High Plain of Heaven. The sun goddess, curious about the awesome noise outside, finally opened the cave door to have a peek at the commotion and to inquire about the reason for so much laughter. Uzume told her that the deities were extremely happy to have among them a divinity superior to her. At this point, the mirror was exposed to her. The sun goddess, being fascinated by the radiant reflection of herself, moved closer to the mirror. As she did so, she was caught by two hidden divinities and pulled out of the cave. Thus, light was again restored to the High Plain of Heaven.

The noisy festival in the front of the cave is believed to be the original form of the Japanese Shinto festivals. The dance by the goddess is the legendary origin of *kagura*, the oldest Japanese dance form, and the inverted wooden tub is the legendary origin of the stage.

Contained within the festival performed in front of the cave are dance, recitation of incantations, verbal interaction, and actions intended to provoke an audience reaction of laughter. The entire gamut of the performing arts is symbolized in this cave story, including dance, song, theater, verbal interaction, stage, and audience. For this reason, the performing arts are a composite of all the arts.

This essay will focus on the Japanese popular performing arts of *manzai* (comic dialogue) and *rakugo* (comic storytelling), especially *manzai*, which pervades all the performing arts in Japan. The survey of the historical development of *manzai* and *rakugo* will include an investigation of the social and cultural functions that they fulfilled during each era and the secularization process of *manzai*. We would like to reappraise Japanese culture, investigating how Japanese humor has been influenced by these performing arts.

HISTORICAL SURVEY

According to folklorist Shinobu Origuchi (1887–1953), *manzai*, which began as part of a festival entertainment, is one of the oldest and most ingrained genres of the performing arts in Japan. A prototype of such festival entertainment can be seen in the story of the rock cave of heaven mentioned earlier. In the Heian period, these types of entertainment took on a more ritualistic form called *okagura*, which developed into a type of performing art. For example, there are two performers in the *okagura*: one represents an anthropomorphic god and the other represents a local deity. The *okagura* consists of dialogues between these two gods. In these dialogues, the anthropomorphic god commands the local deity and tries to make him obey. However, the local deity mocks, disobeys, and makes fun of the anthropomorphic god. In the end, the local community and land are said to be blessed by the local deity succumbing to the anthropomorphic god. This *okagura* reflects the old belief of the Japanese people that a visiting deity from outside comes to bless their land. Festival entertainment is performed to invite the visiting deity. The significance of the two performers found in the *okagura* can be traced to the present-day style of *manzai*. In later years the anthropomorphic god, referred to as *tayu*, and the local deity, called *saizo*, became known as *manzai* performers. They performed by singing and celebrating special and happy occasions.

However, it was not until the Muromachi period (1333–1600) that the concept of making people laugh was incorporated into *manzai* in the celebration of festival occasions. By the Edo period (1600–1868), the commoners in Edo preferred the humorous aspect of *manzai*, in which the cocky *saizo* would misinterpret and mock the serious *tayu*'s phrases. *Manzai* began to emphasize humor over its original function of blessing the local community. In this way, *manzai* slowly began to be secularized in the urban center of Edo, while continuing to retain its original form in the countryside.

During the Meiji (1868–1912) and Taisho (1912–1926) periods, Edo was transformed into the industrialized Tokyo of today. *Manzai* was transported from

Tokyo into the mass society of the commercial and manufacturing center of Osaka. Before *manzai* as it developed in Osaka is studied, let us examine the development of *rakugo*.

Examples of *rakugo* humor can be found in the ancient chronicles of Japan. According to Kazuo Sekiyama's theory, the traditional art of storytelling performed by one person can be traced to the sermons given in the Jodo Buddhist sect. It is also maintained that it has its origin in the old oral tradition of the common people.

According to Hidetoshi Kato, in his *Yose: Wagei no Shusei* [Vaudeville: collection of the narrative arts], the *rakugo* art developed from the *otogi* storytelling tradition found during the age of civil war in the sixteenth century, when sudden attacks were often made. In order to stay awake in anticipation of these unpredictable attacks, even the feudal lords had to keep watch during the night. To ease such long nocturnal vigils, the *otogi* storytellers would be called on to narrate interesting tales to keep the feudal lords awake. There is a theory that these interesting and humorous *otogi* stories led to the development of *rakugo*. It seems most likely that a combination of such theories best explains its development.

Rakugo can be described as a popular comic art performed by one person. One must be able to have the skill of creating a stage, background, and atmosphere in the minds of the audience and also be able to play the parts of the characters that appear in the stories being narrated. An example of such a *rakugo* will be cited here.

One owner of a shop made quite a killing in his business, employing a head clerk and several employees. But when one is successful, one hesitates to use money. So he thought that if he decreased his employees, he could save more money; this, in turn, would mean he would make more money. So he fired one employee after another, until he had fired everyone except his wife and himself. He thought that business would carry on even without his wife, so he kicked her out of the house so that only he remained. He thought that business would be just fine even without himself, so he tied a rope around his neck and hanged himself. *Rakugo* stories are usually about twenty minutes in length. However, the example given above is of a *kobanashi* (short story), which is a short form of *rakugo*.

Rakugo stories usually end with a punchline. It is interesting to examine what kinds of things people laughed at in those days. The standard of living for most commoners in the cities was very low then. There must have been many people within the audience who worked for stingy employers and many who were unemployed. Everyone knew that every penny counted, and many people were leading lives at subsistence levels. Even such silly *rakugo* stories had a real place in their everyday lives. The *rakugo* cited was composed during the Edo period, but its content still signifies a real situation even in these recent times. There are many employers who will do anything for a profit, even to the extent of cutting their own throats. These kinds of occurrences are not confined to Japan alone, but reach across borders of nations such as America. In such ways, many classic *rakugo* stories, although old, still have an appeal beyond time and place.

Toward the end of the Edo period, Encho Sanyutei was rated number one among the professional *rakugo* performers. He established *rakugo* as a more formal and theatrical art that gained much popularity. Sanyutei was not satisfied, however, with the mass appeal of *rakugo*. He tried to restrict the art to storytelling rather than relying on the use of stage settings and other devices. During the Meiji period, his efforts were realized with the establishment of *rakugo* as a form of performing art, but there was no guarantee that the art of *rakugo* would be successfully passed on to future generations. Sanyutei's disciples concentrated on bringing the content of *rakugo* back to the level of the common people. The stance of the *rakugo* performers also changed from that of viewing *rakugo* as a mere art form to that of an all-inclusive way of life. It was Shinsho who faithfully put this new stance into practice. Shinsho influenced and contributed tremendously to the world of *rakugo* by including aspects of real life in his own performances.

The *rakugo* stories developed in the Edo period are called "classic *rakugo*," and there are hundreds. The *rakugo* stories created later by incorporation of new elements found in the later decades are called "new *rakugo*." During the Meiji period, performers in Tokyo such as Enyu and Entaro made the audience laugh at nonsensical humor that satisfied the needs of the common people. Enyu, in particular, as a disciple of Encho, included contemporary customs and issues in his *rakugo*. He made the audience laugh with his unexpected twists and gags in this considerably modernized *rakugo*. He is known as the father of modern *rakugo*.

Rakugo entered another golden age in Tokyo from the end of the Meiji period until the beginning of the Taisho period when many popular and famous *rakugo* performers emerged from workshops that were originally organized by Ensa, a comic storyteller. At the same time, in Osaka *rakugo* flourished owing to the competition between the Sanyu and Katsura schools of *rakugo*. There were about one hundred *rakugo* performers in Osaka during this period. However, with the arrival of radio and movies, *rakugo* gradually began to decline in popularity in both Tokyo and Osaka. Osaka, in particular, began to change its focus from *rakugo*-centered to *manzai*-centered *yose*.

Manzai

During the Meiji period, *manzai* changed its form to modern *manzai*. Entatsu Tamagoya was the first to implement this change by including folk songs and ballads into *manzai*. The religious significance of *manzai* as it was performed to bring blessings and prosperity began to fade. *Manzai* combined with *niwaka*, a performing art whose main feature was improvisation. *Manzai* began to have a more impromptu quality to its humor. This form of *manzai* soon became very popular and many performers joined *manzai* from other fields of the performing arts, including *rakugo*. With the disappearance of the religious form of *manzai*, it was transformed into a more secularized art form.

Almost every *manzai* performance seems to have created new kinds of humor. *Manzai* performers introduced various musical instruments such as the traditional Japanese *shamisen*, *biwa*, and drums. Some introduced Western instruments, such as the violin and accordian, as well as the use of puppets and dolls. *Manzai* alone began to encompass the whole of *yose* (vaudeville) with its mimicry, puppetry, traditional Japanese music, songs, skits, and even *kabuki*. *Manzai* began to have the reputation that one could see everything in it. Musical performance was its central feature, with short stories and comedies performed in between. The audience also often participated in the dialogue. There was an atmosphere within the *manzai* tent of relaxation and carefree conversation between the audience and performers. The audience could relax and enjoy *manzai* performances as if they were in their own living rooms.

Sometimes *manzai* performances were enlightening and educational; old sayings and incantations called *kochi* were discussed by the performers. This allowed for the enhancement of the status of *manzai*. However, since *manzai* performers used obscene language in order to make the audience laugh, *manzai* generally continued to be perceived as a vulgar art. In order to change this image, Sutemaru Sunagawa and his partner, Haruyo, toured Japan trying to convince their audiences that *manzai* could be funny even without the use of such language. At the same time, Entatsu, a disciple of Entatsu Tamagoya, the founding father of modern *manzai*, tried to develop a *manzai* that could be appreciated by all classes of people, not just the lower classes. He also included current news from various regions in his *manzai*, a feature that was greatly appreciated by audiences all over Japan. *Manzai* thus began to serve the purpose of informing people of contemporary news and trends. Two of the most popular new entertainments in those days were radio, and baseball games, especially games between Waseda and Keio. Entatsu and his partner, Achako, performed an imitation radio broadcast of these baseball games in their *manzai* performance. Entatsu and Achako became superstars through their performance of "So-Kei sen," a skit depicting a baseball game between Waseda and Keio University.

Manzai performers wore traditional Japanese costumes or kimono on stage. However, Entatsu and Achako performed in Western suit and necktie, giving *manzai* a new touch. Entatsu dressed like Charlie Chaplin with a moustache and glasses, changing the image of the *manzai* altogether, especially at a time when Western things were greatly in vogue and desirable in Japan. As *manzai* began to be broadcast through the radio, obscene language and crude jokes were gradually filtered out. Many popular *manzai* stars were born through radio broadcasting.

However, with the broadening of the radio audience, it became increasingly difficult to suit the tastes of all the people. At this point, "idea makers" were necessary. The two "idea makers" who appeared were Minoru Akita and Makoto

Nagaoki. Akita masterminded *manzai* plots for almost fifty years; Nagaoki also contributed immensely as the "think tank" of the *manzai* world.

In order for *manzai* to develop into a genre of art, an organizational structure also became necessary. Toward the end of the Meiji period and into the early Taisho period, Taizo Yoshimoto began a chain system of small *yose* theaters. His wife, Yoshi, and her younger brother took over after his death and built Yoshimoto Entertainment Inc. The small *yose* theaters covered the whole Osaka district. Gradually this company grew large enough to include all the major cities of Japan by creating a huge *yose* theater system. Owing to the efforts of the Yoshimoto company, the *yose*, which had developed during the Edo urbanization period, survived the industrialization of later years.

In 1923 many capable *manzai* performers who had been freelancing came back to Osaka after the huge earthquake that occurred in Tokyo that year. As a result, *manzai* became even more interesting, with various new talents gathered together at one place. Yoshimoto Entertainment Inc. took this opportunity to bring *manzai* into its *yose* system. However, since the main feature in the *yose* was the well-established *rakugo*, only well-known performers such as Entatsu and Achako were selected to perform *manzai*. Gradually even Nanyokan Hall of the *yose*, where only *rakugo* had been performed, became exclusively a *manzai* hall. Nanyokan Hall served as the foundation and training ground for *manzai* performers and facilitated the development of *manzai* into what it is now.

Manzai became a generally accepted form of entertainment in Osaka during the Manchuria Incident (1931). Yoshimoto Entertainment Inc. sent Entatsu and Achako to Manchuria on a goodwill tour. Upon their return, they performed *manzai* using incidents and stories they had heard in Manchuria. They portrayed their own experiences in Manchuria, and these were soon taken up and reported by various newspapers with photo clippings as well. This was the first time that *manzai* had ever been portrayed in the newspapers. With the widening acceptance of *manzai* during the 1937 China Incident, it was taken up in newspapers as well as magazines. Even short stories and novels began to include comic and *manzai* characters in them.

Entatsu and Achako both became very famous, and the difference between the *saizo* and *tayu* became difficult to define. They gradually decided to go their separate ways. Yoshimoto Entertainment Inc., however, decided to use Entatsu and Achako as partners in a comedy movie. Their first movie together, entitled *Akireta Renchu* [Those jerks], was produced in 1935 and became a great hit. Several movies followed, including the popular stage show "Mito Komon," which was performed and well received in Osaka at the Kadoza Theater. This stage show starred other comedians such as Minoru Takase and Kingoro Yanagiya, the number one modern *rakugo* performer, who made the audience roar with laughter. This kind of mixture and competition brought great success and created a new structure in *manzai*.

The male/female combination of Wakana and Ichiro introduced the accordion on stage, while Entatsu and Achako's performance relied on dialogue alone.

Wakana and Ichiro included drama, songs, ballads, swordplay, love scenes, and movie narrations in their *manzai*, which made their performance lively and fun. Wakana and Ichiro added a musical component to the dialogue style of Entatsu and Achako.

In Osaka, the performers and the audience had a great deal in common. However, in the countryside and the outskirts of cities in Japan, the lifestyles of the audience were very different from those of the performers, who were generally not local people. Many dialogues in the *manzai* sounded foreign outside of Osaka. Because of this, performances held outside of Osaka stressed the stage show rather than the dialogues. Generally there was a great difference between the *manzai* performed in the urban centers by Yoshimoto Entertainment Inc. and those in the more remote parts of the country.

In 1939, just before the Second World War, the New Entertainment Company was established in response to the new need in entertainment. It began to systematically recruit *manzai* performers, comedians, actors, and singers and to develop a new program for all-round entertainment. Wakana and Ichiro were enticed by this new *manzai*, which suited the objective of the company. The New Entertainment Company featured Wakana and Ichiro as their central stars and soon grew into a company large enough to challenge Yoshimoto Entertainment Inc.

With the advance of the Second World War, it became more and more difficult to have humorous dialogue in the *manzai*. Thus, the New Entertainment Company, which relied less heavily on dialogue and emphasized the stage show, began to have an advantage over Yoshimoto Entertainment Inc. One of the reasons why *manzai* was able to flourish even during the war was, according to Minoru Akita, its ability to adjust to changing social conditions.

The entertainment business was hard hit during and after the war. The two largest companies had to disband owing to their inability to employ large numbers of performers. These established performers formed their own comedy troupes and theatrical groups conducting tours around the provinces. With the decentralization of the entertainment business, several new styles and schools of acting developed. This brought about a variety of performers that had not been seen prior to the war.

In 1946, a *manzai* study group called MZ Kenshinkai was formed under the guidance of Minoru Akita. The members consisted of young *manzai* performers including A-suke and B-suke Akita, Itoshi Yumeji, Koishi Kimi, and Misu Wakana. This group stimulated many young *manzai* performers. In 1947, the first postwar comic radio program, ''Kamigata Enteikai,'' was launched at the NHK radio station, followed by several other radio programs in which *manzai* performers played major roles. These programs sponsored by various radio stations certainly contributed to the popularity of *manzai* in postwar Japan. By 1953, there were 150 pairs of *manzai* performers in the Kansai area and 100 pairs in Tokyo.

In 1955, a radio program developed that starred the *manzai* partners Chocho

Miyako and Yuji Nanto. This program's main feature was the participation of couples (husband and wife) from the audience in an impromptu *manzai* dialogue with Chocho and Yuji on marital problems and experiences. This program was the first of its kind in which *manzai* performers could deal directly with the family and social issues. It became an immediate hit. In 1963, the show was televised, creating a major breakthrough in Japanese culture. Private marital problems and issues (not traditionally discussed in public) were let out of the closet. With Chocho and Yuji's programs on television and radio, *manzai* experienced a boom that continued through the early 1960s.

Although the popularity of *manzai* began to decline, the demand for young *manzai* performers, as well as young *rakugo* performers, increased. They met the qualifications for masters of ceremonies and hosts as well as disk-jockeys, all of whom were highly sought after. There was a rapid increase in all-night radio talk shows, many of which were hosted by a *manzai* performer. One, "Bito Takeshi's All-Night Nippon," allowed people to listen to and talk with the candid and humorous Bito Takeshi. The program catered to the needs of the fast-growing and alienated urban society and was an immediate success. The people listened to all-night radio programs with the hope of establishing some human rapport and escaping their own loneliness. There also developed programs in which amateurs from the audience participated along with the professionals. "Shinkon-san Irasshai" [Welcome, newly-weds] was one such program in which the audience contributed to the creation of the program and the entertainment through their candid discussion of their own interesting or humorous experiences. The host of the program, Sanshi, was a *rakugo* performer who acted the part of *saizo* in order to encourage and maintain an interesting dialogue between the amateur and the professional.

By the early 1960s, the then ubiquitous television led to two separate *manzai* booms, one in the late 1960s and early 1970s and another in the early 1980s. By 1980, *manzai* shows began to appear on prime-time television, and the program entitled "Crash, *Manzai* Bullet Train" recorded an all-time high rating of 27.2 percent. After the start of this particular program, many other stations developed their own *yose* programs.

One of the propelling forces behind the popularity of *manzai* was the Sho No Kai, a study group formed by *manzai* performers and novelists. It must be noted that the efforts of Minoru Akita were highly instrumental in the creation of the Sho No Kai. Inspired by this group, many similar study groups sprang up. In 1979, a *manzai* performed by the Sho No Kai won an outstanding award at the annual art festival in the field of popular performing arts.

The meteoric rise in the popularity of *manzai* was accompanied by the idolization of its performers. Popular *manzai* performers were starring not only on *manzai* programs, but as disk-jockeys, masters of ceremonies, dramatic actors, and so on. Thus, they continued to spread the world of laughter to various areas of the performing arts.

Manzai performers and partners such as "Za Bonchi," B&B," and "all

Hanshin-Kyogin'' created a new trend by becoming idols to young junior and senior high school students. There was a growing tendency to direct humor to specific age groups. Younger performers aimed their humor at their own generation. This age-specific *manzai* heralded the third boom and greatly changed the content of the art. The third boom began with the presentation of a more explicit and realistic humor by ''Shinsuke and Ryusuke.'' ''Two Beat'' in Tokyo was also arranging more realistic performances for their audience. However, by 1982, the oversaturation of *manzai* radio and television created a glut that led to a rapid decline in its popularity.

Rakugo

After World War II, most of the *yose* had disappeared or been burnt down. However, performers such as Shinsho Kokontei and Bunraku Katsura faithfully maintained the essence of *rakugo* in their performances even after the war. In spite of the fact that there were still quite a few *rakugo* performers left, the number of *yose* had declined to only four in Tokyo, which had an urban population of 10 million. (In 1842, when the population was 1 million, there were 200 *yose*.) Although there were few *yose* remaining, *rakugo* continued to be performed in other guises.

The first of many *rakugo* halls, the Mitsukoshi Department Store's Mitsukoshi Theater, was constructed in 1948. Noted *rakugo* performers were invited once a month to the *rakugo* meeting halls where their performances were enjoyed by the audience to the exclusion of all else. On the other hand, *yose* focused attention on other forms of entertainment, leaving little room for *rakugo*. *Rakugo* halls became popular among *rakugo* fans. However, since the older and more established *rakugo* performers had a monopoly on the performances held at these halls, the young and upcoming performers hardly had a chance to appear before the audience.

Because of this, regional *yose* called ''mini-*rakugo*'' began to develop and grew rapidly after 1975. Although these mini-*rakugo* centers began with unestablished performers, there was a gradual appearance of famous *rakugo* performers. These centers, which began to invite support from the public, were usually held at shrine offices, conference halls of companies, public bathhouses, sushi shops, coffee shops, restaurants, and even tour buses. They were performed not only at night, but during lunch breaks for company men. Such regional *yose* were similar to the *yose* when they first appeared in the Edo period; they were performed in response to the needs and demands of the audience.

As more *rakugo* was broadcast on radio and television, it became more popular, creating a boom in the early 1980s similar to the *manzai* boom. Like the *manzai* performers, *rakugo* performers were also idolized. University students formed *rakugo* study groups. In 1981, there was a movement toward the appreciation of classic *rakugo*. In Osaka and Kyoto, performers of the old school such as Shokaku, Beicho, Harudanji, and Kobunshi were given various awards and recognition, thus establishing themselves as the main pillars of *rakugo*. In turn, their disciples further developed new trends in *rakugo*. For example, Beicho's disciple, Shizuyaku, Harudanji's disciple, Fukudanji, and Kobunshi's disciple, Sanshi, as well as Bunchin, all contributed to the creation of the new *rakugo*. In 1981, Sanshi won the Outstanding Laughter Award, and Bunchin enhanced the visual aspects of *rakugo* with the use of laser beams and synthesizers. Recently, there has been a trend in *rakugo* to combine and harmonize other areas of the traditional performing arts such as the puppet theater.

CRITICISM

This section deals primarily with critical reviews and analyses of some of the important sources on the historical development of *manzai* and *rakugo*. The focus is on the impact these performing arts have had on Japanese culture. One book on the history of performing arts in general deserves mention: *Sasuraibito no Geinoshi* [Performing arts history of wanderers] by Haruo Misumi. Misumi's thesis here is that the starting point for most of the Japanese performing arts was in the street or square or an area in front of homes, any of which was temporarily converted into a "stage" on which the wandering performers demonstrated their arts. These members of the agrarian society, who did not own land and were therefore unable to settle down permanently, as well as the extremely poor, were unable to eke out a living for themselves unless they travelled from one village to another like gypsies. The fact that made this itinerant existence possible was the ancient Japanese folk belief that gods came from foreign lands to bless the villages by impersonating human beings. Therefore, although these wanderers were in fact social dropouts, they were welcomed by the residents of the far-flung villages as purveyors of blessings and prosperity.

Because these performers occupied the bottom rung of society themselves, they could deeply sympathize with the hardship and pathos of others. Furthermore, they came directly in contact with the people in various provinces, and through this contact came to understand the mind of the common people. It is in this milieu that the performing arts emerged, and through this history gave forth their varied blooms.

Thus, the well-known and representative performing arts of today, such as *kabuki* and *noh* drama, have their roots in the popular arts (of which *manzai* is one) performed by wandering entertainers. That is why the philosophy of wanderers, as described in Misumi's book, is significant in shedding light on the nature of the popular performing arts.

In one chapter, "Tabi-Geinin" [The travelling entertainers], of his book, *Misemono kara Terebi e* [From exhibition to television], Hidetoshi Kato considers the wandering performers (earlier treated by Misumi) from the perspective of communication. He sees them as cultural cement, connecting the diverse and isolated Japanese villages, each a small universe in itself. He characterizes Japan as linked by each cultural art form in which the human agent is the medium of cultural exchange. In this respect, Kato writes, wandering performers/entertainers were Japan's first public communication specialists since they communicated what they saw and heard in each area to other areas— news of the latest events from the city to the countryside, as well as the latest news from the provinces to the city.

Shunsuke Tsurumi looks at the history of the performing arts as a history of entertainment. A festival, for example, is held in the form of entertainment. Examples of other kinds of entertainment held to bring blessings from outside are *tayu* and *saizo*. The influence of Shinobu Origuchi, the folklorist, can be seen in the treatment of the performing arts by Tsurumi as well as by Kato and Misumi. Tsurumi uses the history of *manzai* to focus on the history of entertainment in his book, *Tayu Saizo Den* [The historical development of *tayu* and *saizo*]. This book presents a decade-by-decade historical development of *manzai*'s social function, with the focus on the philosophical analysis of the social and cultural role of *tayu* and *saizo*.

In his book, *Manzai*, Hiroshi Inoue philosophizes about the roles of *tayu* and *saizo* in much the same way as Tsurumi does. With reference to society at large or, from a more technical viewpoint, in terms of individual daily lives, Inoue asks what meaning the performing arts provide. He suggests that their responsibility is to impose chaos (*saizo*) on the order (*tayu*) of society and our lives. In other words, according to Inoue, the world is made up of multiple pairs of opposites such as order and chaos, common sense and nonsense, hard and soft, responsibility and irresponsibility, mind and body, reality and illusion, sacred and profane. Then, depending on the forces that create the world, of which order is important among them, order must be periodically subjected to a threat of chaos, after which the old order is regenerated and a new order emerges. The complementary forces of order and chaos are both indispensable. This relationship is symbolically represented in the *manzai* performance.

Tsurumi also emphasizes the significance of this relationship between *tayu* and *saizo*. He cautions in his book that if the function of chaos is not allowed to create a new form, problems severe enough to endanger the survival of mankind could emerge.

In the Japanese culture itself, there are multiple pairs of opposites symbolizing order and chaos—indigenous and foreign elements, central and local government, city and country—through whose dynamic interaction the culture has come to be what it is. Tsurumi's work is particularly insightful on the subject of viewing the development of the Japanese culture through the historical development of *manzai*. Unfortunately, this book traces the history of *manzai* only until 1960.

It has already been mentioned that had the idea maker, Minoru Akita, never existed, *manzai* as we know it today would probably not exist—so profound is his influence on this performing art form. His book, *Osaka Warai Banashi* [The history of Osaka comic stories] is indispensable for understanding the historical process of *manzai*. This is because Akita discusses the history of *manzai* from the perspective of a producer of that humor. He has spent more than fifty years

in the direct company of *manzai* performers, and is well qualified to write on
the history of *manzai* from the vantage point of the performers themselves.
Nevertheless, at no point does this intimacy result in sentimentality, nor does it
prevent Akita from acknowledging all the facts.

Akita views the history of humor through the history of *manzai*. In order to
show the function that humor fulfilled in respective eras, many actual scripts are
included. Another aspect treated is the self-regenerative capacity inherent in
manzai. Still, an unfortunate fact with this book, too, is that it treats only pre–
World War II material, giving scant attention to the postwar world of *manzai*.

According to Akita's definition of *manzai*, the humor is contained in the interest
of words and in talking around a subject. A meandering conversation between
two people standing is a suitable setting; a light-hearted conversation or even
gossip is also acceptable. Instead of talking to the audience about the honest
conversation of an ordinary person's daily life, *manzai* is that art in which two
people on stage converse with each other. Therefore, Akita's definition of *manzai*
is slightly different from Tsurumi's, for whom the two interlocutors must represent *tayu* and *saizo*. Tsurumi, in other words, insists on the necessity for a wit
and a fool. In this conception of *manzai*, humor is created by the fool.

Tsurumi's definition is close to Isamu Maeda's definition as expressed in the
book, *Kamigata Manzai Happyakunenshi* [Kyoto-Osaka *manzai*: A history of
eight hundred years]. Inoue incorporates the definitions of both Akita and Tsurumi to describe the world of *manzai*. In other words, he uses both Akita's
concept, which emphasizes the ordinariness of an average man's daily life, and
the wit/fool relationship, emphasized by Tsurumi, to explore the world of *manzai*
humor. The philosophical analysis of the fool's relationship to *tayu* (*shin*—a
modern expression for *tayu*) and *saizo* (*boke* or *tsukkomi*—modern expressions
for *saizo*) in Inoue's book is more readily understood than Tsurumi's analysis.
But Inoue's treatment of *manzai* history is considerably weaker than that of
Tsurumi.

Teiji Kojima, who, like Akita, is a *manzai* scriptwriter, has authored *Manzai
Sesoshi* [A historical survey of *manzai*]. The outstanding characteristic of this
book, one would have to say, is the presentation of *manzai* scripts in the format
of a historical survey. In the case of Tsurumi, Inoue, and particularly Akita,
manzai scripts are treated to some extent, but on the whole the texts consist of
commentaries. Kojima's book is unique in making the scripts the central concern
of his text.

Traditional *manzai* is generally known as "Mikawa *manzai*." Upon reading
Kojima's book, however, one is struck by the various kinds of *manzai* represented—from Hokkaido to Kyushu. This work is particularly significant because
it provides a detailed commentary on each of the *manzai* included. It is also
more significant than others in terms of the commentary on *manzai* activities in
Tokyo. But, again, as is the case with the works of Tsurumi and Akita, this
book too covers the subject only up to the 1960s.

Kamigata Wagei Gei no Sekai [The world of comic arts in the Kyoto-Osaka area], by Kaichiro Furukawa, et al., is the book that best treats the post–1960 material available on *manzai*. This is published by Hakusui Publishers under the guidance of no fewer than six editors. The most useful chapter in this collection is Kaichiro Furukawa's "Sengo Kamigata Owarai kai no Nagare to Sono Shuhen" [The current trend of the postwar Kyoto-Osaka comic world and related subjects]. Here, Furukawa summarizes a theory of *manzai* for each ten-year period, and with this summary as background he provides a deeper analysis.

The significance of this book is Furukawa, et al.'s focus on the historical development of *manzai* and *rakugo* from the postwar era to 1984, a period hardly addressed by Tsurumi, Akita, and Kojima.

As mentioned above, books that describe the historical survey of *rakugo* are exceptionally rare. When they do exist, they are quite different from the historical surveys of *manzai*. Most of them are extremely short and do not offer a very coherent or detailed survey of the historical development of *rakugo*. Among them is one that is somewhat segmented, but at least is representative of the historical current: *Yose: Wagei no Shusei* [Vaudeville: collection of the narrative arts], edited by Geinoshi Kenkyukai. In it is a chapter by Kazuo Sekiyama on the development of *rakugo* as an oral art, a chapter on vaudeville of the Edo period by Shinji Nobuhiro, and one on Encho *rakugo* performers during the Meiji period by Hiroo Nagai.

In considering the historical current, particularly the transformation of *rakugo* from the Edo period up to contemporary times, Hidetoshi Kato's chapter on *rakugo* in the Geinoshi collection is particularly useful. Kato defines Edo vaudeville as a neighborhood art in which neighbors eagerly recognized all members of the audience as intimate friends. But as times changed and strange faces appeared with the shift from a neighborhood society to an urban one, Kato identifies vaudeville as an urban art. Later, as *rakugo* radio and television entered every home, Kato identifies the new form of vaudeville as a home art that has even greater freedom than that of Edo vaudeville. Yet, he somehow doubts whether this is truly a restoration of the Edo freedom. Though this chapter is short, Kato's analysis of his *yose* is profound and complete with many insightful comments.

In his book, *Rakugo no Ronri* [The logic of rakugo], Kenichi Onishi writes that the pleasure and amusement of real *rakugo* must be expanded to provide entertainment for the masses. In this very readable work, he explains the model for that development and relates the logic and philosophy of *rakugo* to Albert Einstein's theory of relativity. In particular, this book should be considered a basic research text for information on the philosophical implications of *rakugo*.

One volume that includes the history of *rakugo* as well as that of *yose* and *manzai* is Hiroshi Takahashi's *Taishu Geino* [Public performing arts]. He provides an especially extensive amount of information in his well-documented history of *yose*, but the treatment of *rakugo* and *manzai* is too simplistic for serious researchers.

Modern *manzai* began in Osaka and continued to develop there. *Rakugo*, on the other hand, emerged and developed in Edo. Hiroshi Inoue, in his book, *Manzai*, referred to above, discusses why *manzai* emerged in Osaka, whereas *rakugo* achieved popularity in Edo. According to Inoue's analysis, the government was the central force in Edo society, which necessitated a vertical hierarchy. In Osakan society, the importance of commerce resulted in a horizontal, merchant-oriented society. Humor in the vertical Edo society was an offensive humor that often disturbed the harmony at large. On the other hand, the humor of Osaka society centered on the conciliatory smile that was indispensable to the horizontal merchant class.

In *Nihonjin no Chie* [Japanese wisdom] by Hidetoshi Kato and others, the humor of *rakugo* and that of *manzai* are described as follows: The humor of *rakugo* is contained in the contrast between the educated person belittling the uneducated one, so that it is a humor based on vertical relationships; but the humor of *manzai* emerges from a difference in perspective based on horizontal relationships. This book also compares the *rakugo* style of Tokyo and the *manzai* style of Osaka from the perspective of communication.

Nihonjin no Warai to Rakugo [Japanese laughter and *rakugo*] is probably the most representative work treating the historical development of *rakugo* humor. The author is Shoichi Fuse. According to Fuse, laughter in the Edo period (1600–1868) is to be understood in the context of *samurai* society and is quite different from the laughter of the townsmen of the period. The *samurai* laughter of the Edo period was transformed into the macho grin fashionable during the Meiji period, with its slogan of "Rich Country, Strong Army." This form of laughter, which did not allow men to expose their feelings openly, gradually became known as the "mysterious Japanese smile." According to Fuse, this laughter is not unique to the Japanese, nor is it characteristic of *rakugo* laughter. The contribution of this book lies not only in its analysis of *rakugo* laughter, but also in its clarification of the historical and social background of the nature of *rakugo*.

Fuse has written that the peak of *rakugo* coincided with the gradual decline of the feudal order. Furthermore, during this era, the merchant class became the most powerful, though the active and energetic merchants ironically ranked the lowest in the strict Tokugawa social order of *samurai*/farmer/craftsman/merchant. Within this social matrix, the repressed energy of the merchants and townsmen gradually expanded beyond the limits imposed by this feudal society. Based on their transcendence from this form, the performing arts emerged, themselves transcending the very form that produced them. Some of these art forms were, for example, *rakugo* and *kabuki*.

Another influence contributing to the formation of these art forms was the two and a half centuries of isolation imposed on the country by the Tokugawa government. This surely was a shaping force in the development of the performing arts.

What was the historical development of Osaka where *manzai* came into being? In response to this question, Michitaro Tada, professor at Kyoto University, has written a very interesting and revealing article, "Osaka wa Mizu no Miyako ka" [Is Osaka the capital of water?]. According to this article, Osaka was developed on land that was originally reclaimed from the sea. Two-thirds of this land was naturally accumulated from river silt, while the other third was man-made following the Muromachi era and finally completed during the Tokugawa era. This was carried out by Osaka leaders who thought that the reclaimed land would be solidified by allowing people to step on it. In order to carry out the plan, they had to bring the people to the land area. The Osaka leaders decided to set up the *misemono* show, which was very popular at that time, to attract people to the land area. In fact, amusement centers did spring up (*yose*), as did shops serving delicious food in the environs. This was the beginning of mass culture in Osaka.

This arrangement, which entertained and amused hordes of people and at the same time achieved the result of firming up the soft reclaimed land, clearly manifests the enterprising spirit of the Osaka business mind. Grasping the historical process of the development of Osaka itself, this article is particularly suggestive and insightful concerning the development of mass culture in Osaka. The important fact to note here is that Osaka is a city that was created out of no form. Because it developed as described above, Osaka is now a chaotically burgeoning city. To describe it in culinary terms, let us say Osaka is, so to speak, a city of "hodgepodge."

Edo, on the other hand, is a world of *makunouchi bento*, which is a very beautifully decorated box lunch. *Makunouchi bento* signifies that beauty is arranged in various ways within a limited form or framework.

From the world of hodgepodge, *manzai* emerged, while from the world of *makunouchi bento*, *rakugo* emerged. *Manzai* is a fluid art form emphasizing form and content, while *rakugo* is an art that stresses form. These two different types are discussed by Hidetoshi Kato as fluid and frozen art forms in his article, "*Manzai* to Nihonjin" [*Manzai* and the Japanese], in *Kato Hidetoshi Chosaku Shu* [The collected edition of Hidetoshi Kato's work]. The style of the frozen art form of *rakugo* was devised by Encho, a popular storyteller during mid-Meiji times (the turn of the last century). After these times, further development of this art form ceased. *Rakugo* has continued to be performed in this frozen and unchanged condition up to the present day.

Kato posits that one expects change, on the other hand, in the fluid form of *manzai*. This aspect reflects the pragmatic nature of the constantly adaptable Osaka merchants. Adaptability and flexibility are positive characteristics of the *manzai*. But *manzai* lacks inner coherence. Its weak point is that it tends to adapt merely to stay alive. This is a point on which Kato focuses. This characteristic of *manzai* can be said to be a characteristic of the Japanese people. Kato's book is invaluable because it sheds light on *manzai* as well as making us reflect on the identity of the Japanese.

Still, *rakugo*'s emergence from, and transcendence of, a form can also be said to be a characteristic of the Japanese people. This is a trait that is mirrored in the frozen art form of *rakugo*. In other words, form is imitated and, by repeating it a number of times, transcended. Through this process the art is refined to completion. *Rakugo* humor that emerged from this paradigm or framework can be categorized as an innovative humor that focuses on improvement within the paradigm. On the other hand, *manzai* humor can be categorized as an inventive humor that is created as a result of interparadigmatic confrontation. The inventive humor is created by the fusion of the opposing forces represented by *tayu* (*shin*) and *saizo* (*boke*).

REFERENCE WORKS AND RESEARCH COLLECTIONS

In comparing reference works related to *rakugo* and those related to *manzai*, one is struck by the abundance of the former. One can surmise various reasons for this state of affairs. One stems from the difference in the characteristics of the two forms. *Rakugo* is a performing art that has matured, like *kabuki* and *noh* drama, within an established form, and within that form the art has been refined. On the other hand, from the perspective of both form and content, *manzai* is more fluid. Because improvisation is a particularly outstanding characteristic of *manzai*, it is extremely difficult to record a performance. But in an art such as *rakugo*, in which the nature of storytelling is clearly defined, the act of recording a performance is much easier. Furthermore, the prestige of *rakugo* as a performing art is much higher. Because *manzai* is thought to be a vulgar performing art, it is seldom written about in book form.

As discussed above, the history of *manzai* is as old as Japanese history itself. But the history of *manzai* that centers on dialogue (which is the sort of *manzai* that comes to mind today) is shallower than that of *rakugo*. This is one possible explanation for its scant treatment as serious literature. Furthermore, *manzai* was spawned and achieved maturity as an art form in Osaka, which may be called a city of business rather than a city of culture. Because of this, writers in general, just as in the case of novelists, all went to Tokyo—the city of culture. Of course, this means that publishers too are concentrated in Tokyo. From this standpoint, then, *rakugo*, devised and nurtured in Tokyo, is definitely in an advantageous position as far as publication is concerned.

Let us now turn our attention to the reference works devoted to a discussion of *rakugo* and *manzai*. With respect to the Japanese performing arts in general, the single most comprehensive bibliographical source is *Japanese Performing Arts: An Annotated Bibliography*, compiled by Masato Matsui, et al. This bibliography consists of a wide variety of materials, including dramatic texts, stage scripts, and musical scores on every conceivable aspect and form of Japan's performing arts. Altogether, there are 1,020 entries, all of which are annotated in English. Nevertheless, of the 1,020, only 38 entries directly relate to popular performing comic arts (*rakugo* and *manzai*). Among these thirty-eight, only two deal with *manzai*.

Perhaps one of the most comprehensive reference works for *rakugo* is *Yose:*

Wagei no Shusei [Vaudeville: Collection of the narrative arts], edited by Geinoshi Kenkyukai. This book delineates the origin and historical developments in the narrative arts of *rakugo* and analyzes their significant features and personalities. From the standpoint of popular performing arts, Hidetoshi Kato's chapter on "Gendai no *Yose*" [Modern *yose*] is the most helpful. The shortest and most comprehensive *rakugo* handbook is *Koten Rakugo no Sekai* [The world of classic *rakugo*] by Shigetami Enomoto. He describes the origin of *rakugo*, its various types, the use of non-verbal *rakugo* gestures, types of punch lines, and "props" related to *rakugo* like fans and hand towels. This book is particularly helpful to beginners as many of the explanations are presented with step-by-step photo illustrations. It includes the following: synopses of fifty well-known classic *rakugo* stories, a directory listing the names of living *rakugo* performers, and addresses of vaudeville theaters as well as other performing theaters in the Kanto and Kansai districts.

Kin Watanabe's *Rakugo no Kenkyu* [*Rakugo* research] aims to provide common orthodox information concerning *rakugo*. He explains its history, types of punch lines, and characteristics of the Osaka variety of *rakugo*.

There is a reference work written especially from the standpoint of ethics. This is Shinichi Ikegami's *Rakugo Rinrigaku* [*Rakugo* ethics], in which forty-five *rakugo* stories are analyzed and discussed. For each story, the meaning of the title is explained, a synopsis of the story is given, and its comical aspects are interpreted. *Rakugo Yuhodo* [*Rakugo* promenade] by Seiichi Yano is a unique book in that the author visits the sites that have become associated with *rakugo* in the public's mind and describes them with the aid of photographic illustrations. This work is an excellent introduction to the *rakugo* world, especially for beginners.

Another unique source is *Rakugo no Sekai* [The world of *rakugo*] by Tsubame Yanagiya, who is a *rakugo* storyteller himself. He explains the steps involved in becoming a full-fledged comic storyteller. The world of *rakugo* is described in terms of his own personal experience. This book is readable for anyone who is interested in *rakugo*. A *rakugo* glossary is appended for reference.

There are several autobiographical works by comic storytellers. The one considered most scholarly is *Anrakuan Sakuden: Hanashi no Keifu* [Anrakuan Sakuden: A genealogy of comic stories] by Kazuo Sekiyama. This is a biography of Anrakuan Sakuden (1554–1642), the author of *Seisuisho*, which is considered to be the first text on *rakugo*.

Another work that should be noted is *Yose Sodachi* [*Yose* upbringing] by Encho Sanyutei (1900–   ), who was born into the *yose* world and was a popular comic storyteller during the Meiji, Taisho, and Showa periods.

Hiroo Nagai's *San Yutei Encho* is a biography of Encho, compiled from fragmentary records left by Encho as well as recollections by his friends.

There are reference works that delineate the relationships between Japanese literature and the narrative art of *rakugo*. Kaname Okitsu's *Nihon Bungaku to Rakugo* [Japanese literature and *rakugo*] is one good example.

Mushu Ui's *Kamigata Hanashi Ko* [Thoughts on comic storytelling in the Kyoto-Osaka area] and Isamu Maeda's *Kamigata Rakugo no Rekishi* [History of *rakugo* in the Kyoto-Osaka area] are two major sources that deal with the historical developments of *rakugo* in the Kyoto-Osaka area. Ui's comments on the rise and fall of *rakugo* in this area are particularly illuminating.

Kenichi Onishi's *Rakugo no Ronri* [The logic of *rakugo*] depicts his philosophical view of this performing art. The sections in which he attempts to relate Shinsho Kokontei's *rakugo* to Albert Einstein's theory of relativity and Werner Heisenberg's quantum theory are difficult reading, but anyone who is interested in the philosophical aspect of *rakugo* may find the effort worthwhile. In *Nihonjin no Warai to Rakugo* [Japanese laughter and *rakugo*], Shoichi Fuse analyzes the contents of classic *rakugo* to explain how it stimulates people to laughter. This book is an essential source for understanding Japanese humor.

For an investigation of the origins and embryonic stages of *manzai*, "Kebozu Ko" [Thoughts of an amateur priest] by the well-known folklorist Kunio Yanagida (1875–1962) is very informative and useful (see *Yanagida Kunio Shu* in the collection of Yanagida Kunio, Vol. IX.)

"The Birth of Japanese Literature" [Nihon bungaku no hassei] in *Origuchi Shinobu Zenshu* [The complete works of Shinobu Origuchi], Vol. 7, by Shinobu Origuchi, who worked with Yanagida, is significant in ascertaining the relationship between the original form of *manzai* and religious festivals.

There are several reference works that trace the changes in the form and content of *manzai* over the years. Shunsuke Tsurumi's *Tayu Saizo Den* [The historical development of *tayu* and *saizo*] is a significant reference source for those interested in the philosophical implications of *tayu* and *saizo* in our society. Tsurumi delineates the social functions of *manzai* generation by generation.

Hiroshi Inoue examines *manzai* as a typical form of Osaka humor from a philosophical perspective in his book, *Manzai*.

Kamigata Warai Gei no Sekai [The world of comic arts in the Kyoto-Osaka area], edited by Kaichiro Furukawa, et al., consists of many essays concerning both *manzai* and *rakugo*. Among them, Furukawa's essay, "Sengo Kamigata Owaraikai no Nagare to Sono Shuhen" [The course of postwar Kyoto-Osaka comic world and related subjects], is most helpful for the purpose of examining the popular performing arts.

Dai Nihon Hyakka Jiten [Encyclopedia Japonica] (edited by Tetsuo Soga), particularly Vols. 17 and 18, is a useful source for those who are looking for a quick overview of *manzai* and *rakugo*, respectively. Likewise, *Nihon Hyakka Dai Jiten* [Japanese encyclopedia] (edited by Showa Shuppan Kenkyujo), Vols. 12 and 13, also provide a brief description of *manzai* and *rakugo*, respectively.

Nihon o Shiru Jiten [Handbook to find out about Japan], by Tatehiko Oshima, et al., contains a brief description of the historical developments of both *manzai* and *rakugo*. One of the very few reference sources written in English is that provided by the *Kodansha Encyclopedia of Japan*, compiled by Kodansha, in which both *manzai* and *rakugo* are briefly described.

While original collections of *rakugo* are limited, there are several comprehensive collections. It must be noted here that all of those collections are, in one way or another, presented in summarized form, with or without commentaries, explanations, and interpretations.

There are two major handbooks that contain a large collection of *rakugo*. The first one is *Rakugo Jiten* [*Rakugo* handbook], written by Nobuo Imamura in 1957. Imamura provides synopses of about 500 well-known *rakugo* stories from Edo times to the present and includes notations and interpretations. This work also presents a brief historical account of *rakugo*, a genealogy of the various schools, and explanations of the punch lines, as well as a directory listing personal histories, performance styles, and addresses of eighty-three living comic storytellers.

A group comprised of ex-members of the Tokyo University Rakugo Research Society decided to revise Imamura's handbook in 1969. They summarized and compiled about 870 *rakugo* stories and included commentaries. It was published as *Rakugo Jiten* [*Rakugo* handbook], edited by Todai Rakugokai. *Rakugo Senshu* [*Rakugo* anthology], edited by Bakusho Yotaro and Nobuo Imamura, is a selected work of *rakugo* with cartoon illustrations. The cartoon illustrations make the book more interesting and readable.

Takashi Hosokubo has written synopses of one hundred *rakugo* stories in accordance with subcategorized specific themes, such as an image of women in *rakugo*. This collection is called *Rakugo Hyakudai* [One hundred topics on *rakugo*]. No explanation or interpretation is given, except for postscript commentaries.

Mushu Ui's *Rakugo no Genwa* [Original sources of *rakugo*] is a compilation of 420 *rakugo* stories, with original source citations and references.

Some collections represent the works of a particular comic storyteller and thus contain different types of *rakugo* works by one comic artist. Such is *Encho-Zenshu* [Complete works of Encho], a collection of the works of Encho Sanyutei (1839–1900). The thirteen volumes in this collection encompass various *rakugo* materials performed by Encho. Some of his correspondence is also included.

A more recent collection of *rakugo* is the *Shinsho Kuruwabanashi* [Shinsho's *rakugo* about the licensed quarters] by Shinsho Kokontei.

With respect to original collections of *manzai*, no comprehensive compilation is available for the reasons indicated above. There are, however, two sources that should be listed here. One of them is Teiji Kojima's *Manzai Sesoshi* [A historical survey of *manzai*]. Kojima, as an author of comic stories, includes as many *manzai* scripts as possible in this book. Likewise, Minoru Akita, another scriptwriter of *manzai*, has written *Osaka Warai Banashishi* [The history of Osaka comic stories], which includes a portion of various *manzai* scripts. However, neither of the books is intended to be a compilation of *manzai* scripts.

BIBLIOGRAPHY

Akita, Minoru. *Osaka Warai Banashishi* [The history of Osaka comic stories]. Osaka: Henshu Kobo Noa, 1984.

秋田実 『大阪笑い話史』 大阪 編集神戸のあ 1984

Enomoto, Shigetomi. *Koten Rakugo no Sekai* [The world of classic *rakugo*]. Tokyo: Kodansha, 1964.

榎本滋民 『古典落語の世界』 東京 講談社 1964

Furukawa, Kaichiro, et al., eds. *Kamigata Warai Gei no Sekai* [The world of comic arts in the Kyoto-Osaka area]. Tokyo: Hakusuichi, 1984.

古川嘉一郎他編 『上方笑い芸の世界』 東京 白水社 1984

Fuse, Shoichi. *Nihonjin no Warai to Rakugo* [Japanese laughter and *rakugo*]. Tokyo: Sanichi Shobo, 1970.

不施昌一 『日本人の笑いと落語』 東京 三一書房 1970

Hosokubo, Takashi. *Rakugo Hyakudai* [One hundred topics on *rakugo*]. Tokyo: Kyoiku Shiryo Shuppankai, 1982.

細窪孝 『落語百選』 東京 教育資料出版会 1982

Ikegami, Shinichi. *Rakugo Rinrigaku* [*Rakugo* ethics]. Tokyo: Tokyo Shobo, 1971.

池上信一 『落語倫理学』 東京 東京武房社 1971

Imamura, Nobuo. *Rakugo Jiten* [*Rakugo* handbook]. Tokyo: Seiabo, 1957.

今村信雄 『落語事典』 東京 青蛙房 1957

Inoue, Hiroshi. *Manzai*. Kyoto: Sekai Shisosha, 1981.

井上宏 『漫才』 京都 世界思想社 1981

Kato, Hidetoshi. *Kato Hidetoshi Chosaku Shu* [The Collected Edition of Hidetoshi Kato's work] Vol. 4. Toyko: Chuokoronsha, 1980.

加藤秀俊 『加藤秀俊著作集 第4巻』 東京 中央公論社 1980

―――. *Misemono kara Terebi e* [From exhibition to television]. Tokyo: Yuanami Shobo, 1965.

『見せ物からテレビへ』 東京 岩波書店 1965

―――. *Toshi to Goraku* [City and entertainment]. Tokyo: Kajima Kenkyujo Shuppankai, 1969.

『都市と娯楽』 東京 鹿島研究所出版会 1969

―――. *Yoka no Shakaigaku* [Sociology of leisure] Kyoto: PHP Kenkyujo, 1984.

『余暇の社会学』 京都 PHP研究所 1984

Kato, Hidetoshi, et al. *Nihonjin no Chie* [Japanese wisdom]. Tokyo: Chuko Bunko, 1973.

加藤秀俊他編 『日本人の知恵』 東京 中公文庫 1973

Kenkyukai, Geinoshi, ed. *Yose: Wagei no Shusei* [Vaudeville: Collection of the narrative arts]. Tokyo: Heibonsha, 1971.

芸能史研究会編 『寄席:話芸の集成』 東京 平凡社 1971

Kodansha. *Kodansha Encyclopedia of Japan*. Vols. 5 and 6. Tokyo: Kodansha International, 1983.

『講談社日本百科事典 第5－6巻』 東京 講談社 1983

Koestler, Arthur. *The Act of Creation*. London: Hutchinson, 1964.

Kojima, Teiji. *Manzai Sesoshi* [A historical survey of *manzai*]. Tokyo: Mainichi Shimbunsha, 1965.

小島貞二 『漫才世相史』 東京 毎日新聞社 1965

Kokontei, Shinsho. *Shinsho Kuruwabanashi* [Shinsho's *rakugo* about the licensed quarters]. Tokyo: Tachikaze Shobo, 1970.

古今亭志ん生 『志ん生廓ばなし』 東京 立風書房 1970

Kurata, Yoshihiro. *Meiji Taisho no Minshu Goraku* [Public entertainment of Meiji and Taisho]. Tokyo: Yuwanami Shinsho, 1980.

倉田喜弘 『明治大正の民衆娯楽』 東京 岩波新書 1980

Maeda, Isamu. *Kamigata Manzai Happyakunenshi* [Kyoto-Osaka *manzai*: A history of eight hundred years]. Osaka: Sugimoto Shoten, 1975.

前田勇 『上方漫才800年史』 大阪 杉本書店 1975

―――. *Kamigata Rakugo no Rekishi* [History of *rakugo* in the Kyoto-Osaka area]. Osaka: Sugimoto Shoten, 1958.

『上方落語の歴史』 大阪 杉本書店 1958

Matsui, Masato, et al., eds. *Japanese Performing Arts: An Annotated Bibliography*. Honolulu: Center for Asia and Pacific Studies Council for Japanese Studies, University of Hawaii, 1981.

Misumi, Haruo. *Sasuraibito no Geinoshi* [Performing arts history of wanderers]. Tokyo: Nihon Hoso Kyokai, 1978.

三角晴男 『さすらい人の芸能史』 東京 日本放送協会 1978

Nagai, Hiro. *Sanyutei Encho*. Tokyo: Seiabo, 1962.

永井敬夫 『三遊亭円生』 東京 青蛙房 1962

Nihon Hyakka Dai Jiten [Japanese encyclopedia]. Vols. 12 and 13. Showa Shuppan Kenkyujo, ed. Tokyo: Shogakukan, 1964.

昭和出版研究所編 『日本百科大事典 第12-13巻』 東京 小学館 1964

Okitsu, Kaname. *Nihon Bungaku to Rakugo* [Japanese literature and *rakugo*]. Tokyo: Ofusha, 1965.

興津要 『日本文学と落語』 東京 桜楓社 1965

Onishi, Kenichi. *Rakugo no Ronri* [The logic of *rakugo*]. Tokyo: Sanichi Shobo, 1973.

大西建一 『落語の論理』 東京 三一書房 1973

Origuchi, Shinobu. ''Nihonbungaku no Hassei'' [The birth of Japanese literature]. In *Origuchi Shinobu Zenshu* [The complete works of Origuchi Shinobu]. Vol. 7. Tokyo: Chuokoronsha, 1976.

折口信夫 「日本文学の発生」 『折口信夫全集第7巻』 東京 中央公論社 1976

Oshima, Tatehiko, et al. *Nihon o Shiru Jiten* [Handbook to find out about Japan]. Tokyo: Shakai Shisosha, 1971.

大島建彦他編 『日本を知る事典』 東京 社会思想社 1971

Rakugokai, Todai, ed. *Rakugo Jiten* [*Rakugo* handbook]. Tokyo: Seiabo, 1969.

東大落語会編 『落語事典』 東京 青蛙房 1969

Sanyutei, Encho. *Encho-Zenshu* [Complete works of Encho]. 13 vols. Tokyo: Shuyodo, 1926–1928.

三遊亭円長 『円生全集 第13巻』 東京 春陽堂 1926-1928

―――. *Yose Sodachi* [*Yose* upbringing]. Tokyo: Seiabo, 1965.

三遊亭円生 『寄席育ち』 東京 青蛙房 1965

Sekiyama, Kazuo. *Anrakuan Sakuden: Hanashi no Keifu* [Anrakuan Sakuden: A genealogy of comic stories]. Tokyo: Seiabo, 1957.

関山和夫 『安楽庵策伝：落語の系譜』 東京 青蛙房 1957

Soga, Tetsuo, ed. *Dai Nihon Hyakka Jiten* [Encyclopedia Japonica]. Tokyo: Shogakukan, 1972.

相賀徹夫編 『大日本百科事典』 東京 小学館 1972

Tada, Michitaro. ''Osaka wa Mizu no Miyako ka'' [Is Osaka the capital of water?]. *Gaku Soso* 4 (1980), 60–69.

多田道太郎 ″大阪は水の都か″ 「学叢々」 第4巻、 pp. 60-69

Takahashi, Hiroshi. *Taishu Geino* [Public performing arts]. Tokyo: Kyoiku Shiryo Shuppankai, 1980.

高橋博 『大衆芸能』 東京 教育資料出版会 1980

Tsurumi, Shunsuke. *Sengo Nihon no Taishubunka Shi: 1945–1980* [The history of the postwar Japanese mass culture: 1945–1980]. Tokyo: Yuwanami Shoten, 1984.

鶴見俊輔 『戦後日本の大衆文化史：1945-1980』 東京 岩波書店 1984

———. *Tayu Saizo Den* [The historical development of *tayu* and *saizo*]. Tokyo: Heibonsha, 1979.

『太夫才蔵伝』 東京 平凡社 1979

Ui, Mushu. *Kamigata Hanashi Ko* [Thoughts on comic storytelling in the Kyoto-Osaka area]. Tokyo: Seiabo, 1965.

宇井無愁 『上方落語考』 東京 青蛙房 1965

———. *Rakugo no Genwa* [Original sources of *rakugo*]. Tokyo: Kadokawa Shoten, 1970.

『落語の原話』 東京 角川書店 1970

Watanabe, Kin. *Rakugo no Kenkyu* [*Rakugo* research]. Osaka: Shinshin Shoten, 1943.

渡辺きん 『落語の研究』 大阪 しんしん堂書店 1943

———. Yanagida, Kunio. "Kebozu Ko" [Thoughts of an amateur priest]. In *Yanagida Kunio Shu* [Collection of Yanagida Kunio]. Tokyo: Tsukuma Shobo, 1962.

柳田国男 『毛坊主考』『柳田国男集 第9巻』 東京 筑摩書房 1962

Yanagiya, Tsubame. *Rakugo no Sekai* [The world of *rakugo*]. Tokyo: Kodansha, 1967.

柳家つばめ 『落語の世界』 東京 講談社 1967

Yano, Seiichi. *Rakugo Yuhodo* [*Rakugo* promenade]. Tokyo: Kyodo Kikaku, 1967.

矢野誠一 『落語遊歩道』 東京 共同企画 1967

Yotaro, Bakusho, and Nobuo Imamura. *Rakugo Senshu* [*Rakugo* anthology]. Tokyo: Rakurakutei, 1953.

爆笑八太郎、稲村信雄編 『落語選集』 東京 楽々亭 1953

5

Popular Film

KEIKO I. MCDONALD

The history of films designed with mass audience appeal in mind has its roots in the Japanese literature with similar aims that appeared four decades earlier. During the early Meiji era in the 1880s, a distinction had already established itself between belles lettres and popular fiction (*gesaku*).[1] While the former continued to offer the aesthetic and intellectual pleasures available to the educated and cultivated minority, the latter kept pace with a growing demand for reading material directed at the general public.

Thus, *gesaku* fiction, which had originated in the Edo period, took its cues from the everyday unspecialized human desire to enjoy the pleasures of escapism and fantasy identification with heroes and values whose appeal is obvious and uncomplicated.

The cinema in due course followed suit, though not in its earliest years. In fact, the concept of a popular film (*taishu eiga* or *taishu goraku eiga*) came only in the 1920s in the wake of that decade's renaissance of interest in art forms with broadly popular appeal.

The beginnings of this movement can be seen in the founding of magazines like *Literature for the Masses* [Taishu bungei]. As its title suggests, this monthly set out to establish modern popular fiction as a literary genre in its own right. Success was immediate and widespread. Mass entertainment novels flooded a ready market, very often in serial form in newspapers and magazines and even on radio.

The film industry was quick to see the potential in this new era of mass communications. By the mid-1920s, studios had achieved genuine mass production capacity based largely on adaptations of popular fiction. Some 650 such films a year were being made by around 150 directors whose purpose may be

seen as an attempt to create a domestic product sufficient in quantity to coun-
terbalance the influx of quality films from abroad.

It must also be said that Japanese popular film has not been given the critical
attention it deserves. Japanese scholars are partly to blame in that they persist
in the belief that popular works are not a fit subject for the serious students of
their country's achievement in cinema. At best, there is a grudging discussion
of the undeniable elements of popular culture at work in the evolution of the
period—or *samurai*—film genre (*jidaigeki*).

Some of the most discussable works themselves help to obscure the distinction
between popular film and so-called "pure-art" film (*jun eiga*), also known as
"artistic" film (*geijutsu eiga*). For example, many of the early films of lower-
middle-class life (*shomingeki*) made by Yasujiro Ozu and Yasujiro Shimazu offer
the rich entertainment of popular film—even as they create complex aesthetic
and intellectual resonances that can be appreciated only by viewers attuned to
them.

English-speaking scholars disposed to judge Japanese popular films on their
own merits have been hampered in their efforts by limited access. A few commercial theaters in Hawaii do specialize in Japanese cinema, yet even they cannot
offer a fully representative sampling of popular film genres. Even in Japan,
screenings of works made as recently as the 1950s and 1960s are few and far
between. Films of more ancient vintage may have to be sought out in museum
collections like those mentioned at the end of this chapter.

No doubt the present-day explosion of film-access technologies will remove
many such obstacles and prepare the way for more thorough and definitive studies
than are possible now. The following brief survey charts a very general course
and shows how much remains to be done by way of interpreting works in an
art form whose development reflects so many complex interactions. As would
be expected, the formation and reformation of the studios in response to changes
in the perceived needs of their audiences have had an important impact on the
industry.

HISTORICAL SURVEY

Popular Film Prehistory (1896–1919)

Though popular film in Japan is seen as a product of the 1920s, Japanese pure
art cinema began with borrowings from native forms with broad popular appeal.
The silent film, for example, was presided over in the early years by a *benshi*,
or narrator-commentator, whose job it was to keep the audience abreast of the
plot and its proper interpretation. This function derived from traditions essentially
plebeian: the *bunraku* (puppet) theater, *narimono* musical accompaniment and
chorus in *kabuki* theater, and traditions of oral narrative like the historical *kodan*
and comic *rakugo* tales.[2]

Theatrical traditions were, in fact, so strong in Japan that the cinema spent its first decade working with dramatic conventions not of its own devising. This burden of tradition worked against the formation of a specifically cinematic grammar, even as it eased the transition from traditionally popular forms of art to the new art of cinema. Thus, audiences could feel on familiar ground with one of the so-called "films of ongoing stage action" (*engeki jissha eiga*), a category that enjoyed immediate success.

This grounding in tradition also led to creative evolution in the new art. Films of a segment of *kabuki* performances on stage were billed as "old drama" (*kyugeki*). By 1917, these were transformed into a type called *shinkokugeki*, whose meaning and *raison d'être* had become displays of violent swordplay. Since swordplay, too, likes a better reason, a further development led to the "period film" (*jidaigeki*).

In some cases, the nature of the dramatic original helped define a type of cinema audience that in turn influenced the films made to attract it. A notable instance here is provided by *shinpa* drama. Itself a creation of forces against the conventions of *kabuki*, the *shinpa* made use of modern settings for a wide range of plays, including comedy and suspense. Its mainstay, however, was melodrama, most often adapted from a domestic novel of unrequited love.

Tear-jerkers in the *shinpa* style were enormously successful with female moviegoers, whose patronage allowed this genre of contemporary film (*gendaigeki*) to prosper as a popular counterweight to the swashbuckling period film (*jidaigeki*).

Acting styles were also transferred from stage to screen in the early days. Some famous *kabuki* actors, in fact, put their art on camera. Danjuro Ichikawa was featured in three "old drama" *kabuki* films: *Two People at Dojoji* [Futari dojoji] (1900), *Nio the Courtesan* [Nio no ukisu] (1902), and *Maple Viewing* [Momiji-gari] (1903).

The "old drama" actor who reached the widest audience was Matsunosuke Onoe. Beginning with *Loyal Retainer Tadanobu* [Goban Tadanobu] in 1909, he made about 1,000 films in a twenty-year career. Physical prowess had something to do with it, since he specialized in *samurai*, gambler, and spy-magician (*ninja*) roles. More than half of his films were directed by his discoverer, Shozo Makino, who believed in sticking to the basics: strong plotting, vigorous acting, and clear photography (something of a technical effect in those early years).

Makino also knew how to capitalize on Matsunosuke's uncommon agility and large, expressive, rather un-Oriental eyes. Together, actor and director popularized a wide assortment of traditional materials drawn especially from the *bunraku* theater repertory and anthologies of *kodan* historical tales.

Though Matsunosuke portrayed any number of loyal *samurai* and great swordsmen, he was most sensational in the costume magician (*ninjutsu*) genre he helped create. In films with titles such as *Superhero Jiraiya* [Goketsu Jiraiya] (1914) and *Tales of the Mysterious Rat* [Kaiki-den] (1915), he portrayed a *samurai* or spy with the magical power to appear in many shapes and guises. This genre was to draw large crowds for many years.

Matsunosuke and Makino also helped launch the thriller. Their classic effort here was *The Yotsuya Ghost: A True Account* [Jissetsu Yotsuya kaidan] (1912), based on a famous *kabuki* play about a wife's revenge on the *samurai* husband who murdered her. This film was the forerunner of the many *Yotsuya Ghost* versions introduced in the 1950s as a regular feature of the *bon* festival during the summer.

When the Nikkatsu Company succeeded in absorbing four other companies in 1912, a monopoly was created with powerful resources for the simultaneous development of types of mass market cinemas. Many Makino-Matsunosuke collaborations were made in Nikkatsu's old Kyoto studio that specialized in "old drama" films. A newer studio in Tokyo (built in 1913) concentrated on the more contemporary idiom borrowed from the *shinpa* tragedy.

Several *shinpa* adaptations made by Nikkatsu in this period are characteristic of a genre that would go from strength to strength as the general public acquired a taste for weeping in the dark. *The Golden Demon* [Konjikiyasha] (1917) dealt with the theme of revenge for unrequited love. Based on a popular Meiji-era fiction by Koyo Ozaki, the story concerns a man whose fiancée jilts him in order to marry into wealth and social position. He revenges himself on her and on money-hungry society by succeeding in the despised profession of usurer. The lasting appeal of this story can be measured in the number of film versions issued—notably in the period after World War II.

Another sentimental staple dates from this era. *The Cuckoo* [Hototogisu] (1917) was based on a popular novel by Roka Tokutomi. Its heroine, separated by war from her loving husband, is subjected to all that melodrama can do by way of a mother-in-law. Her fragile, tragic type of beauty marked her for death from a sickness with so much fiction to recommend it: consumption. The poetry of that beautiful wasting away was not to be lost on the cinema audience of 1917—or those for many years afterward.

Interestingly enough, the box-office hit that saved the Nikkatsu Company from financial reverses at this time was a work on the borderline between pure art cinema and the popular film. This was *Resurrection* [Fukkatsu] (1914–1917), a film in three parts adapted from Tolstoy's novel. Its claim to pure art status lay in elements taken from the so-called New Theater (*Shingeki*) movement, especially the acting technique based on Stanislavsky. Even so, *shinpa* influences predominate in the highly melodramatic treatment given the story. (Part 3 of the series depicts the coming of Nevrudov to Japan.)

Yet changes were being urged in those early years. In 1916, a movement for artistic cinema was demanding technical innovations: Subtitles were to replace the *benshi* commentators, Western music would displace the traditional Japanese, acting would become more realistic, and female impersonators would give way to their natural competition.

These modernizations proved premature and were not really put into effect for several more years. The choice of subject matter was not, in any case, affected, and production continued on numbers of contemporary genre films modeled on the older stylistic methods.

The 1920s: A Decade of Popularization

A number of factors combined to speed the progress of popular films in the 1920s. The pure art cinema movement gradually succeeded in weakening the hold of traditional theatrical influences on all kinds of films. A corresponding emphasis on realism did much to remove two long-standing obstacles to innovation: the female impersonator and the *benshi* commentators.

In terms of sheer quantity, the film industry took a quantum leap forward in these years: from under 2,000 reels in 1920 to over 55,000 in 1926. Progress varied from studio to studio. While Nikkatsu proved slow to replace its female impersonators with actresses displaying the Hollywood style, a bold new competitor did that and more. This was the Shochiku Company, formed in 1920 by an already gigantic syndicate with extensive holdings in theaters and acting troupes.

Moreover, thanks to conflicting ideologies within the company, Shochiku was ready to move ahead on two market fronts at once. The "pure art" market faction was led by Kaoru Osanai, famous for his work in the New Theater movement. His Shochiku Kinema School group succeeded brilliantly with their first production, Minoru Murata's epoch-making *Souls on the Road* [Rojo no reikon] (1921).

Unfortunately, this branch of the company failed to produce other commercially successful works, so Shochiku decided to accumulate capital through popular film ventures before it returned to artistic films with limited audience appeal. Thus, the company favored the Shochiku Kamata Studio branch of its enterprise. It was put in charge of Hotei Nomura, whose first film (shot in just three days) became Shochiku's first real hit in popular film. This was *Evening Paperboys* [Yukan o uru shonentachi] (1921), a tear-jerker based on a newspaper article about two destitute children, a boy and a girl. That success was followed by another, *Mercy in Justice* [Ho no namida] (1921), the story of an impoverished rickshaw man's unsuccessful attempt to kill himself and his children.

Nomura did, however, offer his audience more than a good cry at the movies. He showed great ingenuity at adapting traditional *shinpa* tragedy storylines to the latest techniques imported from the West: close-ups, subtitles, and short cuts.

Then, too, the younger directors on his staff began to modify the *shinpa* narrative format. The long-suffering female victim of traditional feudal family structure was shown emerging in her own right. Such a woman was apt to assert a bit of free choice in matters of love, though such a woman invariably ended badly. Female moviegoers of the day were not offended. On the contrary, their steady patronage of such films helped keep the Shochiku Company in the black.

Other segments of the popular audience soon wearied of Nomura's films, which tended to be deficient in rhythmic variation, not to mention comic relief. The much-needed lighter touch was supplied by Shiro Kido, brought in at the age of thirty to replace Nomura as studio head. Kido's success was based on the comedy of the lower middle classes (*shoshimin kigeki*) with wholesome belly laughs provided by heroes who were happy-go-lucky even in a hostile environment. Eventually Nomura himself followed suit in films like *Collar Button* [Karabotan] (1926), a light-hearted view of the hard-knocks career of a salaryman. Kido's pursuit of this genre paved the way for improvement in the 1930s, when films about the life of the middle or lower middle class (*shomingeki*) became the hallmark product of the Shochiku Company.

The renaissance in popular fiction in the 1920s is seen everywhere in the films of the decade. Afther the Great Tokyo Earthquake, Nikkatsu transferred its contemporary film studio to Kyoto, where it pursued themes indicative of the trend. A number of these films were directed by the former Hollywood actor Yutaka Abe. Among them was *A Mermaid on Land* [Riku no ningyo] (1926), the story of two girls, one rich and one poor, who vie for the love of a sporting man. A girl torn between two suitors was also the subject of Kenji Mizoguchi's *The Cuckoo* [Jihi shincho] (1927). Minoru Murata (whose *Souls on the Road* is mentioned above) joined forces with Tomotaka Tasaka for *Marriage Duet* [Kekkon nijuso] (1928), a film notable for its realistic detail in a story involving a heroine's emotional conflict as she compares her fiancé with the man she really loves. All these films were based on fiction by Kan Kikuchi, a popular writer of newspaper serials.

The Shochiku Company challenged Nikkatsu's success in the contemporary film genre by adapting other Kikuchi novels: *Lady Pearl* [Shinju fujin] (1927), a tale of manners and mores in the upper class (Kinuyo Tanaka appeared as a new face), and *King of the Sea* [Umi no oja] (1927), a Japanese *Romeo and Juliet*.

The period film genre (*jidaigeki*) also came into its own in the 1920s. In 1923, Shozo Makino, who had worked so successfully with Matsunosuke Onoe in this genre, left the Nikkatsu Company to establish his own studio in Kyoto. There he gave the swashbuckling hero of the period a new style and image free of *kabuki* conventions. Makino was apparently under the influence of American films with their emphasis on swiftly paced, action-packed suspense. The entertainment period film exploiting swashbuckling came to be called *chanbara*.

Makino also liberated his scripts from the old-fashioned storyline of *kodan* historical tales, whose protagonist was apt to figure as a moral paragon. In the new period film, the hero was free to exhibit his share of human frailty.

One who did this freely was Ryunosuke Tsukue, a solitary nihilist who killed for pleasure and abused women as a matter of principle. He originated as the protagonist of a famous popular novel by Kaizan Nakazato. *The Great Bodhisattva Pass* [Daibosatsu Toge]. As such, he was pursued by the film industry, though unsuccessfully in the 1920s, thanks to conflicts of interest between novelist and studio. Ryunosuke was to have his day, however, since his exploits were cinematized and dramatized over and over again between 1935 and 1964.[3] Although not filmed until the 1930s, Nakazato's novel was influential during the 1920s. Inspired by it, Rokuhei Susukida directed a number of cliff-hangers featuring Ryunosuke-style heroes. One such was titled *Wood Block Printer: Purple-Hooded Assassin* [Ukiyoeshi murasaki zukin] (1923). Susukida wrote this blood-and-thunder script himself. Its success led to others with titles such as *Assassin at Night* [Kaiketsuo] (1923) and *Bloody Handprint* [Senketsu no tegata] (1924).

A more lasting effect of these films was their discovery of Tsumasaburo Bando, who became a sensational attraction at the age of twenty-three. This Japanese Zorro was an absolutely first-class studio property working with other directors as well, as in Buntaro Futagawa's *Shadow Figure* [Kageboshi] (1925). Bando's image was that of a pale-faced, nervous nihilist never far from issues decided by virtuoso swordplay. He was an early example of the star system establishing itself in popular film. By 1925 Bando had already become a star in his own production company. His second film there was *Serpent* [Orochi] (1925), directed by Buntaro Futagawa. This pioneer work of *chanbara* with swashbuckling realism set every kid on the block to swinging a stick in imitation of Bando's dazzling technique.

Still, Makino Productions remained the premier studio for films in the *jidaigeki* genre. During the golden age of about seven years (ending with sound pictures in 1930), these put the more general film genre (*gendaigeki*) in the shade.

Makino also brought more new talent to the fore as the star system came to dominate the burgeoning *jidaigeki-chanbara* market. Among his new finds was Utaemon Ichikawa, whose wholesome and handsome young swordsman image contrasted usefully with Bando's saturnine ferocity. This difference was made clear in Ichigawa's *Purple-Hooded Assassin* [Murasaki zukin] (1930) sequel to Bando's 1923 picture mentioned above.

Like Bando, Ichikawa became his own producer in films like *Shogun's Idle Retainer* [Hatamoto taikutsu otoko], a series beginning in 1930. The protagonist is a kind of shantytown Robin Hood, a superfluous retainer of the shogunate who lives anonymously in a slum, always prepared to take up arms against the wicked *samurai* oppressors of helpless townsmen. This good-looking hero fighting for justice became Ichikawa's trademark character in films made all through the 1930s and even after the war.

Another handsome Makino protégé was Kanjuro Arashi (first called Chojuro Arashi). He was first cast as the hero of *Acrobats* [Kakubeijishi] (1927), adapted from the popular fiction of Jiro Osaragi. The original material was serialized in a boys' magazine and offers a hero disguised as a masterless *samurai* ready to fight for emperor and common folk in the loyalist-shogunate conflict at the end of the Tokugawa period. The success of this film led to a sequel, *A Loyalist from Kurama* [Kurama tengu] (1930), and to Arashi's complete identification with this warm-hearted, cheerful hero in black hood and loose-fitting formal kimono. Audience demand ultimately supported some twenty-three films in this series before the war, and another seventeen thereafter.

The career of yet another star-turned-producer shows what could be done for popular cinema when box-office charisma put itself in the hands of inspired direction. Chiezo Kataoka made his mark as a bright-eyed youth with a captivating smile. He was fortunate in having directors like Mansaku Itami and Hiroshi Inagaki; they helped him succeed with films based on works by popular writers like Kinka Kimura and Shin Hasegawa.

Itami's gift was the deft sarcasm found in films such as *The Appearance of Thief Genji* [Genji kozo shutsugen] (1931). This parody of a famous series of *Good Thief* [Nezumi kozo] films pokes fun at the good-natured hero who steals from the wicked rich to give to the virtuous poor.

Inagaki used a touch of wholesome comedy to lighten the atmosphere of various Kataoka films in the *jidaigeki* genre (which tended to be gloomy) by allowing the ebullient swordplay to shine through. One of Inagaki's finest efforts in this direction was *Yataro's Travel Hat* [Yataro gasa] (1933). Based on the popular novel by Kan Kobozawa, this film depicts the itinerant gambler's contact with the world of honest men. Another distinguished Inagaki-Kataoka film was *Long Sought-for Mother* [Mabuta no haha] (1932), a uniquely melodramatic *jidaigeki* based on an immensely popular fiction by Shin Hasegawa.

Another director's refinement of the *jidaigeki* genre presaged films of the next decade, when Sadao Yamanaka's work yielded the pure art classic, *Humanity and Paper Balloons* [Ninjo kamifusen] (1935). In a more resolutely popular vein, Yamanaka had directed Arashi a few years before in *The Adventures of Detective Umon* [Umon torimonocho] (1932). This film generated a series destined for tireless elaboration both before and after the war until it became a staple of television.

Individual stars were not the only ones to benefit from the guidance of directors with imagination and good market sense. By the mid–1920s, the Nikkatsu Taishogun Studio found itself bogged down in a formula once so successful with their star performer, Matsunosuke. The studio's approach to the *jidaigeki* genre was too noticeably untouched by the new fluidity and realism being developed elsewhere. Audiences began to weary of the old-fashioned, repetitious long shots sadly needed for an actor long past his prime, surrounded by female impersonators.

After Matsunosuke's death in 1926, the director Daisuke Ito teamed up with the stocky, wide-eyed star Denjiro Okochi to put Nikkatsu in the running as a producer of *jidaigeki*. Okochi figured as the lone outsider in films bearing Ito's trademark of new expressive devices like rapid panning and frequent cutbacks. Together, they made one of the rare masterpieces of cinematic art in the 1920s, the trilogy, *A Diary of Chuji's Travels* [Chuzi tabinikki] (1928).

Ito's brand of social criticism in the *Chuji* films invited a certain amount of thoughtful consideration, yet he and Okochi also made a number of strictly popular films together. For example, the title of *Bloodshed at Takada no Baba* [Chimatsuri Takada no Baba] (1928) speaks for itself. Yasubei Horie, the masterless *samurai* superhero, derives from the *kodan* historical tales and is typically drinking when he is not fighting (and vice versa). Barging into his grandfather's duel, for example, he fells twenty-eight opponents. Audiences fell for him, too.

In Ito's popular trilogy, *Ooka's Trial* [Ooka seidan] (1928), two *kodan* heroes share the limelight. Sazen Tange, played by Okochi, is one eyed and one armed, but no less a *jidaigeki* idol for that. His quest for two famous swords leads to a series of adventures and much derring-do. Echizen Ooka, a *jidaigeki* idol, also figures as a quick-witted city magistrate of the Tokugawa shogunate who could use the legal process like a weapon to protect innocent commoners. The immense popularity of this trilogy led to a number of spin-offs on film with either hero, and in fact its influence can still be seen in prime-time television series featuring Echizen Ooka. Ito's technical mastery in these early silent films is especially notable for the rhythmical narrative effected by quick alternation between subtitles and scenes.

There are other examples of *jidaigeki* popular in the 1920s making their mark on Japanese television. A striking instance is another film from Nikkatsu, *Vice Shogun Komon Mito* [Mito Komon] (1926). This star-studded picaresque was based on *kodan* material, too. The protagonist is the supposedly powerful uncle of the third Shogun Iemitsu. Disguised as an old man accompanied by two comical young bodyguards, he travels around Japan righting wrongs inflicted on the common people by corrupt officials. Filmed over and over again for the movies, the *Komon Mito* series has recently completed its first decade on television.

The Shochiku Company had never become a major force in the *jidaigeki* genre, but it made an inspired choice by way of promoting a star to improve its product. This was Chojiro Hayashi (later renamed Kazuo Hasegawa), a handsome youth of nineteen whose gentle charm derived from his training as a female impersonator in *kabuki* theater. He became an instant success with Shochiku's mainstay—the female patrons of its *shinpa* melodramas.

The highly creative director Teinosuke Kinogasa was put in charge of Hayashi. His previous work included the expressionist film, *The Page of Madness* [Kurutta ippeji] (1926). Turning to popular cinema, he made eighteen successful entertainment films with Chojiro Hayashi, among them *Young Child's Swordsmanship* [Chigo no kenpo] (1927) and *Brave Samurai at Dawn* [Akatsuki no yushi] (1927).

Talkies and the 1930s

The coming of sound tripled the cost of making a film. This disincentive to taking risks with the marketplace was accompanied, nevertheless, by a certain amount of experimenting as companies looked for profitable new trademark genres—and old ones profitably modified.

The Shochiku Company led the way with Japan's first successful talkie, *The*

Neighbor's Wife and Mine [Madamu to nyobo] (1931). Its subject was the trials and tribulations of a playwright distracted by a noisy neighborhood of dogs and cats and squalling brats—and a neighbor's wife who has a jazz band. This was the traditional comedy of the common man (*shoshimin kigeki*) given the benefit of the new realism of everyday noise, and could be defined as a popular film in subject matter. However, the director Heinosuke Gosho exploited this dimension of his story with such skill and sophistication that the prestigious journal *Kinema Jumpo* voted this very popular film the best of 1931. It says something for Gosho's artistry that he avoided the chief defect of so many early sound films, namely, the oversaturation of dialogue and sound effects.

Sochiku also broke new ground in two other early talkies, both directed by Yasujiro Shimazu: *A Girl in the Storm* [Arashi no naka no shojo] (1933) and *Our Neighbor Miss Yae* [Tonari no Yae-chan] (1934). Both also offer valuable insight into the nature of the film about the life of the common people (*shomingeki*) in that they exhibit traits of both popular and sophisticated art. They advance this genre in the direction of today's domestic drama as they vividly portray the first love of a girl in a middle-class family. But Shimazu's style in both is notably sophisticated, making use of repetition and parallels to advance a well-nigh plotless narrative to its predictably everyday conclusion.

Another Shochiku director who resisted the talkie as long as he could was Yasujiro Ozu, by custom now considered the "most Japanese of all their directors."[4] He began with *shoshimin kigeki* like *Pumpkin* [Kabocha] (1928) and *Wife Lost* [Nyobo funshutsu] (1928), the latter based on a prize-winning short story. He then moved on to *shomingeki*. Though his first efforts were aimed at popularity, even the most deliberate slapstick effects were somehow upstaged by Ozu's unmistakable thought-provoking seriousness and a tendency to stylize—both qualities difficult to associate with notions of mass appeal.

A film like *I Was Born, But* . . . [Umarete wa mita keredo] (1932) deals with a favorite Ozu theme, the unfairness of life. This time it is viewed through the eyes of two brothers in elementary school. Ozu's touch throughout is lightly humorous and stylistically sophisticated. His contribution to the *shomingeki* genre can be seen in the transformation of merely technical devices into expressive means. The repetitions and parallelisms and stationary camera—all hallmarks of his mature mastery—are already in place here.

Ozu's actual mass appeal is probably explained by lesser films with titles like *Where Now Are the Dreams of Youth?* [Seishun no yume ima izuko] (1930) and *I Flunked, But* . . . [Rakudai wa shita keredo] (1930). In the latter, a gifted college graduate cannot find a decent job, while a ne'er-do-well classmate succeeds, thanks to his connections.

The Nikkatsu Company allowed its directors to make such "tendency films" (*keiko eiga*) of outright social criticism, but Shochiku preferred to soft-pedal the issues. The company slogan said it all: "A little smile, some tears, a full, warm feeling."

After Japan's military expansion into China in 1931, the *shomingeki* genre

was hampered more noticeably each year by national policy as the government
looked to the popular media for patriotic pap. Even so, Shochiku's commitment
to melodrama expanded in directions having little to do with sacrificing for the
fatherland or the blessings of life down on the farm. The profit motive found
more congenial allies in themes like romantic double suicide. Heinosuke Gosho's
Love Requited in Heaven [Tengoku no musubu koi] (1932) left two lovers
separated by class barriers no choice but death by poison. A box-office sensation
in this case was matched by a rush to Mt. Sakata where the lovers killed themselves. Twenty couples committed suicide ''on location'' in the year of the film's
release.

More benign sentimentalities were at work in films such as Yasushi Sasaki's
White Mount Fuji [Mashiroki Fuji no ne] (1935), based on a true-life story of
male high school students killed in a boating accident. Sasaki explored the
troubled sentiments in the breasts of students from a girl's high school, making
sensitive use of the romantic backdrop of Mt. Fuji soaring up above the beach,
the site for regatta practice.

Shochiku also did its best to exploit the entertainment value of pure art literature. Junichiro Tanizaki, for example, was outraged by the treatment given
his work, *The Story of Shunkin* [Shunkinsho], by Yasujiro Shimazu in *Okoto
and Sasuke* [Okoto to Sasuke] (1935). The novelist considered the acting forced
and vulgar.

Shimazu also offended the novelist Riichi Yokomitsu, who had labored to
give some measure of social insight and psychological depth to his newspaper
serial fiction of love and greed in the world of high finance. The film based on
his work, *Family Conference* [Kazoku kaigi] (1936), ignored the subleties. Worse
yet, Shimazu fleshed out the given love triangle with sensationalized details of
murder and a market fix. The outcome was not high art, but it probably fit its
special occasion: a film to celebrate the opening of the new Shochiku Ofuna
Studio.

Occasionally, the drift of popular cinema was in the opposite direction. Kunio
Kishida's newspaper serial novel was a rather mediocre melodrama of love
intrigue played out against a background of hospital administration. In the film
version, *Warm Currents* [Danryu] (1939), the director Kozaburo Yoshimura
transformed this material into a polished screenplay with vivid dialogue and
sparkling performances by all four main characters.

Shochiku's chef d'oeuvre of melodrama was the four-part hit, *Lover's Vow*
[Aisen katsura] (1938). The original novel by Matsutaro Kawaguchi offered a
standard sentimental plot: A widow with a child falls in love with the son of the
head of the hospital where she works as a nurse, but her child's illness, pressure
from the son's family, and an unsuccessful elopement combine to separate the
lovers, who are ultimately reunited. Hiromasa Nomura's film version starred
Kinuyo Tanaka with Ken Uehara as hero. This melodrama ran for a year and a
half non-stop while its theme song sold millions of recordings.

Shochiku was quick to follow up its advantage with similar films aimed at the sentimental female audience. Success could be measured in round numbers, profits in 1939 being up by 50 percent over 1937. At the same time, Shochiku came under fire from critics who said that its productions were all sentimental with no social consciousness. Certainly the growing imperialist mood of the nation was coming to suppress all manner of self-indulgence, melodrama included. In 1940, therefore, Shochiku turned to a policy of "healthier" entertainment advocating the expected virtues. The resulting lightweight films merely proved that commercial success was not to be found in political potboilers.

Meantime, Shochiku's rival, Nikkatsu, was pursuing a different part of the market. It did continue to support the pure literature movement with various films of contemporary life (*gendaigeki*), but these could not compete with the profit potential of the popular period film (*jidaigeki*) or its more kinetic cousin, the *chanbara* action film.

Moreover, Nikkatsu had plenty of material to choose from as popular historical fiction and rewrites of traditional tales continued to flood the print market. The coming of the star system also helped by matching up proven actor-director combinations. This enabled teams like Daisuke Ito and Denjiro Okochi to repeat their earlier successes in ventures like the sound remake of *One-Armed One-Eyed Swordsman* [Tange sazen] (1933).

Directors such as Sadao Yamanaka and Hiroshi Inagaki also managed to imbue their *jidaigeki* films with a certain seriousness, notably in the form of insight into the social milieu of the late Tokugawa period. Inagaki does this, for example, in *The Shinsen Group* [Shinsengumi] (1935). Yamanaka's efforts in this direction would include films such as *Chuji Kunisada* [Kunisada Chuji] (1935), *Humanity and Paper Balloons* [Ninjo kamifusen] (1935), and *The Village Tattooed Man* [Machi no irezumi mono] (1935).

Both men also managed *jidaigeki* that were more resolutely popular. Yamanaka used Nikkatsu's star ruffian, Denjiro Okochi, for another film in the series whose protagonist really knew how to deliver the damaged goods—thus, *One-Armed One-Eyed Swordsman: A Priceless Pot* [Tange sazen: Hyakuman ryo no tsubo] (1935). Inagaki's contribution in this line was the first film version of that invaluable property from the 1920s, Kaizan Nakazato's *The Great Bodhisattva Pass* [Daibosatsu Toge] (1935).

Mummy's Money [Dokurosen] (1938) was made by that other sure-fire box-office draw, Kanjuro Arashi, directed by Shiro Tsuji. This *jidaigeki* combination of mystery and *samurai* adventure netted profits four times greater than the average release.

No list of superstar pictures from this decade would be complete without two remakes of films from the silent era, both directed by Tomiyasu Ikeda: *Komon Mito on a Journey Around the Country* [Mito Komon kaikokuki] (1937) and *Forty-Seven Loyal Ronin* [Chushingura] (1938). In the former, the old vice-shogun tours the country in disguise, dispensing justice, as mentioned above. In the latter, the forty-seven masterless *samurai* carry out a suicidal pact to avenge their dead master.

Political pressures toward the end of the decade also forced Nikkatsu to shy away from projects at variance with the ethos of imperialism. Thanks to some stars with warrior appeal, the company weathered this difficult period with style and profit in the *jidaigeki-chanbara* film genres.

Nikkatsu was lucky to re-engage Chiezo Kataoka in time for Inagaki's trilogy, *Musashi Miyamoto* [Miyamoto Musashi] (1940–1942). Kataoka was just right for this tale of a master swordsman, because the hero's quest for personal integration was reassuring to the authorities, even as the masses were captivated by the swashbuckling adventures that brought Musashi to his goal. The story was based on a newspaper serial by the prolific popular novelist Eiji Yoshikawa. It had been used in the silent film era, but this sound version established Musashi as a remake perennial in the *chanbara* action film genre.

Nikkatsu also capitalized on a new genre, the *yakuza* or professional gambler film.[5] *Shimizu Harbor* [Shimizu Minato] (1939) featured a special appearance by Torazo Hirosawa, the most popular *naniwabushi* reciter, or reciter of historical and legendary tales. Masahiro Makino directed this adaptation from those traditional sources—which in time furnished series material aplenty. The protagonist is the famous *yakuza* boss Jirocho Shimizu, who figures as champion of the common man oppressed by corrupt officials. Along with another famous *yakuza* boss, the solitary outcast Chuji Kunisada, Jirocho was to become the best-known figure in this genre, thanks to his mass appeal in the character of benevolent father surrogate.

A third major company joined the industry in 1936. It was the Toho block, a conglomerate formed of the Takarazuka Theater, the J. O. Studio, and Photo Chemical Laboratory. Two years later, the name was changed to the Toho Company. Backed by massive capital, Toho began with an impressive roster of directors and an effective management strategy, replacing the old "director system" with a "producer system." Instead of competing with its rivals for particular segments of the popular audience, Toho decided to appeal to every type of moviegoer with vaudeville-style comedy and pop song film genres.

Photo Chemical Laboratory had produced these before Toho was formed. One of its producers, Iwao Mori, had become interested in vaudeville and revue on a tour of Europe. He not only encouraged ventures like the musical, but cast vaudeville players in comedies as well.

This tactic continued at Toho. Among the players in a spate of early comedies were Enoken (Kenichi Enomoto, a man less than five feet in height), Roppa Furukawa, and the duo Entatsu and Achako. Among early box-office hits were Enoken's *Buddhist Priest* [Hokaibo] (1938) and Roppa's *Poppa Roppa* [Roppa no otosan] (1938).

In another hit comedy, *Newlywed's Ghost Mansion* [Shinkon obake yashiki] (1939), Toho added radio show talent to its vaudevillians. This gimmick of borrowing big names from other media anticipated the 1950s rage for drafting pop singers into drama.

While Shochiku continued to concentrate on the female audience, Toho tried reaching out to all viewers in their twenties—the greatest percentage of the moviegoing public. In 1939, however, Toho scored a great coup with a Shochiku-style melodrama, *Song of the White Pony* [Byakuran no uta]. The actress Toshiko Yamaguchi created something of a sensation, advertised as a Chinese national although she was, in fact, a Japanese. Her next such appearance was even more successful. In *China Night* [Shina no yoru] (1940), she played opposite Kazuo Hasegawa in a story of unrequited love between a local girl and a Japanese civilian stationed on mainland China.

The rivalry with Shochiku increased in bitterness when that company succeeded in preventing a Toho-Nikkatsu merger. Nevertheless, Toho's capital resources remained a powerful weapon, as when the company used them to capture Chojiro Hayashi (renamed Kazuo Hasegawa), Shochiku's superstar in the *jidaigeki* genre.

Toho gave itself the benefit of Hasegawa's expertise in films such as *Tojuro's Love* [Tojuro no koi] (1939). Teinosuke Kinugasa also directed him in *Princess with a Snake Guardian* [Hebihime-sama] (1940). Success with these did much to place Toho's productions on a par with Nikkatsu's, whose popular *jidaigeki* films were hitherto much the better.

Wartime Popular Cinema (1940–1944)

In August 1940, the Censorship Bureau of the Home Ministry issued its guidelines to the film industry. Popular films were not to be discouraged, but were expected to reflect wholesome values and "positive" themes. Matters injurious to the public morals were not to be depicted—for example, women smoking, drinking in cafés, and behaving in a flippant manner.[6] Film production, however, had to be cut to an annual quota of forty-eight per company, with footage for each limited to 300 meters (news films excepted). This put an end to double-feature billing.

By mid–1941, national economic priorities forced a reorganization of Japan's ten major film companies into just two. Nikkatsu's assets were divided between Shochiku and Toho.[7] In 1942, however, the politically adroit Masao Nagata managed to form the Dai-Nihon Eiga (Daiei), or Great Japan Motion Picture Company.

That same year, Daiei issued an extremely popular musical fantasy, *The Palace of Singing Badgers* [Utau tanuki goten]. The story's Cinderella theme provides an excuse for the discovery of a bevy of beauties performing a musical revue in a palace deep in a forest.

Daiei was a spin-off of the Shinko Kinema Company, which had specialized in two genres synthesized in this film. One was a straightforward girlie show like the 1939 *Badgers' Palace* [Tanuki goten]. Another was a type of fantasy ghost mystery involving metamorphosis. In *Story of a Monster Cat* [Saga kaibyo-den] (1939), the animal disguised as a human being avenges its master's death.

Daiei also produced some successful entertainment *jidaigeki*. Among them was Tomiyasu Ikeda's *Moon on the Water* [Iga no suigetsu] (1943), the story of a master swordsman's revenge. Another was a *Musashi* film, this time entitled *Discovery of the Two-Sword Style* [Nitoryu kaigan] (1943) and directed by Daisuke Ito.

In contrast to Shochiku's failure to adapt its productions to the changing times, Toho did remarkably well with both patriotic potboilers and entertainment films. The latter included some *jidaigeki* hits like *Kantaro from Izu* [Izu no Kantaro] (1943). Directed by Eisuke Takizawa and starring Kazuo Hasegawa and Isuzu Yamada, this film took its cues from earlier *yakuza* works like the *Chuji Kunisada* and *Jirocho Shimizu* series. Another success was *Hurray for Fishvendor Tasuke!* [Appare Isshin Tasuke] (1945), whose scriptwriter was Akira Kurosawa. This film in the *kodan* oral tradition focused on the adventures of a lowly Tokyoite noted for his courage.

Hasegawa and Yamada worked together again on *The Map of Female Lineage* [Fukeizu] (1942), a melodrama of tragic love set in conventional Meiji society. Like its sequel the same year, it was based on a novel by the Meiji writer Kyoka Izumi.

Popular Film of the Occupation (1945–1950)

Despite chronic shortages of every kind—film, theater space, and personnel—the cinema industry in postwar Japan managed to produce and even to prosper. Censorship, too, remained an obstacle to overcome. The Supreme Commander for the Allied Powers (SCAP) had replaced the wartime government's guidelines with equally strict ones of its own. This time, the "positive" attitude meant playing up democratic values and banishing themes and values associated with the "nationalism" of the past. This policy was especially hard on the *jidaigeki* genre, with its echoes of feudal loyalty and heroic self-sacrifice.

Even so, release from wartime pressures freed audiences anxious to crowd the few remaining theaters (some 530 had been destroyed in the war). These were audiences looking for entertainment, not indoctrination. A large percentage were young students released from wartime service—students whose disrupted education left them ill prepared for the challenge of serious, sophisticated cinema. The popular film was to benefit from this cultural shortfall. Musicals and comedies were made in quick succession and eagerly attended.

Shochiku's first postwar venture was a kind of musical revue, *Breeze* [Soyokaze] (1945). Its hit theme, "Song of Apples" [Ringo no uta], was heard everywhere in war-torn Japan, becoming a symbol of hope for the future. Toho challenged its rival with a musical comedy, *Song to the Sun* [Utae taiyo] (1945), directed by Yutaka Abe. Prewar comedians such as Entatsu and Achako continued to work for Toho, one of their hits being *Five Tokyo Men* [Tokyo gonin otoko] (1946), directed by Torajiro Saito.

The paramount success in the song film genre was Hideo Oba's *Sad Whistle* [Kanashiki kuchibue] (1949). This film took its title theme and performer directly from the then most popular song, "Sad Whistle," sung by the young teenager Hibari Misora. Misora was in constant and sensational demand in hits such as *Roaming Singing Queen* [Horo no utahime] (1950). Her long line of song films enabled Shochiku to turn a profit after expensive failures in erstwhile specialties like melodrama and *shomingeki*.

Daiei was to have its share of troubles, too, losing some important *jidaigeki* performers to another company. In the meantime, Chiezo Kataoka was put to good use in the contemporary film genre with a *Detective Bannai Tarao* series. Daiei's profits began with the first of these pictures, *Thirty-three Steps* [Sanjusan no ashioto] (1948).

Daiei production in 1949 went all-out for melodrama in the so-called "mother" tear-jerker series (*haha-mono*): *Mother and Crimson Plum Blossoms* [Haha kobai], *Three Mothers* [Haha sannin], and *In Search of Mother* [Haha koi boshi]. These films were inspired by the commercial success of *Wildcat Miss* [Yamaneko reijo] (1949), a work in the soap opera vein (like *Stella Dallas*). It stressed the unselfish love and heroic loneliness of a naive and unrefined mother whose daughter has been adopted by a rich family.

These sentimental "mother" films, with their common theme of separation, proved especially appealing to middle-aged rural women. When such a film came to a province, impatient farmwomen would be up at dawn, anxious to begin the long trip to town, each carrying a box lunch as if for a school excursion.

The Toho Company suffered two prolonged strikes in 1946; as a result, its total production was only eighteen films. Most of those were "art" films on democratic themes, though a few comedians did contribute works with mass audience appeal.

A continuing ideological split in the company led to the formation of an anti-strike faction of some ten stars and 450 employees. This group broke away in 1947 to found its own Shin Toho Company. Losses shared with the parent company, however, forced this new venture into overproduction in both artistic and popular genres. Profits in both were uncomfortably modest at first. For example, *A Thousand and One Nights with Toho* [Toho sen-ichi-ya] (1947), the inaugural entertainment film, fell short of popular appeal, though it offered an array of big-name stars and the unique idea of exposing the audience to events taking place inside the studio. Shin Toho's first smash hit was made in the following year with a melodrama in the Shochiku manner: *Three Hundred and Sixty Nights* [Sanbyaku-rokuju-go-ya], directed by Kon Ichikawa.

The Toho Company itself was not restored to full production until 1951. Interestingly enough, a comeback was made possible by yet another in the ever-popular *Musashi* series. This time, Horoshi Inagaki's *jidaigeki* hero took up arms against the title opponent *Kojiro Sasaki* [Sasaki Kojiro] (1951).

A Golden Age of Popular *Jidaigeki*: The 1950s

The film industry was not left out of the Japanese economic miracle in the 1950s. New construction soon restored the number of theaters to the prewar figure of 2,641. By 1959 that number had nearly tripled to 7,401. The return to national independence with the San Francisco Peace Treaty of 1951 had a direct effect on the development of both artistic and popular cinema. *Jidaigeki*, especially the swashbuckling *chanbara* variety, returned to captivate an audience hungry for the source of cultural continuity cut off by the occupation ban on feudal tales.

At this new point of departure, the four existing firms (Toho, Shin Toho, Daiei, and Shochiku) were joined by another, the Tokyo Eiga Company, commonly called Toei. Toei was to make valuable contributions to popular cinema. They began by adapting radio *jidaigeki* for film. Doing this put them in contact with a vast new market of children and teenagers. They also groomed new stars for this genre—and kidnapped some big names from other studios.

In 1954 Toei also put into effect a demanding new market strategy: double features of medium-length films. In their search for material to supply this demand of their own creation, they borrowed again from radio: the enormously popular NHK children's drama series, *New Tales from Various Lands* [Shin shokoku monogatari], which aired from 1952 to 1956. Turning to radio recalled the prewar practice of making films out of serial fiction from boys' magazines. The direct precedent here would be the magic costume films of Matsunosuke.

The first such Toei venture was the three-part *Whistling Boy* [Fuefuki doji] (1954). This mixture of fantasy and adventure pitted boy heroes equipped with swordsmanship and magic against heroic odds. Success with the child-teenager audience was immediate and vast. The new young faces on the screen became instant film idols: Kinnosuke Nakamura (now Kinnosuke Yorozuya) and Chiyonosuke Azuma.

This healthy boost to Toei self-confidence began what was to prove a golden age of entertainment films dominated by this company. The same NHK series was used again for the five-part film, *The Red Peacock* [Beni kujaku] (1954–1955). The same costars appeared with a treasure hunt added to the format. In spite of a simple story rewarding the virtuous and punishing the wicked, *The Red Peacock* far outdistanced *Whistling Boy* as a box-office hit.

Encouraged by success in one area of the market, Toei decided to aim for a much wider audience. In spite of being newcomers to the industry, they assembled an impressive array of craftsmen and stars old and new in preparation for a blockbuster *jidaigeki*. The choice of script was venerable and safe: the traditional *Chushingura* epic, *Forty-seven Loyal Ronin* [Ako roshi] (1956). This classic of cinema history offers any studio plenty of opportunity for putting its stars and resources to a test of spectacle and splendor. Toei did that, calling on all their major talent—which included Utaemon Ichikawa and Chiezo Kataoka. It was Toei's second color film attempt.

Their success set off a *Chushingura* chain reaction in the studios. In 1957 Shochiku came out with its version starring the famous *kabuki* actor Ennosuke Ichikawa. Daiei followed in 1958 with Kazuo Hasegawa in the lead. Toei in 1959 rechallenged its rivals with yet another version starring Chiezo Kataoka.

Toei's commanding lead in the entertainment *jidaigeki* was also established by a series of gambler-boss films about the *yakuza* Jirocho Shimizu: *The Way of Yakuza at Shimizu Harbor* [Ninkyo Shimizu Minato] (1952), *The Way of Yakuza on Tokaido Highway* [Ninkyo Tokaido] (1958), and *The Way of Yakuza on Nakasendo Highway* [Ninkyo Nakasendo] (1959).

The famous prewar *yakuza* Chuji Kunisada was conspicuously absent from this interest in revivals. Chuji's method of operation involved bucking the system in order to be his own man and to do his bit for the downtrodden. In the social and political atmosphere of 1950s Japan, the importance of economic growth led to heavy emphasis on loyalty to the group. Rampant individualism of Chuji's sort was clearly out of style. Jirocho may have been a *yakuza*, but he knew how to run a system within a system. (One imagines his goons grouping to sing "We are family.") The same attitudes may be seen at work in *jidaigeki* plots where threats to feudal clan stability replace the prewar motives of personal revenge.

A new cinematic respectability seemed to flavor revivals generally. For example, when Toei decided to remake part of a popular prewar series as *Shogun's Idle Retainer: Mysterious Haunted Ship* [Hatamoto taikutsu otoko: Nazo no yureisen] (1955), Utaemon Ichikawa was cast again in the lead. In the 1930s series, Ichikawa played a loner who withdrew from the luxury of the palace to live in a slum where his bent for derring-do and doing good could benefit the common folk. Both the hero and his clothes changed dramatically in the 1950s revival. He was dressed more colorfully; while this enhanced the picture's mass appeal as "costume drama," it also signaled a change in status. This new hero was magnificently part of the system, an official emissary given a mandate (in the shogun's own hand) to surprise and punish rebels, wherever they might be. This pattern proved good for a seven-year series ending with the thirtieth film, *Shogun's Idle Retainer: Mysterious Ryujin Cape* [Hatamoto taikutsu otoko: Nazo no Ryujin Misaki] (1963).

In another successful series revival, the hero retained his prewar disguise as a commoner; only the wrongs he redressed were changed. This was Kinnosuke Toyama, a famous town magistrate of the Tokugawa era. In earlier series he fought crimes like murder and theft, whose victim was the individual. In the 1950s he was called upon to defend the system—to thwart plots against the shogunate itself. He too could brandish an official mandate.

For an innovation of a different sort, Toei lured the popular singer Hibari Misora away from Toho for a series of popular *jidaigeki* with titles such as *Young Samurai with an Umbrella Hat* [Hanagasa wakashu] (1958).

While Toei's energy and ingenuity outdistanced the competition in the *jidaigeki* genre, it also created the unremitting pressure of the double-bill marketing strategy. By 1958 a subdivision was formed and put in charge of the mass production of *chanbara* films that peaked in the next few years. This was the Daini Toei (Second Toei, later New Toei) Company.

The double-feature schedule also included films from a police detective series begun in 1954 and continuing for a decade. A total of twenty-four titles were issued, among them *Five Minutes till Escape* [Tobo gofun mae] (1955), *Unlucky Last Train* [Ma no saishu ressha] (1955), and *Crime at High Noon* [Hakuchuma] (1957). This low-budget series, shot on location, favored the documentary mode of focus on the sorts of crime related to poverty caused by rapid economic growth.[8]

Shochiku began the decade with a familiar emphasis on melodrama, especially the *shomingeki* drama of lower-middle-class life. The singer Hibari Misora made more profitable song films with titles such as *The Tokyo Kid* [Tokyo kiddo] (1950), *In Search of Father* [Chichi koishi] (1951), and *Girl in the Apple Orchard* [Ringoen no shojo] (1952). Every Hibari film was a box-office hit and boosted equally impressive sales of her records. She was recruited by Toho in 1955.

Shochiku's highest achievement in the postwar tear-jerkers was the three-part *What Is Your Name?* [Kimi no na wa] (1953–1954), directed by Hideo Oba. A radio thriller by Kazuo Kikuta inspired this film. The original was so spellbinding that the women's side of the public bath was said to be absolutely empty by eight o'clock, its broadcast time.[9]

The plot of this film somewhat resembles the Robert Taylor–Vivien Leigh *Waterloo Bridge*. A boy meets a girl on Sukiyabashi Bridge during an air raid on Tokyo. They part without exchanging names, promising to meet again on the bridge. By the time their paths cross again, the girl is unhappily married. When she does decide to leave her husband, she finds herself pregnant. In the end, the lovers are united—on the bridge.

The magnitude of the box-office receipts for this film suggested that the entire population of Japan saw at least one installment of the trilogy. Though the screenplay of *What Is Your Name?* was mediocre, it broke new ground for the Japanese melodrama. The erstwhile self-sacrificing mother, as in the *haha-mono* series, was now replaced by a new woman: the wife who could think of saying farewell to a domineering husband and mother-in-law in order to live with the man she loved. The new definition was not just "wife," but "object of a man's affection." This new orientation was to become an operative theme with the twist of the wife's infidelity in the television daytime drama of the 1960s.

The Toho Company decided to capture the white-collar market with a comedy series featuring a company president (*shacho*) cast as a benevolent father figure. *Third Rate Company Executive* [Santo juyaku] (1952), directed by Masahisa Haruhara, was based on a popular novel by Keita Genji. The executive in the story gets his rating from his wife. At the office, he is a model of the caring employer and conscientious businessman; at home he is henpecked. A thematic constant in this series of thirty-seven films is a harmony between top management and low-ranking employees (a pattern found in domestic drama as well). Other titles in the series include *Mr. Hope* [Hopu-san] (1951), directed by Kajiro Yamamoto; *Mr. Lucky* [Rakki-san] (1951), directed by Kon Ichikawa; and *The President's Pin-Money* [Hesokuri shacho] (1956), directed by Yasuki Chiba.

Toho is also credited with inventing the Japanese monster science fiction film. The debut film, *Godzilla* [Gojira] (1954), needs no introduction in the West. A sequel appeared in the following year—*Godzilla's Counterattack* [Gojira no gyakushu] (1955)—and was itself followed by spin-offs such as *Radon, Monster in the Sky* [Sora no daikaiju Radon] (1956). Godzilla's career typifies the allegorical conflict in this new type of science fiction: The materialistic society creates the monster that then attacks it. Conflict between monsters good and bad was sure to come, as was television, influenced in its turn by series such as *Ultraman* [Urutoraman] and *Ultra Q* [Urutora kyu] in the 1960s.

Toho also decided to compete in the romance musical market. Using Hibari Misora and the jazz singers Chiemi Eri and Izumi Yukimura, they made a series of such films with titles like *Toss-up Girls* [Janken musume] (1955), *Romance Girls* [Romansu musume] (1956), and *Three Lucky Girls* [Oatari san-shoku musume] (1957). Plots revolved around a mix-up over boys, with couples sorted out by the end.[10] Vocal highlights by the girls led to "reel-long singing" for the finale.

One striking innovation of the 1950s was the teenage sex film. This trend was begun by Shochiku with *Daughter Protests This Way* [Musume wa kaku kogisura] (1952), soon followed by the Shin Toho Company's *Mistakes of Younger Days* [Wakaki hi no ayamachi] (1952).

Daiei was notably successful with art films in the 1950s, producing international prizewinners like *Rashomon* in 1950 and *Ugetsu* in 1953. Their popular film success, however, lay in creating a boom in the subgenre named for their series' title, *Sex Stories of Teenagers* [Judai no seiten] (1953–1954). Plots in such films uniformly showed high school girls paying dearly for losing their chastity.

Another innovation derived from Nikkatsu's difficult position when the company resumed production in 1953. Shortage of capital, experienced staff, and established stars made mass production extremely difficult at a time when double billing had become the accepted market strategy. Then, too, the market seemed neatly divided among the competition: the female audience for Shichiku, the urban for Toho, the teenage for Daiei, and the juvenile and rural for Toei. As the newcomer on the scene, Nikkatsu could only hope to generalize with various quick-return productions.[11]

Prosperity came quite by accident in 1956 with the so-called *Sun-Tribe* [Taiyozoku] film based on the young Shintaro Ishihara's novel, *Season of the Sun* [Taiyo no kisetsu]. Its subject was a group of youngsters whose response to a materialistic society (defined in terms of fast cars and motor boats) was the pursuit of sex and violence. The first film in this genre, directed by Takumi Furukawa, bore the title of the book. Its student hero is a member of a boxing club. Having tired of a casual love affair, he sells his girl to his brother. She becomes pregnant. The student urges abortion. When the girl dies, the student cries at her funeral that adults understand nothing about the younger generation's plight.

A new genre fad resulted in similar productions like *Crazed Fruit* [Kurutta kajitsu] (1956) and *Counter Light* [Gyaku-kosen] (1956). The latter deals with a female "sun tribe" member's relationship with a middle-aged man.

The novelist's younger brother, Yujiro Ishihara, became an overnight sensation after his debut in Nikkatsu's first *taiyozoku* film. The athletic build and rather cool acting style of this new star did much to reverse the company's downward trend. Nikkatsu took full advantage, casting Ishihara in a film a month in 1957. One in particular, made in October that year, marked the peak of the "Yujiro boom": *I Am Waiting* [Ore wa matteiru]. Toei's *samurai* film "Kinnosuke boom" was put in the shade by this. It seemed a good time for Nikkatsu to withdraw from the competition in the *jidaigeki* genre.

Shin Toho's efforts in this decade were devoted to non-popular genres like military films with ultra-conservative overtones. The company did, however, market some cheap popular titles for the working class and rural population. Among these were Masaki Mori's *Yotsuya Ghost Story* [Yotsuya kaidan] (1956), a grotesque version of the famous *kabuki* play, and Toshio Shimura's *The Revenge of Queen Mother Pearl* [Onna shinju-o no fukushu] (1956), which included some tentative female nudity. Thanks to audience curiosity, these titles became great box-office hits, much to the surprise of their makers.

Television and Retrenchment: The 1960s

The 1960s soon began to generate dismal statistics. For example, by 1963 television was reaching 65 percent of the nation's viewing audience. That same year, the film audience shrank to half of its 1955 peak of 1,127 million. Clearly, the film industry would have to retrench and reform its products and marketing strategy in line with audience tastes now apt to reflect influences from this new "motion picture" medium.

Plagued by poor management and a series of strikes, Shin Toho went bankrupt in 1961. The New Toei was also dissolved that year. The parent Toei Company no longer needed help with mass production in a shrinking market—itself a reflection on a *jidaigeki* product perceived as being outmoded in plot and theme.

Toei hoped to replace its lost *jidaigeki* lead with a more timely contemporary *yakuza* (gangsters and professional gamblers) genre film, especially scripted to showcase two stars (sometimes costars): Ken Takakura and Koji Tsuruta. The debut film in this series was *The Theater of Life: Hishakaku* [Jinsei gekijo: Hishakaku] (1963), with Tsuruta directed by Tadashi Sawajima. Tsuruta and Takakura appeared together in sequels like *The Theater of Life: Hishakaku and Kiratsune* [Jinsei gekijo: Hishakaku to Kiratsune] (1968).

The early *yakuza* films set out the basics for many to follow. It should be noted that while all *yakuza* gangster-gamblers are low-life characters, the "good" *yakuza* lives true to the old-fashioned code of honor that the "bad" is willing to violate. The climax of the plot comes when the good *yakuza* has had enough; fed up by the unprincipled violence of the bad guys, he heads for enemy headquarters for the showdown, armed with his short swift sword and quite alone, ready to sacrifice himself for the sake of honor. This pattern shows an interesting reversal of the postwar emphasis on *samurai* heroes acting in support of the system. The *yakuza* has returned us to the prewar loner hero whose moral authority "shines like a good deed in a naughty world."

Toei also produced a number of other *yakuza* series. *The Story of Japanese Yakuza* [Nihon kyokaku-den] was the longest run in the genre, with eleven films from 1964 to 1971. Territorial consolidation was the theme of good-bad confrontation here, with the added novelty of old-new conflict: a get-rich-quick *yakuza* organization in cahoots with politicians tries to wrest power from a traditional *yakuza* group with a healthy interest in protecting law-abiding citizens. *Gambling* [Bakutouchi] was a series of ten films made between 1967 and 1972.

The consistent success of this genre led Toei to try a variation featuring a heroine who was completely feminine, but a fighter nevertheless. Junko Fuji rose to stardom in this role, beginning with *The Scarlet Peony Gambler* [Hibotan bakuto] (1968) and continuing through eight installments until 1972.

Popular *jidaigeki* were crowded out by this competition, or rather displaced into television production. There, prewar and postwar favorites such as *Komon Mito* and *Detective Heiji Zenigata* continued to thrive.

The *yakuza* also crowded out the violent swordplay *chanbara* subgenre of *jidaigeki*. The realistic swordfighting of the 1950s became noticeably bloodier in the early 1960s. While this type of film captured only a fraction of the market, there were some notable successes. Along with artistic *samurai* films like Kurosawa's *Yojimbo* (1961) and Kobayashi's *Harakiri* [Seppuku] (1962), the immensely popular *Story of Zatoichi* [Zatoichi monogatari] (1962) was issued by Daiei.[12]

In this last, Shintaro Katsu was cast as a blind masseur so expert with his cane sword that he could slice a die in two. Katsu himself served as actor-director in most of the series of some two dozen films that followed from 1962 to 1972. His work has been described as parodic and absurdist.[13] However, it was practically the only *chanbara*-style entertainment to succeed in a market dominated by *yakuza*.

The Toho Company, meantime, continued to do well with its *Company President* series. Like the 1950s, this decade remained strong in the Toho specialties of comedy and science fiction. Along with the *Company President* films, Toho's longest-running comedy success in the 1960s was the *In Front of the Station* [Ekimae] series of twenty-three films issued between 1958 and 1969. As titles indicate, these were on-location, local color comedies, as in *Town Developments in Front of the Station* [Ekimae danchi] (1961).

In science fiction, Toho continued to populate the screen with Godzilla and his monster look-alikes. An East-West meeting of monsters was also arranged in a film whose Japanese title has a definite ring to it: *King Kong vs. Godzilla* [Kingu Kongu tai Gojira] (1962).

Next to Toei, the most active company in the 1960s was Nikkatsu, which provided some stiff competition for its rival. This was done by skillful management of established idols like Yujiro Ishihara and by grooming new talent. Thus, Akira Kobayashi, Koji Wada, and Keiichiro Akagi (killed, like James Dean, in a crash in 1961), along with Ishihara, were dubbed "the diamond line" of Nikkatsu.

While Ishihara continued in a series of action comedies, Kobayashi made the *Migrant Bird* [Wataridori] series (1959–1962) with nine titles, and Akagi made the *Gunman* [Kenju Buraicho] series (1960) with five titles. The narrative pattern of the *Migrant Bird* series concerned a drifter who comes to town in time to prevent a *yakuza* takeover of some sort. That done, the hero takes his leave, leaving behind his local female admirer. Similarly, Akagi's series focused on a young gunman who uses his exceptional skill to challenge the underworld bosses. These series did much to solidify Nikkatsu's claim to preeminence in the action film drama.

Despite the general cutback in numbers of films produced, Daiei profits remained substantial, thanks to four action drama series with popular stars: the *Zatoichi* and *Evil Man* [Akumyo] series, both with Shintaro Katsu, running 1961–1969; *Assassin Spy* [Shinobi] with Raizo Ichikawa, running 1962–1969; and the *Black* [Kuro] series, with titles like *Black Test Car* [Kuro no shisosha] (1962), featuring the handsome leading man Jiro Tamiya, running 1962–1964. Katsu, in particular, with his rugged masculine charm, captivated a public whose entertainment appetite moved steadily toward stimulation and excitement in this relatively peaceful decade for Japan.

Even so, a film like the final picture in the *Assassin Spy* series could have artistic ambitions. Director Kazuo Ikehiro added a measure of depth and insight to his violent hero in *Assassin Spy: New Version* [Shinsho shinobi no mono] (1966).

Shochiku fared poorly in the 1960s owing a decline in audience interest in domestic drama, melodrama, and comedy. The public seemed to support only what was unique and new. Then, in 1969 Shochiku's comedy comeback began with the first in a series that continues today: Yoji Yamada's *It's Tough to Be a Man* [Otoko wa tsurai yo]. This parody of the *yakuza* film features the vagabond Tora who never quite manages a break free of his home ties. He falls in love with a beautiful new heroine in each episode, only to find himself perpetually rejected. In some cases, he is accepted, but cannot bring himself to tie the actual knot. This series, affectionately known as the *Tora-san* series, shows how a major film studio can profit by television feedback. Shochiku had done this before, with Yoji Yamada's screenplay adapted to a 1966 film version of the television domestic drama *Miss Ohana* [Ohana-san].

Production Innovation: The 1970s

In a decade of continuing decline, the cinema industry was forced to make adjustments that altered the character of some studios considerably. Daiei vanished altogether, bankrupt by 1971. Nikkatsu scaled down production and eventually stopped making regular feature-length films.[14] Shochiku, Toho, and Toei partook of a new mood of extreme caution.

Nikkatsu's change of character was most complete. It began with the introduction of a new genre requiring somewhat lower budgets, fewer staff, and reduced production time. This was the so-called *roman poruno*. (The American designation would be "soft porn.")

Back in the 1960s, many "pink" movies focusing on sexual scenes were made by independent filmmakers, but the 1960s audience did not respond with much enthusiasm; a new market strategy may have helped change this in the 1970s. While the other studios were being eased out of the double-feature business by rising costs, Nikkatsu pursued it with pairs of these hour-long soft porn films. Some 500 such works were circulated this way by Nikkatsu in the 1970s.

Plots were necessary only to the extent that they provided excuses for sexual encounters with a soft porn emphasis on female nudity. Censorship in Japan being what it was and is, these films left rather more to the viewer's imagination than their American counterparts. Representative titles included *Sayuri Ichijo: Wet Desire* [Ichijo Sayuri: Nureta yokubo] (1972), by Tatsumi Kamishiro; *Eros Behind the Room Partition* [Yojo-han fusuma no urabari] (1974), also by Kamishiro; and *Madame Emanuele of Tokyo* [Tokyo Emanyueru fujin] (1975), by Akira Kato. The last was apparently inspired by the French box-office hit. An interesting change brought about by the fugitive film careers of actresses in this genre was a break with the star system, which for seventy years had sustained the "program film."

Faced with the declining commercial value of stars like Tsuruta and Takakura, Toei introduced a successful new series: Kinji Fukasaku's five-part *yakuza* film, *Combat Without Code* [Jingi naki tatakai] (1973–1974). Covering the twenty-five years from 1945 to 1970, this film traced the rise and fall of various *yakuza*. Its contribution to the genre was a radical shift in the direction of violence, exploring its contagious, chaotic, purposeless character. The success of *Combat Without Code* made Bunta Sugawara into an overnight sensation.

The accent on violence also paid off in another Toei breakthrough. After eighteen years away from the genre, the company gambled on a revival of the *chanbara* action *samurai* film with *The Intrigue of the Yagyu Clan* [Yagyu ichizoku no inbo] (1978). Also directed by Kinji Fukasaku, this film offered the viewer sensational displays of violence. (It was released in English as *Shogun's Samurai*.)

At the Shochiku studio, the director Yoji Yamada continued the vastly popular *Tora-san* series with another twenty installments in the 1970s. No doubt a feeling that family solidarity was becoming a thing of the past had something to do with making Tora-san a national hero. Under Yamada's skillful direction, this vagabond vendor was shown to be nostalgically attached to his homeplace, sister, and relatives (his parents being gone), despite his wayward character.

Toho did not do particularly well in popular genres in the early 1970s. Their comedies became hackneyed, and audiences turned away from their *jidaigeki* offerings. A profitable exception was the *Lone Wolf with a Child* [Kozure okami] (1972) series with Tomisaburo Wakayama, Shintaro Katsu's brother. Its hero was a banished retainer of the shogun, a figure whose comic book origins are most apparent in displays of swordfighting reminiscent of gunfighter shootouts in American westerns.

Toho's precarious finances were given a shot in the arm by an adaptation of Sakyo Komatsu's best-selling book, *Japan Sinks* [Nihon chinbotsu] (1973). Thus, a major studio found its fortunes propped up by a disaster film of the *Earthquake* or *Towering Inferno* variety. Toho's downward trend was reversed in the mid–1970s when the singing star Momoe Yamaguchi was cast as a heroine opposite the young Tomokatsu Miura in a succession of films. This so-called "golden combination" made nineteen box-office hits, both artistic and popular, before their marriage in 1980.

The Kadokawa Publishing Company entered the cinema industry in 1976, with results that were to be far reaching in the future. Their Kadokawa Film Company ignored double billing in order to pour their immense capital into single large-scale popular features. Their first production was based on the popular mystery novel by Seishi Yokomizo and directed by Kon Ichikawa: *The Inugami Family* [Inugamike no ichizoku] (1976). This and every other production turned a handsome profit for Kadokawa. Two other titles worthy of mention would be *Proof of Manhood* [Ningen no shomei] (1978) and *Proof of Savagery* [Yasei no shomei] (1978), both directed by Junya Sato.

Kadokawa's publishing connections were the silver lining of their enterprise. Massive advertising campaigns were organized to promote best sellers, film versions, and sound track recordings simultaneously. For example, before *Proof of Savagery* was released, Kadokawa ran daily ad headlines: "Read the Novel Before the Film or See the Film After the Novel." This kind of reinforcement from radio, television, and newspapers helped *Proof of Savagery* outrank Toei's biggest box-office hit of the year, *The Intrigue of the Yagyu Clan*. Under these circumstances, a newcomer like Kadokawa could pose a major threat to the established companies fighting in a bearish market.

Midway Through a Decade: The 1980s

As the number of serious films continues to decrease, the cinema industry seems likely to reconsider its future in terms of popular cinema. Kadokawa continues to exemplify the leading edge of production and marketing. Now that teenagers form a majority of the audience, the company's policy of grooming young talent seems likely to continue. They began as early as 1978, with stars such as Hiroko Yakushimaru, who was scouted from high school and turned into a singing actress. Yakushimaru has turned out box-office hits one after another while her songs rank high on the Hit Parade. Kadokawa's "kill three birds with one stone'' advertising blitz still works with combinations of best sellers, film versions, and recordings.

Kadokawa's commercial triumph thus far has been the *jidaigeki* film, *Story of Eight Heroes with Eight Different Virtues* [Satomi hakken-den], released for the 1984 New Year's holiday season. This could be called the popular film for the 1980s: a hugely expensive production featuring Hiroko Yakushimaru surrounded by big-name stars in service of the ultimate in entertainment—a heady mixture of mystery, science fiction, romance, and adventure.

By 1984 Shochiku's *Tora-san* was in its fifteenth year with more than twice that number of installments. Declining attendance figures, however, indicate that even the longest-running popular series must end sometime. Then, too, the star comedian Kiyoshi Atsumi cast as Tora-san is past fifty and may no longer summon up the charisma required by the romantic subplot of his script.

In June of 1984, Shochiku sought to mend its fortunes by reviving the television series, ''A Band of Assassins'' [Hissatsu], in a film adaptation. Its success with this title derived from a wide range of audience—from the teens to the middle-aged. No doubt carefully planned casting helped, giving the adult audience its familiar comedian Makoto Fujita with a constellation of teen idol stars.

Toho has set itself a new direction in science fiction with the large-scale *Goodbye, Jupiter* [Sayonara Jupita] (1984). Sakyo Komatsu, a popular novelist, has adapted his own work here, functioning as scriptwriter, producer, and director-in-chief. Toho also produced a *Godzilla* revival for the 1985 New Year's holiday season—thirty-one years after the original appeared.

Toei has managed to capture a share of the teen idol market cultivated so successfully by Kadokawa. No doubt this owes something to Toei's power as distributor to theaters under contract. Nikkatsu continues to concentrate on softcore pornography for the male audience.

Undoubtedly the youth of the filmgoing audience will continue to affect the future of the industry. At the same time, the older generations, considered more attuned to sensitive and sophisticated craftsmanship and artistry, appear content with the revival of popular *jidaigeki* television series that offer the pleasures of identification with the likes of Vice Shogun Komon Mito, Detective Heiji Zenigata, and Magistrate Kinshiro Toyama.

REFERENCE WORKS

Works in English

To date, no single reference work in English is devoted to the Japanese popular film. The following books, however, provide helpful background reading and in some cases touch on popular film as it relates to the history of Japanese cinema in general.

Japanese Cinema: Film Style and National Character (1971) by Donald Richie is a classic study by the foremost Western authority on the subject. This work offers an excellent evocation of the beauty, subtlety, and sophistication of Japanese cinema. Richie brings historical and aesthetic perspectives to bear on representative films and discusses the thematic and stylistic characteristics of major directors. However, popular works by those same directors are not treated since this book is devoted to the artistic cinema in the most exacting sense of the term.

The Japanese Film: Art and Industry (1982) by Joseph L. Anderson and Donald Richie is a comprehensive historical survey of the subject from the earliest days to the mid–1970s. This illuminating work discusses the origins of various popular genres and shows how they developed under market and industry pressure. Popular cinema researchers will find the treatment of the period 1920–1960 especially informative. Though originally published in 1959 and expanded for reissue in 1982, the book contains little on popular films after 1970.

The Encyclopedia of Japan (1983) contains an excellent entry on Japanese film by Joseph L. Anderson. This concise, critical survey moves from the beginning to 1976. Along with mainstream artistic developments, Anderson offers an overall view of genres associated with mass entertainment.

The Japanese Movie by Donald Richie (revised edition, 1982) provides valuable information on the popular *samurai* films made in the silent era. Again, the bias is toward art cinema.

The Samurai Film by Alain Silver is a useful book for basic research. Though half of the works discussed belong to art cinema by directors such as Kurosawa, Kobayashi and Shinoda, the remainder do represent popular *jidaigeki* films. Every work is treated as an object of serious study. Silver emphasizes the intertextuality of each as revealed in its stylistic and thematic devices.

Works in Japanese

Even researchers not conversant with Japanese may be interested to know that the following reference tools exist in the native language.

Nihon Eiga Hattatsushi [History of the development of Japanese cinema] (1976) by Junichiro Tanaka is the most comprehensive survey to date. These five volumes were apparently the prime source for the Anderson-Richie book mentioned above. Tanaka's focus is on artistic cinema, but he frequently offers detailed discussion of the sometimes subtle relations between artistic and popular films at various stages of development. This work was issued in 1976, so coverage ends with 1975.

Nihon Eigashi no Soshutsu [A history of Japanese cinema in the making] (1983) by Motohiko Fujita is a collection of individual essays examining the contributions made by various popular culture genres to Japanese cinema.

Kinema Jumpo [Bi-monthly journal of cinema] is the most prestigious film journal in Japan. It offers up-to-date coverage of works in all genres issued by the major studios. This magazine is taken seriously by Japanese readers as a source of insight and criticism independent of the film industry. Dedicated researchers into popular film have, in addition, any number of Japanese magazines to choose from, many of them issued for young readers.

Sekai no Eiga Sakka [Film directors of the world] is a series published by the Kinema Jumpo Company. It profiles figures like Yoji Yamada and Kinji Fukasaku, both considered popular film directors by Japanese audiences. Unfortunately, coverage of directors still active stops with the date of publication (1972–1974)—a serious disadvantage, given the growing importance of popular cinema.

Volume 31 in the series *Nihon Eigashi* [History of Japanese cinema] is one of the best critical surveys of the Japanese film to 1975. It is a collection of essays done by various leading film critics. Though the bias is, again, toward art cinema, this volume contains a number of cogent observations on some popular genres.

RESEARCH COLLECTIONS

Sources in the United States

Most U.S. film distributors of Japanese films along with art museums offer artistic titles almost exclusively, as does the Film Center of the Museum of Modern Art in New York City. However, a few distributors have begun to list some installments from popular *jidaigeki* series such as the *Blind Swordsman* [Zatoichi].

Two major Japanese companies have established branches in the United States. Toei in New York offers a number of its own science fiction and *yakuza* films. Shochiku Films of America, Inc., in Los Angeles, distributes that company's films as well as many from Daiei, although most of the former are thirty-five millimeter.

The most complete popular cinema collection in the United States is housed in the Pacific Film Archive in Berkeley, California. This repository of Shochiku, Daiei, Toho, and Nikkatsu films circulated in the United States contains about 600 titles both popular and artistic. A published catalog edited by Linda Provinzano, *Films in the Collection of the Pacific Film Archive, Vol. 1 Daiei Motion Co. Ltd. Japan*, contains all Daiei holdings. Those of other companies are not yet completed. Only the card catalog at the library is complete. Screenings are on site, by appointment, for a fee.

The few theaters devoted full-time to Japanese cinema are concentrated in Los Angeles, San Francisco, and Hawaii, but they do offer a valuable cross-section of genres.

The Japan Film Center of the Japan Society (established in 1979) sometimes offers weekend film series of popular titles, stars, and directors. The center, located in New York City, imports some of the newest releases directly from Japan.

Sources in Japan

The Film Center of the Tokyo National Museum of Modern Art (established in 1952) houses some 6,000 titles. Most are artistic films, though the center often screens popular works in its regular director-genre series. Research access is available upon application.

The Japan Film Library Council in Tokyo makes its collections of sources and reference materials available to researchers.

The dedicated researcher in Japan will not neglect the wide and various offerings of local commercial theaters and public organizations, though they are generally limited to postwar films. The monthly magazine *Pia* contains schedules for every sort of entertainment in Tokyo and its satellite cities, and is an extremely useful guide for anyone interested in popular cinema.

NOTES

1. For further information on the *gesaku* writing of the early Meiji era, see Mitsuo Nakamura, *Modern Japanese Fiction* (Tokyo: Kokusai Bunka Shinkokai, 1968), pp. 9–17.

2. The *kodan* are recited tales of heroes from the Tokugawa period. For a more detailed treatment of the influence of the *kodan* on the *jidaigeki*, see Joseph Anderson and Donald Richie, *The Japanese Film: Art and Industry*, expanded edition (Princeton: Princeton University Press, 1982), pp. 315–17.

3. The newest version by Kihachi Okamoto (1964) was released in English as *Sword of Doom*.

4. Donald Richie, *Ozu* (Berkeley: University of California Press, 1972), p. xi.

5. Before the war, the *yakuza* genre dealt with Tokugawa-era professional gamblers, but after the war this genre became associated with films about gangsters/professional gamblers.

6. Anderson and Richie, p. 129.

7. Ibid., p. 142.

8. Hajime Nagasaki and Kikuo Yamamoto, "Sen-kyuhyaku-gojunendai" [The 1950s], in N. Chiba, et al., *Sekai no Eiga Sakka: Nihon Eigashi* [Film directors of the world: History of Japanese cinema], Vol. 31 (Tokyo: Kinema Jumpo, 1976), p. 188.
長崎一、山本喜久男 「１９５０年代」 『世界の映画作家ー日本映画史』
東京　キネマ旬報　１９７６　p.１８８

9. Anderson and Richie, p. 260. See also Junichiro Tanaka, *Nihon eiga Hattatsushi* [History of the development of Japanese cinema], Vol. 3 (Tokyo: Chuo Kuran, 1976) , p. 36.

10. Anderson and Richie, p.260.

11. Ibid., p. 264.

12. I consider Kurosawa's *jidaigeki* artistic films; by borrowing the framework of what appears to be an entertainment film—a medium accessible to the masses—he conveys his social and moral vision.

13. Joseph L. Anderson, "Japanese Cinema" in *Encyclopedia of Japan* (Tokyo: Kodansha International, 1983), p. 274.

14. Anderson and Richie, *The Japanese Film*, p. 454.

BIBLIOGRAPHY

Anderson, Joseph L. "Japanese Cinema." In *Encyclopedia of Japan*. Tokyo: Kodansha International, 1983.

Anderson, Joseph L., and Donald Richie. *The Japanese Film: Art and Industry*. 1959; rpt. New York: Grove Press, 1960. Expanded edition, Princeton: Princeton University Press, 1982.

Chiba, Nobuo, Kenji Iwamoto, Hajime Nagasaki, and Kikuo Yamamoto. *Sekai no Eiga Sakka: Nihon Eigashi* [Film directors of the world: History of Japanese cinema] Vol. 31. Tokyo: Kinema Jumpo, 1976.

千葉伸夫、岩本憲児、長崎一、山本喜久男 『世界の映画作家－日本映画史』
３１巻　東京　キネマ旬報　１９７６

Fujita, Motohiko. *Nihon Eigashi no Soshutsu: Jidai o Utsusu Kagami* [A history of Japanese cinema in the making: The mirror which reflects the era]. Tokyo: Goryushoin, 1983.

藤田元彦　『日本映画史の創出－時代を映す鏡』　東京　五柳書院　１９８３

Kodama, Kazuo and Chieo Yoshida. *Showa Eiga Sesoshi* [History of social currents in films of the Showa period]. Tokyo: Shakai Shisosha, 1982.

児玉一夫、吉田知恵男　『昭和映画世相史』　東京　社会思想社　１９８２

Kotoda, Chieko, ed. *Sekai no Eiga Sakka: Fukasaku Kinji: Kumai Kei* [Film directors of the world: Kinji Fukasaku; Kei Kumai]. Vol. 22. Tokyo: Kinema Jumpo, 1974.

小藤田千栄子編　『世界の映画作家　深作欣二　熊井啓』　２２巻　東京
キネマ旬報　１９７４

―――, ed. *Sekai no Eiga Sakka: Kato Tai: Yamada Yoji* [Film directors of the world: Tai Kato; Yoji Yamada]. Vol. 14. Tokyo: Kinema Jumpo, 1972.

小藤田千栄子編　『世界の映画作家　加藤泰　山田洋治』　１４巻　東京
キネマ旬報　１９７２

McDonald, Keiko. "Kinji Fukasaku: An Introduction." *Film Criticism* 8, no. 1 (Fall 1983), 20–32.

Matsuura, Kozo, ed. *Nihon Eigashi Taikan* [Tables of a history of Japanese film]. Tokyo: Bunka Shuppankyoku, 1982.

松浦幸三　『日本映画史大鑑』　東京　文化出版局　１９８２

Provinzano, Linda, ed. *Films in the Collection of the Pacific Film Archive: Vol. 1 Daiei Motion Picture Co. Ltd. Japan*. Berkeley: University of California Art Museum, 1979.

Richie, Donald. *Japanese Cinema: Film Style and National Character*. Garden City, N.Y.: Anchor, 1971.

―――. *Ozu*. Berkeley: University of California Press, 1972.

―――. *The Japanese Movie*. 1966; rpt. Tokyo: Kodansha International, 1982.

Silver, Alain. "Samurai." *Film Comment* 11, no. 5 (September-October 1975), 10–14.

―――. *The Samurai Film*. Cranbury, N.J.: A. S. Barnes, 1977.

Svensson, Arne. *Japan: Screen Guide*. New York: A. S. Barnes, 1970.

Tanaka, Junichiro. *Nihon Eiga Hattatsushi* [History of the development of Japanese cinema]. 5 vols. Tokyo: Chuo Koron, 1976.

田中純一郎　『日本映画発達史』全５巻　東京　中央公論社　１９７６

Uriu, Tadao. *Sengo Nihon Eiga Shoshi* [A short history of postwar Japanese cinema]. Tokyo: Hosei University Press, 1981.

瓜生忠夫　『戦後日本映画小史』　東京　法政大学出版局　１９８１

6

Japanese Television

BRUCE STRONACH

In the eyes of world, Japan* is technology. Its high-tech, high-quality consumer goods are found from Bangor to Bangladesh, and one of the first symbols of Japanese technological superiority was the color television. Although the world is aware of Japan's ability to produce television sets, few know anything about what is broadcast in Japan.

In this chapter I shall briefly attempt to convey the development of television in Japan, contemporary programing, and some aspects of the relationship between Japanese society and television. Japan is considered an anomaly by many: the only non-Western postindustrial society, and hitherto essentially inexplicable. It is hoped that through the information found in this chapter, the reader will gain not only a greater insight into the history, roles, and functions of television as one of the world's mass media, but also a greater understanding of Japan through its particular use of television.

HISTORICAL SURVEY

In Japan, television has reached a diffusion rate of almost 100 percent and has become the main source of both home entertainment and information for members of all age groups.

* Japanese place and organization names and the titles of Japanese television programs will be translated into English, if a relatively precise translation can be made. Japanese personal names are presented surname first and given name last.

I would very much like to thank my good friends Ms. Iwao Sumiko and Mr. Peter Evans for reviewing the manuscript and making many invaluable corrections and comments. I would also like to thank Ms. Sugiyama Mieko of the NHK Public Opinion Research Institute for her helpful comments on Japanese television.

Broadcasting was originally under the control of the government, which created the Nippon Hoso Kyokai (NHK or Japan Broadcasting Association) as its broadcasting and propaganda service. NHK was the only broadcaster in Japan until the end of the American occupation. During the American occupation, reforms were instituted allowing public access to NHK and paving the way for the eventual commercialization of Japanese broadcasting.

Contemporary television broadcasting is divided into two systems: public broadcasting on NHK Sogo (NHK-G or General) and NHK Kyoiku (NHK-E or Educational) and the commercial networks and independent stations. NHK operates under the Broadcast Law, depends upon mandatory receiver contract fees for its operating budget, and is relatively free from government interference. The commercial stations also operate under the Broadcast Law, as well as Ministry of Posts and Telecommunications guidelines, and are divided into networks based upon key stations in Tokyo. There are four of these with a fifth quasi-network.

Although Japan has a long history of research in television technology dating back to the 1920s, the development of Japanese television hardware and software was much influenced by the United States because of American control over Japanese broadcasting during the occupation, the advanced condition of American television technology at the time, and the lack of production facilities in Japan. American programing on Japanese television reached its peak in the early 1960s, but began to drop off as the Japanese movie industry began to cooperate with the television industry and the Japanese developed their own production facilities. While there are now few imported programs on Japanese television, the United States accounts for about 77 percent of total imported programing. By the 1980s Japan had become a net exporter of programing, 56 percent of which was animation. The United States imports 90 percent of all Japanese programing exports.

Programing on the commercial stations consists of various kinds of dramas—home, police, children's, and *samurai* dramas—wide shows, news and information, cartoons, documentaries, variety, game/quiz, and sports shows. While NHK-G broadcasts some of the most popular dramas on Japanese television, its main role is to provide cultural and enlightening programing. It has been especially important in keeping alive the traditional arts by making them available to all Japanese. Commercial stations attempted educational broadcasting in the 1960s, but NHK-E is now the only educational broadcaster and has almost 100 percent educational programing.

Contemporary programing reflects the Western influence on Japanese society, especially the continuing American influence, but the emphasis on form and the subordination of content reflect its Confucian heritage and is the most important factor in Japanese programing.

The two most severe criticisms of Japanese programing are the high level of violence on a wide range of programing and the unhealthy nature of much of children's programing.

Japan is now incorporating into its communications system many new media that will give the public more access to information, increase the quality of television reception in remote areas and eventually widen the range of programing available to the Japanese public.

The Current Situation

Within Japanese television broadcasting, there exist two systems, public and commercial. The Nippon Hoso Kyokai (NHK or Japan Broadcasting Association) is a public, non-profit organization, originally created as the government broadcasting and propaganda office but now operating with legal independence from the government. NHK operates under the regulations of the Broadcast Law and relies on mandatory receiver contract fees for most of its operating budget. As of 1988 the contract fee per household was 900 yen for color television (¥ 35 = $1) and 540 yen for black and white television. The mandatory receiver contract system was instituted in order to ensure that NHK would have financial freedom from government interference. NHK broadcasts over two television networks, NHK Sogo (NHK-G or General), mainly responsible for news, cultural, and entertainment broadcasting, and NHK Kyoiku (NHK-E or Educational), mainly responsible for educational broadcasting. Other NHK services include two megawatt (AM) radio networks, one FM network, and an overseas shortwave broadcasting network (the latter does receive some government support).

NHK is controlled by a board of governors consisting of twelve members appointed by the prime minister. The board is responsible for the overall operation of NHK, including creation of the budget and meeting the Standards of Domestic Broadcasting set forth under the Broadcast Law. In addition, the president is appointed by the board of governors, and he in turn appoints a vice president and seven to ten directors, all of whom constitute the board of directors.

Under Article 44 of the Broadcast Law, NHK is charged with "elevating the level of civilization" of the people, maintaining local as well as national programs, preserving a knowledge of the past, conducting regular opinion polls, and creating the Standards of Domestic Broadcasting. The standards, which apply to all domestic broadcasts, include contributions to the ideal of world peace, respect for basic human rights and democracy, character building through the promotion of culture, and the preservation and diffusion of knowledge about traditional culture.

Commercial broadcasters also operate under the Broadcast Law and are supervised by the Ministry of Posts and Telecommunications, which issues guidelines for broadcasting and broadcasting licenses and reviews those licenses every three years. Commercial television broadcasting is based upon "key station" nationwide networks. The key stations are the television broadcasting stations that first developed in Tokyo and then sold their services to others around the country lacking either the production facilities or the geographical proximity to

Tokyo necessary to maintain quality entertainment and news programing. Most of the programing for the network is developed in the key station. There are now five commercial VHF television broadcasting stations in Tokyo, four of which are key stations for national networks. They are Nippon Television (NTV/ Channel 4), Tokyo Broadcasting System (TBS/Channel 6), Fuji Television (Fuji-TV/Channel 8), and the Asahi News Network (TV Asahi/Channel 10). The fifth Tokyo commercial television broadcasting station is TV Tokyo (Channel 12) and is not a key station by a precise definition of the phrase, but its programing is used by a loose network of local stations around the country.

There is no doubt that Japan is a fully developed *joho shakai* (information society). As of 1983, NHK operated 6,797 television broadcasting stations (general and educational), while ninety-nine private companies operated 5,562 commercial broadcasting stations. It is difficult, however, to estimate the exact number of television sets in this land of 112 million people. This is because ownership statistics are taken from the NHK receiver system, in which every household must pay a standard fee for black and white or color television, no matter how many sets are in the house. Therefore, one knows only how many households have televisions and not how many television sets are in each household. Even the former figure is not totally reliable, since many households with televisions, evade the regulation (even in this relatively obedient society) and do not purchase contracts to receive NHK broadcasts. Enforcement of the regulation is quite lax as the inspectors, who make nominal door-to-door checks for compliance, have no authority to enter the home without the householder's permission. Keeping the above caveat in mind, at the beginning of 1983, there was a total of 30,403,046 households contracted to receive NHK broadcasts.[1] The Economic Planning Agency has estimated from that figure the total number of television sets in Japan to be approximately 35 million, with a diffusion rate of 98.5 percent.[2]

Table 1 shows us that the Japanese watch between three and four hours of television daily. It is obvious from this table that the amount of time spent watching television is directly related to age, with people watching progressively more television as they grow beyond the teen years. Although the Japanese are avid consumers of all the mass media, television has grown rapidly since 1958 to become the most popular source of information and entertainment among all the mass media (see Tables 2 and 3).

The Development of Broadcasting and Television

The first radio broadcasts in Japan were transmitted from the Tokyo Broadcasting Station on March 22, 1925, to 3,500 contracted receivers. Broadcasting at this early stage was controlled by the Ministry of Communications (since changed to the Ministry of Posts and Telecommunications), which decreed that there should be one radio station in each of Japan's three major cities: Tokyo, Osaka, and Nagoya. In August 1926, a year after regular broadcasting had started from these three stations, they were consolidated under the newly established Nippon Hoso Kyokai in order to give the government much tighter control over programing. These controls included a ban on political analysis, prior censorship of all broadcast copy, the right of the censor to cut off a program if anything objectionable was broadcast, the exclusion of any material that could possibly be construed as decadent or radical, and the elimination of any reference to the Imperial family not in keeping with their divine status.

Movement toward television broadcasting was begun four years later with the establishment of the NHK technical laboratories about eight miles west of the Tokyo Broadcasting Station in Atagoyama, in downtown Tokyo. Professor Takayanagi of the Hamamatsu College of Engineering had successfully broadcast an image in March 1928, but it was not until the mid–1930s that television research really began to take off.

Japan was to host the 1940 Olympics, and wanted to impress the world with the level of its technological development by televising the games. In May 1939 the first experimental broadcast was successfully undertaken, and this was followed the next spring by the experimental broadcast of a television drama, "Before Supper."

Unfortunately, international conflict forced the cancellation of the 1940 Games, and research on television declined as NHK and its facilities were pressed into service for the duration of the Pacific War. After the bombing of Pearl Harbor, NHK broadcasting was limited to a single frequency for the whole nation. During the war NHK was mainly concerned with the broadcast of government propaganda to the nation, to overseas allies, and to enemy and occupied areas. One of the most popular NHK programs of the war years, "Zero Hour," was broadcast to the enemy in order to lower morale. From late 1943 it featured a number of Japanese women announcers with sultry voices collectively called "Tokyo Rose" by the Allied troops. When American soldiers finally occupied Tokyo, the mythical Tokyo Rose was first on the press corps' interview list.

The American occupation of Japan was founded on two principles: democratization and demilitarization. Gen. Douglas MacArthur, Supreme Commander for the Allied Powers (SCAP), had a classic black-top image of the Japanese in that he felt most people did not really support militarism, but had had no choice before the war as all aspects of society had been controlled by a small elite of militarists and their supporters. MacArthur believed that elimination of these militarists and the institutions they had used would allow democracy to flourish in Japan. SCAP therefore initiated a number of sweeping changes in the Japanese political, economic, and social systems.

SCAP was well aware of the importance of the broadcast media in political control and socialization, and one of the top priorities of the occupation was to redefine the role of broadcasting in Japan. One of the earliest directives from SCAP dealt with radio's role in allowing the free expression of opinions and unbiased news reporting that are necessary for the development of a democratic

Table 1

Television Viewing Time (in hours and minutes)

		1970	1975	1980
National Average		3.19	3.58	3.50
Male	10-15 yrs.	2.73	2.89	2.96
	16-19 yrs.	2.60	2.94	2.70
	20s	2.48	2.81	2.73
	30s	2.67	3.21	2.78
	40s	2.64	3.21	3.21
	50s	3.45	3.54	3.63
	60s	3.52	4.32	4.45
	over 70	----	4.38	4.71
Female	10-15 yrs.	2.61	2.86	2.63
	16-19 yrs.	2.56	2.66	2.56
	20s	3.29	3.68	3.30
	30s	3.68	3.92	3.36
	40s	3.44	3.98	3.69
	50s	3.78	4.34	4.28
	60s	4.28	4.43	4.69
	over 70	----	4.34	4.87

Source: Naomichi Nakanishi, Changes in Mass Media Contact Times (Tokyo: Nippon Hoso Kyokai, 1982), p. 13.

Table 2

Mass Media Preference

	Male	Female	Total
Television	82%	82%	82.3%
Newspapers	85%	73%	78.2%
Radio	38%	36%	37.0%
Books	29%	29%	28.8%
Weekly Magazines	22%	15%	17.9%
Sporting Papers	30%	07%	17.5%
Monthly Magazines	14%	13%	13.3%
Comics	12%	07%	09.2%

Source: Nippon Hoso Kyokai, Nihonjin to Terebi [The Japanese and television] (Tokyo: Nippon Hoso Kyokai, 1981), p. 28.

Table 3

From Which Medium Do You Get Your Information?

	1958	1961	1964	1966
Television	02%	31%	56%	68%
Newspapers	51%	36%	33%	24%
Radio	43%	28%	10%	06%

Source: Nippon Hoso Kyokai, Saikin Shicho Tokusei [Contemporary characteristics of people's interest] (Tokyo: Nippon Hoso Kyokai, 1981), p. 2.

participatory political culture. However, it was also made clear that news reflecting badly on the Allied Powers could not be tolerated.

During the occupation, NHK broadcasting was under the control of the Civil Information and Education Service (CIES), the Civil Censorship Detachment (CCD), and the Civil Communications Section (CCS). SCAP issued a radio code vague enough to ensure control of broadcast content. Everything broadcast was censored by CIES and CCD, including sports and entertainment programs, to eliminate militarist influences and instill the proper atmosphere for the growth of democracy.

Programing during the occupation was specifically designed to encourage the expression of opinion and unbiased news reporting. Some of the most popular programs of the time aired man-in-the-street interviews and interviews with political prisoners of the past regime. There were programs that began to educate women and other groups previously discriminated against as to their new roles in a democratic society. There was also a new emphasis on entertainment and comedy. Songfests, comedies, and quiz programs, all of which became standard fare on Japanese television, began on NHK during the occupation.

There is no doubt that the United States had a very important impact on Japanese broadcasting, and it was the occupation that created the precedent. Of all the effects of the occupation on broadcasting, perhaps the most important was the creation by SCAP of the three broadcasting laws that would become the foundation for the development of broadcasting in modern Japan. The Radio Law regulates the licensing of broadcast stations and the operation of facilities. The Broadcast Law regulates public broadcasting under NHK and also sets standards for commercial broadcasting. The Radio Regulatory Commission Law instituted that organization as the body responsible for overseeing and executing the regulations of the Radio and Broadcast Laws. The part of this package most difficult for the Japanese government to accept was the placing of control in the hands of the commission rather than in those of the Ministry of Communications. Given MacArthur's adamant support of the measure, the government was forced to support it, but in August 1952, after sovereignty had been restored, the ministry took control of broadcasting.

By the end of the decade, there was a growing desire for the creation of Japanese television broadcasting, fueled by both previous Japanese efforts and the reality of American television broadcasting since the late 1940s. U. S. Senator Carl Mundt had claimed in 1951 that, by utilizing Voice of America services, the Japanese could institute regular television broadcasting for as little as 4.6 million dollars. A former president of the *Yomiuri* newspaper, Shoriki Matsutaro, used the idea as the basis for creating a commercial television network, the Nippon Television Network Corporation (NTV). He planned to set up stations, with American assistance, in Tokyo, Osaka, and Nagoya with a series of relays for nationwide broadcasting. In October 1951, NTV was the first to file an application with the Radio Regulatory Commission for a license to operate a television station. This application was important not only in itself, but also for the galvanizing effect it had on NHK and other prospective commercial broadcasters. That which had been viewed as a possibility sometime in the middle future now seemed much closer to fulfillment as NHK and four commercial radio companies filed their own license applications shortly after NTV.

The years between NTV's first license application and the eventual beginning of regular broadcasts in 1953 were filled with acrimonious debate between NHK and NTV in the Radio Regulatory Commission. Central to this was the question of whether the commission would adopt a six- or seven-megahertz band, and it was thought that whichever side won would be the first to receive a license from the commission. The six-megahertz band was used in the United States and was therefore supported by NTV, which was using American equipment. The seven-megahertz band was supported by NHK, which was relying on domestically produced equipment, using the argument that the six-megahertz band would be inadequate for future color broadcasting. The last day of existence for the Radio Regulatory Commission was July 31, 1952, after which date control of broadcasting would be turned over to the Ministry of Posts and Telecommunications, following a licensing decision. As is often the case with Japanese consensus decision making, the discussion went on well into the night, literally to the last minute, when it was finally decided that the six-megahertz band would be adopted and NTV would be granted the first license. The decision was based partially on the fact that the NHK budget would have to wait for Diet (Japanese legislature) approval, and any licensing grant would be worthless until such approval was given. It was understood, however, that when the Diet finally did pass the NHK budget, a license would be granted.

Meanwhile, the development of television continued with hardware and production imports from the United States. American experts were brought over to teach production and direction as well as to help in the creation of facilities. While NHK was more self-sufficient in hardware and had more experience in television programing, both stations relied heavily on American assistance.

NTV was the first to receive its license, but NHK (which received its license on December 26, 1952) was the first to begin regular programing—on February 1, 1953. From the beginning, NHK had to rely on receiver contracts for its revenue (initally 200 yen per household), and, given the number of television sets and the economic conditions of the day, the financial picture was not very bright, particularly since NHK thought it necessary to go into operation before the "free" commercial stations if it were to have a chance of success.

After having some problems procuring RCA equipment from the United States, NTV went into operation six months after NHK. In 1954 there were three NHK stations and one NTV station operating in Japan. Seven years later there were eighty-seven NHK and sixty-one commercial stations.

While the rapid diffusion of television was important to both NHK and the commercial broadcasters, it was perhaps more crucial to the commercial companies as they had their private funds invested and depended on audience size to sell advertising. For this reason, NTV created the "plaza TV" concept of putting television sets in public places in order to increase the number of viewers at a time when the cost of ownership was prohibitive for the vast majority of Japanese. NTV installed sets in railway stations, on street corners, in plazas— anywhere people normally congregated. Coffee shops, bars, barber shops, restaurants, and similar establishments also began installing televisions in order to draw customers. Some interurban railroad companies even went so far as to install televisions in their cars. Because of these efforts, television in the mid– 1950s became much more popular than might be inferred from the number of sets sold.

The development of domestic television set production began to take off with the Japanese economic miracle. Income rose as the economy developed, and television prices dropped as production increased. In 1954 most televisions were imported from the United States at a minimum of 170,000 yen. However, Japanese production increased from 613,000 sets in 1957 to 2.8 million sets in 1959, dropping the price of a domestically produced set to 50,000 yen.[3] As prices dropped, television ownership (as judged by NHK receiver contracts) increased from 165,666 in 1955 to 6,860,472 in 1960. A 1956 NHK survey of children's viewing habits found that 16 percent of the children watched television in their own homes, while 84 percent responded they watched television outside in restaurants (32 percent), radio shops (25 percent), or at the barbershop (23 percent). By 1958, 60 percent responded that they watched television in their own homes and only 9 percent watched television outside the home. The number of commercial broadcasters was also increasing. Radio Tokyo's KR-TV became Tokyo's second television station in 1955, and both Osaka and Nagoya got their first stations in 1956.[4]

Early programing consisted mainly of variety entertainment, news, quiz and sports programs that could be easily transferred, along with their audiences, from radio to television, with the new addition of foreign movies and television programs. Sports played an especially important role in developing audiences, and four events that were to become lasting favorites of Japanese audiences— professional wrestling, *sumo* wrestling, professional baseball, and the annual high school baseball tournaments—attracted large crowds to television in the early 1950s. Professional baseball has been particularly crucial to NTV, as its parent company owns Japan's most popular baseball team, the Yomiuri Giants.

The development of television in Japan had a significant effect on the radio and movie industries. Until 1958 radio and television sales grew together, but then radio receiver contracts began a steep decline while television sales continued to soar. Radio contracts, which had peaked at about 15 million in 1958, dropped to about 1.5 million by 1967. From 1954 to 1964, NHK's first radio network audience rating dropped from 24 to 3 percent in the evening, 8 to 1 percent in the afternoon, and 11 to 2 percent in the morning.[5] NHK tried to reverse the trend by reducing the cost of radio receiver contracts, finally eliminating them in 1968. Especially damaging to radio was the loss of advertising revenues to television. In 1956 radio advertising accounted for 17.4 percent of all media advertising revenues (13 billion yen), while television accounted for 2.8 percent (2 billion yen). By 1964 radio revenues had been reduced to 4.9 percent of the total (17 billion yen), while television had risen to 31 percent (108 billion yen).[6] Radio eventually rebounded by moving into areas that did not compete with television—such as all-music, late night disk-jockey, and commuter programing—but never again caught up with television in advertising revenues.

The effect of television on the movie industry was similar to that on radio. Japanese movie attendance peaked at 1.1 billion in 1958, but declined to 373 million in 1965. In the early years, the movie industry had attempted to defend itself against a television industry desperate for attractive programing by not allowing its films to be broadcast. The strategy was eventually self-defeating, as it forced television to turn to foreign films and programs, which led to a boom in American programing.

One interesting feature of the growth of Japanese television is that the desire to televise a particular event has often encouraged the development of the industry as a whole. During the 1930s the impetus was the 1940 Olympics, and every decade since the war has witnessed its own notable advance. In 1952 the pattern for remote broadcasts was set by the coverage given the crown prince's departure from Yokohama Harbor to Queen Elizabeth's coronation ceremonies. In 1959 it was the desire to televise the crown prince's wedding that brought changes to the industry. When the prince came of marriageable age, there was much popular speculation as to who the bride would be. When it was announced that a commoner, Shoda Michiko, had been chosen, the empathy of the people with the princess-to-be manifested itself in the desire to watch the wedding on television, which created a nationwide boom in television sales.

Only NHK, which acted as a pool for all other broadcasters, was allowed inside the Imperial Compound, but coverage of the postwedding parade was open to anyone. In order to handle the enormous task of covering the event most efficiently, the two Tokyo commercial stations broadcast along a network of all twenty-eight commercial broadcasting companies in Japan. Previous to the wedding, all commercial broadcasters were totally independent and broadcast specifically for their local areas. During the era of radio broadcasting, this independence created few problems, but television programing had become more complicated, especially since most major news and entertainment events occurred in Tokyo. After the wedding, full-fledged networks were formed around the two Tokyo commercial stations. KR-TV became the key station for the Japan New Network (JNN), and NTV eventually spawned two more networks: Fuji-TV and TV Asahi.

In 1957 the Ministry of Posts and Telecommunications, then headed by Tanaka Kakuei (prime minister during the Lockheed scandal), set down a list of government guidelines for the issuance of television licenses that placed emphasis on "the limitation of monopoly and concentration of mass communications media."[7] It included specific provisions that kept any broadcasting company from owning more than 10 percent of another broadcasting company, any television company from having exclusive rights to broadcast the programs of any other broadcasting company, and newspaper publishing companies and television broadcasting companies from having overlapping directorships. The principles outlined in the ministry guidelines were essentially anti-network, but nevertheless by 1975 massive ties had developed between stations and between newspapers and television companies.

The next event that signified a drastic change in Japanese television broadcasting was the Tokyo Olympics. The October 1964 Games, like the 1940 Games before them, were quickly perceived as an opportunity to show the rest of the world Japan's rapid postwar economic and political development. The Olympics kicked off a giant construction boom in Tokyo (and all over Japan), which included not only the transformation of part of the Yoyogi district into an Olympic park, but also the building of the Shinkansen (Bullet Train), new expressways, and public buildings. In order to display this New Japan properly, great emphasis was placed on total television coverage, including the use of satellite relay broadcasts.

Shortly after satellite relays began with the launching of Telstar by the United States, NHK's Technical Research Laboratory began working on telecommunication satellite technology. Its efforts culminated in the construction of a parabolic antenna and earth station by November 1963. Through some quirk of fate, the early satellite broadcasts between the United States and Japan were to be linked with tragedy. The first was scheduled for November 23, 1963, but instead of receiving the planned 5:30 a.m. statement from President Kennedy, the people of Japan were shocked to find they were watching coverage of his assassination. A second shock came in March 1964, when Ambassador Reischauer was stabbed by a Japanese youth a day before a simultaneous broadcast was planned. The broadcast had to be used to calm feelings on both sides of the Pacific.

The main goal of these efforts was to broadcast the Olympics to the rest of the world. The first experimental broadcast had taken place almost one year before the Olympics, but the technology involved was still quite new and fragile.

After receiving final agreement from NASA to use the Syncom III satellite, the Japanese had only three months to perfect the technology necessary to complete the U.S.-Japan connection. This was accomplished by sending the video signal via Syncom III and the audio signal over the trans-Pacific submarine cable. These two signals were then joined at Point Mugu, California, and broadcast by microwave to Montreal, where they were taped and sent by special jet courier to Europe. The successful satellite relay of the 1964 Olympics led to more international programing, which became commonplace after Intelsat II went into stationary orbit over the Pacific in January 1967.

The importance of the 1964 Olympics was not all international, however, as domestic television sales again soared, this time including color television sets. The first color broadcasting was begun in 1960 by both NHK and the commercial stations, but it was the Olympics that provided the incentive for the first real wave of color television purchases. By 1966 the networks had changed over to nationwide microwave color broadcasting, and in the following year all news broadcasts were in color. While all stations in Japan were capable of broadcasting in color by 1968, only 50 percent of the programing at that time was in color. It was also in 1968 that NHK began charging a special receiver contract rate for color television, even though the household diffusion rate was still only 1.6 percent. Color television production increased dramatically in the early 1970s, however, and by 1976 the diffusion rate had climbed to 70 percent.

During the late 1950s and early 1960s, American programing had a great impact on Japanese television. The total number of American series on Japanese television jumped from nine in 1956 to forty-five in 1960, and reached fifty-four in 1963–1964.[8] No single type of program accounts for this increase as Japanese audiences were continually changing their tastes in American programing. In 1959 the most popular imports were dramas, but gave way in the next two years to westerns, which peaked at thirteen shows in 1961 and then dropped off rapidly to only four in 1962. The detective show grew in popularity at the same time, peaking with eleven shows in 1961.[9] At the height of American programing, in 1963 and 1964, the Japanese could watch a wide variety including fourteen dramas, fourteen comedies, and eighteen sports shows. A viewer on a Friday night in August 1960 could have watched the "Roy Rogers Show" on NET at seven o'clock, the "Alfred Hitchcock Show" on Fuji-TV at eight o'clock, over to NTV at nine o'clock for "Wyatt Earp," switched to "Ben Casey" on TBS at nine-thirty, and then back to Fuji-TV at ten-fifteen for "Gunsmoke." Two of the most popular series in Japanese television history were "Laramie" (41 percent audience share) and "Rawhide" (35 percent), which can still be seen on late night reruns.

One of the main reasons for the large amount of imported programs at this time was the inability of the domestic industry to keep up with the demand for viewing time. During the end of the 1950s and the beginning of the 1960s, many new stations were beginning to broadcast, but the production facilities needed to fill the additional air time did not exist. The film industry also was not willing to allow its films to be broadcast, thereby removing an important source of domestic programing. The movie industry did not change its policy until 1962, and it did not begin to sell older films to television until 1964—the peak year of American programing.

Given the special relationship between the United States and Japan since the occupation and the advanced state of production technology in the United States, it is no surprise that American programs accounted for—and continue to account for—more than 90 percent of imported programing. Importation of American programing began to decline rapidly by 1965 as film companies began to sell films to the networks and share production facilities, and the stations themselves began to develop facilities adequate for large-scale production.

The new facilities were used to create a wide range of programing in the mid–1960s, most of which has continued to be very popular. One of the most important programing innovations was the development of the "wide show" format. The idea for this format was taken from early morning American programing (especially the "Today" show), and included a genial host and a supporting cast who covered a wide range of topical events, news, gossip, sports, and information in short segments. This format had the advantage of allowing a busy morning audience to tune in and out without really missing anything. The original Japanese wide show was "Norio Kijima's Morning Show," which was quickly followed by imitations on all other networks, including NHK. This format soon broke the restraints of its morning slot and moved into the afternoon for housewives who watched television intermittently during their daily chores. It then moved to late night television, where NTV's "11 P. M. Show" has been one of the most popular programs for many years. This show has maintained its popularity by combining the rapidly changing segments of a wide show with talk show–style interviews and a liberal dose of erotica.

Two other important developments that date from this time are the "home drama" and lavish variety spectaculars. Home dramas are about family and home life in Japan and cover roughly the same range of subjects and emotions found in "soap operas"—mother/daughter-in-law relationships, unwanted pregnancies, the seamy side of hospitals, housewife alcoholism, infidelity, and the like. In Japan these types of programs are not confined to afternoon programing, but are also very popular on "golden hour" (prime-time) slots in the evening. Variety/entertainment shows have been a part of Japanese broadcasting since the occupation, but the increase in facilities in the mid–1960s led to an increase in lavishness and a boom in popularity. The contemporary format, based on teenage idols in song-dance-comedy sequences, dates from this period. As the technical quality of such programs improved, so did their ratings and the demand for more entertainment programing. Programing available in the Tokyo metropolitan area in 1965 consisted of 52 percent entertainment programs, 15 percent educational/cultural programs, and 13 percent news programs. People spent 75 percent of their viewing time watching shows that combined entertainment with education and culture.[10]

NHK also set trends in drama, especially with morning serial dramas and historical dramas. In 1961 NHK-G began broadcasting serialized dramas for fifteen minutes each morning at eight-fifteen and these have remained extremely popular ever since. Their content is usually sentimental and similar to home dramas. Also popular are the NHK-G Sunday night historical dramas, which began in 1963 and continue today. While both types of programs are billed as cultural entertainment, both are long on entertainment and short on culture. This is indubitably why they are usually NHK's most popular programs. Indeed, the two programs with the highest nationwide rating in 1983 were the morning serial "Oshin" and the historical drama "Tokugawa Ieyasu." While the commercial stations were polishing their entertainment programing in the mid–1960s, NHK actually reduced its entertainment programing and introduced more educational/cultural programing during prime time. The network has developed a very engaging mixture of cultural and information-oriented (as opposed to entertainment-oriented) documentaries, educational quiz shows, and informational panel and discussion shows, all of which remain very popular.

Educational Television

The Japanese government's desire to have the broadcast media play a significant role in education is clearly stated in the Broadcast Law and the Ministry of Posts and Telecommunications' 1957 licensing guidelines. A further cause was the drive during the occupation to create a democratic political culture through the wide dissemination of knowledge and opinions. Radio broadcasts to the Japanese school system (then extremely disorganized) by SCAP-controlled NHK were begun in December 1945. At that time evacuated students were scattered around the countryside, many facilities were damaged, and censorship of prewar textbooks left them all but unusable. SCAP saw radio as the best way to circumvent these difficulties, and begin educating Japanese children in the principles of democracy. As few radios existed at the time, SCAP distributed 2,735 free radio receivers to elementary schools throughout Japan.

At first, programs broadcast for both pupils and teachers were heavily oriented toward civics and the participatory aspects of democracy, but by 1948 these broadcasts had expanded on both the first and second networks to cover a much wider area of subjects for students, teachers, and parents. In 1953 all such programing was transferred to the second network, which had a coverage of 93 percent and consisted of 15 programs per day broadcast for three and a quarter hours.

During the earliest years of television, most educational programing was broadcast over NHK, and the commercial stations wanted NHK to concentrate exclusively on educational programing. NHK argued that it should have a separate channel for educational programing while maintaining its existing channel for cultural and entertainment programing. The debate was resolved in NHK's favor when the 1957 licensing guidelines were issued. The guidelines stated that NHK would be required to establish a separate educational television station.

NHK-E began broadcasting over its Tokyo station in January 1959, and expanded during the next year to a twenty-seven-station network. Much of the programing was intended for classroom viewing and had a significant effect on Japanese education. In 1961 there was an average of 1.3 television sets in each of Japan's elementary schools and junior high schools, but by 1970 that figure had increased to 8.2 for elementary schools and 3.4 for junior high schools. By 1974, 81.5 percent of Japan's kindergartens, 94.6 percent of the elementary schools, 45.2 percent of the junior high schools, and 51.9 percent of the senior high schools were making use of NHK's educational broadcasts in the classroom.[11] The diffusion of educational television was nationwide, but its impact was most important in the rural areas of Japan, where schools had fewer resources and materials than schools in highly populated areas.

One very important function of NHK-E is its correspondence course facility. At the end of the war, these courses were in great demand, and the NHK station in Sendai set aside a few minutes each week to have teachers give students helpful study hints. This idea was eventually incorporated into the national NHK network and culminated in the establishment of NHK's Correspondence High School in 1963. The school broadcasts classes that the students take at home and supplement with occasional visits to the school's facilities in the western suburbs of Tokyo. Because high school enrollment has skyrocketed since the end of the war, there is a question as to how much longer the service will be needed. In keeping with current demands, NHK-E now broadcasts college-level courses and a "University of the Air," modeled on the BBC's "Open University" began broadcasting in 1985.

Commercial stations also had a role in the beginning of educational television in Japan. In 1957, licensing guidelines were meant to encourage the development of educational television on commercial stations as well as NHK. They created three categories of licensing—ordinary stations with 30 percent educational/cultural programing, semi-educational stations with 29 percent educational and 30 percent cultural programing, and exclusively educational stations with 50 percent educational and 30 percent cultural programing.

There were two major experiments in commercial educational television. The first was Nippon Educational Television (NET), which began broadcasting just a few weeks after NHK-E. NET patterned its broadcasting after that of NHK-E and concentrated on broadcasting to schools. Five years later, Tokyo-TV Channel 12 began operating as the second such station. Tokyo Channel 12 was initiated to broaden science and technology education in Japan, and was supported by the Japan Science Foundation. It started a correspondence school, hoping that the growing science and technology companies in Japan would use its programing for personnel training. Unfortunately, neither Tokyo Channel 12 nor NET was able to compete for advertising money with the much more popular entertainment-oriented stations. In 1970 NET became the Asahi News Network and had its license changed to ordinary status, with Tokyo Channel 12 following suit in 1973.

International Aspects of Japanese Television

It comes as no surprise to learn that Japan is a net exporter of television sets, but it may come as one to learn that Japan is also a net exporter of television programing. Programing imports have been drastically reduced since the peak of the mid–1960s, and in 1980–1981 Japan imported 2,631 programs totaling 2,332 hours, or 5 percent of programing for the year.[12] Not only was this one of the lowest percentages in the world, it was also equivalent to half of the 4,585 hours of programing exported. The United States, however, still maintains a surplus in the bilateral balance of programing (see Tables 4 and 5) and contributed 77.4 percent (1,800 hours) of Japan's total imported programing, followed by Great Britain, which contributed 8.8 percent. The United States was also the leader in coproductions, accounting for 27 percent of the total as compared with 20 percent for multinational productions and 8 percent for British coproductions.

TV-Tokyo led all Japanese stations by importing 10.8 percent of its total programing, twice the national average. This relatively high percentage may have had two causes. TV-Tokyo is not a key station, so its production facilities are more limited than those of the network centers; its programing also relies more heavily on popular documentaries, which are easier to buy than produce.

In comparing imported and domestically produced programs, dramas accounted for 85 percent of imports but only 23 percent of domestic fare. At the same time, non-fiction programing accounted for 11 percent of imports and 65 percent of domestic fare. This is one indication that the Japanese are more interested in entertainment than information from abroad. Those programs ostensibly about foreigners and their countries are often made by the Japanese to suit the Japanese image of the rest of the world.

While foreign programing makes up only a small percentage of the total, much of it is shown in prime time—especially movies. Many of the movies shown on Japanese television are imported and shown on the prime-time movie slot—9:00 to 11:00 p.m. on Sundays, Mondays, Wednesdays, Thursdays, and Saturdays—thus creating a higher viewing rate for imported programing than domestic programing during those time slots. Other than the evening movie slot, foreign television serials such as "Magnum P. I.," "The Fall Guy," "Twilight Zone," and "Rawhide" have been broadcast in the late evening-early morning time slot.

It should be noted here that most films and television programs imported from abroad are dubbed into Japanese, with the exception of the occasional art film or BBC production of Shakespeare on NHK. However, one of the most important technological innovations in recent years has been the widespread use of multiplex broadcasting. This has been put to many uses, including facsimile trans-

Table 4

Imported Programs by Top Ten Countries of Production
(October 1980 - September 1981, Kanto)

Country	Number of Programs	Broadcast Times hrs/mins	%total	Average Household Viewing Rate
1. USA	1,972	1,804:24	77.4%	5.4%
2. Great Britain	209	204:27	8.8%	5.6%
3. Italy	69	111:11	4.8%	6.4%
4. France	53	69:43	3.0%	5.1%
5. West Germany	38	37:33	1.6%	4.9%
6. USSR	26	19:42	0.8%	3.4%
7. Canada	29	16:00	0.7%	2.9%
8. Hong Kong	8	14:37	0.6%	15.7%
9. Sweden	8	8:28	0.4%	7.6%
10. Spain	4	6:07	0.3%	4.0%

Source: International Television Flow Project on Japan, Report 3, Japanese Television Programme Imports and Exports (Tokyo: International Television Flow Project on Japan, 1982), p. 12.

Table 5

Program Exports Broadcast in Japanese or Native
Language by Type and Country in Percentage (1980)

	USA Jpnese	USA dubbed	Brazil Jpnese	Brazil dubbed	Hong Kong Jpnese	Hong Kong dubbed
News	4.3%	0.5%	40.5%	----	----	----
Education/Culture	2.4%	20.9%	1.6%	----	----	0.3%
Music	5.4%	0.6%	24.4%	----	100%	0.5%
Comedy	2.7%	1.0%	----	----	----	----
Drama	67.0%	19.3%	8.8%	----	----	19.9%
Animation	5.2%	50.0%	----	----	----	79.3%
Sports	6.0%	6.9%	24.8%	----	----	----
Other	6.9%	0.7%	----	----	----	----

Source: International Television Flow Project on Japan, Report 3, Japanese Television Programme Imports and Exports (Tokyo: International Television Flow Project on Japan, 1982), p. 27.

mission and broadcasting for the deaf, but its main use has been to broadcast programs in an additional language. One is able to listen to the broadcast in Japanese on one channel and in its original language on the other. In addition, many important domestic programs, including the evening news and sports events, are broadcast in English on the multiplex channel. English is the second language of Japan and accounts for 96.4 percent of bilingual broadcast time.

The development of Japanese domestic programing can be judged by the increase in programing exports, which jumped from 2,200 hours in 1971 to 4,585 hours in 1980–1981. Again, the American connection was the most important, with the United States importing 90 percent (1,357 hours), followed by Italy (768 hours), and Hong Kong (391 hours). Twenty-seven percent of all exported programs were in the Japanese language, of which 97 percent went to the United States and 3 percent to Brazil, while the remaining 73 percent were dubbed. The United States has seven television stations—in Hawaii, California, and New York—that broadcast in Japanese, while Brazil has two in São Paulo.

Exports were led by animated programs (56 percent), followed by dramas (23 percent), and educational/cultural (12 percent). The importance of animation among exports to non-Japanese-language broadcasting stations is demonstrated by the fact that 80 percent of all dramas exported were in Japanese and therefore not primarily intended for non-Japanese-speaking audiences, while only 1 percent of the animated exports were in Japanese. Japanese cartoons have an exceptionally large audience in Western Europe, which accounted for 40.7 percent of total animation exports in 1980–1981. Italy alone consumed 740 hours of Japanese cartoons. Asia accounted for 35.3 percent of animated exports; North America imported only 3.7 percent. The popularity of Japanese cartoons in Europe and Asia is due to their high degree of technical skill and interesting story development, but an increasing concern about the violence in Japanese cartoons has led to a decrease in the number imported by Asian countries.

Contemporary Programing

In order to describe contemporary programing more readily, this section will follow the results presented in Tables 6, 7, and 8. Table 6 is a time survey of all VHF stations in the Tokyo area conducted by the author in late February 1984. All stations surveyed—with the exception of TV Tokyo—are key stations for nationwide networks; it is assumed that they are representative of the nation as a whole. The data in Table 6 are listed in order of magnitude of weekday broadcasting and are measured in average minutes broadcast on weekdays and weekends by the two NHK stations and the five Tokyo commercial stations. Table 7 gives the viewing rates for both the two NHK stations and an aggregate rate for the five commercial stations by time of day for 1982 and 1983. Table 8 lists the Nielsen ratings for the Kanto area (Tokyo and vicinity) for the period February 20–26, 1984.

Table 6

Average Broadcast Time in Minutes Per Weekday and
Weekend Day for NHK-G, NHK-E, and Commercial Stations

	Weekday			Weekend		
	Comm.	NHK-G	NHK-E	Comm.	NHK-G	NHK-E
1. Dramas	289.9	70.0	-----	122.0	107.5	-----
2. Wide Shows	220.6	141.6	-----	77.4	37.5	-----
3. News/Weather	127.6	228.6	-----	86.4	145.5	-----
4. Cartoons	103.4	30.0	-----	51.9	15.0	-----
5. Info/Misc.	94.3	112.0	115.0	106.6	57.0	-----
6. Variety	59.6	56.6	-----	145.8	65.0	-----
7. Movies	46.7	-----	-----	62.7	57.5	-----
8. Documentaries	46.2	-----	-----	52.0	-----	-----
9. Sports	41.2	31.6	20.0	239.6	150.0	180.0
10. Quiz/Game	33.2	-----	-----	46.4	20.0	-----
11. Talk Shows	30.0	30.0	13.3	33.0	12.5	30.0
12. Music	25.0	46.6	8.3	29.0	77.5	45.0
13. Children's	16.0	40.0	5.0	10.5	12.5	-----
14. Education/Cul.	15.0	267.0	854.0	109.0	300.0	795.0

Source: International Television Flow Project on Japan, Report 3, Japanese Television
Programme Imports and Exports (Tokyo: International Television Flow Project on
Japan, 1982), p. 27.

Dramas are by far the most popular fare on television and receive the most
air time. Commercial stations air an average of almost 290 minutes of drama
per weekday and 122 minutes on weekends. In addition, dramas account for
seven of the top thirty programs in the Nielsen ratings, including the top two
positions.

At the top in 1983 was NHK's morning drama, "Oshin," the story of a
young girl who comes from a small village and is indentured by her family to
a rich family in Osaka. She marries the owner of a small shop and through
her efforts builds it into a successful business. The extraordinary popularity of
"Oshin" is due to the ability of most Japanese (especially women) to empath-
ize with the heroine's suffering, patience, hard work, and perseverance. The
program is also effective because it portrays all stages in Oshin's life, and
therefore creates sympathy among all age groups. While "Oshin" does not

Table 7

Viewing Rates for NHK-G, NHK-E, and
Commercial Stations by Year and Time

		Comm.		NHK-G		NHK-E	
		1982	1983	1982	1983	1982	1983
Weekdays	morning	4.5%	4.2%	7.0%	7.9%	0.3%	0.3%
	afternoon	7.9%	7.8%	4.4%	4.8%	0.1%	0.1%
	evening	23.0%	23.3%	7.8%	7.6%	.03%	.04%
Saturday	morning	3.5%	3.5%	6.4%	7.6%	.03%	0.3%
	afternoon	7.3%	7.3%	4.8%	5.0%	.01%	0.3%
	evening	26.6%	27.1%	5.9%	6.2%	.03%	0.5%
Sunday	morning	6.9%	6.8%	5.3%	5.6%	.03%	0.4%
	afternoon	8.9%	12.7%	7.5%	6.6%	0.4%	0.4%
	evening	23.8%	22.5%	9.6%	10.1%	0.4%	0.4%

Source: "Terebi, Rajio Shicho no Genkyo" [The present condition of interest in
television and radio], Hoso Kenkyo to Chosa [Broadcast research and survey] 34
(February 1984), 48.

technically fit the home drama category, it is representative of the genre in
that it presents a highly sentimentalized and romanticized version of the audience's lives.

As mentioned previously, NHK devotes less air time to dramas than the
commercial stations, but its morning dramas and Sunday evening historical
dramas are often at the top of the ratings. While not included in this listing, one
of the most popular programs in early 1984 was "Mountains and Rivers Ablaze"
(30 percent audience share), NHK's Sunday evening historical drama about
Japanese-Americans in the United States during the 1930s and 1940s.

There are several reasons for the popularity of these NHK dramas. Even though
the emphasis may be on drama (as opposed to historical accuracy), the viewer
knows that NHK is the cultural station and therefore feels less guilt than when
watching dramas on a commercial station. Many viewers believe that watching
the Sunday evening historical drama is an educational experience. Secondly, the
morning dramas are more obviously middle-lowbrow but retain their grip on the
audience in two ways. Each episode is short (fifteen minutes), so the harried
householder can watch it while gulping breakfast. It is also shown for a second
time, later in the morning, so that the housewife can sit and relax after the

husband and the children have left the house. In addition, each segment ends with a "hook" that keeps the audience in suspense until the next installment.

The second most popular show is "Mito Komon," one of four *samurai* dramas (the others are "Toyama Kinsan" [# 18], "Murder Is My Business" [# 19], and "Abarembo Shogun" [# 30]), listed in the top thirty. In all but "Murder Is My Business," the hero is a relative of the shogun who goes around the countryside incognito sniffing out injustice and wrongdoing. When the hidden hero has given the venal official or underworld crook enough rope to hang himself, he reveals himself as a high official and, aided by his minions, begins the inevitable swordfight. The *samurai* drama has its roots in the *chanbara* (swordfighting) movies of the 1950s and 1960s, of which *The Seven Samurai* is the best known. In *samurai* dramas the plot is usually secondary to minutely choreographed and highly stylized swordfighting scenes that emphasize artistry of movement rather than gore.

Although wide shows have the second largest exposure time on commercial stations with an average of 220 minutes per weekday and rank third on NHK-G with 141 minutes, only one appears on the Nielsen ratings. NHK-G's early morning "News Wide" (# 4) is atypical of most morning shows in that it has much more hard news reporting, commuter and weather information, and public information mixed with its light features. Other shows in the same time slot tend to concentrate on lurid crimes, movie star scandals, weddings and divorces, and assorted peccadilloes of the famous. "News Wide" is broadcast approximately one hour earlier than the others in order to capture the working audience as it prepares to leave the house, while the others are aimed at the housewife after the family has left for the day.

"News Wide" is popular because the Japanese are voracious consumers of news and information. New programs are consistently among the most popular in Japan. NHK-G devotes more weekday time to news than to any other type of programing (228.6 minutes). News ranks third on the commercial stations (127.6 minutes). In addition, four of the Nielsen top thirty (including "News Wide") are news programs.

As can be seen in Table 3, television overtook newspapers as the preferred source of information for most Japanese during the mid-1960s. However, it was not until approximately ten years later that television revenues began to outstrip those of newspapers (see Table 9). The extensive coverage given the Vietnam War in Japan was a major reason for the increased popularity of television news as it demonstrated quite clearly the impact and immediacy of television reportage.

NHK-G news programing is the most popular in Japan (NHK-E does not have news programing). Not only does NHK-G have three of the four news programs in the Nielsen top thirty and an average of one hundred minutes more news programing per day than the commercial stations, but seven of the top twenty NHK-G programs are news programs.[13] This is one indication that NHK-G's reputation as the "serious" station is directly related to both the quality and the quantity of its news programing.

Table 8

Kanto Area Nielsen Ratings (February 20-26, 1984)

Program	Rating
1. Oshin (NHK home drama)	62.5%
2. Mito Komon (TBS samurai drama)	38.1%
3. Quiz Derby (TBS quiz)	37.5%
4. News Wide (NHK 7:00 a.m. weekday news)	35.4%
5. Of Course, the World! (Fuji-TV quiz)	35.0%
6. Amusing Quiz Seminar (NHK quiz)	34.8%
7. 1984 International Women's Relay Marathon (NTV)	34.3%
8. Kinchan's Open Variety Show (TV Asahi variety)	33.1%
9. The Best Ten (TBS music hit parade)	30.2%
10. Kindon! (Fuji-TV comedy/variety)	29.7%
11. Sazaesan (Fuji-TV cartoon)	29.1%
12. "How Much?" Around the World (TBS quiz)	28.5%
13. Japanese Folktale Cartoons (TBS cartoon)	28.0%
14. Word Association Game (NHK game)	27.8%
15. Pitashikankan (TBS quiz)	26.4%
16. Laughter Score (NTV comic storytelling)	26.3%
17. Fuji Family Wide Show (Fuji-TV murder case special)	25.4%
18. Toyama Kinsan (TV Asahi samurai drama)	25.1%
19. It's All Right to Laugh Special (Fuji-TV comedy wide show)	25.0%
20. Murder Is My Business Part IV (TV Asahi samurai drama)	25.0%
21. News/Weather (NHK 7:00 p.m. weekday news)	24.7%

Table 8 (cont.)

22. Front Line Special Detective (TV Asahi police drama)	24.2%
23. Ask 100 People Quiz (TBS quiz)	23.8%
24. Stewardess Story (TBS romance drama)	23.2%
25. Sunday Evening Report (NTV Sunday evening news)	23.1%
26. Star Mimicry Contest (NTV game/variety)	23.0%
27. Paman (TV Asahi cartoon)	22.9%
28. News/Weather (NHK weekday noon news)	22.3%
29. World Pro Wrestling (TV Asahi sports)	22.3%
30. Abarembo Shogun Part II (TV Asahi samurai drama)	22.2%

Source: "Data Station," Za Terebishion 3 (March 10-16, 1984), 106.

NHK generally reports only weighty domestic and international "hard" news, such as legislative debates, reports from the ministries, international financial news, and Soviet-American negotiations. Stories about other subjects that do appear on NHK also tend to be on the dry side and include such things as the announcement of cultural prizes, archeological discoveries, and very soberly reported crimes. Public scandals are rarely reported on NHK until they become too sensational to ignore. The gravity of the news presented on NHK is accentuated by the staid delivery of the conservatively dressed announcers, who rarely smile or comment on the news they read.

The commercial stations have not been able to match NHK in the seriousness of its news programs and have therefore adopted an American-style "happy news" format. The most popular of these shows is NTV's "Sunday Evening Report," the only commercial news program to be found in the Nielsen ratings (# 25). Broadcasts often begin with whimsical sketches of the day; there is occasional banter between the announcers during the presentation, and "off the cuff" comments are sometimes given; short items of local color or human interest are presented at the end of the show. Of course, even in the happy news format, priority is given to hard news, but on the commercial stations the hard news stories tend to be more crime/vernacular than political/economic.

NHK began to lighten its newscasting a little in 1984 in order to compete with the "happy news" format being offered by many of the commercial stations. It added more human interest and local color stories to the 7:00 and 9:00 p.m. reports and introduced a new program at 10:30 for sports and international news. The format of the sports program is especially upbeat and features a jolly reporter who sometimes does comment on the stories of the day.

Two good examples of the differences in NHK and commercial stations' news

Table 9

Newspaper and Television Advertising Revenues: 1965-1982 (¥ billion)

	Newspapers		Television	
	advertising revenues	increase over previous year	advertising revenues	increase over previous year
1965	123.3	95.1%	111.0	102.7%
1966	133.7	108.4%	124.7	112.3%
1967	161.1	120.5%	150.9	121.0%
1968	188.4	116.9%	174.5	115.6%
1969	225.0	119.4%	204.2	117.0%
1970	265.3	117.9%	244.5	119.7%
1971	268.1	101.1%	259.4	106.1%
1972	302.4	112.8%	284.1	109.5%
1973	372.1	123.0%	352.2	124.0%
1974	394.5	106.0%	391.7	111.2%
1975	409.2	103.7%	420.8	107.4%
1976	455.0	111.2%	509.3	121.0%
1977	506.8	111.4%	584.7	114.8%
1978	570.2	112.5%	653.5	111.8%
1979	655.4	114.9%	750.8	114.9%
1980	708.6	108.1%	788.3	105.0%
1981	757.2	106.9	838.9	106.4%
1982	793.3	104.8%	905.5	107.9%

Source: Nihon Minkan Hoso Renmei, 1983 Nihon Minkan Hoso Nenkan [1983 Japanese commercial broadcasting yearbook] (Tokyo: Nihon Minkan Hoso Renmei, 1984), p. 499.

broadcasting are election returns programs and the coverage given to the Glico/ Morinaga case. NHK consistently runs very statistical and analytical coverage of election returns and is perceived by the Japanese as the representative of the political system. The commercial stations tend to treat the election returns shows as variety shows. The panels analyzing the returns will include comedians and singing talent, as well as legitimate political analysts; the programs will include comedy skits and humorous polls mixed with straight reportage. In the Glico/Morinaga candy-poisoning case, NHK presented a number of very sober reports following police procedure, analyzing videotapes, and interviewing important police officials. The commercial stations played up the police's helplessness in the case for months and vociferously called for a solution. The commercial stations' coverage has also been much more likely to treat criminals as folk heroes who have outwitted the police.

The Japanese cartoons so successful overseas are also popular in Japan. One can find a wide variety of cartoons in Japan, most of which are broadcast betweeen 4:00 and 7:00 p.m. in order to catch the children between school and supper. Of the three listed in the top thirty of the Nielsen ratings, "Sazaesan" (# 11) is a representative family cartoon. It portrays a stereotypical Japanese family of grandparents, parents, and two children going through humorous incidents typical of Japanese middle-class life.

"Japanese Folktale Cartoons" (# 13) is representative of the cultural/educational cartoons that have been gaining in popularity. These cartoons relate famous folktales and fables with morals suitable for young viewers. In addition, there are cartoons and puppet shows that portray famous episodes in Japanese and Western history.

"Paman" (# 27) is one of the many fantasy/comedy cartoons on Japanese television in which apparently normal children have superpowers at their command to use in good deeds. Other popular cartoon themes include girls' romances featuring blond-haired blue-eyed heroines and boys' science fiction adventures.

Television in Japan, like programing in any country with commercial broadcasting, is very sensitive to changes in audience demand. This sensitivity leads to fads in a boom-and-bust cycle. Quiz and game shows are the latest type of program to go through the boom cycle. Quiz shows still have a relatively small amount of air time, but their popularity is demonstrated by the six shows listed in the top thirty, and five in the top fifteen.

Recently the most popular shows tend to be a mixture of information and entertainment, and so NHK offers educational quiz and game shows. NHK's "Amusing Quiz Seminar" (# 6) and "Word Association Game" (# 14) are high on the Nielsen ratings, and are the second and fifth most popular shows on NHK as ranked by a November 1983 survey.[14] In "Amusing Quiz Seminar" a genial host asks historical, scientific, and literary questions to four teams of celebrity guests. When possible, the answers are demonstrated on stage with minilectures on the subject of the day given by experts in the field. The "Word Association Game" is a close copy of the American show "Password," in which two teams of star contestants compete in guessing the synonym of a word read out by the team leader or moderator. The only Japanese innovation is to separate the teams by sexes.

The most popular type of quiz show on commercial television is what might be called the travelogue quiz, made popular by "Of Course, the World!" (# 5).

In this program a member of the staff is shown participating in an unusual situation either in Japan or in a foreign country. The contestants must then answer questions pertaining to the situation. This particular program became so popular it produced a clone called "How Much Around the World" (# 12) in which the contestants have to guess the price of objects in different parts of the world. This type of program continues to be so popular that every commercial station in Tokyo now has its own version.

Tables 6 and 8 do not accurately depict the popularity of sports programing since the surveys were conducted at a time of few major sports events. Only the International Women's Relay Marathon (# 7) appears on the Nielsen's. The Japan Commercial Broadcasters Association's rankings for 1982[15] listed twelve sports programs among the top thirty, including eight baseball games and four *sumo* wrestling matches. While the predominance of weekend sports broadcasting holds true throughout the year, during the baseball season (April-October) there are night games that rotate between the commercial stations almost every evening from 7:30 to 9:00 p.m. NHK also broadcasts an occasional day or night game. One of the peculiarities of sports programing in Japan is that a game goes off the air when the time for that particular slot runs out, not when the game ends. Consequently, one is often left to listen to the end of an exciting game on radio.

The most popular amateur sports events since broadcasting began are the annual spring and summer high school baseball tournaments, broadcast only by NHK. Following professional and amateur baseball in popularity is the traditional Japanese sport of *sumo* wrestling. There are six professional *sumo* tournaments held in Japan every year, each of which consists of fifteen days of bouts. These tournaments are broadcast on NHK-G from 3:30 to 6:00 p.m. daily. Among other sports broadcast from both home and abroad are golf, track and field, rugby, soccer, and tennis.

As can be clearly seen in Table 6, the lion's share of educational/cultural programing is on NHK, but none of the programs comes near the top of the ratings. Most of NHK-E's programing is educational, with occasional sports or arts programing. NHK-G includes a much wider range of programing and emphasizes the cultural. Important programs on NHK-G that have not been mentioned are documentary series on foreign and domestic topics of interest, classical music performances, and contemporary theater. In addition, on almost any day of the week, NHK-G presents traditional storytelling, *kabuki* theater, *noh* drama, traditional puppet plays, *shamisen*, *koto*, and *shakuhachi* music, and a wide range of other traditional arts. One of NHK's most important roles is to preserve the traditional arts and make them available to a far wider audience than was previously possible. The role of the traditional arts in Japan, as a living part of a high-tech society, is in great part due to NHK.

The majority of viewers think of NHK as a supplement to the entertainment-oriented programing available on the commercial stations. A look at Table 2 shows that while NHK-G is most popular in the morning (owing to the morning drama serial and "News Wide"), the commercial stations are more popular in the other time slots—especially during prime time. On the other hand, individual NHK shows tend to have a high popularity. The top eight shows on the 1982 Commercial Broadcasters Association's ratings all came from NHK,[16] and NHK-G accounted for half of the top thirty shows.

As pointed out earlier, Japanese variety shows depend heavily on a Western song-dance-comedy format that is long on atmosphere and short on talent. The music on these programs tends to be popular music or *enka*, the country and western music of Japan. The most popular form of comedy is the two-man stand-up routine called *manzai*. *Manzai* went through a popularity boom in the 1970s but has been recently declining in popularity.

No discussion of variety shows in Japan can be complete without mentioning the precursor of them all, the single most popular program every year since the occupation—the "White Group vs. Red Group Singing Contest." This program has been broadcast live by NHK every New Year's Eve since 1945 and is a lavishly staged singing contest between twenty of the best male and twenty of the best female singers in Japan. Its rating every year stands at either side of 70 percent and it has become a New Year's tradition for many Japanese families. Whether or not a singer is included in the show is a gauge of his or her success in the Japanese music industry.

Critique

There is a debate in the field of Japanese Studies over the uniqueness of Japan. Some argue that its ethnic development, high population density, and lack of racial mixing have created a singular homogeneity among the Japanese. Others argue that the industrialization and the American occupation have westernized Japan to the extent that there are many similarities between it and the rest of the First World. When Japan is examined through its image on television, it is enigmatic and eccentric but not unique. Certainly the form of Japanese television is overwhelmingly influenced by Western, and specifically American, culture. The format for most kinds of programing, from wide shows to dramas to news, has been heavily influenced by, if not directly adopted from, American television. Commercials often reflect Western values and attitudes and star Western talent.

In other and more subtle ways, Japanese television is beginning to reflect a more Westernized society. In the past few years, programs for young people that invite a very non-Japanese satire and criticism of society have sprung up. "We Are the Satire Group" (Fuji-TV) is a new Saturday night prime-time show quite popular with young viewers that parodies both television and society in general. While it has none of the biting satire of Britain's "Monty Python" or America's "Saturday Night Live" and never directly attacks important figures in politics or society, it is adventurous enough to be ranked second by Japanese mothers among the shows they would least like their children to watch.[17] "You" (NHK-E) is another Saturday night program that has gained a significant teenage and young adult audience through its critical appraisal of those aspects of society that affect people in their teens and twenties. The openness of the set and the close contact between the audience and the guests are designed to heighten the confrontation with and criticism of the subject.

Western influences have been important in creating similarities between television in Japan and the West, but there exist many differences, both subtle and blatant. Most important is the difference between the Japanese and Western concept of form and content. In any country television shows have formulas from which little variation is allowed. Once a program becomes popular, plot and characterization tend to be stereotyped in order to ensure continuance of the original popularity. The difference in Japan is that, rather than simply being a means to ensure continued success, this stereotyping is a product of fundamental societal values.

Confucian influences in Japanese art emphasize form over content and stress the modeling of classic forms. These influences have a very strong impact, both positive and negative, on Japanese television. One of the most negative is the repetition of plot and characterization found in most Japanese dramas. The extent to which plots are repeated on Japanese dramas cannot be overstated. In almost every show, events happen in the same sequence week after week. *Samurai*, police, children's, and home dramas rely upon stock formulas and characters that have remained unchanged for years in some cases. Once one has seen a few of these shows, it becomes very easy to predict what will happen in any further episodes. Characters tend to be one-dimensional; acting range is secondary to the precise portrayal of a specific role. For the above reasons, Japanese dramas have little spirit or spontaneity.

The unimportance of content applies to other kinds of programing as well as dramas. Entertainers who appear on variety or game shows have very few apparent individual talents, but are well packaged to appear as *talento*; they seem to base their reputation on appearance rather than entertainment skill. Perhaps it would be more accurate to say that their appearance *is* their entertainment skill. The result is that entertainment in variety shows comes not from the individual talent being showcased, but from the overall effect of the lighting, choreography, and set design of the production numbers. There is also a lack of imagination in scriptwriting, production, and format. Generally, shows on Japanese television are so stereotyped as to become parodies of themselves. Few producers seem to have the ability to go beyond the limits of precedent.

Another negative consequence is the continuance of various discriminatory stereotypes on Japanese television. Female characters are rarely given roles of authority; they are often included for prurient value and are always secondary to male characters. Almost every news, variety, and quiz show is hosted by a male/female team, but the leading role is always the male partner's. The female is, at best, confined to reinforcing or repeating what the other has already said.

In addition, the image of foreigners presented on Japanese television is quite unrealistic. Westerners are presented as being bigger than life in either a positive or a negative way—better athletes, for example, or worse criminals. Third Worlders are at best presented as being likably laughable. In either case, the difference between foreigners and the Japanese is what is most often stressed.

The most positive aspect of the primacy of form and the perfection of role is the creation of excellent images. The Japanese concern with the visual, in combination with their advanced technology, ensures that Japanese television is often very pleasing to the eye. Sets are technically well designed and the photography is excellent. Commercials (regarded by many as the best thing on Japanese television) are the best example of the above, as they are forced to condense their presentation and rely on visual images.

If television is used as a means of relaxation and escape, as opposed to education and enlightenment, it may be very enjoyable to lose oneself among the images without having to bother with the search for ideas. The pleasure of relaxation is heightened, since programs are like oft-read books that can be left and then returned to without losing one's place. Some use television as they would meditation, as a means to empty the mind. Japanese television is very well suited for this type of viewing.

There are some aspects of Japanese television, however, that do not seem to accurately represent the society. The Japanese have a well-deserved reputation for being polite, law abiding, friendly, and peaceful, but one would never know this by watching television. It appears as though there is as much violence on Japanese television as on American television, although the type of violence may be different.[18] Gratuitous violence, including extensive gun fights filmed in slow motion, is an integral part of police dramas. All *samurai* dramas include slashing swordfights. Many children's cartoons and dramas revolve around the destructive powers of beast or machines. Professional wrestling has remained one of the more popular sports since the beginning of television in Japan and is based on blood, screams, and grimaces.

Another problem is the amount of sex and scatology, especially on children's programing. In a survey done by NHK on those programs mothers least want their children to watch,[19] only one of the top ten was violent—professional wrestling. The rest were mentioned because of bad language, bad attitudes, or too much scatalogical humor. At the top of the list (36 percent) was one of the most popular children's programs for many years, "Let's Get Together at 8 O'Clock!" It is a Saturday night variety program starring the Drifters, a comedy group, and is an odd mixture of innocent fun and gross sexual and scatalogical humor. Skits are sometimes staged around flatulence or defecation, and the actors sometimes wear genital symbols.

The prevalence of "cute" scatology in Japanese children's programing is very difficult to explain, but is best portrayed by "Dr. Slump" (# 8 on the Nielsen's and 8 percent on the mothers' worst survey). It is the story of an inventor, his wife, and their robot children. The cartoon seems like many others in the country: The story line is inventive, the characters are creative and humorous, and there are parodies of the real world to amuse the adult audience. However, the favorite game of the main character of the show, Arare-chan, the robot daughter of Dr.

Slump, is playing with feces that have dropped by the side of the road. In one episode, her body was damaged in a fight with a bad robot and Dr. Slump was forced to put her head on a male body while he repaired her real body. She then went around showing all her school friends her new penis. This show is aired on Wednesdays at 7:00 p.m. and is aimed at a preteen and teen audience.

The New Media

This essay is not specifically concerned with the technology of television, but it would be incomplete without mentioning the recent attention in Japan given to the "new media." These consist of new communication technologies including facsimile transmission, videotex or Character And Pattern Telephone Access Information Network System (CAPTAIN), Video Response System, super-high-frequency broadcasting, optical fiber cables, information network systems, cable television, and satellite broadcasting. The broadcast and print media and the government have enthusiastically heralded the advent of revolutionary changes in society that will be brought about by these new technologies.

The new media having the closest relationship to traditional television broadcasting are cable television, satellite broadcasting, and videotex. The emphasis in all of these has been on greater public access to information or increased quality of television reception, rather than access to a wider range of programing.

A new medium that has allowed television to play an expanded role in the dissemination of information has been videotex, in Japan called CAPTAIN, which allows information to be retrieved from data banks and displayed on the home television screen via telephone lines. Experiments in CAPTAIN began in the 1970s and have developed to the point where the first commercial CAPTAIN system has already begun service for the Tokyo area. The service allows consumers to enjoy "talkback" programs, twenty-four hour news services, shopping catalogs, business information, and other information services through their home television sets.

One of the most important events of the new media wave was the launching of Japan's first broadcast satellite in 1984. The stationing of the satellite above Japan and the private sales of parabolic antennas have ensured clear reception for homes in rural communities surrounded by mountains or urban homes blocked by skyscrapers.

In the past, the primary role of both UHF and cable television has been to increase reception in rural and urban areas, respectively. The reception, as opposed to programing, role of cable and UHF is indicated by the existence of only one cable system in Tokyo—and this specializes in English-language broadcasting for apartment complexes and hotels. In addition, there are only two UHF stations in the Tokyo area.

For all the advances in Japanese television technology, the range of programing available is very traditional. Companies are now applying for licenses that will allow them to increase the role of cable broadcasting in the future, but there is nothing to match the entertainment explosion that has occurred in the United States as a result of the development of pay channels such as Home Box Office and Music Television. There is no doubt that the new media will continue to have a significant effect on Japanese society, but it will not be until the early 1990s that the technologies will have an impact on programing.

In areas other than entertainment broadcasting, there is a lag between the development and application of new media technologies—a lag that needs to be explained. The new media cross many traditional boundaries and have created a conflict between the Ministry of Posts and Telecommunications and the Ministry of International Trade and Industry over control and regulation. The interbureaucratic struggle between these two heavyweights has significantly delayed the application of some new media.

Government regulations that control the new media are hard to change, and Japanese society itself is very conservative and slow to change traditional patterns of behavior. Housewives who use their daily shopping trips as social outings are not likely to do their shopping by videotex. A business community that emphasizes interpersonal relations is less likely to use a video conference.

The newspaper/broadcasting giants have a great deal of political clout and are well aware that the wide range of entertainment broadcasting available on cable television in the United States has reduced the major networks' prime-time audience by over 14 percent from 1979 to 1984. They will take whatever steps are necessary to ensure that their companies are not hurt by the new media.

Finally, it may be that Japan is letting other countries take the lead in operationalizing these new technologies in order to learn from their mistakes.

REFERENCE WORKS

The most basic problem confronting foreigners interested in researching Japanese television is the lack of resources in languages other than Japanese. The few non-Japanese-language resources that are available are primarily in English, but they tend to be limited to general overviews of broadcasting history and the broadcasting system or non-analytic compilations of data. There are very few works in English that offer a comprehensive analysis or criticism of any aspect of Japanese television.

The most comprehensive work in English is NHK's *Fifty Years of Japanese Broadcasting*. It is a 430-page narrative history of Japanese broadcasting buttressed by statistical information gathered by various NHK research organizations over the years. Although a description of events in Japanese broadcasting takes precedence over analysis, the book does provide some insight into the ''whys'' of Japanese television broadcasting—past, present, and future. In addition, it contains many valuable sources of data, a chronology of Japanese broadcasting, some primary documents, and maps of the various television broadcasting systems in Japan. This should be the first book read by researchers who cannot read Japanese.

John A. Lent's *Broadcasting in Asia and the Pacific* includes information similar to that found in *Fifty Years*, but most of it is a distillation of the original work. *Broadcasting in Asia and the Pacific* gives a good comparative view of broadcasting in all the various countries of Asia, but because of its scope, the amount of information included on each country is rather limited.

Three very important sources of information in Japanese are the Hoso Kankei Kenkyukai's *Hoso Kankei Bunken Somokuroku*, a bibliography; NHK's *NHK Nenkan*; and the Nihon Minkon Hoso Renmei's *Nihon Minkan Hoso Nenkan*, both yearbooks. The *Hoso Kankei Bunken Somokuroku* is the complete bibliography of all books dealing with broadcasting. The latest edition was published in 1983 and covers all books published from 1967 to 1979. Books published before that are covered in the 1968 edition. The books are categorized under the headings of general broadcasting, broadcast production, commentaries, programing, education and broadcasting, viewer interest, broadcasting and the world, and advertising, to name but a few.

The importance of the above bibliography is rivaled only by the two yearbooks. The format of the two works is similar, but the contents vary. The NHK yearbook reports on the new media, the organization of NHK, NHK facilities around the country, the programs broadcast by NHK over the year, viewer interest, research conducted by NHK, and international broadcasting. The *Nippon Minkan Hoso Nenkan* covers television production and programing, the programs shown over the year, viewer interest, the new media, advertising, and a description of most of the commercial broadcasting companies in Japan.

Japanese government, or semi-public, agencies produce a number of reports, pamphlets, and booklets relevant to Japanese television. The Foreign Press Center publishes a series of booklets entitled ''About Japan'' that includes *Japan's Mass Media*, a description of all Japanese mass media, print and broadcast, with statistical information. The Prime Minister's Office has a research division that constantly monitors Japanese society and often produces papers in English on the results of their findings. Those interested in the relationship between the broadcast media and other forms of leisure activity should read their work, *Basic Survey of Life in Japan: People's Daily Hours and Leisure Activities*. The Ministry of Posts and Telecommunications produces a *Report on the Present State of Communications in Japan*, which describes not only present conditions, but government policies toward the various communication media in Japan.

The single largest organization conducting research on television is NHK. NHK produces a wealth of information every year through its own publishing house; this includes compilations of statistics like *Nihonjin to Terebi* as well as more analytical and descriptive works like *Terebi Jiyannarizumu no Sekai: Genba kara no Hasso*. The first work reports the findings of surveys on the viewing habits of Japanese families, the impact of television on the family structure, and differences in viewing habits between the various regions of Japan. The second is a more descriptive and analytical look at what goes into the reportage of news on Japanese television.

There are two works, one in English and the other in Japanese, that place Japanese television in its international context. The International Television Flow Project's report on Japan, *Japanese Television Programme Imports and Exports*, includes a lengthy analysis of the relationship between imported and domestic programing in Japan and the effect of Japanese programs on the rest of the world. In addition, there are a few appended articles on related subjects, including one excellent article by the late Ithiel de Sola Pool and Iwao Sumiko on the effect of the television program "Shogun" on American and Japanese audiences. Kawatake Kazuo's *Terebi no naka Gaikoku Bunka* covers parallel topics like the impact of foreign programing on Japanese audiences, television news as international communication, and the impact of American programing, but with more narration and description and less statistical data.

There are any number of descriptive and critical works on Japanese television in Japanese, and only a few of the best and most recent will be mentioned here. One should read Kinoshita Egi's *Shosetsu NHK* as it not only criticizes Japanese television generally, but singles out NHK and its broadcasting policy. It is a good balance to the strong pro-NHK bias that runs through much publishing on Japanese television (especially as much of the publishing done is by NHK). Okamoto Yoshihiko's *Terebi yo Ogorunakare* is a very potent criticism of the lack of humanism in contemporary Japanese television, and in some way represents a backlash against the thraldom of high-tech culture. An older work, but still relevant today, is Kanazawa's *Terebi no Ryoshin: Johoka Shakai ni okeru Kadai*. Kanazawa discusses freedom of conscience in information societies and the need for broadcasters to police their own standards of broadcasting.

Some of the more descriptive works include Sato Tadao's *Terebi no Shiso: 1960 nendai—1970 nendai*. This wide-ranging book gives the author's views on the development of television in the 1960s and 1970s, including the effect of television on the arts, television as a business, the eclipse of the movie industry, and vulgarity on television. NHK's *Terebi de Hataraku Ningenshudan* looks at the different groups of people involved in television, the jobs they do, and their contribution to Japanese culture. Shirai Ryuji's *Terebi Shoseki* is an amusing anecdotal narrative history of the fledgling years of Japanese television as told by an insider. Both *Terebi Shoseki* and *Hoso Bunka Ron*, edited by Tsuganezawa Satchiro and Tamiya Takeshi, are collections of articles covering a wide range of related subjects including culture in broadcasting, the socialization of broadcasting, broadcasting and language, and the effects of advertisements.

The recent new media "boom" is reflected by the number of books in the field recently published. Most of them, like *Niyu Medeia no Jidai: Hoso Esei no Subete*, edited by Hoso Kenkei Kenkyukai, and *Hoso to Niyu Medeia*, edited by Sunobe Yoshio, are descriptions of the present condition of satellite broadcasting, facsimile transmission, and videotex and a look into the future of broadcasting technology. Others, like Shiga Nobuo's *Terebi, Niyu Medeia 1984*, take a more critical approach to both the application of the new media and television broadcasting's use of the new technologies.

There are a number of popular weekly or biweekly magazines with titles like *The Television* and *Television Guide* that combine weekly program listings with articles on popular entertainers, shows, and ratings. While the subject matter is by necessity very light, they should not be discounted as valuable research sources of information. They give a very good subjective picture of the trends of the broadcasting industry, including consumer demand, audience tastes, and culture mores.

The best "serious" journals are two monthly publications, NHK's *Hoso Kenkyu to Chosa* [Broadcast research and survey] and the privately published *Hoso Bunka* [Broadcast culture]. These two journals are relatively similar and contain analytical articles on various topics including the effect of television on viewers; the role of the new media; and television and socialization. There are also regular features that include sections on international and domestic broadcasting and ratings and a bibliography covering books and periodical articles on television and broadcasting. The major differences between the two journals stem from *Hoso Kenkyu to Chosa*'s NHK connection. It publishes much more hard statistical data because it has the research facilities of the NHK organization supporting it. On the negative side, however, most information presented in the journal tends to be about NHK, to the exclusion of information about commercial broadcasters.

RESEARCH COLLECTIONS

Anyone interested in doing research on public broadcasting in Japan should first make contact with the NHK Public Opinion Research Institute. The institute, staffed by some forty members, conducts research on a wide range of subjects related to television and broadcasting. Its special area of interest is audience/ broadcaster relations.

While it is helpful to have a personal introduction to someone on the staff, the staff is generally helpful, friendly, and willing to aid researchers. Although it is best to speak Japanese, there are some members of the staff who may be able to help English speakers. The institute is located in the heart of Tokyo at 2–1–1 Atago, Minato-ku, and anyone wishing to visit should call them at 03–433–5211.

The NHK Broadcast Museum and Library are located in the same building ·as the Public Opinion Research Institute and are also helpful and interesting. The library is a bit smaller than it should be (relative to the research capabilities of the institute), but it contains a good selection of periodicals and books as well as the Japanese and English publications of the Public Opinion Research Institute.

The Nihon Minkan Hoso Renmei (Japanese Commercial Broadcasters' Association or Nikan) also has an excellent research facility and library available to researchers. Those wishing to research commercial television, as opposed to

NHK, should contact Nikan at 03–265–7481. They are located on the fifth floor of the Bungeishinju Building in the Kioii-cho section of Minato-ku, downtown Tokyo. For those who cannot speak Japanese, ask for the International Department and you will be connected with an English-speaking staff member.

The National Diet Library is the library for the national legislature and is a repository for books on all areas of Japanese Studies. Most of the Japanese-language books on Japanese television can be found there, but their English-language collection is rather slim (but, then again, there are few books on the subject in English). The library itself is located next to the Diet and can be contacted at 03–581–2331.

Another very helpful institution is the Foreign Press Center, located on the sixth floor of the Japan Press Center. The Foreign Press Center has a reading room containing numerous government and semi-government publications in English, which are intended to help foreign journalists in Japan, but the service can be used by the public as well. Some of the publications available are free, but even those that must be purchased are generally very inexpensive. For more information on Foreign Press Center services, call 03–501–3401/4; many staff members can speak English.

The reader is advised to secure a personal introduction, however tenuous, to some member of the above institutions. All of these institutions are willing to help researchers, but they also have a host of demands on their time. Given the strong emphasis on interpersonal relations in Japanese society, a personal introduction tends to open more doors and better facilitate the researcher's entrée into the field.

NOTES

1. Ministry of Posts and Telecommunications, *Report on Present State of Communications in Japan* (Tokyo: Japan Times, 1984), p. 54.

2. Foreign Press Center, *Japan's Mass Media* (Tokyo: Foreign Press Center, 1982), p. 38.

3. Nippon Hoso Kyokai, *Fifty Years of Japanese Broadcasting* (Tokyo: Nippon Hoso Shuppan Kyokai, 1977), p. 227.

4. Ibid., p. 231.

5. Ibid., pp. 247, 351.

6. Ibid., pp. 248–59.

7. Ibid., pp. 238–39.

8. Ibid., p. 267.

9. International Television Flow Project on Japan, Report 3, *Japanese Television Programme Imports and Exports* (Tokyo: International Television Flow Project on Japan, 1982), p. 8.

10. NHK, *Fifty Years of Japanese Broadcasting*, p. 334.

11. Ibid., pp. 289–90.

12. Unless otherwise stated, all data presented in this section are taken from *Japanese Television Programme Imports and Exports* and refer to the year 1980–1981.

13. "Terebi, Rajio Shicho no Genkyo" [The present condition of interest in television and radio], *Hoso Kenkyu to Chosa* 34 (February 1984), 48.
「テレビ、ラジオの視聴の現況」　放送研究と調査　３４　１９８４．２：４８
14. Ibid.
15. Nihon Minkan Hoso Renmei, *1983 Nihon Minkan Hoso Nenkan* [1983 Japanese commercial broadcasting yearbook] (Tokyo: Nihon Minkan Hoso Renmei, 1984), p. 508.
日本民間放送連盟　「１９８３　日本民間放送年鑑」　東京　日本民間放送連盟　
１９８４　ｐ．５０８
16. Ibid.
17. Ken Sugano and Yoshimitsu Abe, "Hahaoya ga Yoji ni Misetakunai Bangumi" [Programs mothers don't want their little children to watch], *Hoso Kenkyu to Chosa*, 33 (November 1983), 37.
菅野謙、阿部喜充　「母親が幼児にみせたくない番組」　放送研究と調査　３３
１９８３．１１：３７
18. Sumiko Iwao, Shigeru Hagiwara, and Ithiel de Sola Pool, "Japanese and U. S. Media: Some Cross-Cultural Insights," *Journal of Communications* 31 (Spring 1981), 32.
19. Sugano and Abe, p. 37.

SELECTED BIBLIOGRAPHY

Eguti, H. and H. Ishinobe, eds. *International Studies of Broadcasting with Special Reference to Japanese Studies.* Tokyo: Nippon Hoso Shuppan Kyokai, 1971.
Eto, Fumio, et al., eds. *Taisho Bunka no Sozo* [The creation of popular culture]. Tokyo: Kenkyusha, 1979.
江藤文夫他編「大衆文化の創造」　東京　研究社　１９７９
Foreign Press Center. *Japan's Mass Media.* Tokyo: Foreign Press Center, 1982.
Geller, Judith F. *Japanese Public Broadcasting, A Promise Fulfilled: A Report to the Aspen Institute and the Carnegie Commission.* New York: Aspen Institute for Humanistic Studies, 1979.
Hoso Bangumi Kojo Kyogikai, ed. *Goraku Bangumi to Sono Hoko wo Saguru: Joho Shaiai ni okeru Hoso to Kurashi* [A study of entertainment programs and where they are going: Life and programs in the information society]. Tokyo: Gendai Journalism Shuppankai, 1971.
放送番組向上協議会編　「娯楽番組とその方向をさぐる――情報社会における放送と暮らし」　東京　現代ジャーナリズム出版会　１９７１
Hoso Hiyo Kondankai, ed. *Niyu Medeia no Jidai: Hoso Esei no Subete* [New media age: All about satellite broadcasting]. Tokyo: Kioii Shobo, 1981.
放送批評懇談会編　ニューメディアの時代――放送衛星の全手」　東京　紀尾井書房　１９８１
Hoso Kankei Kenkyukai, ed. *Hoso Kankei Bunken Somokuroku: 1967–1979* [Bibliographical catalog of broadcasting: 1967–1979]. Tokyo: Nigai Association, 1983.
放送関係研究会編　「放送関係文献総目録　１９６７～１９７９」　東京　内外アソシエーツ　１９８３
Inoue, Hiroshi. *Terebi to Shakaigaku* [Television and sociology]. Kyoto: Sekai Shishosha, 1979.
井上宏　「テレビと社会学」　京都　世界思想社　１９７９

International Television Flow Project on Japan. *Japanese Television Programme Imports and Exports*. Report 3. 101 Tokyo: International Television Flow Project on Japan, 1982.

Kanazawa, Kakutaro. *Terebi no Ryoshin: Johoka Shakai ni okeru Kadai* [The conscience of television: Subjects of the information society]. Tokyo: Tokyodo Shuppan, 1970.

金沢覚太郎　『テレビの良心ーー情報化社会における課題』　東京東京堂出版

１９７０

Kawatake, Kazuo, ed. *Terebi no naka Gaikoku Bunka* [Foreign culture in television]. Tokyo: Nippon Hoso Shuppan, 1983.

川竹和夫編　『テレビの中の外国文化』　東京　日本放送出版　１９８３

Kinoshita, Egi. *Shosetsu NHK* [NHK novel]. Tokyo: Sanichi Shobo, 1983.

木下英治　『小説ＮＨＫ』　東京三一書房　１９８３

Kishida, Isao. *Terebi Hosojin: Watashi no Shigoto* [Television broadcaster: My job]. Tokyo: Tokyo Keizai Shinposha, 1979.

岸田功　『テレビ放送人ーー私の仕事』　東京　東洋経済新報社　１９７９

Kobayashi, Yosoji. *Vocation Culturelle de la Television au Japon*. Paris: Institut de France, 1977.

Kondo, Haruo. *Masukomi: Bunka no Tenbo* [Mass communication: A cultural view]. Tokyo: Rishosha, n.d.

近藤春雄　『マスコミーー文化の展望』　東京　理想社

Kuramoto, So. *Shin-Shinterebi Jijo* [Aspects of new television]. Tokyo: Bungeshunji, 1983.

倉本聡　『新新テレビ事情』　東京　文芸春秋　１９８３

Lent, John A., ed. *Broadcasting in Asia and the Pacific*. Philadelphia: Temple University Press, 1978.

Ministry of Posts and Telecommunications. *Report on Present State of Communications in Japan*. Tokyo: The Japan Times, 1984.

Nakanishi, Naomichi. *Changes in Mass Media Contact Times: Analysis of Results of National Time Use Survey*. Tokyo: NHK Public Opinion Research Institute, 1982.

Nakano, Osamu. *Gendai no Joho Kodo* [Modern man's information behavior]. Tokyo: Nippon Hoso Kyokai, 1981.

中野　収　『現代人の情報行動』　東京　日本放送協会　１９８１

Nihon Minkan Hoso Renmei. *Nihon Minkan Hoso Nenkan* [1983 Japanese commercial broadcasting yearbook]. Tokyo: Nihon Minkan Hoso Renmei, 1984.

『日本民間放送年鑑』　東京　日本民間放送連盟　１９８３

Nippon Hoso Kyokai. *Fifty Years of Japanese Broadcasting*. Tokyo: Nippon Hoso Shuppan Kyokai, 1977.

————. *A Guide to the NHK Public Opinion Research Institute*. Tokyo: NHK Public Opinion Research Institute, 1982.

————. *Kazoku to Terebi* [The family and television]. Tokyo: Nippon Hoso Shuppan Kyokai, 1981.

日本放送協会　『家族とテレビ』　東京　日本放送出版協会　１９８１

————. *Nihonjin to Terebi* [The Japanese and television]. Tokyo: Nippon Hoso Shuppan Kyokai, 1981.

『日本人とテレビ』　東京　日本放送出版協会　１９８１

————. *1983 NHK Nenkan* [1983 NHK yearbook]. Tokyo: Nippon Hoso Shuppan Kyo-kai, 1984.

「１９８３ＮＨＫ年鑑」　東京　日本放送出版協会　１９８４

————. *Saikin Shicho Tokusei* [Contemporary characteristics of people's interest]. Tokyo: Nippon Hoso Shuppan Kyokai, 1981.

「最近視聴特性」　東京　日本放送出版協会　１９８１

————. *Terebi de Hataraku Ningenshudan* [Human groups working in television]. Tokyo: Nippon Hoso Shuppan Kyokai, 1980.

「テルビで働く人間手段」　東京　日本放送出版協会　１９８０

————. *Terebi Jiyannarizumu no Sekai: Genba kara no Hasso* [The world of television journalism: An on-the-spot report]. Tokyo: Nippon Hoso Shuppan Kyokai, 1981.

日本放送協会　「テレビジャーナリズムの世界－－現場からの発想」　東京　日本放送出版協会　１９８１

Okamoto, Yoshihiko. *Terebi yo Ogorunakare* [Television, don't be so proud of yourself]. Tokyo: Bakushusha, 1983.

岡本義彦　「テレビよおごるなかれ」　テレビ　麦秋社　１９８３

Prime Minister's Office. *Basic Survey of Life in Japan: People's Daily Hours and Leisure Activities*. Tokyo: Foreign Press Center, 1982.

Sato, Tadao. *Terebi no Shiso: 1960 nendai-1970 nendai* [Thoughts and ideas on television: 1960s-1970s]. Tokyo: Chikuna Shuppansha, 1978.

佐藤忠男　「テレビの思想－－１９６０年代～１９７０年代」　東京　筑摩出版社　１９７８

Shiga, Nobuo. *Terebi, Niyu Medeia 1984* [Television and the new media: 1984]. Tokyo: MG Shuppan, 1984.

Shirai, Ryuji. *Terebi Shoseki* [On television novel]. Tokyo: Kioii Shuten, 1983.

白井隆二　「テンビ創世紀」　東京　紀尾井書房　１９８３

Shizawa, Shigeru. *Documento. Terebi Jidai: 25 nenshi no Ningen Dorama* [Documentary. The age of television: The 25-year history of human drama]. Tokyo: Kodansha, 1978.

塩沢茂　「ドキュメント　テレビ時代－－２５年史の人間ドラマ」　東京　講談社　１９７８

Sunobe, Yoshio, ed. *Hoso to Niyu Medeia* [Broadcasting and the new media]. Tokyo: Nippon Hoso Shuppan, 1983.

須之部淑男編　「放送とニューメディア」　東京　日本放送出版　１９８３

Terebi [Television]. Tokyo: Kawade Shobo, 1983.

「テレビ」　東京　河出書房　１９８３

"Terebi, Rajio Shicho no Genkyo" [The present condition of interest in television and radio]. *Hoso Kenkyu to Chosa* [Broadcast research and survey] 34 (February 1984).

「テレビ、ラジオの視聴の現況」　放送研究と調査　３４　１９８４．２：４８

Tokyo Television Staff, eds. *Terebi no Uragawa Marumie Joho* [A real behind-the-scenes look at television]. Tokyo: Seinen Shokan, 1984.

東京テレビジョンスタッフ、編　「テレビの裏側まるみえ情報」東京　青年書館　１９８４

Tsuganezawa, Satchiro, and Takeshi Tamiya, eds. *Hoso Bunka Ron* [Comments on broadcast culture]. Tokyo: Minerva Shoten, 1983.

津金沢聡広、田宮武編　『放送文化論』　東京　ミネルヴァ書店　１９８３

United Nations Educational, Scientific, and Cultural Organization. *Rural Television in Japan: A Report on an Experiment in Adult Education*. Paris: UNESCO, 1960.

7

Sports

WILLIAM R. MAY

Sport is one of a variety of cultural expressions that can serve as a text for the examination and interpretation of a society's lived culture. In the sports that a group of people choose to play and that capture their imaginations, one is provided with vivid portrayals of the system of meanings that inform that society's orientation to experience.*

This cultural approach to sport begins with Clyde Kluckhohn's definition of culture as "those selective ways of feeling, thinking, and reacting that distinguish one group from another—ways that are socially transmitted and learned (with of course, some changes through time) by each new generation."[1] Clifford Geertz has suggested that an interpretation of culture requires an analysis of the symbols and symbolic processes that provide the handles for the thoughts and feelings, actions and reactions specific to a culture.[2] In this vein, Howard Slusher in his philosophical contemplation of sport has observed that sport offers "a grouping of myths, symbols, and rituals that facilitate the total experience."[3]

Sport is not merely the manifestation of the system of meanings that guide the culture, but is also an important vehicle for the transmission of the values that must be learned to participate in the culture. Sport is an important venue for the study of popular culture and the source of yet keener insights into the nature of a culture.

A few of the questions that a cultural approach to sport in Japan might seek to understand are: Why has baseball become the national passion? Why does cricket remain one of the few Western sports in Japan to have never enjoyed an ardent following? Why do thousands of spectators pack the Kokugikan every year to watch *sumo*, while only a handful of admirers attend the semi-annual

---

* Japanese names in this essay are in the Japanese order of family name, given name.

kemari exhibitions? Why do individually oriented activities, such as kendo, judo, golf, and tennis, have millions of adherents, while team sports, such as soccer and basketball, attract only a fraction of that number? Cursory and superficial explanations of these questions have been offered, often within the realm of some "*samurai*" notion of sport. This essay, however, is an attempt to stimulate and encourage a deeper and more carefully considered interpretation of sport in Japan.

What is sport? This question has been confronted by a number of scholars from a variety of intellectual orientations, often demonstrating that it may be impossible to arrive at clear-cut definitions for play, games, and sport. One need only to briefly consider Christian K. Messenger's compilation of descriptions of sport to begin to appreciate the "welter of meanings" and the "multiplicity of associations" that have already accumulated in the short course of sport studies.[4] Sport has been described as its own system, an institutionalized game, a dramatic model for our psychological lives, a natural religion, and the rationalization of the Romantic in the modern world, to list a few of the models of sport listed by Messenger.

The task of defining "sport" is further complicated in Japan by its association and confusion with the martial arts tradition and its location within the objectives of physical education. Western sports introduced to Japan before the Pacific War underwent a process of Japanization that emphasized the spiritual aspects of sports training and recast sports vocabulary in martial terms, giving words like *yakyudo* (the way of baseball) currency before the war. The martial arts, on the other hand, underwent processes of "sportification," and more recently "salaryman-ization," in order to fit the rhythms of modern Japanese life.[5] Efforts to describe the martial arts as the traditional sports of Japan may be misguided since the martial arts were developed for combat effectiveness and later spiritual refinement, not for athletic competition. The other complication in attempting to discuss sport in Japan is its equation with the idea of *taiiku* (body nurturing). While the term *supotsu* has come into common usage in Japanese today, *taiiku* is still used interchangeably for physical education and sport. The objectives of sport are seen as extensions of physical education's goals of nuturing strong, healthy bodies and resilient spirits.

Although the problems of defining "sport" are manifold, a working definition to guide this essay has been borrowed from Allen Guttman's *From Ritual to Record: The Nature of Modern Sports*.[6] Guttman defines "sport" as those physical contests within a category of competitive games that are a subset of organized play, or, in short, "playful physical contests." He then separates modern sport from earlier sports of ancient, medieval, and preindustrial societies by listing seven characteristics he has observed in modern sport: secularism, equality of opportunity to compete, and, in the conditions of competition, specialization of roles, rationalization, bureaucratic organization, quantification, and the quest for records.

This essay approaches sport in Japan as those "playful physical contests" that have developed in and along with the emergence of a modern Japan. As an aspect of Japan's popular culture, sport is seen as an object of popular imagination as well as a mass participatory phenomenon. Yet, having arrived at this understanding of sport, one realizes that modern sport in Japan was shaped by a number of influences from the past. Therefore, the first step is backward.

HISTORICAL SURVEY

To suggest that the development of sport in Japan is a necessary aspect of her modernization is not to deny that a "playful" spirit or "competitive" activities existed in early and medieval Japan. Indeed, the activities and attitudes held by the early Japanese regarding play, as well as physical and spiritual discipline, have had a profound influence upon the shape of sport in modern Japan.

Looking back into the mists of Japanese mythology, it was a *sumo* wrestling match that determined which tribe would exercise sovereignty over the archipelago. As recorded in the *Kojiki* [The record of ancient matters] (A.D. 712), the brash young son of the ruler of Izumo (Japan), Takeminakata-no-Kami, sought a test of strength with the messenger of the divine race, Takemikazuchi-no-Kami. Upon clasping hands, the young mortal realized the folly of his challenge and quickly capitulated. This tale is obviously part of the mix of mythology and genealogy compiled by the Yamato court as an official history designed to legitimate the clan's rule and glorify their reign. Nevertheless, this meeting of Japanese titans hints at a couple of important considerations.

Hikoyama Kozo noted that as a result of the victory, "the divine race took over the land and succeeded in effecting an important national and social unity over the race."[7] Although written just prior to the Pacific War during a time when Japanese writers were celebrating the superiority of the Japanese race, Hikoyama's assertion is but one example of the "uniqueness of the Japanese" myth that has informed the Japanese worldview throughout the ages.

Representative of the divine will as it was, *sumo* was bound to Shinto rituals and observances. P. L. Cuyler notes that the results of *sumo* matches performed at shrine festivals in early Japan were considered oracles of good fortune and bountiful harvest or of hard times.[8] The early Japanese court also enjoyed watching ceremonial *sumo* matches, staged for their pleasure by wrestlers from the outlying provinces.

The early histories are concerned with the nobility and their divine ancestry and reveal little about the mass of people who populated the islands and their physical activities. It can be assumed, however, that rather than having the time for recreational pursuits, the ancient Japanese were preoccupied with survival, sustenance, and security. Archery, *sumo*, and dance developed from the utilitarian activities of hunting for food, training for battle, and praying for abundant crops.

Along with the dancing and ceremonial *sumo* wrestling of shrine observances, the Japanese hoped to elicit the favor of the gods with offers of *sake*. They believed that liquor would make the gods as happy as it made mortals. From the earliest Chinese dynastic histories that reported that people of the Wa (Japan) were "fond of liquor," to Jared Taylor's recent critical view of the Japanese, in which he insists that drinking is a Japanese excuse to "behave like children," inebriation has been and is fundamental to the Japanese approach to relaxation and play.[9]

The sixth and seventh centuries witnessed several social and cultural changes in Japan wrought by the importation of Chinese civilization. Among the continental pastimes embraced by the Japanese nobility, *kemari* (kickball) especially appealed to the refined sensibilities of those who were at leisure to engage in parlor games of verbal ingenuity and delight in *yukikorogashi* (rolling snowballs).[10]

Kemari in Japan was not a competitive game as it had been in China, but rather a cooperative effort by the players to keep the ball in the air through an intricate pattern of kicking and passing. The symbolism is rich, and all aspects of the game are intended to enhance the aesthetic experience of the players who act out a sense of universal order and harmony. The playing area is bounded by four trees for the four seasons. A stick of incense times the play. Even the ball, made of bamboo and deerskin, reverberates with a hollow and lonely "pon" when kicked.

Kemari has enjoyed a minor role in Japanese history and literature. The young leaders of the Taika Reforms of 645 were brought together during a game of *kemari*. *Kemari* became an integral part of the Fujiwara culture of elegant pursuits described in the *Tale of Genji* (c. A.D. 1000). The heroes of Lady Murasaki's novel, Genji and Kaoru, were described as connoisseurs of the game.

Another view of court life is revealed in the *Chojugiga* [Animal scrolls] (c. 1200), which made a burlesque of the decadence of the nobility. As an early form of cartoon, the scrolls were illustrations of animals in human dress engaged in a variety of activities including wrestling, archery, and swimming.

When the power of the increasingly effete court was usurped by military forces, the emphasis in sports also changed. Although some of the *bushi* (warriors) affected the lifestyle of the court, others honed their martial skills, giving rise to various schools of martial arts and the use of weapons. *Sumo* was no longer performed merely for the amusement of the court, but became an important part of the warriors' training, more like jiujutsu than the modern sport known in Japan today. The *bushi* also sharpened their archery skills with *yabusame* (mounted archery) and *inuoumono* (shooting dogs).

The tendency in Japan's sport and martial history is to emphasize the development of the martial arts from the rise of the *samurai* class in the twelfth century to the decline of the Tokugawa shogunate in the mid-nineteenth century. This view stresses the evolution of bodies of techniques into schools of spiritual discipline. Over 9,000 different schools of martial arts have been cataloged.[11] *Samurai* education in the Tokugawa clan schools pursued an ideal of *bunbu ryodo*, the unification of literary and martial skills. However, the *samurai*-centered scheme of Japanese sport history fails to provide an adequate picture of the recreational activities of other classes of Japanese society.

The emerging class of merchants in Tokugawa Japan developed their own bawdy diversions and pleasures. *Sumo*, *kabuki*, and the amusement quarters were the major attractions, or distractions, of the monied sons of Edo and Osaka. Professional *sumo* began to assume some of its modern characteristics in an environment away from war and sustained by the merchants' patronage. Recreation that might be seen as physical exercise for the merchant class of this time—such as riding boats and going for hikes—however, was less for health reasons and more for a chance to appreciate the beauty of nature.

For the people who had neither the leisure nor the money, recreation was offered by the many shrine festivals. These were opportunities for drinking, dancing, and other raucous behavior, such as carrying the *mikoshi* (a portable Shinto shrine) through the village or ward of the local shrine. The *mikoshi* is borne upon the shoulders of a crowd of people who dance and chant their way through the streets and alleys of the community. The violent shaking of the *mikoshi* is thought to reflect the turbulent nature of the diety within the shrine. Festivals were also occasions for tests of strength like *sumo* or *chikara ishi*, which was an early form of weightlifting in which the contestants lifted huge rocks, bales of rice, and barrels of *sake*.

The Tokugawa period of Japanese history is often depicted as a period of seclusion, although the Japanese remained informed of international developments through their contacts with the Dutch in Nagasaki and their dealings with the Chinese. One history of sports in Japan notes that the Dutch put on a demonstration of fencing, social dance, and horseback riding for the shogun in the early eighteenth century. *Komo Zatsuwa* [Tales of the redhairs] reported in 1787 that foreign seamen on their island in Nagasaki were seen playing badminton.[12]

The period of seclusion was brought to an end when Commodore Perry concluded a treaty with the shogunate. In addition to treaty negotiations, both sides engaged in some early sports diplomacy. On the Japanese side, a number of *sumo* wrestlers "enormously tall in stature and immense in weight of flesh" wrestled before their American guests, although the foreign observers labeled it a "disgusting exhibition" and a "very unsatisfactory trial of strength."[13] It may have been, though, that these were reactions to the defeat of three American sailors by the wrestler Koyanagi. The Americans, for their part, put on a minstrel show and gave a demonstration of the manly art of pugilism.[14]

Realizing their precarious position before the advancing empires of the West, the Japanese raced to affect the trappings of Westernization, spurred on by the proponents of "civilization and enlightenment." The leading expositor of this notion, Fukuzawa Yukichi, wrote extensively about conditions in the West and the requirements of education for a new Japan, but seems to have ignored, or at least not trifled with, physical education or sport.

Fukuzawa, however, did recognize the importance of physical exercise. He recalls in his autobiography that he grew up with hard work and exercise. He studied *iai* (the art of drawing the sword) as a youth, and, when he left home to take up Western studies, took along a practice sword for exercise. In his later years, Fukuzawa's move away from ideas of "civilization and enlightenment" was accompanied by an end to his "coddling" himself and a renewed interest in practicing *iai* and pounding rice.[15] Kimura Kichiji has drawn from Fukuzawa's many writings in an attempt to demonstrate that the idea of physical exercise was fundamental to his approach to notions of people's rights, the rights of nations, and later the idea of "rich nation, strong military."[16]

Several Japanese, like Fukuzawa, scoured Europe and America for the institutional and technological knowledge that would inform Japan's modernization. Sport, although not on the agenda of desired information, was prominent in the societies the Japanese chose to visit and formed a separate body of knowledge brought home by Japan's early overseas students. Hiraoka Hiroshi was one of the early travellers and spent time in Boston studying English, learning about railroads, and developing a passion for baseball. When Hiraoka returned to Japan in 1877, he brought along a number of bats, balls, and gloves and in 1879 formed the Shimbashi Club Athletics—a collection of railway employees from Shimbashi and their American advisors.

Sport was also an integral aspect of the culture brought to Japan by foreign merchants and missionaries. Baseball already had firm roots in Japan by the time Hiraoka put together his team. When and where baseball was first played in Japan, however, remains open to discussion. Edward Seidensticker reports that the first games in Japan were played on the grounds of a mansion belonging to an ally of the Tokugawa shogunate.[17] Horace Wilson and E. H. Mudgett are usually credited with teaching their students at Kaisei Gakko the fundamentals of baseball in 1873. Other sources suggest that the first baseball team was a group of students at Sapporo Agricultural College.

The Educational Code of 1872 made no provision for physical exercise beyond primary school, although foreign teachers expressed their concern for the "narrow intellectualism" of Japanese education. The foreign educators considered their students "docile," lacking in "fire, energy and manly independence."[18]

The Ministry of Education decided to establish an Institute of Physical Education in 1878 and selected Dr. George A. Leland of Amherst College to develop a national program of physical fitness for Japan. Donald Roden suggests that Leland's emphasis on "light calisthenics" in the institute was rooted in two beliefs. One, Leland's own sense of cultural relativism led him to believe that the Japanese were incapable of rigorous physical activity. Two, Leland feared that competitive sports would foster an athletic elite within the *samurai* legacy.[19]

Other foreign instructors, notably Englishman Frederick Strange, believed in the benefits of healthy competitive games and utilized sports as one way to teach the Japanese the ways of the West. Strange promoted rowing and track and field, always stressing the virtues of sportsmanship and gentlemanly behavior for his students at the Tokyo University Preparatory School. As sports grew in popularity on Japanese campuses, it was crew, then baseball that became the passion of the student elite.

Sport was the source of much prestige for the students of the higher schools and universities in Japan. Because the Primary School Ordinance of 1886 limited primary, middle, and normal schools to a regime of military calisthenics, sport became the privilege and preserve of the student elite. The importance of sport in student life can be appreciated if one considers that seven of the nine original clubs in the First Higher School's Society of Friends were sports clubs—baseball, crew, judo, kendo, archery, tennis, and track.[20]

The growing sense of Japanese nationalism in the 1890s and 1900s was grounded in a linking of Social Darwinism and neo-traditionalism, locating the values of manliness and strength in Japan's pre-Meiji past. It was only natural that the sports at the higher schools were recast in Japanese terms and that baseball became the "new *bushido*."[21]

At this time, there were repeated calls by the Japanese for revision of the unequal treaties they were burdened with, and repeated invitations by the First Higher School to the Yokohama Athletic Club (YAC) for an international showdown on the baseball diamond. The Americans in Yokohama had long rejected such a game on the basis of the inferiority of the Japanese. However, on May 23, 1896, the Japanese students handed the YAC a twenty-nine to four loss in the first game between Japanese and Americans. Subsequent games were often equally embarrassing for the American side. The games had a profound influence upon the image the Japanese had of themselves and made the First Higher School team members national heroes overnight, reinforcing their claims as the future leaders of Japan. Lindsay Russell, president of the Japan Society in 1914, called those first games a "landmark" in inter-Pacific relations.[22]

In the early 1900s, Japan's growing diplomatic and military reputation was paralleled by athletic achievements. The Waseda University baseball team was invited to the United States in 1905 to play American university teams, and returned with a seven-nineteen record. The following year, a University of Tokyo pole vaulter, Fujii Minoru, cleared the world record height of 3.9 meters and had the performance entered in the almanac of the United States Amateur Athletic Union. Pierre de Coubertin sought a Japanese team for the tenth anniversary games of the modern Olympics to be held in Athens in 1906. Although this first invitation was not acted upon, a second invitation for the 1912 Olympics in Stockholm was routed to Kano Jigoro.

Kano's name is most often associated with the establishment of the Kodokan and the founding of judo. Kano has been described as a traditionalist in Japanese sport, but his approach to judo was influenced by the British educational principles he absorbed as a student at Tokyo University. Indeed, one might argue that it was Kano's reputation as a progressive educator that led the Foreign Affairs Ministry to send the Olympic invitation to him. In 1910 Kano became Japan's first International Olympic Committee member, and in 1912 he led a Japanese delegation of four to Stockholm.

The development of sports in Japan in the early twentieth century has often been attributed to the student elite. Saeki Toshio argues, however, that the students lacked the funds to be serious promoters of sport and insists that it was the newspaper industry, which recognized the selling value of sports news, that popularized sport in Japan.[23] While the newspapers of the early Meiji period had been political opinion sheets, newspapers at the turn of the century in Japan were business enterprises that built their commercial success on simplified writing, news from the wars with China and Russia, and the development of "third page" journalism, consisting mainly of social gossip and sports news. The *Asahi Shimbun* and *Mainichi Shimbun*, the giants of Japanese journalism, inflated their circulations, in part, by sponsoring and promoting sports events.

The infatuation with international and domestic sport continued throughout the 1920s. The Waseda-Keio baseball rivalry was considered by the Japanese to be one of the three great collegiate sports events in the world—along with the Cambridge-Oxford regatta and the Harvard-Yale gridiron classic. The Japanese government subsidized their Olympic team for the first time in 1924 with a grant of 60,000 yen. The Olympic delegation in Paris that year marched behind a flag presented to them by Chichibunomiya, the emperor's younger brother. Sports magazines and books flourished, while the modern boys and girls of urban Japan were enthralled with "the three S's—sports, screen, sex."[24]

The liberal veneer of the 1920s obscured an undercurrent of traditionalism and ultranationalism, which crept toward the surface throughout the 1930s. The sports and recreation of urban Japan, however, appear to have been unaffected until 1938. The highlight of the decade was Babe Ruth's barnstorm tour of Japan in 1934. Ruth, Lou Gehrig, and the other American major leaguers toyed with their Japanese competition on the way to a seventeen-zero record. The tour, however, generated the momentum for the creation of Japan's first professional baseball team and the establishment of Japan's own professional baseball league.

Japanese athletes enjoyed much success at the Los Angeles and Berlin Olympic Games and have been described by Richard D. Mandell as "symbols of a nation desperate for success."[25] The Japanese desired to hold the 1940 Games in Tokyo and set about to win that honor. The Tokyo Municipal Office offered a polished brochure, *Tokyo: Sports Center of the Orient*, in 1934 that began:

To set the Twelfth Olympiad against the background of a civilization thousands of years old, against the national celebration of the Empire's 2600th anniversary under a single Imperial Dynasty, would lend to the competitors an added interest, a complementary attraction.[26]

The bid was successful and plans were made for the Tokyo Olympics and an international exposition. However, Japan's invasion of China created international criticism and talk of an Olympic boycott. In July 1938, the Japanese Cabinet withdrew plans to stage the Olympics and suggested a "Japanese Olympics" promoting the health and strength of the Japanese.[27] The Meiji Shrine

Games, Japan's national sports festival since 1924, became increasingly militaristic, with new events in running obstacle courses, throwing grenades, and carrying sandbags.[28]

American football provides a revealing case study of Japanese sports during Japan's growing militarism. Originally known as *beishiki shukyu* (American-style football), the game became *gaikyu* (armor ball) in response to demands that foreign influences be expurgated from Japanese life. The patrons of each sport went to great lengths to rationalize their sport's contribution to Japanese life and the nation's spiritual strengthening. In March 1943, the Ministry of Education canceled all physical training activities except for judo, kendo, and *kyudo*. The *gaikyu* clubs reorganized as *kaigun-shiki tokyu* (navy-style war ball) and attempted to continue play until July 1943 when the military authorities ordered all university clubs disbanded.[29] With that and similar measures, sports activity in Japan came to a halt until the end of the war.

After the war, the occupation's objectives for the demilitarization and democratization of the Japanese were aimed at the martial influences in Japanese society. Physical education programs were developed "along democratic lines." The more immediate concern of the Japanese people's morale was attended to by a national sports festival held in 1946 in Kyoto—the one place saved from the bombings of the war. As Japan regained its footing, however, a new sense of confidence was encouraged by the international performances of Furuhashi Hironoshin, the "Flying Fish of Fujiyama," a world record–shattering swimmer; Tanaka Shigeki, winner of the 1951 Boston Marathon; and Shirai Yoshio, Japan's first world champion in professional boxing. Professional wrestler Rikidozan, whose karate chop did in a number of foreign bad guys, benefited enormously from the renewed national self-esteem and the introduction of television to Japan.

Perhaps nothing in Japan's postwar history has been as important symbolically to the Japanese as the staging of the 1964 Tokyo Olympics. With the same sense of unity and purpose that guided their economic recovery, the Japanese focused their energies upon making the Games a showcase of Japanese diligence, hospitality, and athletic prowess.

Architecture critic Kojiro Yuichiro reflected upon the construction that went on in preparation for the Games and provided a unique glimpse at conflicting Japanese self-images. He admired the displaced center design of the Yoyogi Gymnasium and the *origami* lines of the Komazawa Gymnasium—styles that drew their inspiration from the "basic forms underlying a still-living culture." In the Budokan, Kojiro saw a style trapped in the Japan of old; its Oriental pretenses gave him the impression of a "fascist building."[30]

Athletically, the Games reasserted the Japanese spirit. Before an entire nation crowded in front of their televisions, Hatta Ichiro's wrestlers and the women's volleyball team driven by Daimatsu Hirofumi led an unprecedented harvest of gold medals. This reassured the Japanese that their unique spirituality could overcome any disadvantage their nation might encounter.

Sports critic Matsumoto Kenichi has suggested, ironically, the Tokyo Olympics marked the end of the spirit that had made the Games such a success for the Japanese. Matsumoto characterizes the first one hundred years of Japan's modern era as a century of struggling and enduring under a "condition of privation." The economic recovery and the success of the Olympics, on the other hand, ushered in a "condition of abundance."[31] The Japanese spirit, bound to tradition and a longing for one's hometown, tenacious and indomitable, gave way to a spirit of recreation, spawned by the post-Olympic prosperity. Swimming has been eclipsed by surfing. Would-be marathoners jog. The theatrical posturings of professional grapplers excite more emotions than the legitimate labors of the freestyle wrestler.

The Tokyo Olympics had, indeed, stimulated an interest in sport and recreation. Economic conditions allowed an increasing number of people the leisure and means to enjoy sport and recreational activities. The Japan Amateur Sports Association began to promote a "Sports for All" philosophy. An unlikely catalyst for this popularization of sport was the widespread campus unrest between 1965 and 1975. Until that time, sports clubs in Japanese universities had represented their schools in intercollegiate competition and had monopolized university athletic facilities. Training and discipline within these clubs had always been strict, but incidents of severe hazing and the reactionary attitudes of some of the clubs discouraged many students from joining. These problems became points of contention during the student-university administration confrontations. After the disturbances, several campuses witnessed the establishment and growth of sport appreciation clubs, whose objectives were recreation and intramural competition. In these clubs, and in a growing number of private sports schools (tennis, swimming, golf, etc.), the idea of recreation remains incompatible with the seriousness of the students' approach to their game. As in schools of the traditional arts, emphasis is placed on correct forms and spiritual refinement.

In recent years, businesses unrelated to sport have discovered the promotional advantages of sponsoring glossy, made-for-the-consumer athletic events. Japanese corporate giants bring internationally renowned sports personalities and teams to Japan in order to associate their name and product with a famous face or popular sport.[32]

Observing these spectacles, one might argue that the Japanese could be an extreme illustration for Lewis Mumford's criticisms of mass sport. Mumford's rather pessimistic view considered sport to be part of the "universal regimentation of life—for the sake of private profits or nationalistic exploit."[33] Competition has become secondary, except for possible attempts at records. The athletes have become popular heroes, and the spectators are more concerned with their personalities than their performances. The aim of the spectacle is to gather a record-breaking crowd to testify to the success of the event and, at the same time, to make the venture profitable. However, while sport has become an increasingly complex institution in Japanese life, the simple pleasures—a local shrine festival, a game of catch, a cold beer—remain the foundations of a popular appreciation of sport in Japan today.

Sports and Society

Throughout the last half of the nineteenth century, the Japanese were known as "essentially feeble and pusillanimous," and Japan was described as "a nation whose men flew kites, studied flower arrangement, enjoyed toy gardens, carried fans, and manifested other effeminate customs and behavior."[34] These views were an extension of a set of attitudes, supported "scientifically" by the tenets of Social Darwinism, held by the West regarding not only Japan, but the whole of the Orient.

Stewart Culin's *Games of the Orient* (originally published in 1885 as *Korean Games, with Notes on the Corresponding Games of China and Japan*) is the very model of a work generated by this exotic view of the Orient. Culin described several Oriental amusements, such as indigenous card games, tops, and kite fighting, in an attempt to "connect the remote past with the present." As an archeologist, Culin was interested in providing evidence to support his theory that the pastimes of "civilized men" had their origins in the sacred and divinatory activities of "barbarous people." East Asia presented itself as Culin's most likely laboratory because of the "remarkable survivals of primitive social conditions" there.[35]

"Exotic Japan" has always been a favorite image for Western observers of Japanese culture and society. Even in sports literature, the emphasis has been on the exotic and un-Western—*sumo*, the martial arts, and "*samurai* baseball." These expositions of the exotic, however, reveal more about the attitudes of their authors toward Japan than anything meaningful about Japanese culture and society.

Much of the English-language literature regarding Japanese sport is informed by a notion of *bushido*, which is as much a Western construct as it is a Japanese historical reality. Aside from the development of the code of the *samurai* from the twelfth to the nineteenth centuries, the idea of *bushido* was molded, in large part, by Nitobe Inazo in *Bushido: The Soul of Japan*. Appearing in 1899, *Bushido* was an important statement of Japanese intellectual currents, reasserting the role of the Japanese character in the "Japanese spirit–Western technology" formula for success in Meiji Japan. Further, in response to accusations that the Japanese had no religious or moral system, Nitobe wanted to demonstrate that Japan indeed had a living system of values. One should remember, however, as Kinoshita has pointed out, that Nitobe's *bushido* was not the feudalistic *bushido* of the Edo period, but rather a "Meiji *bushido*" embodied in the Imperial Rescript to Soldiers and Sailors and the Imperial Rescript on Education.[36] Meiji *bushido* became the ideal for the whole process of the "*samurai*-ization" of Japan.

The development of the idea of *bushido* is inextricably bound to the idea's reception by the West, as Colin Holmes and A. H. Ion have convincingly demonstrated in "Bushido and the Samurai: Images in British Public Opinion, 1894–1914." Concern for the condition of the British Empire at the turn of the century had led some social critics to search for alternative models of society. Some of the discontented observers were attracted to *bushido* since the ideal was easily assimilated into romantic notions that emphasized the importance of society over self. The *samurai* were the ideal guardians of H. G. Wells's modern utopia.[37] This appropriation and redefinition of *bushido* continues today by contemporary dissidents seeking alternative lifestyles, models of society, and approaches to sport.

Writings about *bushido* and the martial arts are varied in approach and uneven in quality. The student of popular culture can begin by eliminating the numerous "how-to" martial arts books and focusing upon some of the statements involving *bushido* as a search for self. Eugen Herrigel's *Zen and the Art of Archery* is most representative of this genre of martial arts literature. Herrigel's religious pursuit should not be confused with or spuriously assigned to sport. Herrigel explains quite clearly that archery becomes "a ceremony which exemplifies the 'Great Doctrine.' . . . Even if the pupil does not, at this stage, grasp the true significance of his shots, he at least understands why archery cannot be a sport, a gymnastic exercise."[38]

Another book often read and frequently misinterpreted is Miyamoto Musashi's *A Book of Five Rings*; the most recent travesty is its application to business strategies. *Five Rings*, however, formed an integral part of Miura Yuichiro's personal search in *The Man Who Skied Down Everest*. This "*samurai* of the snows" borrows heavily from Miyamoto Musashi in his quest to discover the meaning of life.

The notion of "spirit" has always been an integral aspect of *bushido*. Like a fine blade, the spirit is an object to temper and polish. In this sense of the word, E. J. Harrison has attempted to unfold the many aspects of Japan's martial culture in *The Fighting Spirit of Japan*.

Robert Frager and Thomas P. Rohlen have approached *seishin*, or "spirit," from a cultural anthropologist's perspective and noted that "despite its history as a panacea of nationalist and militaristic movements, the Japanese orientation to *seishin* has a much broader and deeper basis in the ongoing life of most Japanese, regardless of their political persuasion."[39] In "The Future of a Tradition: Japanese Spirit in the 1980s," Frager and Rohlen discuss the complex of attitudes and practices that form this aspect of Japanese life and its relation to the lifecycle in Japan.

Bushido terms were first applied to Western sports by the baseball players of the First Higher School in the 1890s. Although the *bushido* perspective was consistent with prevailing attitudes in the 1890s and has contributed significantly to the climate of sport in Japan today, it has not been without its undesirable consequences. Kawamoto Nobumasa argues in his chapter on Japanese sports in *Supotsu no Gendaishi* [A modern history of sport] that the *bushido* perspective implies parallels between losing in athletic competition and death on the battle-field. This has fostered a win-at-all-costs mentality among Japanese coaches and athletes that places an inordinate amount of pressure on Japan's top-level competitors. Kawamoto pursues this argument while seeking an answer for marathon runner Tsuburaya Koji's suicide in 1968.

Jacques Barzun once advised, "Whoever wants to know the hearts and minds of America had better learn baseball." The same may also be said about the Japanese for whom baseball is a year-round obsession. This passion has not gone unnoticed, yet descriptions of Japanese baseball emphasize the exotic and unusual. Cultural anthropologist Izumi Seiichi has suggested, on the other hand, that it is possible to divide the world into those people who play baseball and those people who play football (soccer).[40] This hints at the curious possibility that there may be some common characteristic held by North Americans, Latin Americans, and East Asians alike.

The most widely read book in English on Japanese baseball is Robert Whiting's *The Chrysanthemum and the Bat*. Whiting's amusing anecdotes and catchy notion of "*samurai* baseball" provide an entertaining, yet somewhat disappointing look at baseball in Japan. He seems to confuse the *tatemae* (appearance) with the *honne* (actuality) of the game, and his focus on the Yomiuri Giants and professional baseball does not lead him to an adequate explanation for baseball's popularity in Japan. His examination of the important ideological factors buried in his "Samurai Code of Baseball" that influence Japanese perceptions of the game are, however, necessary for any basic understanding of sports as popular culture in Japan.

The Japanese translation of Whiting's book, *Kiku to Batto*, has enjoyed immense popularity because of its implications for *Nihonjinron*, or theories of "who are the Japanese." Baseball has become a natural venue in which to play out this Japanese obsession with their uniqueness. Iwakawa Takashi provides a vivid example of this genre of Japanese literature in his "Nihonjin to Kyojingun" [The Japanese and the Giants] for *Bungei Shunju*. An abridged English translation for the *Japan Echo* reveals some of the popular clichés of *Nihonjinron*. Iwakawa notes that the Giants and Japanese businessmen share a "willingness to sacrifice personal ambition and individuality and strive with single-minded purpose toward victory [that] must appear strange and disturbing to foreign eyes."[41] He expresses concern for a new breed of individualistic players who might mean the downfall of the Giants, and he concludes that "the collapse of the Giants would certainly indicate changes in Japan's social structure or in the Japanese character."[42]

The Yomiuri Giants are descendants of Japan's first professional baseball team, the Dai-Nippon Tokyo Yakyu Dan (Greater Japan Tokyo Baseball Club), which faced the American entourage in 1934. The force behind this international series (and behind the Giants and Japanese professional baseball as well) was *Yomiuri* newspaper president Shoriki Matsutaro. In his biography (*Shoriki: Miracle Man of Japan* by Edward Uhlan and Dana L. Thomas), Shoriki is portrayed larger than life as a judo expert, baseball promoter, and journalistic visionary. Oh

Sadaharu, the postwar sports hero of Japan, on the other hand, comes across as incredibly human in David Falkner's penetrating look into Oh's life, *Sadaharu Oh: A Zen Way of Baseball*. One expects from the title a solid dose of martial mysticism to color Oh's achievements, but learns that the martial arts were employed purely to enhance concentration in Oh's single-minded dedication to hitting baseballs.

Touching upon the international aspects of the game, two journal articles provide valuable insights into Japanese baseball. Donald Roden's "Baseball and the Quest for National Dignity in Meiji Japan" in the *American Historical Review* not only colorfully recounts the events of the first Japanese-American series between the First Higher School and the Yokohama Athletic Club, but re-creates the entire tenor of the 1890s social climate in Japan. Any serious consideration of baseball in Japan must begin with Roden's perceptive piece. Richard C. Crepeau traces the developments of prewar baseball diplomacy and its coverage by the American sports press in "Pearl Harbor: A Failure of Baseball?" in the *Journal of Popular Culture*. While baseball exchanges had been vigorous between Japan and America before the war, Americans were lost for an explanation as to how the "people who took so well to the game of democracy could turn out to be the archenemy of the greatest democracy on earth." The *Sporting News* concluded that while the Japanese had developed their technical skills, they had never acquired the "soul of our National Game" and that "if the spirit of the game had ever penetrated their yellow hides," Pearl Harbor would never have happened.[43]

The "*samurai* baseball" perspective has been the lens through which a number of newspaper and magazine articles have been filtered. However, because this view focuses upon the social psychology of the players, it has obscured an understanding of baseball's popular appeal in Japan. This is to suggest that it is time to move beyond the narrow limits of vision imposed by this view.

In 1965, Ralph Andreano made some of the same observations that Whiting was to describe in his book. He noted the traditional patterns of loyalty, an emphasis on skills, and the strong corporate backing of Japanese baseball. He also noted that baseball is a slow game, which "fits the tempo of Japanese life." It might be more accurate to say that as a slow game, baseball provides a respite from the pace of Japanese life. Stepping through the turnstiles, walking down the tunnels, and emerging in the stands to gaze upon the playing field is like stepping into a dream world where time and space are suspended. The slowness of the game encourages attention to details and to the small gestures important to the game, while the game's occasional moments of action highlight its bland meanderings.

Baseball is a pastoral game, a form of art in which everything exists in harmony.[44] The view is holistic and the movements circular. Humanities professor Tada Michitaro submits in *Asobi to Nihonjin* [Play and the Japanese] that one of the pleasures of the baseball fan is to sit in the bleachers and watch the players act out a sense of order and harmony.[45] As pastoral art, baseball asserts the importance of a communion with nature, a point that would resonate with Japanese sensibilities. The textures of the game are organic,[46] though this is threatened by the introduction of artificial turf and aluminum bats.

Baseball also allows for a close interaction between players and spectators. The many pauses in a game invite the fans to enter into a dialogue with the players. It is a game where the distance between the performers and the spectators is lessened, which is to say that it is a highly personal game in which the audience is bound to the performance.

The spectators are able to participate because the game, though subtle, is easily comprehended. The statistics of baseball are readily computed and meaningful. Baseball's simplicity also makes it a game that is readily played and enjoyed, adding to its popular appeal, both as a participant and as a spectator sport. "Rubberball" baseball has contributed immensely to baseball's overall appeal in Japan and is the number one participant sport activity among men in Japan.

As a form of popular drama, baseball, like *kabuki*, has several familiar characters and famous scenes (with variations) in which "the main actor can demonstrate his individuality and skill."[47] The concept of *shobu* (showdown) between the pitcher and batter contributes to the drama of the game. The moments between pitches, like the *shikiri* in *sumo*, heighten the tension and anticipation of the spectators. This duel adds the ginger-like piquancy to the tofu blandness of the game.

Baseball, finally, "is old-fashioned right from the start; it seems conceived in nostalgia."[48] This would seem to be an important key for understanding baseball in a nation as bound to tradition as Japan. Many Japanese have recollections of Koshien high school baseball tournaments. Ian Buruma has described these meets as celebrations of "the cult of youthful purity."[49] Others, like baseball historian Ikei Masaru, conjure up memories of the Tokyo Six University League, most notably, Waseda-Keio rivalries. For Americans, the nostalgia of baseball is located in America's small-town, preindustrial past. For the Japanese, it is the magic of the Meiji period, the fifty years of Japan's modern transformation. The myth of Japan's modernization underlies baseball's continuing popularity. Baseball was one of the most visible, most easily comprehended, and most successful applications of the Japanese spirit to a Western body of knowledge. More than a game that merely alludes to the swashbuckling fictions of the *samurai*, Japanese baseball invokes the spirits of the Meiji men who mastered Western civilization yet whose hearts remained quintessentially Japanese. In the end, however, the interpretation of baseball in Japan will be determined by how one chooses between the Japan of Kurosawa's *samurai* movies and Ozu's nostalgic studies of everyday Japanese.

If baseball is the story of Japan's successful union of Japanese spirit and Western technique, *sumo* presents the myth of Japan's divine origins. This can be seen in the raised *dohyo* (*sumo* ring), the mythic proportions of the wrestlers, and the ritualism surrounding the tournaments and bouts. This view is further reinforced by *sumo*'s designation as the *kokugi*, "national sport," which carries with it the subtle implication that the Japanese and only the Japanese have the necessary qualifications (i.e., spirit) to do *sumo*. *Sumo* officials, wrestlers, and devotees share a self-satisfied complacency knowing that outsiders cannot assault this final bastion of Japan's uniqueness. As a result, foreigners who perform well send seismic shocks through the *sumo* world, endangering the myth of divine origins and uniqueness.

In addition to professional *sumo*'s immense popularity with the Japanese, the sport holds a magnetic attraction for the Western community in Japan, despite its latent xenophobia. The English-language newspapers and journals in Japan all have their resident *sumo* experts who explain the intricacies of this exotic Japanese passion to the uninitiated. This keen interest in professional *sumo* and its wrestlers has generated column after column of print, but unfortunately this does not translate well into scholarship.

The materials in English about *sumo* are largely explanatory, providing a historical background, an explanation of the traditions and symbolism of *sumo*, and an introduction to the wrestlers and winning techniques. Of these works, P. L. Cuyler's *Sumo: From Rite to Sport* is the most ambitious, attempting a detailed and comprehensive history of *sumo*'s development and a scrutinizing look at *sumo* today. In her effort to be complete, however, Cuyler may have jeopardized her reliability. She reported, for example, that the popular Hawaiian wrestler Takamiyama would retire in 1979,[50] although this did not occur until five years later. A revised edition of Cuyler's book by Doreen Simmons has attempted to correct some of these problems. Takamiyama's own book (under his Hawaiian name, Jesse Kuhaulua), *Takamiyama: The World of Sumo*, is the most informative for its many insights into *sumo* that only an insider could provide. *JESSE! Sumo Superstar* by Andrew Adams and Mark Schilling is an endeavor to augment Takamiyama's autobiography with more recent information.

The only English-language general history of sport in Japan is the 1977 issue of *Sports in Japan* by the Japan Amateur Sports Association. Its brevity, however, and some serious flaws in its English detract from its usefulness.

Because the student elite at the turn of the century was so influential in the establishment and development of sport in Japan, Donald Roden's work is invaluable to any probe into Japanese sport. His "Baseball and the Quest for National Dignity in Meiji Japan" has been quoted earlier, but for a broader picture of the role of sport in the culture of Japan's student elite, his chapter on "The Culture of Ceremony" in *Schooldays in Imperial Japan* is also indispensable.

Jacqueline G. Haslett's doctoral dissertation, "A History of Physical Education and Sports in Japan from 1868 to 1972," is an attempt to pull together the ideas that have influenced physical education in Japan's modern century. Haslett summarizes the period from 1868 to 1945, and then turns to a deeper analysis of developments from 1945 to 1972. The scope of this project and Haslett's focus on educational trends limit the contribution this work can make to the study of sport as an aspect of Japan's popular culture.

Of the many Japanese histories of sport and physical education in Japan, most are narrative recollections of the development of sport in Japan and the activities of the coaches and athletes who contributed to that development. Two histories, however, are conspicuous for their attempts to relate sport to other developments in Japan. Kinoshita Hideaki's *Supotsu no Kindai Nihonshi* [A history of sports in modern Japan] links the social and cultural trends in Japan to developments in sport from the Meiji period. A companion volume to Kinoshita's work is Kimura Kichiji's *Nihon Kindai Taiiku Shiso no Keisei* [The intellectual foundations of modern sport in Japan]. Kimura begins with the thoughts of Fukuzawa Yukichi, then explores the intellectual biography of Kano Jigoro, and relates other currents of thought to sport in Japan. Other histories of note are Imamura Yoshio's *Nihon Taiikushi* [A history of Japanese physical education] and Kimura Ki's *Nihon Supotsu Bunkashi* [A cultural history of Japanese sports].

Josei Taiikushi Kenkyukai's *Kindai Nihon Josei Taiikushi* [A women's history of physical education in modern Japan] is a collection of biographical essays about the pioneers of women's physical education in Japan. The feminist may find the collection disappointing since four of the first six sketches are about men. The study of women in sport in Japan remains an undeveloped area.

Nakamura Toshio adds a comparative perspective to the historical studies of sport in Japan. His *Supotsu no Fudo* [The climate of sport] is an attempt to draw out some of the characteristics of sport in England, America, and Japan that have risen naturally out of the history of each nation's sport. Nakamura chooses to focus upon the fraternal spirit of English sport, the functionalist, industrial approach of the Americans to sport, and the Japanese emphasis on *shobu* and its implications for training and discipline.

In 1964, David N. Plath examined some of the questions of leisure and recreation advanced by Japan's modernization in *The Afterhours: Modern Japan and the Search for Enjoyment*. He noted, for example, that drinking in Japan is seen as an opportunity for a person to demonstrate his ability to enter into "relationships of human feeling and intimacy," as is expected in Japan.[51] Since Plath, however, the study of leisure in Japan by Western scholars has remained dormant.

On the Japanese side, however, Tada Michitaro in *Asobi to Nihonjin* [Play and the Japanese] has examined the many forms of play in Japan and has arrived at some creative conclusions. Tada suggests that *pachinko*, the popular Japanese pinball game, is an expression of Japan's adaptation to industrialization as a form of communion with machines. In the realm of theories of "who are the Japanese," Tada has taken the notion that Japan is a *naru* (to be) culture as compared with the Western *suru* (to do) cultures, and found confirmation of this in the Japanese love for baths. While other peoples seek relaxation by doing something—jogging, playing games, or tending a garden—the Japanese find a fundamental form of leisure by *being* relaxed in the bath.

There is no shortage of critical works regarding sport in Japan. Sakuta Keiichi looks incisively at the myths that surround Koshien high school baseball and Daimatsu Hirofumi's ideas about the Japanese spirit in his *Haji no Bunka Saiko* [The shame culture reconsidered]. Kawamoto Nobumasa has challenged some of the win-at-all-costs doctrines that animate Japanese athletics. He criticizes combining sports science with the notion of the Japanese spirit as a dehumanization of the athlete. In his previously mentioned book, he also directs some critical comments at the Japanese national sports festival and university athletics. Also of interest are the critical essays of sport sociologist Saeki Toshio, who writes for the *Ekonomisuto*. He often criticizes the sports business establishment that dictates how sports in Japan will be enjoyed.

Before the mass of Japanese people were able to participate in the recreational activities of the various elites, their moments of recreation and leisure were provided by the festivals of the local shrines. Today, sports events bear many similarities to Japanese festivals, so an understanding of these festivals and the people who attend them may provide some clues to the popularity of sports in Japan. *Nihon no Matsuri* [The Japanese festival] by Yanagita Kunio is considered a classic in Japanese folk studies, but Michael Ashkenazi's doctoral dissertation, "Festival Change and Continuity in a Japanese Town," may be more the sort of description and analysis that lends itself to an understanding of sport. The first chapter in Ian Buruma's *Japanese Mirror*, "Mirror of the Gods," is valuable for its insights into the meanings surrounding shrines and the "whole range of sensual nature worship, folk beliefs, ancient deities and rituals"[52] to which the Japanese remain tightly bound.

A catalytic force behind the popularization of sport in Japan has been the media. Indeed, the evolution of the popular press and sports in Japan may be seen as reciprocal developments, the existence of one benefiting the other. The media have always expressed the values of a society in their packaging, presentation, and interpretation of sports news, forming a natural union between these two aspects of popular culture. Today, the five sports dailies control 12 percent of Japan's newspaper circulation, serving up a steady diet of sports, gambling, gossip, and news from the entertainment world. Sports magazines abound and sports programs on television are among the most popular. *Sogo Jaanarizumu Kenkyu*, a journalism research journal, published special issues in 1980 and 1984 that focused upon the sports-media link. These criticisms are very general in nature, concerned more with sports magazines and television than the other media, but these collections of essays may offer a first step in an exploration of sport's relationship with the media.

The media are not limited to the print and broadcasting. The values of a society embodied in sport can be played out in a number of vehicles of expression. Sports movies and television dramas would be lively possibilities, but remain untouched. While Natsume Soseki was reputed to have been an avid fan of the First Higher School's baseball team, he appears to have chosen not to use sportsmen in his novels. An analysis of athletes and athletic images in Japanese literature, in fact, has yet to be attempted. Messenger has demonstrated what is possible with his analysis of sportsmen in American literature, while, in the Japanese context, Plath has provided a model for this work with his brief analysis of the film *Anata Kaimasu* in *Afterhours*. Mishima Yukio, Japan's postwar renaissance man, contributed several reflections on sports in his short life to Japanese newspapers and magazines. A collection of these essays, *Jikkanteki Supotsuron* [Essays on the essence of sport], reveals the complex ideas and elaborate style that Mishima brought to his contemplation and descriptions of sport. Frederik L. Schodt has explored the many implications of values expressed in the ubiquitous Japanese comic books in *Manga! Manga! The World of Japanese Comics*. His chapter on "The Spirit of Japan" captures some of the importance assigned to the Japanese spirit in Japanese life as it is portrayed in the pages of sports and martial arts comics.

The complex and many-faceted phenomenon that is sport in Japan can provide subtle insights into the values and meanings that guide Japanese existence. Sports have captured the Japanese imagination because they are living expressions of the deeper currents that move Japanese life. Yet, without a more sensitive understanding of Japanese sports, we will continue to use the worn-out lens of "*samurai* sports" and to arrive at the same conclusions about Japanese sports, Japanese life, and Japanese culture that have prevailed since the nineteenth century.

REFERENCE WORKS

The reference materials relevant to sport and physical education in Japan are many and varied. Indeed, one would get the impression that generating, collecting, and indexing information are among the favorite pastimes of the Japanese.

To appreciate the volume of work that has been generated in Japan regarding sport, one can begin by perusing the *Taiiku Supotsusho Kaidai* [A bibliographic introduction to the literature of physical education and sports] compiled by sport historians Kinoshita Hideaki, Nose Shuichi, and Kimura Kichiji. The editors have compiled a list of over 15,000 titles of books about sports that have been published from the Meiji period to the present. In each entry, the *Kaidai* notes the libraries in which the book is located. A similar section for newspapers, magazines, and journals has also been compiled. The index arranges the titles by category—for example, history, medicine, games, and martial arts—and lists the authors and research groups that have contributed to this preponderance of work.

The Nihon Taiiku Gakkai (Japanese Society of Physical Education) is an important outlet for much of the physical education research being conducted in Japanese universities. Tanimura Tatsumi's two-volume *Taiikugaku Kenkyu Bunken Bunrui Mokuroku* [Classified bibliography of Japanese research in physical education] is a summary view of the research papers that have been presented at Japan Society of Physical Education congresses from 1950 to 1969. Volume 1 lists the titles of the papers presented at JSPE congresses and notes those that have been selected for the congress bulletins. Volume 2 summarizes the work that is available in individual university journals.

The Japanese Ministry of Education and the Center for Academic Publications Japan have given foreign scholars some relief from the tortures of doing research in the Japanese language by providing two English-language aids to this enormous body of research. The ministry's *Index of Researches on Physical Education and Sports Science in Japan* reveals the wide variety of research topics attended to by scholars before 1964. The Center's *Current Contents of Academic Journals in Japan* first appeared in 1971 and provides a highly selective view of sports and sports medicine research from *Taiikugaku Kenkyu*. All articles listed are in Japanese with English abstracts.

For encyclopedic treatments of sport and physical education, the recently published *Gendai Taiiku Supotsu Taikei* [Modern physical education and sport], in twenty-nine volumes, is truly a Herculean exploration into modern sport by editors Asami Toshio, Miyashita Mitsumasa, and Watanabe Toru. The first twelve volumes examine the larger questions of sport philosophy, history, sociology, health, and education, while the remaining volumes are devoted to individual sports—their history, rules, training techniques, and strategies.

A single-volume work that provides basic information regarding sport in Japan is the *Supotsu Daihyakka* [Cyclopedia of sports] published by the Japan Amateur Sports Association. A colorful volume with several pictorials, the *Daihyakka* is divided into a general survey of sport in Japan, descriptions of individual sports, and a section of records and meet results. A brief "Who's Who" in Japanese sport and a chronology of domestic and international sports developments from 1927 make the work a comprehensive collection of sports information.

To augment the final sections of the *Daihyakka*, one could consult one of three sources. The *Taiiku Jinmei Jiten* [Biographical dictionary of physical education], compiled by the Tokyo Taiiku Kagaku Kenkyukai (Tokyo Sport Science Research Group), contains brief sketches of noted athletes, coaches, educators, and scholars in Japan and overseas. Imamura Yoshio's *Taiikushi Shiryo Nenpyo* [Chronology of sports and historical sources] and the *Kindai Taiiku Supotsu Nenpyo* [Chronology of modern sports and physical education], edited by Kishino Yuzo, are indispensable for their chronological presentations of sport in Japan and for their citations of the historical sources consulted.

Imamura's chronology reaches back over two millenia (38 B.C.–1968), which is to say that the first entries taken from the early Japanese histories are mythological accounts of the divine Imperial ancestors. The historical entries on early Japan are from diaries noting when the emperors played *kemari*, hunted, or watched *sumo*. Medieval Japan is marked by entries of the martial activities of the shogun and the *samurai* houses. Beginning with early modern Japan, Kishino's chronology (1800–1972) dovetails with Imamura's but offers more detail by presenting his calendar in four parts—social developments, general sports, sports in schools, and Western sports.

Where these two chronologies overlap before 1873, one encounters the problems of dates determined by the lunar and solar calendars. To illustrate, Imamura notes that the *sumo* wrestler Koyanagi defeated three of Perry's sailors in a wrestling match on the sixteenth day of the second month of the seventh year of the Kaei reign, while Kishino records the same event on March 24, 1854, with a "[2.26]" notation indicating the lunar calendar's date. The ten-day discrepancy in lunar dates may be attributed to a variance among different historical sources.

To investigate questions of terminology, Imamura Yoshio's and Miyahata Torahiko's *Shinshu Taiiku Daijiten* [Newly compiled dictionary of sport] is an easy-to-consult dictionary of Japanese and Western sport terms. The *Zusetsu Nihon Budo Jiten* [The illustrated dictionary of Japanese martial arts] of Sasama Yoshihiko provides definitions of the many weapons and techniques of the martial arts, as well as a brief list of books relevant to each martial art and a section on their rules and conduct.

Foreign contributions to the reference materials for sport in Japan suffer serious limitations. Robert W. Smith's 1959 *Bibliography of Judo* is dated, while the *Japan Sports Guide* by Andy Adams, Arthur Tansley, and John Robertson is more a directory for the would-be athlete and martial artist than a research tool. Clyde Newton's *Makuuchi Rikishi of the Showa Period* provides the vital information concerning *sumo*'s upper-division wrestlers since 1925, and painstakingly records their tournament records. The focus of this work is so narrow, however, that it will appeal only to the most devoted of *sumo* enthusiasts.

RESEARCH COLLECTIONS

The Imperial family has always had its sports fans. The Meiji emperor was a patron of *kemari* at a time when the things of Old Japan were being submerged in the high tide of Westernization. The Showa emperor regularly attends *sumo* tournaments in Tokyo, while other members of the Imperial household make appearances at a number of athletic events every year, including the National Sports Festival.

Yet, the Imperial family's true sport fanatic may have been Prince Yasuhito, the younger brother of the Showa emperor. Chichibunomiya, as the prince is more popularly known, enjoyed a number of sports, but is remembered most fondly as an avid rugby enthusiast. Appropriately, the rugby stadium next to the National Stadium bears the prince's name—as does the most extensive collection of materials pertaining to sport housed in Japan.

Chichibunomiya Kinen Supotsu Toshokan (Chichibunomiya Memorial Sports Library) within the National Stadium complex holds over 15,000 books, ranging over the many aspects of sport, and 220 magazine titles. The interested scholar who does not possess a reasonable command of Japanese might feel lost, however, since none of the books and only a handful of the magazines are in English. Chichibunomiya Kinen Supotsu Hakubutsukan, the sports museum adjacent to the library, provides one with an enchanting stroll through the history of sport in Japan. The "Sports of Japan's Past" display features the traditional garb of *kemari* and *yabusame*. There are displays from past Olympics and sports festivals. In one remote corner is the MacArthur Cup from the MacArthur Games, competitions in tennis, rubberball tennis, and table tennis held during the occupation. A special room is devoted to Chichibunomiya memorabilia.

The library of the Japan Amateur Sports Association and the Japanese Olympic Committee in Kishi Kinen Taiiku Kaikan (Kishi Memorial Hall) is another valuable collection of books, journals, and films. There is a limited collection of foreign language materials, including the Japanese Olympic Committee publication, *Sports in Japan*. This annual summarizes the international and domestic sports activities of the Japanese and is one source of up-to-date information. One must forgive, however, the cheerleading for Japanese athletes that goes on within the pages of this magazine. The 1977 issue contains a summary of Japan's sport history, following the outline set out by former Chichibunomiya librarian Kinoshita Hideaki. The 1978 issue features a similar review of Japan's Olympic history.

Small collections of the limited range of English-language materials are available at the libraries of the Japan Foundation and the International House of Japan, which cater to foreign scholars of Japanese studies. Since sport in Japan has yet to be developed into a serious academic concern of Japanologists, the holdings of these two libraries are largely martial arts books reflecting, again, the dominant bias in thinking about sports in Japan.

Outside of Japan, the Applied Life Studies Library, coupled with the Asian Studies Library, at the University of Illinois at Urbana-Champaign may offer the most likely place to do research. The extensive holdings of the Applied Life Studies Library include many of the limited writings regarding Japanese sport and physical education. A few martial art books also dot the collection. The strength of the Illinois collection is its ability to support comparative studies of Japanese sports through a wide range of works.

NOTES

1. Quoted in David W. Plath, *The Afterhours: Modern Japan and the Search for Enjoyment* (Berkeley: University of California Press, 1964), p. 70.

2. Clifford Geertz, *The Interpretation of Cultures* (New York: Basic Books, 1973).

3. Howard S. Slusher, *Man, Sport, and Existence: A Critical Analysis* (Philadelphia: Lea and Febiger, 1967), p. 127.

4. Christian K. Messenger, *Sport and the Spirit of Play in American Fiction: Hawthorne to Faulkner* (New York: Columbia University Press, 1981), p. 6.

5. Kishino Yuzo, "Bunka toshite no Budo: Dento Budo to Kyogi Budo" [Budo as

culture: Traditional martial arts and competitive martial arts], *Taiikuka Kyoiku* 32, no. 1 (January 1984), 21.

[4] 岸野雄三 「文化としての武道－伝統武道と競技武道」 体育科教育 ３２巻１号 １９８４.１ p.２１

6. Allen Guttman, *From Ritual to Record: The Nature of Modern Sports* (New York: Columbia University Press, 1978), pp. 1–55.

7. Hikoyama Kozo, *Sumo: Japanese Wrestling* (Tokyo: Board of Industry, Japanese government, 1940), p. 13.

8. P. L. Cuyler, *Sumo: From Rite to Sport* (New York: Weatherhill, 1979), p. 22.

9. Tsunoda Ryusaku, William Theodore de Bary, and Donald Keene, *Sources of the Japanese Tradition* (New York: Columbia University Press, 1958), p. 7; Jared Taylor, *Shadows of the Rising Sun* (New York: William Morrow, 1983), p. 245.

10. Ivan Morris, *The World of the Shining Prince: Court Life in Ancient Japan* (Tokyo: Charles E. Tuttle, 1978), pp. 150–54.

11. Donn F. Draeger, *Classical Bujutsu* (New York: Weatherhill, 1973), p. 21. See also Yamada Tadachika and Watatani Kiyoshi, *Bugei Ryuha Daijiten* [Dictionary of martial arts schools] (Tokyo: Shinjinbutsu Oraisha, 1969).

山田忠史、綿谷雪 「武芸流派大辞典」 東京 新人物往来社 １９６９.

12. Imamura Yoshio, *Nihon Taiikushi* [A history of Japanese physical education] (Tokyo: Fumaido Shuppan, 1970), pp. 329–30.

今村嘉雄 「日本体育史」 東京 不昧堂書店 １９７０, p.３２９－３０.

13. Cuyler, pp. 10, 12.

14. Kinoshita Hideaki, *Supotsu no Kindai Nihon-shi* [A history of sports in modern Japan] (Tokyo: Kyorin Shoin, 1970), p. 2.

木下秀明 「スポーツの近代日本史」 東京 杏林書院 １９７０ p.２

15. Fukuzawa Yukichi, *The Autobiography of Yukichi Fukuzawa* (New York: Columbia University Press, 1966), pp. 329–32.

16. Kimura Kichiji, *Nihon Kindai Taiiku Shiso no Keisei* [The intellectual foundations of modern sport in Japan] (Tokyo: Kyorin Shoin, 1975), pp. 1–17.

木村吉次 「日本近代体育思想の形成」 東京 杏林書院 １９７５ p.１～１７

17. Edward Seidensticker, *Low City, High City: Tokyo from Edo to the Earthquake* (Tokyo: Charles E. Tuttle, 1983), p. 166.

18. Donald Roden, ''Baseball and the Quest for National Dignity in Meiji Japan,'' *American Historical Review* 85, no. 3 (June 1980), 514.

19. Ibid., p. 515.

20. Donald Roden, *Schooldays in Imperial Japan: A Study in the Culture of a Student Elite* (Berkeley: University of California Press, 1980), p. 115.

21. Roden, ''Baseball and the Quest,'' p. 520.

22. Ibid., p. 531.

23. Saeki Toshio, ''Nihonjin no Supotsu Raifu: Sono Haikei to Hoko'' [Japanese sports life: Its background and direction], *Nihon Hyakkaten Kyokai Kaiho* no. 1030 (August 1979), 6.

佐伯聡夫 「日本人のスポーツ・ライフーその背景と方向」

日本百貨協会会報 １０３０号 １９７９.８ p.６

24. Edwin O. Reischauer and Albert M. Craig, *Japan: Tradition and Transformation* (Tokyo: Charles E. Tuttle, 1978), p. 207.

25. Richard D. Mandell, *Sport: A Cultural History* (New York: Columbia University Press, 1984), p. 245.

26. Tokyo Municipal Office, *Tokyo: Sports Center of the Orient* (Tokyo: Tokyo Municipal Office, 1934), pp. ii, iii. The "2600th Anniversary" is from the sum of 1940 and the mythological date of the foundation of the Japanese Empire, 660 B.C.

27. Kinoshita, p. 211; Mandell, p. 246.

28. Kinoshita, pp. 213, 214.

29. Nihon American Football Kyokai, *Kagirinaki Zenshin: Nihon Amerikan Futtoboru Gojunenshi* [Forever forward: A fifty-year history of American football in Japan] (Tokyo: Nihon American Football Kyokai, 1984), pp. 90, 91.

ニホンアメリカンフットバール協会　「限りなき前進：ニホンアメリカンフットバール
五十年史」　東京　ニホンアメリカンフットバール協会　1984、pp．90，91

30. Kojiro Yuichiro, "Building for the Olympics," *Japan Quarterly* 11, no. 4 (October-December 1964), 445.

31. Matsumoto Kenichi, "Doryokukei kara Shumikei e: Supotsu no Sesoshi" [From endurance to enjoyment: A social history of sport], *Seiron*, no. 135 (May 1984), 50–61.

松本健一　「努力系から趣味系へ」　正論　1984．5　p．50～61

32. Roy Garner, "How Business Profits from Sport," *Intersect* 2, no. 1 (January 1986), 10–15.

33. Lewis Mumford, "Sport and the Bitch-Goddess," in *Technics and Civilization* (New York: Harcourt, Brace and World, 1934), p. 307.

34. Quoted in Roden, "Baseball and the Quest," p. 513.

35. Stewart Culin, *Games of the Orient* (Rutland, Vt.: Charles E. Tuttle, 1958), pp. xvii-xviii.

36. Kinoshita, p. 144.

37. Colin Holmes and A. H. Ion, "Bushido and the Samurai: Images in British Public Opinion, 1894–1914," *Modern Asian Studies* 14, no. 2 (1980), 322.

38. Eugen Herrigel, *Zen and the Art of Archery* (London: Routledge and Kegan Paul, 1953), p. 57.

39. Robert Frager and Thomas P. Rohlen, "The Future of a Tradition: Japanese Spirit in the 1980's," in *Japan: The Paradox of Progress* (New Haven: Yale University Press, 1976), p. 256.

40. Quoted in Kawamoto Nobumasa, *Supotsu no Gendaishi* [A modern history of sport] (Tokyo: Taishukan Shoten, 1976), p. 37.

川本信正　「スポーツの現代史」　東京　大修館書店　1976　p．37．

41. Iwakawa Takashi, "The Mystique of the Yomiuri Giants," *Japan Echo* 11, no. 3 (1984), 63.

42. Ibid, p. 64.

43. Richard C. Crepeau, "Pearl Harbor: A Failure of Baseball?" *Journal of Popular Culture* 15, no. 4 (Spring 1982), 72.

44. Murray Ross, "Football and Baseball in America," in *Sport and Society: An Anthology* (Boston: Little, Brown, 1973), p. 103.

45. Tada Michitaro, *Asobi to Nihonjin* [Play and the Japanese] (Tokyo: Chikuma Shobo, 1974), p. 76.

多田道太郎　「遊びと日本人」　東京　筑摩書房　1974　p．76

46. George Grella, "Baseball and the American Dream," *The Massachusetts Review* 16 (Summer 1975), 556.

47. Sakakibara Yasuo quoted in Ralph Andreano. "Japanese Baseball," in *Sport and Society: An Anthology* (Boston: Little, Brown, 1973), p. 73.

48. Ross, p. 103.

49. Ian Buruma, *A Japanese Mirror: Heroes and Villains of Japanese Culture* (Middlesex, England: Penguin Books, 1985), p. 147.

50. Cuyler, p. 129.

51. Plath, p. 87.

52. Buruma, p. 3.

SELECTED BIBLIOGRAPHY

Adams, Andrew, and Mark Schilling. *JESSE! Sumo Superstar*. Tokyo: Japan Times, 1985.

Adams, Andy, Arthur Tansley, and John Robertson. *Japan Sports Guide*. Tokyo: Bat Publications, 1978.

Andreano, Ralph. *No Joy In Mudville: The Dilemma of Major League Baseball*. Cambridge: Schenkman Publishing Co., 1965.

Asami, Toshio, Miyashita Mitsumasa, and Watanabe Toru, eds. *Gendai Taiiku Supotsu Taikei* [Modern physical education and sport]. Tokyo: Kodansha, 1984.

浅見俊雄、宮下充正、渡辺融編 『現代体育スポーツ体系』 東京 講談社 １９８４

Ashkenazi, Michael. "Festival Change and Continuity in a Japanese Town." Ph.D. dissertation, Yale University, 1983.

Barthes, Roland. *Empire of Signs*. Trans. Richard Howard. New York: Hill and Wang, 1982.

Center for Academic Publications Japan. *Current Contents of Academic Journals in Japan*. Tokyo: Center for Academic Publications Japan, 1971–1986.

Crepeau, Richard C. "Pearl Harbor: A Failure of Baseball?" *Journal of Popular Culture* 15, no. 4 (Spring 1982), 67–74.

Culin, Stewart. *Games of the Orient*. Rutland, Vt.: Charles E. Tuttle, 1958.

Cuyler, P. L. *Sumo: From Rite to Sport*. New York: Weatherhill, 1979.

Frager, Robert, and Thomas P. Rohlen. "The Future of a Tradition: Japanese Spirit in the 1980's." In *Japan: The Paradox of Progress*. Ed. Lewis Austin. New Haven: Yale University Press, 1976, 255–78.

Guttman, Allen. *From Ritual to Record: The Nature of Modern Sports*. New York: Columbia University Press, 1978.

Harrison, E. J. *The Fighting Spirit of Japan*. 1955; rpt. Woodstock, N.Y.: Overlook Press, 1982.

Haslett, Jacqueline G. "A History of Physical Education and Sports in Japan from 1868 Through 1972." Ph.D. dissertation, Boston University, School of Education, 1977.

Herrigel, Eugen. *Zen and the Art of Archery*. Trans. R. F. C. Hull. London: Routledge and Kegan Paul, 1953.

Holmes, Colin, and A. H. Ion. "Bushido and the Samurai: Images in British Public Opinion, 1894–1914." *Modern Asian Studies* 14, no. 2 (1980), 309–29.

Ikei, Masaru. *Hakkyu Taiheiyo wo Wataru: Nichi-Bei Yakyu Koryushi* [Baseballs across the Pacific: A history of Japan-America baseball exchanges]. Tokyo: Chuo Koronsha, 1976.

池井優 「白球太平洋を渡る：日米野球交流史」 東京 中央公論社 １９７６

————. *Tokyo Roku Daigaku Yakyu Gaishi* [An unofficial history of the Tokyo Six University Baseball League]. Tokyo: Baseball Magazine-sha, 1977.
池井優 「東京六大学野球外史」 東京 ベースボール・マガジン社 １９７７

Imamura, Yoshio. *Nihon Taiikushi* [A history of Japanese physical education]. Tokyo: Fumaido Shuppan, 1970.
今村嘉雄 『日本体育史』 東京 不昧堂書店 １９７０

Imamura, Yoshio, and Miyahata Torahiko, eds. *Shinshu Taiiku Daijiten* [Newly compiled dictionary of sport]. Tokyo: Fumaido Shuppan. 1976.
今村嘉雄、編 「新篇体育大事典」 東京 不昧堂書店 １９７６．

————. "Special Lecture: Traditional Sports in Japan." In *Proceedings of International Congress of Sports Sciences, 1964*. Tokyo: Japanese Union of Sport Science, 1964, 28–35.

————. *Taiikushi Shiryo Nenpyo* [Chronology of sports and historical sources]. Tokyo: Fumaido Shoten, 1969.
今村嘉雄 『体育史資料年表』 東京 不昧堂書店 １９６９

International Young Women and Children's Society. *Swimming in Japan*. Tokyo: International Young Women and Children's Society, 1935.

Iwakawa, Takashi. "The Mystique of the Yomiuri Giants." *Japan Echo* 11, no. 3 (1984), 60–64.

————. "Nihonjin to Kyojingun" [The Japanese and the Giants]. *Bungei Shunju* 62, nos. 6 and 9 (June and September 1984), 132–48, 168–84.
岩川隆 「日本人と巨人軍」 文芸春秋 ６２巻６号(１９８４．６)
１３２～１４８ 「日本人と巨人軍:part2」 ６２巻９号(１９８４．９) １６８～１８４

Japan Amateur Sports Association. *Sports in Japan*. Tokyo: Japan Amateur Sports Association, 1950– (annual publication).

————. *Supotsu Daihyakka* [Cyclopedia of sports]. Tokyo: Japan Amateur Sports Association, 1982.
「スポーツ大百科」 東京 日本体育協会 １９８２

Japanese Government Ministry of Education. *Index of Researches on Physical Education and Sports Science in Japan*. Tokyo: Ministry of Education, Physical Education Bureau, 1964.

Josei Taiikushi Kenkyukai, ed. *Kindai Nihon Josei Taiikushi* [A women's history of physical education in modern Japan]. Tokyo: Nihon Taiikusha, 1981.
女性体育史研究会編 「近代日本女性体育史」 東京 日本体育社 １９８１．

Kawamoto, Nobumasa. *Supotsu no Gendaishi*. [A modern history of sport]. Tokyo: Taishukan Shoten, 1976.
川本信正 『スポーツの現代史』 東京 大修館書店 １９７６

Kenrick, Doug. *The Book of Sumo: Sport, Spectacle, and Ritual*. New York: Weatherhill, 1969.

Kimura, Ki. *Nihon Supotsu Bunkashi*. [A cultural history of Japanese sports]. Tokyo: Baseball Magazine-sha, 1978.
木村毅 『日本スポーツ文化史』 東京 ベースボール・マガジン社 １９７８

Kimura, Kichiji. *Nihon Kindai Taiihu Shiso no Keisei* [The intellectual foundations of modern sport in Japan]. Tokyo: Kyorin Shoin, 1975.
木村吉次 『日本近代体育思想の形成』 東京 杏林書院 １９７５

Kinoshita, Hideaki. *Supotsu no Kindai Nihonshi* [A history of sports in modern Japan]. Tokyo: Kyorin Shoin, 1970.
木下秀明 『スポーツの近代日本史』 東京 杏林書院 １９７０

Kinoshita, Hideaki, Nose Shuichi, and Kimura Kichiji. *Taiiku Supotsusho Kaidai* [A bibliographic introduction to the literature of physical education and sports]. Tokyo: Fumai Shuppan, 1981.

木下秀明、能勢修一、木村吉次　『体育スポーツ書解題』　東京　不昧堂出版

１９８１

Kishino, Yuzo. "Bunka toshite no Budo: Dento Budo to Kyogi Budo" [Budo as culture: Traditional martial arts and competitive martial arts]. *Taiikuka Kyoiku* 32, no. 1 (January 1984), 18–21.

岸野雄三　「文化としての武道ー伝統武道と競技武道」　体育科教育　３２巻１号

（１９８４．１）

————, ed. *Kindai Taiiku Supotsu Nenpyo* [Chronology of modern sports and physical education]. Tokyo: Taishukan Shoten, 1973.

岸野雄三編　『近代体育スポーツ年表』　東京　大修館書店　１９７３

Kojiro, Yuichiro. "Building for the Olympics." *Japan Quarterly* 11, no. 4 (October-December 1964), 439–45.

Kuhaulua, Jesse, with John Wheeler. *Takamiyama: The World of Sumo*. Tokyo: Kodansha International, 1973.

Mandell, Richard D. *Sport: A Cultural History*. New York: Columbia University Press, 1984.

"The Marathon Craze." *Japan Quarterly* 25, no. 4 (October-December 1978), 395–98.

Matsumoto, Kenichi. "Doryokukei kara Shumikei e: Supotsu no Sesoshi" [From endurance to enjoyment: A social history of sport]. *Seiron*, no. 135, (May 1984), 50–61.

松本健一　「努力型から趣味型へ：スポーツの世相史」　正論　（１９８４．３）

５０～６１

Mishima, Yukio. *Jikkanteki Supotsuron* [Essays on the essence of sport]. Tokyo: Kodansha Tsushinsha, 1984.

三島由紀夫　『実感的スポーツ論』　東京　共同通信社　１９８４

Miura, Yuichiro, and Eric Perlman. *The Man Who Skied Down Everest*. New York: Harper and Row, 1978.

Miyamoto, Musashi. *A Book of Five Rings*. Trans. Victor Harris. London: Allison and Busby, 1974.

"Muscular Cramp." *Japan Quarterly* 20, no. 2 (April-June 1973), 135–38.

Nakamura, Toshio. *Supotsu no Fudo: Nichi-Ei-Bei Hikaku Supotsu Bunka* [The climate of sport: A comparison of Japanese, English, and American sports culture]. Tokyo: Taishukan Shoten, 1981.

中村敏雄　『スポーツの風土』　東京　大修館書店　１９８１

Newton, Clyde. *Makuuchi Rikishi of the Showa Period*. Tokyo: Japan Printing Co., 1982.

Nihon Taiiku Gakkai. "Supotsu Shido to Konjoron" [Coaching and fighting spirit]. *Taiiku no Kagaku* [Journal of Health, Physical Education and Recreation]. Vol. 34, no. 2 (February 1984).

「スポーツ指導と根性論」　体育の研究　３４巻２号（１９８４．２）

Nitobe, Inazo. *Bushido: The Soul of Japan*. 1899; rpt. Rutland, Vt.: Charles E. Tuttle, 1969.

Oh, Sadaharu, and David Falkner. *Sadaharu Oh: A Zen Way of Baseball*. Tokyo: Kodansha International, 1984.

Plath, David W. *The Afterhours: Modern Japan and the Search for Enjoyment.* Berkeley: University of California Press, 1964.

Prime Minister's Office. *Basic Survey of Life in Japan, 1981: People's Daily Hours and Leisure Activities.* Tokyo: Foreign Press Center, 1982.

Roden, Donald. ''Baseball and the Quest for National Dignity in Meiji Japan.'' *American Historical Review* 85, no. 3 (June 1980), 511–34.

―――. *Schooldays in Imperial Japan: A Study in the Culture of a Student Elite.* Berkeley: University of California Press, 1980.

Saeki, Toshio. ''Kenko Bumu ni Hisomu Kiken'' [Dangers hidden in the health boom]. *Ekonomisuto*, June 7, 1977, pp. 58–62.

佐伯聡夫 「健康ブームにひそむ危険」 エコノミスト （１９７７．６．７）
５８～６２

―――. ''Kigyo ga Kaishimeru Amasupotsu'' [Amateur sports cornered by business]. *Ekonomisuto*, August 25, 1981, pp. 86–91.

佐伯聡夫 「企業が買い占めるアマ・スポーツ」 エコノミスト （１９８１．８．
２５） ８６～９１

―――. ''Nihonjin no Supotsu Raifu: Sono Haikei to Hoko'' [Japanese sports life: Its background and direction]. *Nihon Hyakkaten Kyokai Kaiho*, no. 1030 (August 1979), 3–7.

佐伯聡夫 「日本人のスポーツ・ライフーその背景と方向」 日本百貨店協会会報
１０３０号(１９７９.８) ３～７

―――. ''Supotsu Bumu Sasaeru Shakai Johyo'' [Social circumstances that bolster the sports boom]. *Ekonomisuto*, April 12, 1983, pp. 42–47.

佐伯聡夫 「スポーツ・ブーム支える社会状況」 エコノミスト （１９８３．４．
１２） ４２～４７

―――. ''Supotsu Bumu to Kigyo Senryaku'' [The sports boom and business strategies]. *Ekonomisuto*, April 17, 1979, pp. 86–90.

佐伯聡夫 「スポーツ・ブームと企業戦略」 エコノミスト （１９７９．４．１７）
８６～９０

Sakuta, Keiichi. *Haji no Bunka Saiko* [The shame culture reconsidered]. Tokyo: Chikuma Shobo, 1967.

作田啓一 『恥の文化再考』 東京 筑摩書房 １９６７

Sargeant, J. A. *Sumo: The Sport and the Tradition.* Rutland, Vt.: Charles E. Tuttle, 1959.

Sasama, Yoshihiko. *Zusetsu Nihon Budo Jiten* [The illustrated dictionary of Japanese martial arts]. Tokyo: Kashiwa Shobo, 1982.

笹間良彦 『図説日本武道辞典』 東京 柏書房 １９８２

Schodt, Frederik L. *Manga! Manga! The World of Japanese Comics.* Tokyo: Kodansha International, 1983.

Smith, Robert W. *A Bibliography of Judo.* Rutland, Vt.: Charles E. Tuttle, 1959.

Sogo Jaanarizumu Kenkyu-jo. ''Special Edition: Sports Journalism.'' *Sogo Jaanarizumu Kenkyu*, April 1980.

「特集スポーツ・ジャーナリズム」 総合ジャーナリズム研究 （１９８０．４）

''Special Edition: Sports Journalism 1984.'' *Sogo Jaanarizumu Kenkyu*, July 1984.

「特集スポーツ・ジャーナリズム１９８４」 総合ジャーナリズム研究
（１９８４．７）

" 'Sports Animals.' " *Japan Quarterly* 24, no. 2 (April-June 1977), 142–47.

"Supotsu Shido to Konjoron" [Coaching and fighting spirit]. *Taiiku no Kenkyu* 34, no. 2 (February 1984).

「スポーツ指導と根性論」 体育の研究　３４巻２号（１９８４．２）

Supreme Commander for the Allied Powers, Civil Information and Education Section, Education Division. *Education in the New Japan.* Vols. 1 and 2. Tokyo: SCAP General Headquarters, 1948.

Tada, Michitaro. *Asobi to Nihonjin* [Play and the Japanese]. Tokyo: Chikuma Shobo, 1974.

多田道太郎　『遊びと日本人』　東京　筑摩書房　１９７４

Tanimura, Tatsumi. *Taiikugaku Kenkyu Bunken Bunrui Mokuroku, Dai 1-, 2-kan* [Classified bibliography of Japanese research in physical education. Vols. 1 and 2]. Tokyo: Fumaido Shuppan, 1970, 1975.

谷村辰己　『体育学研究文献分類目録』第１、２巻　東京　不昧堂出版　１９７０
１９７５

Tokyo Taiiku Kagaku Kenkyukai. *Taiiku Jinmei Jiten* [Biographical dictionary of physical education]. Tokyo: Shoyo Shoin, 1970.

東京体育科学研究会　「体育人名事典」　東京　シォヲォ書院　１９７０

Uhlan, Edward, and Dana L. Thomas. *Shoriki: Miracle Man of Japan.* New York: Exposition Press, 1957.

Van Dalen, Deobold B., and Bruce L. Bennett. *A World History of Physical Education: Cultural, Philosophical, Comparative.* Englewood Cliffs: Prentice-Hall, 1971.

Watanabe, Toru. "Budo to Nihon no Supotsu Fudo" [Martial arts and the climate of Japanese sports]. *Taiiku-ka Kyoiku* 32, no. 1 (January 1984), 22–24.

渡辺融　「武道と日本のスポーツ風土」　体育科教育　３２巻１号（１９８４．１）
２２～２４

Whiting, Robert. *The Chrysanthemum and the Bat: The Game the Japanese Play.* Tokyo: Permanent Press, 1977.

Yanagita, Kunio. *Nihon no Matsuri* [The Japanese festival]. Tokyo: Kadokawa Shoten, 1956.

柳田国男　『日本の祭り』　東京　角川書店　１９５６

8

Popular Music

LINDA FUJIE

Among both scholars and laymen, any discussion of the definition of "popular music" is apt to produce a wide variety of definitions.* Taking the first component of the term literally, one must first ask, "popular among whom?" since different kinds of music are popular among different segments of a given society. As John Blacking has pointed out,

[Popular music] is music that is liked or admired by people in general, and it includes Bach, Beethoven, and the Beatles, Ravi Shankar, Sousa's marches and the "Londonderry Air." . . . The music that most people value most is popular music; but what that music is, varies according to the social class and experience of composers, performers and listeners.[1]

Even ignoring such societal differentiation, and using, for example, sales figures of recordings as the basis for determining "the music that most people value most" within a single country, difficulties persist. How does one label the songs written in a style similar to "hit" songs but that do not sell well? On the other hand, if popular music were to be defined not on the basis of some artificial index of "popularity" but on the basis of a particular musical style, how would one account for the wide range of musical styles found among the music of Bob Dylan, Barbra Streisand, and the Grateful Dead, all of which has been labeled "popular music" of one type or another.

The editors of a periodical entitled *Popular Music* offer the opinion that "from one point of view 'popular music' exists in any stratified society. It is seen as the music of the mass of the people . . . as against that of an elite."[2] The im-

* Japanese names in this essay are in the Japanese order of family name, given name.

plication of this statement—that the music a so-called elite listens to is therefore never in the realm of popular music—is highly questionable.

Owing in great part to confusion regarding the "popular" element of popular music, the size of the body of music referred to as such differs widely according to the speaker and context. In its most encompassing sense, the label "popular music" is used to include traditional "folk music." The *New Oxford Companion to Music*, for example, defines popular music as "all the various kinds of music that might not be considered under the general heading of 'serious' or 'classical' music."[3] However, this broad usage seems to have fallen out of favor of late.[4] In the most specific usage of "popular music," one finds "popular" or "pop" music differentiated from "rock," "folk," or "new wave" music as different subcategories under the rubric of "popular music."

Clearly there are a myriad of problems inherent in defining the concept of popular music. However, the term is widely used in many different cultures, and some points of agreement do seem to exist between the various ways in which it is used. This essay will explore specific genres of Japanese music that the Japanese themselves label "popular music." In the course of reading about these genres, those familiar with popular music of other cultures may find points of confluence between the Japanese definition of popular music and those of other cultures.

In the Japanese case, both the terms *minshu ongaku* and *taishu ongaku* can be translated as "popular music" or "music of the masses." More recently, the term *popyura ongaku* (the English "popular" plus the Japanese for "music") has also come into use.[5] Idiomatically, the term *kayokyoku*, which refers to the whole range of popular song, is probably used most often to refer to Japanese popular music in general.[6]

It is important to note here that any discussion of popular music in Japan must concentrate primarily on vocal music. The major categories of *kayokyoku—enka*, Japanese pops, and "new music"—all consist of vocal music, mostly solo songs. In addition, this essay will deal almost exclusively with the popular music performed by—and, in most cases, composed by—Japanese.[7] While Western popular music in the broadest sense (including jazz, country-western, soul, and rock) makes up an important element of the current music scene in Japan, this discussion will limit itself to music produced in its original form by the Japanese record industry.

There are several characteristics of *kayokyoku* that it has in common with much of the music identified as popular elsewhere; these differentiate such music from folk and art music. These characteristics include the facts that (1) the composer and lyricist are known; (2) the music is promulgated mainly through the mass media capable of sound reproduction—television (both live and video), radio, recordings; and (3) the average "lifespan" of a piece—the period when it is frequently heard over the mass media and sells the most records—is relatively short, generally a few weeks. Musically, typical *kayokyoku* songs have in common with Western popular songs a relatively short length (on the average, about

Figure 1
Major Types of *kayokyoku*

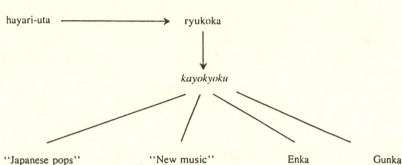

three to five minutes) and a structure consisting of simple strophic form with refrain. The vocal part or parts are generally set off by an instrumental introduction and the insertion of an instrumental interlude between strophes.

Some of the categories used in Japanese popular music are shown in Figure 1. A major problem with the terms used to subdivide the general category of "popular song" is that record companies, the general public, and scholars alike use them with little consistency and have applied them to different music at different times. An informal telephone survey of major record companies conducted in February 1985 indicated that the companies themselves have no clear-cut policy as to how they classify different types of *kayokyoku*. Rather, songs are placed into categories of *kayokyoku* according to who sings them; a certain singer is pegged by a record company as a singer of "new music," for example, and almost anything he produces will be classified as "new music," even if the style of the song is similar to another kind of popular song.[8]

Ryukoka is a term that originally was associated with popular song spread by means of the mass media, but that has generally been replaced with the term *kayokyoku*, which refers to the all-encompassing category of popular song.[9] *Enka*, one of the major types of popular song, is a song, written by a known composer and lyricist, that generally uses pentatonic scales (as opposed to Western heptatonic scales) and whose sentimental lyrics concern love and nostalgia. The other categories of popular song listed in Figure 1 will be defined and discussed later in the course of this essay.

HISTORICAL SURVEY

Before surveying the historical background of popular music in Japan, it will be useful to review the general characteristics of traditional music in that country. Some knowledge of the indigenous musical culture of the Japanese can enable one to discern ways in which popular music has drawn from, or strayed away from, traditional Japanese music.

A warning must first be made, however, that formulating theoretical generalizations that apply to all genres of Japanese music is a difficult task. This is because a comprehensive body of musical theory does not exist in the Japanese tradition. Musical concepts that apply to specific genres have been developed but widely applicable concepts are rare.

The method of vocal production, for example, differs with each genre of vocal music. Small differences in timbre, created by the method of vocal production, have traditionally set off different genres of song. Thus, *kiyomoto*, or song that is used to accompany *kabuki* dance, is sung with a different method of vocal production than *nagauta*, the general music of the *kabuki*. This differentiation holds true to some degree for popular music as well; the style of vocal production differs from one type of popular music to another, and this, in turn, partly determines how that music is categorized.

Vocal production in Japanese music is usually of the *uragoe* (falsetto) or *jigoe* (natural voice) variety. Koizumi defines *uragoe* as "made by producing a soft utterance while controlling a part of the vocal band to achieve uniform pitch," while *jigoe* is "made by producing a strong utterance at a relatively high pitch while keeping the vocal band and surrounding area tense."[10] Most Japanese vocal music is produced by the *jigoe* technique; *hanagoe* (nasal voice), a type of *jigoe*, is often used in *naniwabushi*, a narrative form of music that strongly influenced some forms of popular song. All of these varieties of vocal production differ from the *bel canto* style of singing in the West, which strives for a more brilliant tone color, and from the common vocal styles of Western popular music.

One specific vocal ornamental technique used in different vocal genres is also important to some forms of popular song. *Yuri*, a "swinging" of the voice to slightly alter a pitch, somewhat resembles the Western ornamentation technique of vibrato. The technique involves "going to the next tone of a melody while causing the melody to spin a bit," and its purpose is to "add luster to the melody line."[11] The exact width, pitch-wise, of the "vibrato" and its speed vary according to the genre of music in which *yuri* is used. The *yuri* heard in most popular songs is similar to the kind of *yuri* found in *shamisen*[12] vocal music and some types of folk song.

Most Japanese music has rhythm of a uniform beat structure; the main exception is the folk song of the *oiwakebushi* type, named after packhorse driver songs. These are lacking in a regular beat and contain melismatic treatment of the melody line. Music with a uniform beat structure is usually in duple meter, such as music for the *shamisen*. Some music for the *koto*, a thirteen-stringed zither, is in quadruple time and *noh* music is generally in units of eight beats, though not necessarily using a continuous, uniform beat. Triple meter in Japanese music is very rare.

It is not easy to make general statements concerning the structure of traditional vocal music, as this is highly flexible even within particular genres. In the various genres of vocal music accompanied by *shamisen*, for example, the music is highly susceptible to the influence of the structure of the lyrics, especially in the case of accompanied drama. The most basic elements of the structure of any given song consist of purely instrumental sections and vocal sections with instrumental accompaniment (though in the case of *gidayubushi*,[13] spoken narrative also enters in as a third element), and how these are alternated differs widely.

Traditional music with both instrumental and vocal parts displays an important aspect of the relationship between voice and instrument in Japanese music: what Malm describes as "an example of heterophony, for both parts seem to be performing the same melody with simultaneous variations." He further explains that "the reason behind this style in Japanese vocal music acccompanied by the *shamisen* seems to be that since both parts tend to perform the same melodic line, it is necessary for the singer to delay or anticipate the sound of a given tone on the *shamisen* in order that the text can be clearly heard."[14] This same effect can be found in some popular songs, a heterophonic interplay between the vocal line and some instrument simultaneously playing the melodic line, often a guitar instead of a *shamisen*.

The scales used in Japanese music differ according to the genre and instrument used, but a few that affect popular music will be presented here. The so-called *minyo* scale, used often in folk music, is equivalent to the natural minor scale with the second and sixth steps omitted: LA–DO–RE–MI–SOL–LA (or A–C–D–E–G–A). Another common scale is the *miyakobushi* scale: MI–FA –LA–SI–DO–MI (E–F–A–B–C–E).

The *shoka* school songs composed in the Meiji period used a new set of scales that later affected military songs and *kayokyoku* in general. They are labeled the *yonanuki* scales because the fourth (*yo*) and seventh (*na*) degrees of the Western major and minor scales are omitted. Thus, the *yonanuki* major scale contains DO–RE–MI–SOL–LA–DO (C–D–E–G–A–C); the *yonanuki* minor scale proceeds LA–SI–DO–MI–FA–LA (A–B–C–E–F–A). These two types of pentatonic scales are particularly important to the development of many popular forms of song in Japan.

A brief survey of the main genres of Japanese music should begin with one of the oldest surviving Japanese music forms, *gagaku*. Known as the court orchestral music of Japan, *gagaku* can be traced to China, India, and Korea, and it is said to have been first introduced to Japan in the seventh century. *Gagaku* ensembles utilize a combination of percussion, wind, and string instruments and can still be heard today in the Imperial Palace, as well as at many shrines and temples throughout the country.

Noh drama derived from popular forms of entertainment that were transformed and codified in the fourteenth and fifteenth centuries by Kannami Kiyotsugu and his son, Zeami Motokiyo. The accompanying instrumental ensemble is called *hayashi*, and consists of the *nohkan*, a transverse bamboo flute, and three kinds of drums, the *kotsuzumi*, the *tsuzumi*, and the *taiko*. A chorus, called *ji*, sings *yokyoku* (the vocal genre of *noh*), also called *utai*. This kind of singing-chanting is based on *shomyo*, or Buddhist chanting, which also has had an important impact on the Japanese music tradition.

The music of the Edo period (1615–1867) best reflects the tastes of urban common people in the premodern period. The *koto* was used for both solo and ensemble compositions, most of which were composed during the Edo period. One important form written for the *koto* is the *jiuta*, which alternates vocal sections with instrumental interludes. Strictly instrumental pieces exist as well, such as *shirabemono*, in which a basic theme is presented, followed by sections of variation with new melodies inserted. The popular instrumental ensemble of the time consisted of *koto*, *shamisen*, and *shakuhachi* (an end-blown flute) or *kokyu* (a bowed fiddle), and these ensembles were known as *sankyoku*.

The literature for solo *shakuhachi* developed mainly during the Edo period, when men known as *komuso* played in the streets wearing large baskets over their heads and sometimes acted as spies. The *shakuhachi* can be heard both in ensembles (as the *sankyoku*) as well as in solo pieces.

The *shamisen* played an important role in Edo period music, particularly in narrative traditions. The genre created by and named after Takemoto Gidayu, *gidayubushi*, utilizes the *shamisen* to accompany the drama of the puppet theater. The narrator-singer and the *shamisen* player sit next to one another to one side of the stage. The narrator speaks the lines of the puppet-characters and sings commentary as well, while the *shamisen* accompanies him and adds instrumental interludes.

Another genre of *shamisen* music popular during the Edo period was the *kouta*, literally "short song." The *kouta* was usually based on a romantic or descriptive text and was sung with *shamisen* accompaniment at small gatherings. *Kouta*, which influenced some early forms of popular song, utilizes the *hanagoe*, or nasal, form of vocal production.

Another important genre using the *shamisen* instrument is *nagauta*, the music of the *kabuki*. The voice and *shamisen* perform the same basic melody in a *nagauta* ensemble, which also includes drums and flutes. *Nagauta* can also be performed independently of the theater; *ozashiki nagauta* is for concert performance only.

Finally, Japan has a long, rich folk song (*minyo*) tradition. Many types of folk songs exist—work songs, game songs, love songs, etc. The voice is often accompanied by drums, *shimisen*, *shakuhachi*, and/or bamboo flutes. *Minyo* is often associated with a particular region, and part of its popularity in the cities derives from the nostalgia felt by those reminded of their home towns as they listen to these folk songs. Surveys have shown that *minyo* is the most popular form of traditional music in Japan, and it has continued to gain popularity in recent years.[15]

The history of *kayokyoku*—popular song with a known composer, primarily disseminated by means of the mass media—can be traced to a period when songs in theatrical plays were made into recordings and then used in movies. One of the first songs to undergo this process was "Kachusha no uta" [The song of Katiusha (the Russian diminutive for Katherine)], which first appeared as a song in a Japanese production of Tolstoy's "Resurrection." As the song gained widespread popularity in Tokyo, the Orient Record Company decided to release a recording of it by singer Matsui Sumako in 1915; this sold about 20,000 copies, a large amount for that time.[16] After this experience, recording and movie companies became involved with the promotion of well-received songs from the stage. In this period, a prospective song had to first prove its popularity with the theater public before being issued on a record or made into the theme song of a movie.[17] "Sendo kouta" [Boatman's *kouta*] was another song that followed this pattern.

The composer of "Kachusha no uta" and "Sendo kouta" was Nakayama Shimpei, who became a major figure in the development of popular song in Japan. Trained at the Tokyo Music School, Nakayama wrote songs that mixed Western and Japanese musical elements in a way that pleased the general public. "Kachusha no uta," for example, uses the Japanese *yonanuki* pentatonic scale for the melody and Western instruments for the background accompaniment. This combination of a melody using a pentatonic scale with Western instrumental accompaniment remains a popular combination among *kayokyoku* to the present day.

The musical beginnings of popular songs such as those mentioned above are said to belong primarily to two types of short song often heard in the Meiji period, the *shoka* and the *gunka*. *Shoka* are songs that were composed in the late nineteenth century to introduce Western-style music and singing to schoolchildren. These songs, as well as the *gunka*, or military songs, which were popular from the time of the Sino-Japanese War through World War II, also incorporated Japanese musical elements, specifically the use of *yonanuki* pentatonic scales.

Here the confusing etymology and use of Japanese popular music terms again come to the foreground. Nakayama is generally considered the first composer of *ryukoka*, though that particular term derived from a different reading of three Chinese characters that could also be read *hayariuta*. (The meaning of the characters themselves is "popular song.") The earlier term *hayariuta* was applied in the early Meiji period to short songs that were sung in the streets to relate the latest news events.

In its earliest use from the Meiji period through the Taisho period, the term *kayokyoku* referred to the lied, or art song, of Western classical music. However, toward the end of the 1920s, the newly formed Nippon Hoso Kyokai (NHK), or Japan Broadcasting Corporation, began to question the use of the term *ryukoka* for the popular songs they broadcast. Their concern derived from the fact that the literal meaning of *ryukoka*—"songs that are popular"—may not have applied to all the songs they broadcast that were in the popular style but not necessarily "popular." In the end, NHK decided to call all new popular music *kayokyoku*, and this usage gradually spread to the general populace.[18] However, the term *ryukoka* was still used for many years and is still sometimes used to refer to popular song in general.

As recording technology became more sophisticated from the 1920s to the 1930s, the quality of music recordings improved and phonographs became cheaper and more widely available to the general public in Japan. During this same period, the influence of record companies grew to the point that they decided almost exclusively which singers and songs would become popular nationwide. With the growth of the record industry, a system developed whereby record companies and movie companies cooperated to simultaneously release the recording of a song and a movie that featured that song. This system gave immediate maximum exposure to a song, making it possible for *kayokyoku* to become popular all over the country at the same time. Examples of this trend can be found in the songs of Sato Chiyako. Her songs, such as "Habu no minato" [The port of Habu], composed by Nakayama Shimpei and released in 1928, are representative of the darkly dramatic *kayokyoku* of this period.[19]

The relationship between popular song and traditional Japanese music was further strengthened in the 1930s, when *geisha* emerged as *kayokyoku* singers with songs that resembled *kouta*, the short-song genre mentioned earlier. One such song is "Gion kouta," composed by Sasa Koka and issued in 1930. In addition, popular songs written in traditional folk song style also became hits during this period. Songs such as "Tokyo ondo" (composed by Nakayama Shimpei and issued in 1933) were considered popular songs when they were released, but today are played at *bon odori* and similar folk events. Given their folk song style and the context in which they are played, many younger Japanese think that such songs are "pure" folk songs. Songs of this style often use scales common to folk songs and intersperse the vocal part with cries known as *kakegoe*, which are used in some varieties of folk song performance.

From the early 1930s, the composer Koga Masao became an important influence in prewar Japanese popular song, and he also reflected the closer relationship with traditional music. Koga's songs, most of which were sung by Fujiyama Ichiro, tended to include melodic lines that used *yuri* ornamentation from traditional music. His songs, such as "Sake wa namida ka tameiki ka?" [Sake is my tears or my sighs?] (issued in 1931), often used the *yonanuki* pentatonic scale.

The song "Wakare no buruzu" [The blues of separation], composed by Hattori Ryoichi in 1937, obviously borrowed the song type named in the title from the American song form, but was actually written in a Japanese "blues" style, which meant using a *yonanuki* minor scale in a slow, 4/4 rhythmic structure. The singer who made this particular song popular, Awaya Noriko, made many hit records of Japanese-style blues and became known as the "Queen of the Blues."

Gunka, the military songs that grew out of the Meiji period, have already been mentioned in connection with their influence on the beginnings of *kayokyoku*. In the midst of events that led up to World War II, such as the Manchurian Incident and the outbreak of hostilities with the Chinese, military songs regained popularity. They often resembled Western marches, with brisk tempos and heavily accented beats within a 4/4 meter. Usually using the *yonanuki* major or minor scales, the *gunka* often had an orchestral accompaniment, with drums and brass particularly highlighted and trumpet fanfares common. One highly popular *gunka* composed by Koseki Yuji and recorded in 1937 was called "Roei no uta" [The song of the bivouac], which firmly established him as the foremost composer of *gunka*.

In the prewar period, radio stations gained a major role in disseminating and influencing the popularity of *kayokyoku*. Because of the relatively poor quality of recording equipment, most music was performed live on the air.[20] This situation changed only after the war, with the proliferation of commercial radio stations and the increased use of better-quality recording equipment.

The end of World War II brought many new changes to popular song in Japan, both in the product itself and in the way in which it was produced. Western influences, from American popular songs to French *chansons*, strongly affected much *kayokyoku* written in this postwar period. In contrast to songs that displayed many elements of traditional Japanese music, such as the *yonanuki* scales and *yuri*, the postwar songs tended to use natural minor scales and melodies uninfluenced by *yuri*. One of the first hits after the war with this new Western-oriented sound was "Ringo no uta" [Apple song], sung by Namiki Michiko and released in 1945. Another such song, whose title reveals its American ties, is "Tokyo Boogie Woogie" (composed by Hattori Ryoichi and released in 1947), which uses a dotted dance rhythm and a major scale.

Even as Western-influenced songs flooded the market, a few hit songs still had musical links with the more Japanese-influenced, prewar *kayokyoku*. One was "Yu no machi ereji" [Hot springs elegy], composed by Koga Masao and sung by Omi Toshiro in 1948. The melody of this song was in a *yonanuki* scale, and the instrumental accompaniment consisted of not a full orchestra but a guitar, which lent a plaintive air reminiscent of the *shamisen*. The trend of using a guitar accompaniment in the background, popular from the 1950s on, was stimulated by this song.

Dramatic changes in how singers and songs were marketed affected almost every aspect of the popular music world in the 1950s. The creation of private broadcasting companies in 1951 and the development of television in 1953 stimulated the growth of so-called *geino* (artistic) production companies. Whereas record companies, sometimes in cooperation with movie companies, had previously coordinated the songwriter, lyricist, and singer in the production of a song, these production companies became involved with every step of the production of *kayokyoku*. They performed all the tasks from planning and selecting the song to negotiating with the record companies and the television and radio stations on behalf of the singer.

As they grew in power, some production companies had seemingly total control over all production aspects of a song and over all who were involved in its creation. The most powerful of these, Watanabe Productions, for example, not only had control over the contracts of a stable of singers, composers, and musicians, but also held the copyrights of all songs produced by their employees. Having acquired their own sheet music-publishing company, Watanabe Productions also had a monopoly on the publication of the songs in their possession.

The careers of singers were completely at the mercy of these production companies, who could decide to hard sell singers one year or ignore them the next. As a result of this complete control, new singers who joined the company could gain immediate, solid backing and assured record issues, but established singers who wanted to become independent had a difficult time. Since the production company had the copyrights to all their hit songs, they had to start out on their own with a whole new repertoire, obviously a great drawback to an established artist. This situation lasted until the 1970s, when television companies took over some of the former duties of the production companies.

Another side effect of this method of production was that a particular song came to be so closely associated with a particular singer that the producers, as well as the public, came to perceive their relationship as a symbiotic one. This perception was related to the way particular singers and songs were sold as a package to record companies and television stations.

One female singer who debuted in 1949 and sang in the Japanese style came to enjoy continued popularity for many years after the end of the war—Misora Hibari. Misora's singing was marked by the use of Japanese-style vocal production, which made a particularly strong impact in the postwar period when so many singers were imitating the West. She was skilled in singing in the *jigoe*, or natural voice, style and in the use of *yuri*. The tune "Ringo oiwake" was sung with a free rhythm, in folk song style, and "Tonko-bushi" [Coalminer's song] used the *minyo* scale. Another popular female singer of the time who used Japanese elements in her singing was Shimakura Chiyoko. Well-known male singers of this period include Kasuga Hachiro, Mihashi Michiya, and Minami Haruo. These artists also performed many songs that used the *yonanuki* scale, *yuri* techniques, and dotted rhythms and long melismatic sections reminiscent of folk song.

Running parallel with this 1950s trend of incorporating Japanese elements into popular song, American popular songs and jazz spread also throughout Japan, particularly aided by the presence of American military bases. Some American hits were translated into Japanese and became hits in versions sung by Japanese. Eri Chiemi made the Japanese version of "Tennessee Waltz" famous in 1952, and Yukimura Izumi recorded the Japanese translation of "The Last Waltz" [Omoide no warutsu], popular in 1953. This move to record American popular hits in Japanese developed into the so-called "Rockabilly" movement, a representative of which was Kosaka Kazuya's 1956 version of "Heartbreak Hotel," the Elvis Presley hit.

In the late 1950s, two rather incongruent styles of music simultaneously garnered popularity popularity in the record market—American pop songs and sentimental songs that used Japanese-style vocal production and melodic minor scales. An example of the latter is Frank Nagai's "Yurakucho de aimasho"

[Let's meet at Yurakucho], composed by Yoshida Tadashi. Singing in a similar style, male singing groups with a featured singer also appeared, such as Wada Hiroshi and the Minor Stars. Such groups were known as "mood chorus groups."

As Japan began its tremendous economic growth after the war, the middle class grew at a correspondingly fast pace. As a result, more songs appeared that were meant to appeal to the urban, white-collar class. Younger singers emerged, many in their twenties or late teens, and the songs they sang extolled youth and platonic love. More groups also were formed, in contrast to the overwhelming number of soloists who dominated the popular music scene.

The predilection the Japanese have for absorbing foreign music, imitating it, and then producing their own unique musical culture based on this experience is a recurring cycle in Japanese music history. Perhaps it is not surprising, therefore, that following the influx of Western popular music after the war, the 1960s saw the rise of so-called "Japanese pops." One highly popular example of this is the song "Ue o muite aruko," composed by Nakamura Hachidai and sung by Sakamoto Kyu, which was one of the few Japanese popular songs to become a big hit in its original form in the United States, there under the title "Sukiyaki."[21] Songs composed by Nakamura tended to have melodies set syllabically, used minor scales, and included such devices of Western harmony as modulations and borrowed chords.[22] Another well-known composer of the 1960s, Izumi Taku, also wrote in this Japanese pops style.

Kayokyoku, which incorporated the traditional scales, made another comeback in the latter half of the 1960s with female singers like Miyako Harumi and Suizenji Kiyoko. From this period it became common to call those songs that used the *yonanuki* scales and *yuri* techniques "*enka*," as opposed to "Japanese pops."[23]

The word *enka* and the music to which it has referred has its own historical background. The beginnings of *enka* can be traced to the 1880s, when the popular rights movement (*jiyu minken undo*) arose to demand less centralization of political, authority and a constitutional form of government. The participants of this movement began a campaign of informing the populace of their goals by composing songs about their movement that they felt would appeal to the public. The lyric sheets of these songs were then sold for profit.[24] The melodies were apparently influenced by traditional folk songs. Some songs had a strong, military-like style, such as "Oppekepe-bushi," composed by Kawakami Otojiro. With the establishment of the National Diet in 1890 and victory in the Russo-Japanese War, people lost interest in the political content of these songs, and the associations that promoted them were disbanded.

After the turn of the century, *enka* received another boost in popularity with the songs performed by Soeda Azembo. His songs, such as "Rappa-bushi," had a touch of social irony, and in general the lyrics of *enka* of this period tended to concern historical or current events. As opposed to the strong influence of traditional folk songs on earlier *enka*, the melodies of Soeda's songs tended to show the influence of *shoka* school songs and *gunka* military songs. From around

1907, the Western violin was used as an accompanying instrument in many of these songs.

During the Taisho period (1912–1926), professional *enka* singers grew in numbers, and these *enkashi* sang songs that often dealt with themes of male-female relationships. Some *enkashi* worked as minstrels, carrying a guitar or accordian from one bar to another and singing the requested songs of customers or accompanying the customers themselves as they sang. In the 1930s, *enka* could be heard both over the radio and on records, though maintaining the sentimental, sometimes teary atmosphere of the *sakaba*, or drinking place. After World War II, many famous *enka* composers and performers came out of the ranks of the old *enkashi*.

Enka underwent a stylistic change after the late 1960s, when singers like Mori Shinichi and Aoe Mina sang songs with a looser beat and in a heterophonic manner. This influenced the singing style of other *enka* singers into the 1970s, a decade during which *enka* underwent another boom in popularity.

Returning to the history of *kayokyoku* in general from the 1960s, the influence of television grew stronger as more households purchased the sets. This medium, in addition to the movies, brought many new singers to prominence.

In the early 1960s, Western musical groups and musicians such as the Beatles, Bob Dylan, and Joan Baez became popular and exerted a strong influence on two Japanese popular music movements: the "folk" movement and the "group sounds" movement. Under the influence of these movements, amateur students began to participate in their own music making by buying instruments, performing, and singing. Folk singers of the late 1960s include Mike Maki, Moriyama Yoko, and Jackie Yoshikawa and the Blue Comets.

The Tigers, the Tempters, and the Wild Ones were all groups formed in these years that came to represent the group sounds movement. The performance style of these groups tended to be affected by the more overtly expressive Western musicians, such as swaying back and forth while singing. The vocal quality of these groups imitated that of Western popular singing. In this period, more groups began to write their own music, in contrast to the former situation in which composer and performer were almost always different. Instruments used in the group sounds were those common to British and American rock groups of the 1960s, including electric guitar and percussion sets. Later, in the 1970s, some singers of the group sounds movement (like Sawada Kenji of the Tigers) left their groups and went solo.

This period also saw the rise of protest songs related to American conduct in the Vietnam War and the renewal of the U.S.-Japan Security Treaty, an issue that also became a focus of intense anti-war activity. Tied to this brand of song was a growing feeling on the part of some musicians that the mass media and recording companies treated singers as commercial objects and neglected the close relationship between singer, song, and listening public. Like the group sounds musicians, folk and rock singers wrote more of their own music in a move to close the gap between singer and song.

In the 1970s, the folk and rock movements drew together to form what was branded "a new kind of sound," represented by Yoshida Takuro and Minami Kosetsu. Their songs—the majority of which were written by themselves— generally use the natural minor scale, short phrases, and long rests between those phrases. The lyrics, which tend to have a more "personal" point of view, are often set syllabically.

By the late 1970s, this new development in the folk movement came to be considered sufficiently different from the previous folk style—particularly in the self-expressive nature of the lyrics—that the word "folk" was thought to be inappropriate. From this time, the label "new music" came into being. In the year 1978, albums of music considered new music sold 40 percent of the total sales of the year, and several of these songs were used in television.[25]

It is difficult to define the musical characteristics specific to new music, which is said to draw not only from the folk movement but also rock, group sounds, and pops. For instance, while folk, rock, and pops can be differentiated to some degree by instrumentation,[26] so-called new music does not have one specific kind of instrumentation. Typically, new music instrumental accompaniment contains different combinations of the common popular music instruments. The songs tend to stress melodic content over the presence of a strong beat, as found in rock music and some group sounds music. While considered, on the one hand, an urban, sophisticated brand of popular song, new music also sometimes incorporates elements of traditional music, such as the background use of Japanese instruments.

Many early new music performers wrote their own music and lyrics (to the point where the designation singer-songwriter became common), but more recent performers also use separate lyricists and songwriters. Texts of new music songs are more prose-like than the more poetic texts of some forms of *enka*, for example, and generally are written from an introspective, self-absorbed point of view.[27] In the themes of their lyrics as well as in musical style, this new music seems to reflect the thoughts and lifestyle of the young generation of Japanese who never experienced the Second World War and have generally grown up amid a standard of living unparalleled in the history of Japan.

Like the folk performers before them, many new music singers perform frequently in live concerts in locations outside of Tokyo like Hokkaido, Tohoku, and Kyushu, and do not appear often on television.

A different but highly visible phenomenon is the emergence of *kawaiko-chan*— the "cute," mostly female singers in their teens who appeal to young teenagers. These singers are packaged (discovered and given an image, attendant musical repertoire, and performing style) and promoted by production companies. *Kawaiko-chan* frequently appear on musical variety television shows, performing in costumes that accentuate an image of youth and innocence. Girls' costumes are often miniskirts or sometimes more elaborate costumes, and boys generally sport casual clothes. Their singing is accompanied by hand gestures and body movements that are especially designed for each song by a choreographer.

Typically, singers in this group maintain their popularity for two or three years before declining. Those who do last longer begin to sing more sophisticated *kayokyoku* as they outgrow the age limit for *kawaiko-chan*. Artist production companies are therefore constantly searching for new talent to replace aging *kawaiko-chan*. Sometimes singers in this category also debut as a group that later breaks up, each member becoming a soloist. This was the case, for example, with Kondo Masahiko, who was originally a member of the Tanokin Trio.

The lyrics of the songs sung by *kawaiko-chan* frequently include a few English words, which are often used in ways that seem out of context to a native speaker. Even the Japanese language is sometimes used incorrectly. For example, a song by the male singer Kondo Masahiko called "Kejimenasai" should actually be *kejime o tsukenasai* in grammatically correct Japanese.[28] There are several instances of grammatically incorrect Japanese phrases entering the language as slang after being used in popular songs.

Under the rubric of *kayokyoku*, or popular song in Japan, numerous categories of song exist, many of which have been already mentioned. The large categories of *kayokyoku* are *enka* and Japanese pops. Within each category, it is possible to distinguish several subtypes. The following is one possible way of subdividing the category of *enka*. Obviously, the boundary lines between these subtypes are flexible and singers may cross over from one kind of *enka* to another.

1. The type of *enka* that has been influenced by *naniwabushi*.[29] Singers of this kind of *enka* are expected to have a strong, thick voice. The singers' costumes are Japanese kimono, often rather bright and gaudy. The singers themselves tend to be in their late thirties to fifties and some were originally *naniwabushi* (also known as *rokyoku*) singers. Representative of this category are the singers Murata Hideo, Minami Haruo, and Futaba Yuriko.

2. Songs that concern life in general. These songs resemble the *naniwabushi* type of *enka* to some degree in the kind of costumes worn, style of vocal production, and voice color. Themes of this kind of *enka* often concern *giri* and *ninjo* (the Japanese values of obligation and humaneness), the love between brother and sister, and the ties between parent and child. The titles of these songs frequently end in–*jingi* (which can be translated as either "moral duty" or "humanity") or–*minato* (port), and masculine names are common in the lyrics. Male and female singers usually wear Japanese clothing and range in age from the middle twenties to the forties. Singers such as Miyako Harumi and Kitajima Saburo often sing songs of this type.

3. *Enka* that has been influenced by *minyo*, or traditional folk song, of the countryside. The singers of this type of *enka* are generally in their late twenties to late thirties; the women wear Japanese kimono (though not as brightly colored as those of the above group), and the men wear business suits. Many of the titles of the songs in this category contain names of rural areas. Singers who generally fit into this category include Mihashi Michiya and Kanazawa Akiko.

4. Songs that concern love and loss of love. This is the largest category of *enka*. The singers of these *enka* usually begin their careers as *enka* singers and are of various ages, from the late twenties and older. In performance, the female singers often wear

long dresses and the male singers wear suits. The titles of the songs themselves can contain the names of large cities like Tokyo and Osaka, being more oriented toward the city than the *enka* in the above category. The lyrics are often about an impossible or a lost love, and the use of images that allude to the emotions of sadness and loneliness is important. Male singers often sing about the feelings of a woman. Typical singers of this kind of *enka* are Mori Shinichi and Yashiro Aki.

The lyrics of the *enka* in this category typically contain the following themes, evoked by certain key words: *sake* and drinking (e.g., drinking, drinking alone, bar, getting drunk), cold and the north (northern Japan, winter, winter wind), rain (drizzle, clouded windows, blowing rain), and sadness (tears, crying). The sentimentality of these songs is not limited to the lyrics, but is also expressed in the vocal production of the singers, who often use a wide vibrato, and in their facial expressions as they sing.

In an attempt to discern the ideals by which the Japanese public judge their favorite singers, Koizumi has focused on the performer Mori Shinichi, who is mentioned above as a singer of the "romantic" type of *enka*. He lists the reasons for Mori's popularity as follows:

1. Mori sings about women's feelings, particularly their feelings about love, which endears him to that segment of the audience.

2. He sings in the style of *shinnaibushi*,[30] which Koizumi believes is a genre of traditional music still close to the hearts of the Japanese.

3. Mori's songs use the *yonanuki* scales in a "blues" style (meaning a slow, 4/4 beat structure), thus maintaining a "Japanese" atmosphere.

4. Mori is handsome and yet looks "like he could be easily hurt."[31] Koizumi claims that, from the viewpoint of the Japanese female in particular, this characteristic is important for the male singer who sings about the feelings of women. Koizumi summarizes: "A small-framed 'handsome boy'-type, always dressed properly in Western suit, singing songs in the style of *shinnaibushi*, knitting his brows and looking somehow in pain, to the background of Western instruments—this could be called the epitome in which is concentrated all the elements of contemporary *kayokyoku*."[32] By this last statement, we may surmise that Koiumzi was generalizing particularly about *enka*, as other forms of *kayokyoku* can have rather different standards.

The general category of Japanese pops can be subdivided into the following types of songs:

1. Songs concerning adult love. Singers of this type usually sing in a clear, Western-style voice and are in their mid-twenties to mid-thirties. The music often uses the Western minor scale, sometimes modulating to the major scale midway. Singers wear costumes that represent the latest urban, adult fashions. Koyanagi Rumiko, Fuse Akira and Sawada Kenji could be placed in this category.

2. Songs appealing to teenagers, sung by *kawaiko-chan* singers. This type of song has been described above.

3. Songs performed by groups. Pop songs that fall into the first two categories are often sung by soloists. Musically, the songs in this group are influenced by the group sounds movement of the 1960s, which has also been described above.

More Japanese listen to the type of music described here as *kayokyoku* than to any other kind of music. A 1982 survey conducted by NHK shows that *kayokyoku* was at the top of the list of "styles of music people most enjoy listening to." Of the various types of *kayokyoku* mentioned in this essay, *enka* appears to be particularly popular at the present time, but audience age is also an important factor in this determination.[33]

In attempting to evaluate the current state of popular music in Japan, it must first be noted that the highly developed electronic technology of Japan has made a strong impact on the music-listening habits of the Japanese, as it has on the rest of the world as well. A survey finds that an average of 40 percent of Japanese listen to records during their leisure hours, and the percentage goes up to 86.5 percent among male teenagers. In the ten-year period from 1969 to 1979, record sales jumped from 60.4 billion to 171.4 billion yen annually; cassette tape sales also nearly tripled in the same period.[34] Recordings—both LPs and tapes—are played in public places such as coffee shops and *pachinko* parlors, as well as in private homes. The popularity of walk-around stereos has meant that people do not even have to remain stationary to listen to their favorite music.

Music programs are frequently broadcast over radio and television. On television, musical variety shows, countdowns of the most popular songs of the week, and song contests for either new or established artists appear almost nightly. A survey of one week of television programs broadcast in Tokyo in January 1985 showed a total of seven daytime shows and ten evening shows more or less exclusively devoted to the presentation of *kayokyoku* of one kind or another.[35] More people listen to music performed over television than over any other media form.[36] One result of this close tie between popular song and television is that visual expression of a song—that is, the singer's facial expression and gestures, as well as the set and costumes—becomes closely tied to the communication of the emotional content of the song. In other words, the aural and the visual elements have become inseparable in the perception of much popular music in Japan today.

Another aspect of the close relationship between popular music and television lies in the use of popular songs for television show themes and for commercials. It is not uncommon for popular songs to become hits as a result of appearing in these television contexts.

One important mass media and cultural event of the year in Japan is the Kohaku Utagassen, the "Red-White Song Competition." This show, broadcast every year on New Year's Eve until almost midnight, features the most popular male and female singers of the year—though the process by which these are chosen is certainly subject to various pressures. Females on the "red" team compete against males on the "white" team, with a final decision rendered at the end of the evening by a panel of judges as to which team as a whole won. Watching this show, which is performed before a live audience in Tokyo and broadcast nationally, listening to favorite singers, and waiting to see which team will win has become a modern ritual of the New Year's season in Japan.

Radio remains a common means for listening to popular music, particularly FM radio. Statistics show that over 80 percent of the programing on FM radio consists of *kayokyoku*.[37] Detailed program schedules listed in popular magazines allow people to plan their listening schedule, should they choose to do so.

A technological development that has had a major impact on the popular music world was the invention of *karaoke*, sometimes called "music minus one." Literally meaning "empty orchestra," *karaoke* involves a singer singing into a microphone to a prerecorded tape that contains the background music for that song. The equipment used can be anything from a simple tape recorder–microphone device to an elaborate apparatus that can measure how far off tune the singer is singing. *Karaoke* gained enormous popularity in the mid–1970s and is still doing well in bars, where it can stimulate business, as well as in individual homes across Japan. Sales of home equipment in 1982 went as high as 625 million dollars.[38] The latest technological development has been the *karaoke* video, by which a singer can tape himself against a videotaped landscape, specially designed for a particular song, and later watch himself on television.[39]

Music video tapes are being created in greater numbers in Japan today, partly spurred on by the popular American videos that are frequently shown on Japanese television. Some are short "promo" videos, but others are lengthier video tapings of concerts that are sold in stores.[40]

An interesting phenomenon in the world of Japanese *kayokyoku* has been the rise of some foreign singers, particularly from other Asian countries. Singers such as Agnes Chan from Hong Kong and Judy Ong from Taiwan gained popularity in the 1970s singing in the Japanese language. A recent television song contest featured singers from several Asian countries competing in the performance of *enka*.[41] Some popular Japanese singers have returned the favor by gaining large audiences in several parts of Southeast Asia.

The exchange of popular singers with the West has been mainly a one-sided affair, from the West to Japan.[42] Exceptions to this rule have included the aforementioned hit song "Sukiyaki," the group Yellow Magic Orchestra, and— for a short time—the female duo Pink Lady, who for a brief period, had their own television show in America. Some singers, such as Itsuki Hiroshi, make a substantial income from performances abroad in such locations as Las Vegas, but their audiences are almost exclusively Japanese nationals or Japanese Americans.

REFERENCE WORKS

Virtually no bibliographical sources dealing with Japanese popular music exist in the English language. The best source for lists of the best-selling Japanese songs, for example, would be English-language newspapers, such as *The Japan Times*, which publish such lists periodically. Otherwise, comprehensive lists of titles would have to be procured from record catalogs from various companies, which are all in Japanese.

In the Japanese language, the *Original Confidence Annual Report* and the monthly magazine *Original Confidence* give thorough listings of current records, as well as commentary aimed at the business side of popular music promotion. Several other popular magazines also give schedules and background for *kayokyoku* of various kinds. Dealing with all different genres of *kayokyoku*, but specifically with regard to FM radio, there are magazines such as *Shukan FM* and *FM Fan*, which contain detailed sales charts, schedules, and notices of newly released records. Also of general interest is the monthly magazine *Music Magazine*, as well as other popular titles such as *Kayokyoku*, *Music Steady*, *Music Life*, and *Takarajima*. *Enka* is featured in the quarterly magazine *Enka Journal*. For listings of current popular music activity in Tokyo, the bi-weekly magazine *Pia* gives information on live concerts, newly issued recordings, and music schedules on FM radio and television.

While recently issued recordings are readily available in stores throughout Japan, obtaining copies of rare, older issues may be a problem even in that country. The best method of obtaining these is to contact the issuing company directly or to locate individuals with comprehensive popular music collections. One source of aid in such a search is the Association of Record Companies in Japan.

Outside Japan, it may be possible to obtain Japanese popular records, particularly in areas with large settlements of Japanese. In the United States, for example, cities such as San Francisco and New York have several bookstores for Japanese nationals that maintain a small stock of records and tapes. Even *karaoke* recordings are generally available at such locations. Some major American cities also carry Japanese television programing, and this, too, can be a source for gathering popular music materials, as popular music shows are often included in this programing.

For scores of popular music, a comprehensive collection is contained within the *Kayokyoku Zen-on Dai-zenshu*, which includes popular songs from the *Kayokyoku Zen-on Dai-zenshu*, which includes popular songs from 1884 to 1981 in five volumes. One major publisher of popular music scores is Shinko Shuppan.

While several books and articles in the English language are concerned with traditional Japanese music, very few deal specifically with popular music. *Japanese Music and Musical Instruments* by William Malm is an important work that surveys the various major genres and instruments. Eta Harich-Schneider's *A History of Japanese Music* provides a comprehensive historical account of the development of Japanese music, particularly in regard to pre-Tokugawa musical life. The late musicologist Koizumi Fumio's Japanese essay on the elements of Japanese music, "Theory," has been published in English in an abridged form in *East Magazine*.

In addition to receiving passing treatment in the above survey works, popular music has lately been the topic of a few articles in English, such as those by Judith Ann Herd and Mitsui Toru. Their articles deal with specific topics in the field of popular music; the former deals with trends in popular music as perceived through a popular music contest and the latter investigates a unique aspect of the recording industry in Japan.

There is relatively little scholarly research on popular music in the Japanese language. The book by Sonobe, Yazawa, and Shigeshita entitled *Nihon no Ryukoka* [Japanese popular song] has chapters dealing with specific types of popular song and issues in the popular music world. Okada's articles in *Ongaku Daijiten* provide a historical survey of *kayokyoku* in general and *enka* in particular.

Koizumi's book, *Kayokyoku no Kozo* [The structure of *kayokyoku*] is a collection of essays that analyzes various types of *kayokyoku* from the musical point of view. Koizumi identifies the various scale types used in Japanese popular song and traces the musical relationships these songs have with other forms of Japanese music. The book also has a valuable chronological table of postwar popular music edited by Okada.

For survey statistics on contemporary attitudes toward music in Japan, see the NHK publication, *Gendaijin to ongaku* [Contemporary man and music], which presents detailed public opinion surveys on the subject of music.

RESEARCH COLLECTIONS

There are, unfortunately, no research collections specifically devoted to the subject of popular music or recordings of popular music in Japan, according to the Association of Record Companies. Perhaps the most comprehensive collection of records of all kinds issued in Japan is contained in the National Diet Library in Tokyo. However, users are warned that the collection is far from complete with regard to popular music, and recordings of popular music are not cataloged by subject, making it necessary to look up each specific recording by each specific artist.

In the United States, several archives, particularly those specializing in ethnomusicology, contain a wealth of examples of traditional Japanese music (which are also readily available on records), but, to my knowledge, there are none that include representative examples of popular music.

The libraries of music colleges in Japan are probably the best source for secondary sources concerning Japanese popular music. Since these colleges specialize in Western music and musical performance, materials dealing with Japanese music account for only a small part of their collections. However, these libraries can be expected to have major Japanese popular music titles. The National Diet Library would also have such titles.

216   Linda Fujie

NOTES

1. John Blacking, "Making Artistic Popular Music: The Goal of True Folk," *Popular Music* 1 (1982), 13.

2. Richard Middleton, "Editor's Introduction to Volume I," *Popular Music* 1 (1982), 3–7.

3. Peter Gammond, "Popular Music," *The New Oxford Companion to Music*, vol. 2, ed. Denis Arnod (Oxford and New York: Oxford University Press, 1983), pp. 1467–77.

4. On this topic, Blacking notes that "popular music was generally thought to include folk songs" until elitists among folk music performers and scholars emerged who disdained popular music as "contaminated" and "commercial," as opposed to "pure" or "authentic" folk music (Blacking, p. 11).

5. Entries of subjects classified as "popular music" in a recently issued major music encyclopedia, *Ongaku Daijiten*, appear under the titles "Kayokyoku," "Enka," and "Popyura Ongaku" [Popular music]. The first two categories refer specifically to Japanese musical genres. The article on popular music presents a summary of popular music in the West.

6. "*Kayokyoku*" is also used to describe the category of so-called "Japanese pops"— that is, popular songs strongly influenced by Western, particularly American, popular songs in instrumentation, scale, vocal style, and arrangement. To avoid the confusion that this double usage can create, the term *kayokyoku* will be used in this essay only to refer to the broad category of popular music.

7. Koizumi includes in the category of *kayokyoku* foreign popular songs that have been translated into Japanese and (presumably) are sung by Japanese singers: "[*Kayokyoku*] includes not only Japanese-manufactured pops but also foreign pop and ['new'] folk songs which are familiar to us translated into Japanese" Koizumi. Fumio *Kayokyoku no Kozo* [The structure of *Kayokyoku* (Tokyo: Tojusha, 1984), p. 190.

小泉文夫　『歌謡曲の構造』　東京　冬樹社　1 9 8 4　p . 1 9 0

8. Personal communication with Naito Hisako, February 13, 1985.

9. The broadest definition of *ryukoka* is that of Koizumi, who equates *ryukoka* with *kayokyoku* in his writing: "Usually included in the category of contemporary Japanese '*ryukoka*' are, besides *kayokyoku*, pops, folk, television show themes, commercial songs, camp songs, recreation songs, student songs, group association songs and folk songs of olden times—really, every kind of song." Koizumi Fumio, *Kayokyoku no Kozo* p. 189.

10. Koizumi Fumio, "The Theoretical Elements of Japanese Music," *East Magazine* 18 (1983), 30.

11. Shigeshita Kazuo, "Enka—Sono Oto to Utaikata" [Enka—Its sound and way of singing], in S. Sonobe, T. Yazawa, and K. Shigeshita, eds. *Nihon no Ryukoka* [The *ryukoka* of Japan] (Tokyo: Otsuki Shoten, 1980), p. 44.

繁下和雄　「演歌――その音とうたいかた」　園部、矢沢、繁下編『日本の流行歌』

大月書店　1 9 8 0　p .　4 4

12. The *shamisen* is a three-stringed instrument that is plucked with a large plectrum.

13. The musical accompaniment to the *bunraku* puppet theater.

14. William Malm, "Some of Japan's Musics and Musical Principles," in Elizabeth May, ed., *Musics of Many Cultures: An Introduction* (Berkeley: University of California Press, 1980), p. 57.

15. Asian Cultural Centre for UNESCO, *Traditional Forms of Culture in Japan* (Tokyo: Asian Cultural Centre for UNESCO, 1975), p. 40.

16. Shigeshita, p. 36.

17. Okada Maki, "Kayokyoku," in *Ongaku Daijiten* [Encyclopaedia musica], Vol. 2 (1982), p. 622.

岡田真紀　「歌謡曲」『音楽大事典』　第2　1982　p.　622

18. Tokumaru Yoshihiko, "Kayokyoku no Shomondai" [Minor issues concerning Japanese popular songs], *Ongaku Geijutsu* 27 (1969), 23.

徳丸吉彦　『歌謡曲の諸問題』　音楽芸術27(7)　1969　p.　23

19. Okada, "Kayokyoku," p. 622.

20. Yazawa Tamotsu, "Hayarase no Shikakenintachi" [Those who make the songs popular], in Sonobe, Yazawa, and Shigeshita, p. 139.

矢沢保　「流行せの仕掛人たち」　『日本の流行歌』　1980　p.　139.

21. This song was re-released in the United States in 1980 under the same title but set to English lyrics and sung by an American female duo called Taste of Honey. Figuring prominently among the background instruments was a *koto*, and their performance on music videos showed them clothed in kimono.

22. Okada, "Kayokyoku," p. 623.

23. As noted earlier, this kind of song is more commonly known as *kayokyoku* in the narrow sense of songs influenced by the scales, vocal techniques, and harmonies of Western popular music. In order to avoid confusion, however, the term "Japanese pops" is used here to refer to this category.

24. Okada Maki, "Enka," in *Ongaku Daijiten* [Encyclopaedia musica], Vol. 1 (1982), p. 252. 岡田真紀　「演歌」『音楽大事典』　第1　1982　p.　252

25. Yazawa Tamotsu, "Nyu Myujikku to Wakamonotachi" [New music and young people], in Sonobe, Yazawa, and Shigeshita, p. 60.

矢沢保　「ニューミュージックと若者たち」　園部、矢沢、繁下編『日本の流行歌』
東京　大月書店　1980　p.　60

26. Typically, "folk" music is accompanied by acoustical guitar, "rock" uses electric guitar, electric organ, and percussion set; and "pops" has an orchestra, with heavy use of strings and woodwinds, in the background. These descriptions, of course, represent only broad generalizations; many overlapping cases exist.

27. Yazawa, "Nyu Myujikku to Wakamonotachi," pp. 69, 77–78.

28. This phrase is difficult to translate into English, but is one that might be used by a parent to a child to remind him of what behavior is expected of him. It is used by persons of higher status to those of lower status in requesting that they adhere to expected duties and obligations.

29. *Naniwabushi* is a dramatic, narrative form of music that is accompanied by *shamisen*. It has been previously mentioned as a case in which *hanagoe*, or nasal vocal style, is used.

30. This is another form of traditional narrative music, also accompanied by *shamisen*, which tends to be less overtly dramatic than *naniwabushi*.

31. Koizumi, *Kayokyoku no Kozo*, pp. 32–38.

32. Ibid., p. 38.

33. NHK Hoso Seron Chosa Shohen, *Gendaijin to Ongaku* [Contemporary man and music] (Tokyo: Nippon Hoso Kyokai Shuppansha, 1982), p. 629.

NHK放送世論調査所編『現代人と音楽』東京　日本放送協会出版社　1982

34. Yazawa, "Hayarase no Shikakenintachi,"pp. 132, 134.

35. Personal communication with Motegi Kiyoko, February 2, 1985.

36. NHK, p. 38.

36. Yazawa, "Nyu Myujikku to Wakamonotachi," p. 75.

38. "Closet Carusos: Japan Reinvents the Sing-along," *Time Magazine*, February 28, 1983, p. 47.

39. Judith Ann Herd, "Trends and Taste in Japanese Popular Music: A Case-Study of the 1982 Yamaha World Popular Music Festival," *Popular Music* 4 (1985), 83.

40. Ibid.

41. Personal communication with Motegi Kiyoko, February 2, 1985.

42. The enormous influence of European and American popular music on Japanese popular music has not been treated in this essay, but it continues, particularly since the end of World War II, to maintain a large share of the Japanese audience.

BIBLIOGRAPHY

Asian Cultural Centre for UNESCO. *Traditional Forms of Culture in Japan*. Tokyo: Asian Cultural Centre for UNESCO, 1975.

Baily, John. "Cross-cultural Perspectives in Popular Music: The Case of Afghanistan." *Popular Music* 1 (1982), 105–22.

Blacking, John. "Making Artistic Popular Music: The Goal of True Folk. *Popular Music*, 1 (1982), 9–14.

"Closet Caruso: Japan Reinvents the Sing-along." *Time Magazine*, February 28, 1983, p. 47.

Gammond, Peter. "Popular Music." *The New Oxford Companion to Music*. Vol. 2. Ed. Denis Arnold. Oxford and New York: Oxford University Press, 1983, pp. 1467–77.

Harich-Schneider, Eta. *A History of Japanese Music*. London: Oxford University Press, 1973.

Herd, Judith Ann. "Play It Again, Isamu!" *Manichi Shinbun*, July 9, 1984, p. 9.

———. "Trends and Taste in Japanese Popular Music: A Case-Study of the 1982 Yamaha World Popular Music Festival." *Popular Music* 4 (1985), 75–96.

Izumi, Dan. *Taikenteki Ongakuron* [Musical theory through practical experience]. Tokyo: Otsuki Shoten, 1976.

いずみだん 『体験的音楽論』 東京 大月書店 １９７６

Keil, Charles. "Music Mediated and Live in Japan." *Ethnomusicology* 28 (1984), 91–96.

Kikkawa, Eishi. *Nihon Ongaku no Seikaku* [The character of Japanese music]. Tokyo: Ongaku no Tomosha, 1979.

吉川英史 『日本音楽の性格』 東京 音楽之友社 １９７９

Koizumi, Fumio. *Kayokyoku no Kozo* [The structure of *kayokyoku*]. Tokyo: Tojusha, 1984.

小泉文夫 『歌謡曲の構造』 東京 冬樹社 １９８４

———. "Musical Forms." *East Magazine* 18 (1983), 21–25.

———. "Rhythm: Transitional Aspects of Music in Time." *East Magazine* 18 (1983), 25–31.

———. "The Theoretical Elements of Japanese Music." *East Magazine* 18 (1983), 25–31.

———. ''Theory.'' In *Nihon no Ongaku* [Japanese music]. Ed. Kokuritsu Gekijo Jigyobu. Tokyo: National Theatre of Japan, 1974, pp. 65–93.
　〃セオリー〃「日本の音楽」　東京　国立劇場事業部　１９７４．

Kojima, Tomiko. ''Shoka.'' In *Ongaku Daijiten* [Encyclopaedia musica] 3 (1982), 1215–16.
小島美子「唱歌」『音楽大事典』　第３巻１２１５‐１６　１９８２

———. *Uta o Nakushita Nihonjin* [We Japanese who have lost song]. Tokyo: Ongaku no Tomosha, 1981.
小島美子『歌をなくした日本人』　東京　音楽之友社　１９８１

Lamb, Andrew. ''Popular Music.'' In *The New Grove Dictionary of Music and Musicians* 15 (1980), 87–121.

Malm, William. *Japanese Music and Musical Instruments*. Rutland, Vt.: Charles E. Tuttle, 1959.

———. ''Some of Japan's Musics and Musical Principles.'' In *Musics of Many Cultures: An Introduction*. Ed. Elizabeth May. Berkeley: University of California Press, 1980, 48–62.

Middleton, Richard. ''Editor's Introduction to Volume 1.'' *Popular Music* 3 (1984), 107–20.

Mitsui, Toru. ''Japan in Japan: Notes on an Aspect of the Popular Music Record Industry in Japan.'' *Popular Music* 3 (1984), 107–20.

———. ''Popular Music.'' In *Ongaku Daijiten* [Encyclopaedia musica] 5 (1982), 2356–58.
三井徹「ポプュラー音楽」『音楽大事典』　平凡社　１９８２

NHK Hoso Seron Chosa Shohen. *Gendaijin to Ongaku* [Contemporary man and music]. Tokyo: Nippon Hoso Kyokai Shuppansha, 1982.
ＮＨＫ放送世論調査所編『現代人と音楽』東京　日本放送協会出版社　１９８２

Okada, Maki. ''Enka.'' In *Ongaku Daijiten* [Encyclopaedia musica] 1 (1982), 252.
岡田真紀「演歌」『音楽大事典』　第１巻２５２　１９８２．

———. ''Kayokyoku.'' In *Ongaku Daijiten* [Encyclopaedia musica] 2 (1982), 621–24.
岡田真紀「歌謡曲」『音楽大事典』　第２巻６２１‐２４　１９８２

Shigeshita, Kazuo. ''Enka—Sono Oto to Utaikata'' [Enka—Its sound and way of singing]. In *Nihon no Ryukoka* [The *ryukoka* of Japan.] Ed. S. Sonobe, T. Yazawa, and K. Shigeshita. Tokyo: Otsuki Shoten, 1980, 8–57.
繁下和雄「演歌ーーその音とうたいかた」　園部、矢沢、繁下編『日本の流行歌』大月書店　pp.８～５７　１９８０

Sonobe, Saburo, Tamotsu Yazawa, and Kazuo Shigeshita. *Nihon no Ryukoka* [The *ruykoka* of Japan]. Tokyo: Otsuki Shoten, 1980.
園部三郎　矢沢保、繁下和雄『日本の流行歌』　東京　大月書店　１９８０

Tanabe, Akio. *Nihon no Kayokyoku* [Japanese popular song]. Tokyo: Otsuki Shoten, 1981.
田辺明雄『日本の歌謡曲』　東京　講談社　１９８１

Tokumaru, Yoshihiko. ''Kayokyoku no Shomondai'' [Minor issues concerning Japanese popular songs]. *Ongaku Geijutsu* 27 (1969), 18–23.
徳丸吉彦『歌謡曲の諸問題』　音楽芸術２７(７):１８‐２３　１９６９

Tomioka, Taeko. *Uta—Kotoba—Nihonjin* [Song—words—Japanese]. Tokyo: Soshisha,
    1972.
富岡多恵子 『歌－－言葉－－日本人』 東京 草思社 １９７２

Yazawa, Tamotsu. ''Hayarase no Shikakenintachi'' [Those who make the songs popular].
    In *Nihon no Ryukoka* [The *ryukoka* of Japan]. Ed. S. Sonobe, T. Yazawa, and
    K. Shigeshita. Tokyo: Otsuki Shoten, 1980, 123–74.
矢沢保 「流行せの仕掛人たち」『日本の流行歌』 園部、矢沢、繁 下 「日本の流行歌」
東京 大月書店 ｐｐ．１２３－１７４ １９８０

―――.''Nyu Myujikku to Wakamonotachi [New music and young people]. In *Nihon
    no Ryukoka* [The *ruykoka* of Japan]. Ed. S. Sonobe, T. Yazawa, and K. Shigesita.
    Tokyo: Otsuki Shoten, 1980, 60–96.
矢沢保 「ニューミュージックと若者たち」 園部、矢沢、繁下編『日本の流行歌』
東京 大月書店 ｐｐ．６０－９６ １９８０

9

Japanese Comics

JOHN A. LENT

> The comic strips showed decapitations, cannibalism, people bristling with
> arrows like Saint Sebastian, people in flames, shrieking armies of marauders
> dismembering villagers, limbless people with dripping stumps, and, in gen-
> eral, mayhem. The drawings were not good, but they were clear. Between
> the bloody stories there were short comic ones and three of these depended
> for their effects on farting: a trapped man or woman bending over, exposing
> a great moon of buttock and emitting a jet of stink (gusts of soot drawn in
> wiggly lines and clouds) in the captors' faces.
> — Paul Theroux, *The Great Railway Bazaar.*[1]

It is true that Japanese comic books are oftentimes brutal, vulgar, and in poor
taste as described by Theroux, but they are more—innovative, pioneering, and
gigantic in format and profits. It was in Japan that the first inexpensive, mass-
produced, regularly scheduled comic books appeared in the 1920s, a decade
before their advent in the United States; that the first professional association of
cartoonists, Manga Kourakukai, was created in 1918, and that the first comic
art museum was opened in 1966—the City Museum of Cartoon Art in Omiya.
Japan has, in Kawasaki City, the only temple devoted to cartoons. Known as
Mangadera (Cartoon temple), it houses cartoons collected by a Buddhist priest
who gave cartoonists refuge after World War II.

Like so many Japanese mass media, the comic book industry is immense, as
is the format of the magazines. It is not unusual to have a comic book of 350
pages with as many as fifteen serialized stories. Usually, book publishers compile
serialized comic magazine stories into books, with a minimum of 200 pages,
sold in hardback and paperback versions. Their circulations are phenomenally
large; the five largest boys' comics boast a combined weekly circulation of about
9 million. The largest, *Shonen Jump*, sometimes sells 3 million copies a week.

Annually, 1.16 billion copies of comics are produced in Japan, constituting 27 percent of the total books and magazines.

HISTORICAL SURVEY

Beginnings

The history of caricature in Japan is no less impressive in longevity; some scholars have traced it to the sixth and seventh centuries.[2] Caricatures of animals, people, and phalli, dating to that time, have been found in the Toshodaiji and Horyuji temples of Nara. In the twelfth century, narrative picture scrolls, some as long as eighty feet, accompanied by text used caricature styles. A monk of the Tendai Sect, Bishop Toba Sojo, drew the *Chojugiga* [Humorous pictures of animals and birds], satirizing the religious hierarchy of the time through the humorous actions of monkeys, rabbits, foxes, and frogs. During the Kamakura era (1192–1333), the picture scroll in cartoon format gained more popularity, notable examples being *Jigoku Zoshi* [Hell scrolls], *Gaki Zoshi* [Hungry ghosts], *Tengu Zoshi*, and *Yamai Zoshi* [Disease scrolls]. Frederik Schodt wrote of these: "Suffering is depicted with sledgehammer realism: grossly deformed demons mock cowering humans; famished grotesqueries devour corpses and human excrement with gusto; the frailty of mortals is pounded home with a parade of maladies and aberrations—a man with hemorrhoids, a hermaphrodite, an albino."[3]

Blyth, in *Japanese Humour*, said *Yamai Zoshi* was a single scroll of fifteen pictures of sick people, meant as a reference work for physicians. He said one, "A Dwarf," showed a man and a priest pointing at a dwarf and two boys dancing with joy over his deformity. Others showed a man without an anus who defecates through his mouth, a woman with a mole on her face, and a man with many anuses. These scrolls were usually done in a mocking caricature form.

Scrolls, when they were not religious in nature, often went to the extreme of depicting farting and phallic contests. *Hohigassen* [Farting contests], suspected to be the work of Bishop Toba, showed a group of men eating sweet potatoes and then competing in a game where they collected wind in bags, "releasing it in each other's faces, farting, and using a fan for self-defense."[4] Blyth said Bishop Toba drew *Shukyuzu* [Stinking fart picture] to get a laugh out of Emperor Eayu, who was suffering from hypochondria.[5] Japanese television and comic magazines today carry on that tradition with *unko manga* (shit comics). Toba also received credit in some circles for the scroll, *Yobutsu Kurabe* [Phallic contests], showing men comparing "their huge erect members and using them in ingenious feats of strength."[6]

The Tokugawa era (1603–1868) was important in the development of caricature. Blyth said the period was "one of caricature, military and political resistance to it, and popular resistance to that resistance through caricature."[7]

By this time, a type of religious cartooning, *zenga* (Zen pictures), also appeared. *Zenga* were, according to Schodt, "circles drawn to represent the Void. They could suggest a profound beauty or be very off-color."[8] Humorous Zen pictures, as with all art, were meant for the upper classes. The common folk were served by cartoons sold only near the town of Otsu in Gifu Prefecture and known as *Otsu-e* (Otsu pictures). *Otsu-e* began as Buddhist amulets for travelers, but according to Schodt, became "uninhibited, secular cartoons with stock themes: beautiful women, demons in priests' garb, and warriors."[9] The *otsu-e*, begun in the Kanei era (1624–1643), were done quickly and cheaply by uneducated artists. Caricature for peasants' amusement also was available on *netsuke*, small toggles used to attach pouches and other personal articles to the sash of a kimono. Carvers of *netsuke*, beginning in the seventeenth century, depicted lighthearted good humor, "no subject, except of course the Imperial Family, [being] immune from the good-natured irreverence with which *netsuke* carvers approached their craft." Nathan Rogers quoted one authority as describing the *netsuke* as "forerunners of contemporary cartoons or caricature."[10]

That the authorities were concerned with caricature is evident in the case of Hanabusa Itcho (1652–1724), a true caricature artist, arrested and exiled to an island for twelve years for his book of pictures, *Hyakunin Joro*, which rashly depicted the fifth shogun, Tsunayoshi. Itcho used humor and caricature as the keynotes to his work. David Chibbett wrote that probably no other Japanese artist gave so many different humorous facial expressions to animals.[11]

The genre that definitely served popular consumption was the woodblock print that became popular in the early seventeenth century. Most popular were the *ukiyoe*, illustrations of the "Floating World," described by Schodt as a "term suggestive of life's uncertainties and the search for sensual pleasures to sweeten one's feelings of hopelessness."[12] Originally, *ukiyoe* showed life in Yoshiwara, the prostitute district of Tokyo, but eventually they showed the "pastimes of the day—fashions, popular places to visit, the latest *kabuki* theater idols, and oft-told historical tales—in flowing lines and multiple colors."[13]

Much has been written about *ukiyoe*. Takahashi said they developed into a "kind of newspaper" portraying events of the day.[14] He pointed out that *ukiyoe* artists, faced with extinction as real newspapers appeared during the Meiji Restoration, then published *Nishikie News*, pictorial representations of newspaper articles in rapid succession. When this paper failed after five or six years, *ukiyoe* artists, such as Yoshitoshi Tsukioka and others, turned to established newspapers as outlets for their illustrations.

The woodblock pictures, combined into twenty or more pages with or without text and bound with thread or opened in corrugated fashion, may have been the world's first comic books. Schodt reported that in 1702, Shumboku Ooka started a cartoon book, *Tobae Sankokushi*, "depicting mischievous, long-legged little men frolicking in scenes of daily life at Kyoto, Osaka, and Edo."[15] In Osaka, these books became popular and were known as *Toba-e* (Toba pictures). At the end of the eighteenth century, *kibyoshi* (yellow cover) booklets, made up of monochrome prints and captions, were popular among adults, stressing "topical subjects for townspeople in a humorous fashion."

Author James Michener, a devotee of *ukiyoe*, said they astonished with their eroticism, in turn becoming "the most bold, frank and explicit sex pictures ever produced by major artists."[16] In the erotic works, called *shunga*, commoners triumphed over noblemen by creeping into the beds of their wives. Michener added that *ukiyoe* was

always an art of social protest. It was an art of gentle ridicule and it was an art that thumbed its nose at the Tokugawa dictatorship. In none of its other manifestations did *ukiyoe* exhibit its true character more than in its unending barrage of *shunga*. Often the duped husbands were pompous *samurai*, the men the princesses ran off with were commoners. The young blade who crept into the nobleman's bed while he lay snoring was the gardener.[17]

Richard Lane wrote that *ukiyoe* were principally "sex manuals and guides to the courtesans, erotica exquisitely designed for members of a lively class of connoisseurs." Citing the caricature style of numerous *ukiyoe* artists, Lane said the woodblock prints they created can "distort reality and depart so much from it and yet still express a sensitive human beauty." Giving reasons for the demise of *ukiyoe* in the nineteenth century, he listed declining talent among artists, overproduction for a mass audience, and deteriorating taste for prints on the part of a changing public. He said in a century and a half, the prints had gone from being "decorations for a connoisseur's chamber to pin-ups for the laborer and clerk."[18]

Frank Whitford held that artists "not only wanted to shock and scare, they also wanted to amuse, and many of their prints show people humorously deformed, or strange beasts with bizarre proportions acting like humans." He said that embedded in many of the prints was a multiplicity of meanings, politically motivated under the repressive shogunate. Thus, some of the prints may have acted as political cartoons of the day.[19]

Among the chief *ukiyoe* artists were Katsushika Hokusai (1760–1849), who did illustrations for books of *kyoka* (humorous verse of thirty-one syllables) and *Hokusai Manga*, a book on painting techniques with numerous caricatures, and Ichiryusai Hiroshige (1797–1858), considered the last of the great *ukiyoe* artists. Hiroshige also published many *kyoka*.[20]

Western Influences

As Japan ended centuries of isolation in the mid-nineteenth century after Commodore Perry's arrival and the succeeding Meiji Restoration, Western influences seeped into the cartoon world. European-style cartoons were introduced by expatriates Charles Wirgman, an Englishman, and Georges Fernand Bigot, a Frenchman. Wirgman, a correspondent for the *Illustrated London News*, contributed a British-style, monthly humor magazine, *The Japan Punch*, for the foreign residents of Yokohama. With a circulation of about 200, the magazine, which survived from 1862 to 1887, featured mostly text but also low-key cartoons by Wirgman.[21] A writer who later analyzed *The Japan Punch*, wrote it was:

lithographed on soft paper, 14 1/2'' by 9 3/4'', the letter press being a reproduction of the actual writing of the Editor, and each issue abounds with cartoons and caricatures. Most of the articles and illustrations are obviously of a topical character, and the point of many of them, therefore, is lost on the present-day reader.

In the first issue, the editor wrote:

It had been our intention to have published an "Overland Punch," but having remembered the very seedy appearance of some editors after the issue of theirs, we enquired the reason, and discovered that it arose from want of sleep. These infatuated men spent six nights in getting the "Overland" published. They assured us that it was impossible to do it in the daytime. We at once resolved for ever to abandon our original decision, and adhere to our motto "Idleness is the Parent of Happiness!" We have consigned the midnight oil to perdition, and firm in our intentions of never taxing our constitutions with over-exertion, we intend to keep our minds in a perpetual state of vernal freshness, free from anxious thought or care, and happy as a bull terrier with a rat. We will never do today what we can put off till some future period of our sublunar career. "Honi soit qui mal y pense." Verb. Sap.[22]

The Japanese were so fascinated with *The Japan Punch* that they published a translated version, and for a considerable time called all cartoons *ponchie*. The magazine became a model for Japanese humor magazines such as *Nipponchi* (1874), *Maramaru Chimbun* (1877), and *Tokyo Puck* (1905). Wirgman's own influence was also great in that Japanese cartoonists copied his illustrative style, while others, such as Goseda Horyu and Kiyochika Kobayashi, trained under him.

Bigot arrived in Japan later, in 1882, and within five years helped found *Tobae* (after Bishop Toba), a bi-weekly, French-type humor periodical of thirteen pages. Bigot contributed cartoons that satirized Japanese society and government, the latter often reacting strongly against him.[23] Wirgman and Bigot introduced elements still important to Japanese comics—the word balloon and arrangement of cartoons in a sequence. From Westerners such as Wirgman and Bigot, the Japanese learned about faster and less expensive printing techniques than woodblock—copperplate printing, zinc etching, lithography, metal type, and photoengraving.[24]

Of the Japanese humor magazines inspired by the Westerners, the most famous was *Marumaru Chimbun*,[25] started in 1877 as a weekly by Fumio Nomura. It, like *Punch* and *Tobae*, came out of Yokohama. The covers were drawn by Kinkichiro Honda, who, over the years, did a number of satirical cartoons on human rights, civil liberties, and other political affairs. Honda was fond of atrocious puns, one of which was entitled "Minken Tohai" or "Howling Dog of the People." Honda completed the pun by drawing a "huge dog howling over some government officials and thus produced a humorous statement on the growing demand for human rights."[26] An 1880 Honda cartoon parodying the parliamentary government resulted in a year of imprisonment for the magazine's editor. Beisaku Taguchi also drew for *Marumaru Chimbun*, mainly topical cartoons on current events such as the need for labor laws.[27]

Horn claims that by the end of the nineteenth century, the inspiration for Japanese cartoonists emanated from the United States, not Europe.[28] Rakuten Kitazawa and Ippei Okamoto, two of Japan's greatest cartoonists, helped popularize comics and cartoons. Kitazawa first worked for an American magazine in Yokohama, the *Box of Curios*. Horn wrote of Kitazawa:

He went on to become one of the most versatile and skilled cartoonists to emerge in Japan and is today the only one with a mission [temple] in his honor. When he cartooned with a pen, as was usual, his drawings had the tight lines and attention to anatomy and perspective that characterize Western cartoons. When he used a brush, he could draw in the loose, simple, and subjective style the Japanese excelled at. His political cartoons had a sharp international perspective that makes those of Japan today look insipid by comparison.[29]

He innovated often: In 1902, Kitazawa started the first serialized comic strip with regular characters, "Tagosaku to Mokube no Tokyo Kembutsu" [Tagosaku and Mokube sightseeing in Tokyo], run in a color Sunday supplement called *Jiji Manga*, and three years later he founded *Tokyo Puck*, the first Japanese magazine devoted to political and humorous cartoons.[30] Probably the "most international magazine ever produced in Japan," *Tokyo Puck* carried cartoons with captions in English, Chinese, and Japanese and had a circulation of over 100,000.

Okamoto, like Kitazawa, showed that cartooning did not have to remain solely a vocational sideline. From 1912, he worked as cartoonist-journalist for *Asahi Shimbun*. After a trip to the United States, Okamoto described U.S. comics and their characters for *Asahi* readers, the result being that a number of U.S. comic strips were translated and serialized in Japan. Japanese comics, such as "Nonki no Tosan" [Easy-going daddy] by Yutaka Aso, often imitated U.S. prototypes.

The early 1920s also was when children's comics first appeared in newspapers (works of Katsuichi Kabashima and Shigeo Miyao) and when the first comic books appeared. Sometimes in color, these books on pulp paper were published monthly. The books were so popular that lending libraries for children, *kashibonya manga*, specialized in distributing them and later in producing them for rent. These lending library producer-distributors lasted until the 1960s, and many successful cartoonists began their careers in rental books.[31]

Also in the 1920s, further politicization of cartooning occurred as artists accepted anti-establishment, and often Marxist, viewpoints. In 1925, *Musansha Shimbun* [Proletariat news] was founded and acted as an outlet for Marxist cartoons; other periodicals of a similar ilk followed, such as *Senki* [War banner]. *Musansha Shimbun* boasted the works of propaganda agitation artists such as Masamu Yanase, Keiichi Suyama, and Fumio Matsuyama. Yanase was perhaps the most feared political cartoonist of his day. Dedicated to the cause of the masses, he regularly hit the capitalists and eventually joined the Communist party. In 1932, he was arrested, suffered prolonged torture, and was sent to prison. As the militaristic government of Japan became stronger, he was prohibited from drawing. Suyama, who helped form Nihon Mangaka Renmei (Japan Cartoonists Federation),[32] also suffered the wrath of the government. After joining the Communist party in 1933, he was arrested and imprisoned for two years. When he was released, he found a situation where political cartoonists could not find work and their lives were threatened. Thus, he turned to writing a series of books on the history of cartoons. Matsuyama, who edited the Nihon Mangaka Renmei periodical, *Humor*, drew for *Rodo Manga* [Labor cartoons] and *Nomin Manga* [Peasant cartoons], both critical of the government. He spent three years in prison in the early 1930s.

Other cartoonists also aimed their pens at political and governmental authorities. Hidezo Kondo, for example, did political cartoons critical of the government's treatment of labor unions and was later involved in *nansensu manga* (nonsense comics). He joined the *Manga Man* [Cartoon man] staff in 1929 and produced many cartoons in *ero* (erotic) and *guro* (grotesque) styles of the nonsense genre. This innovative magazine, which introduced some U.S. cartoons and comics and was partially in color, was closed by the government in 1931.[33]

Discussing the increasing thought control of Japanese police, Schodt wrote that artists and their editors were forced into self-censorship, with arrest the result when editors did not comply. He added, "It happened so often that some magazines designated an employee as 'jail editor'—he who had the honor of taking the rap and saving the company."[34] Many artists, as a result, worked in safer genres, such as the *ero-guro-nansensu*, or were coopted to draw for the government.

Despite the restraints placed on comic artists, the industry prospered, with monthly children's magazines such as *Shonen Club* and others becoming fatter with episodes of twenty pages or more, and with children's classics emerging.

As Japan became more heavily involved in its war effort, the cartoonists fell into step. Most cartoonists' organizations were obliterated and replaced by the government-backed Shin Nippon Mangaka Kyokai, and government policy was strictly followed. Shin Nippon Mangaka Kyokai published the monthly, *Manga*, the only cartoon magazine that existed throughout the war. Hidezo Kondo acted as editor, creating some of his most memorable political cartoons, depicting "evil demons" Roosevelt, Churchill, and Stalin. Cartoonists allowed to continue drawing during wartime worked either in harmless family comic strips, single-panel cartoons, or in *manga* or other Japanese media, depicting the enemy in the most unfavorable manner, and, with the government and military service propaganda corps, designing graphics to be used against the enemy.[35]

Strips were used on the domestic front to promote conservation, loyalty, and production and to exhort the people to "annihilate the Satanic Americans and British!" while overseas, they attempted to persuade Asians that the Japanese were liberators and to sow dissension among Allied troops. Thus, leaflets with comic figures telling Allied troops that their spouses were being unfaithful back home were dropped, as were those telling Asian populations that the Japanese came as friends.[36]

Among Japanese artists working for the American cause was Taro Yashima, who drew "Unganaizo," a twenty-panel comic leaflet done for the U.S. Office of War Information. The cartoon was realistic enough that it was often found on the bodies of dead Japanese soldiers. In 1943, he created *New Sun*,[37] a narrative with captioned drawings that showed the pressures and restrictions brought upon artists.[38]

The postwar period saw the flourishing of comic art again, despite paper shortages and the Allied occupation censorship. Horn described the period:

After an initial period of prostration, the Japanese cartoonists also rebounded with their legendary resiliency. The American occupation had the benefit effect of cutting the Japanese strip loose from some of its more desiccated story telling traditions, and Japanese comics acquired a more occidental look, with forays into science fiction ("Fushigina Kuni no Putcha"), jungle adventure ("Shonen Oja"), and even domestic humor ("Sazae-san").[39]

Political topics were second in priority to subjects dealing with average families trying to cope and "lovable little children." Most popular of this genre was "Sazae-san" [Mrs. Sazae], drawn by Machiko Hasegawa and carried in *Asahi Shimbun*. "Sazae-san" is most representative of funny comics of the postwar years, applying a personal philosophy and way of looking at the world that is presented in a microcosmic society. Taihei Imamura likened "Sazae-san" to the U.S. strip, "Blondie," claiming the humor derived from the contradiction between the ideology and the actual life of the middle-class family.[40]

Children, in particular, were topics of comic art. Children's magazines, such as *Shonen Club*, reappeared and small-scale publishing companies began issuing "red book" comics—inexpensive, with red-ink covers, printed on rough paper and sold in the streets. These books attracted a number of young artists, including a medical student, Osamu Tezuka, who revolutionized the appearance of comics. In his autobiography, Tezuka wrote:

I felt [after the war] that existing comics were limiting. . . . Most were drawn . . . as if seated in an audience viewing a stage, where the actors emerge from the wings and interact. This made it impossible to create dramatic or psychological effects, so I began to use cinematic techniques. . . . French and German movies that I had seen as a schoolboy became my model. I experimented with close-ups and different angles, and instead of using only one frame for an action scene or the climax (as was customary), I made a point of depicting a movement or facial expression with many frames, even many pages. . . . The result was a super-long comic that ran to 500, 600, even 1,000 pages. . . . I also believed that comics were capable of more than just making people laugh. So in my themes I incorporated tears, grief, anger, and hate, and I created stories where the ending was not always "happy."[41]

In 1947, Tezuka drew "Shintakarajima" [New treasure island], using the above-mentioned movie effects; the 200-page magazine sold between 400,000 and 800,000 copies. He also drew for boys' magazines, such as *Manga Shonen* and *Shonen*, what were to become classics—"Jungle Taitei" [Jungle emperor] and "Tetsuwan Atom" [Ambassador atom, which later became Mighty atom]. Japan's first cartoon serial in 1963, "Tetsuwan Atom" [by then Astro boy], was produced by Tezuka. The animated cartoon now has a worldwide audience.

The magazine, *Manga Shonen*, like Tezuka, had a lasting impact upon the industry. Founded in 1947 by Kenichi Kato, it was important as one of the first children's magazines to concentrate on comics. Many contributors to the magazine in the early 1950s became the best known of Japanese cartoonists. Some of them had worked for *kamishibai* (pay libraries) in the 1950s, using the cinematic style and novel plot developed by Tezuka. The genre that developed during this time became known as *gekiga* (drama pictures).

One of the most popular *gekiga* comics was "Kamui-den" [Legend of Kamui], begun in 1964 by Sampei Shirato, a *kamishibai* artist. Although it epitomized a purpose Hidetoshi Kato ascribed to *gekiga*, that is, to provide the "intellectual vitamins for Japan's ultra-leftist student movement," initially "Kamui-den" readers were mainly low-income townsfolk.[42] "Kamui-den" is still very popular, attracting millions of readers, especially alienated young urban intellectuals and politically active students. By 1971, the story had grown to twenty-one volumes of paperbacks of 300 pages each, or 50,000 frames of pictures. Another forty volumes are expected, making it the longest story in the history of the comic books. Set in eighteenth-century Japan, "Kamui-den" is the story of feudal exploitation and the resultant agrarian revolt. Sadao Yamane, Leo Loveday, and Satomi Chiba gave credit for the boom in comics in the 1950s and 1960s to the rise of *gekiga* such as "Kamui-den."[43]

Also, perhaps the severe competition of children's magazines in 1955 helped to establish a better market for the comic books. As a circulation gimmick, the magazines began giving their subscribers two or three comic books of thirty-two to sixty pages each. At the time, the children's magazines also had several comic strips, so that the readers saw about ten types of comics monthly. Kanji Hatano said the content of the comics also underwent changes in the 1950s; until then, the treatment of the hero was an imitation of Western comics—for example, a beautiful princess saved by a skillful fencer.[44] "Developmental" comics, also known as *Konjo manga*, or spiritual comics, made their debut after 1954, featuring judo, wrestling, and other action that fostered high aspirations of becoming a champion, and showed boys and girls, through suffering, attaining character training and harmony.

In summary, children's comics in the 1950s took three forms: (1) serial comics in boys' and girls' magazines, each of which devoted one-third of its space to comics; (2) comic books, which, with first printings of 5,000 to 10,000, sold for twenty-eight to fifty-six cents; and (3) cheap comic books, which children obtained from toy shops or *zokki* book stores. The latter, according to Hatano, issued in first editions of 5,000 to 30,000, were one-half the size of U.S. books, lacked artistic originality, and used poor paper, printing, and color.[45]

When, in 1959, Kodansha issued *Shonen Magazine* as the first weekly devoted to comics, the circulations skyrocketed and the industry took on some of its present-day characteristics. For example, in 1966, *Shonen* had 1 million circulation. By 1981, the figure was often 3 million. Schodt described the traits carried over from the 1960s:

[The industry] was predominantly located in Tokyo. Television and comics were firmly intertwined in a symbiotic relationship. Major book publishers supported themselves with sales of comics, first serialized in magazines and then compiled into series of paperbacks. Meanwhile, the average age of the readership was steadily rising, resulting in the appearance of comics for adults. Women had finally entered the field in force as artists for girls' comics.[46]

But this boom came at great costs—color printing disappeared, as did political and editorial cartoons and the humor magazines that imitated *The New Yorker* or *Punch*.

The Industry Today

The hugeness of the Japanese comic art industry has no parallel in the world. A number of magazines top 1 million circulation, and cartoonists are among the highest-paid individuals in the nation. Speaking of the cartoonists, Schodt said, "In Japan, artists are usually independent and individually responsible for the conceptualization and completion of their work, even if they have assistants helping them."[47] Many are rich and their names are household words; they are social celebrities and asked to comment on their lives and domestic or foreign affairs in the press and on radio and television. As many as 10,000 people regularly attempt to become professional cartoonists. The efforts of the few hundred who succeed are prodigious. Tezuka, for example, had drawn over 150,000 pages in thirty-five years; another artist was known to draw 500 pages in a month.

In 1980, comic books and magazines were a billion-dollar industry, accounting for 17 percent of all books published, 24 percent of all monthly magazines, and over 14 percent of all weeklies. Over 2,000 new volumes of comic paperbacks appeared that year; one publisher, Kodansha, published 279 new volumes in 47 million copies. Sixty publishers bring out the weekly, bi-weekly, and monthly comic magazines, and thirty others publish the paperback comic books. Large publishers such as Kodansha and Shogakkan have near monopolies in both the children and the adult markets. Kodansha publishes at least twelve comic magazines and compiles their serialized stories into paperbacks at the rate of twenty to thirty volumes monthly. As other examples of successes, "Doraemon," the adventures of an atomic-powered robot cat, has appeared in a twenty–six-volume collection with 50 million dollar sales, and "Dr. Slump" in 1980 sold 15 million copies in a seventeen-volume collection. There are also numerous spin-offs from the comics that are equally profitable—animated cartoons for film and television, toys, stationery, clothes, candy, records, radio drama stories, and plays. In fact, the revenue received by Japanese comics producers exceeds that of the world's largest steel company.

Why the enormous popularity of comics? One source listed reasons as being a shift from the print to the pictorial medium because of the influence of television, the need for escape in a highly pressurized society, youthful rebellion against classic forms, the amount of money available to young people who often live with their parents until they marry, and the ease of reading of comics.[50] Schodt said Japan developed a comics phenomenon of this size because the Japanese are predisposed to visual communication because of their calligraphic writing system, because the country is a very crowded, urban nation with little physical space for children's play, and because the gruelling educational system is so demanding that students must escape to easy-to-read comics.[51]

Most popular of the various genres are boys' comics (*shonen manga*); few magazines of any type in the world can match the 3 million weekly circulation of *Shonen Jump*. Also popular are the forty-five *shojo manga* (girls' comics), a number of which have circulations of over 1 million. Only two are weeklies. These magazines are not as action packed as boys' comics and emphasize dreams, human relationships, and employ a visual style that features fashion and highlights the "orblike" eyes of the characters.[52] Horn wrote that because of the "consciousness of sex roles, girls' comics tend to be peopled by extremely serious, romantic, starry-eyed, Caucasian-looking characters."[53] Women have increasingly become the artists of *shojo manga*, two of the most popular being Yoshiko Tsuchida and Machiko Satonaka. Tsuchida is unique as she draws a gag strip for girls' comics, using homely characters who perform the outrageous. Her most famous work was "Tsuruhime Ja!" [Here's Princess Tsuru!]. Satonaka has made a major contribution to *shojo manga*, writing consistently on themes of love, at the same time adapting herself to a wide range of ages and readers and interweaving her plots with controversial subjects such as racial discrimination, the Vietnam War, and the Nazi persecution of Jews. Women artists are exploited often in their brief careers.

Samurai (warrior) comics, like most others, have changed radically during the last generation. No longer are they popular in children's comics, but rather in comic magazines for young men (*seinenshi*), and their themes have moved from the dichotomy of good versus evil to themes of violence, sex, and philosophy. However, they do not stress war, according to Schodt, because of Japan's "total defeat and the needless deaths of millions" during World War II. To advocate war-like behavior in comics would be considered bad taste. Schodt added that "Japanese comics may be among the most violent in the world, but when World War II is portrayed romantically the emphasis is usually on the bonds formed between men under stress; on death, not of the enemy but of Japanese troops . . . or on the machinery of war."[54]

Some artists have gone out of their way to ridicule wartime values, while one, Keiji Nakazawa, himself a survivor of the atom bombing of Hiroshima, has spent a lifetime chronicling that event in his serial, "Hadashi no Gen" [Barefoot Gen]. Described by Horn as one of the most moving comics ever created, the semi-autobiographical "Hadashi no Gen" is the story of Gen Nakaoka, a second grader, who, with his mother, survived the bombing.[55] The strip, which shows Gen struggling for survival in the post-bombing period, emphasizes compassion, perseverance, and the will to live. Originally serialized in 1973 in the weekly comic book, *Shonen Jump*, the strip since has been compiled and published in several four-volume editions with over 600,000 volumes sold, made into a movie, and translated into an English version for overseas consumption, the first Japanese comic book to have that honor. In 1977, Project Gen was started as a volunteer group to convey the strip's anti-war message to the world.

Other types of *samurai* comics are *yakuza* (gangs of the underworld) and *samurai* sports. An example of *yakuza* is "Golgo 13," the story of a professional assassin who hires himself out to the highest bidder. The story debuted in 1969. *Samurai* sports, the most popular of male comics, got a boost in 1952 with Eiichi Fukui's series, "Igaguri-kun" [Young Igaguri].[56] Since then, they have dealt with most sports and serve as an "acceptable surrogate" for war comics.

Also featured in boys' comics are themes connected to work: showing how "perseverance in the face of impossible odds, craftsmanship, and the quest for excellence" paid off (*konjo mono*, or perseverance tales) and parodying the "pathetic existence" of the middle-class worker (salaryman or *sarariman*).[57] One of the first *konjo mono* comics was "Kugishi Sabuyan" [Sabu the pin artist], carried in *Shonen Magazine* in the early 1970s. Another, published in 1972, depicted the life of former Prime Minister Kakuei Tanaka as he worked his way up from poverty to being a millionaire by age twenty-seven.[58] Schodt wrote that "the heroes of most work comics are apprentices, and the more traditionally Japanese the occupation the more potential there is for psychological drama."[59]

Sarariman (salaryman) comics, concentrating on white-collar rank-and-file employees, have been especially popular since Japan's economic boom of the 1960s. The hero of these comics, a middle-class common employee, lives a miserable life, according to Schodt, as he is "married to an ugly woman, dreads going home, and hangs his head low after being scolded by the boss."[60] *Sarariman*, usually shorter than most other Japanese comics, appear in newspapers as well as in weekly news magazines, adult comic magazines, and paperback collections.

A genre of comics devoted to play—especially gambling-oriented activities such as *mah jongg*, horse racing, and *pachinko*—has grown up in the last half decade. These magazines, with circulations of 150,000, are meant primarily for male audiences.

Among the funny comics, the most popular in the 1970s was the already mentioned "Doraemon," a series by Fujio-Fujiko, which spawned a paperback of about 30 million circulation and an animated television series. The hero, Doraemon, is a robot of the future, resembling a cat with snowman-like features. He and a primary school pupil, Nobita, get into a number of difficult situations, all with a similar theme. Nobita, lacking in spirit, strength, and intelligence, must be helped by Doraemon, who applies supernatural powers to everyday objects—a toy helicopter capable of flying, television sets able to see into the future, and lipstick that makes everyone speak in a flattering manner.

"Doraemon" typifies the funny comics that are based on everyday life situations. Others that have been popular are: "Boy Policeman" [Gaki-deki] by Tatsuhiko Yamagami, featuring a boy who wears a policeman's uniform and gets involved in a number of farcical situations; "Hang on, Tabuchi" [Ganbare Tabuchi-kun!] by Hisaichi Ishii, portraying a clumsy but determined professional baseball player; "The Part-timer," following the trail of a poor university student who takes odd jobs to pay his way; "Tensai Bakabon" [The idiot genius], by Fukio Akatsuka; "Cheerleaders" by Do-o-kuman; "Parkside Police Station" by Osamu Akimoto; "Shoji'" by Sadao Shoji, featuring a low-ranking employee of a company; and "The Section Manager" by Shunji Sonoyama.[61] The importance of everyday events in these drawings is related by Yamane: "Even when political and economic affairs are taken up in the cartoons, they appear only to the extent that they affect the everyday lives of the cartoons' characters. Thus, such cartoons lack a feeling of satire or parody and seek to amuse the reader with their intrinsic humor."[62] Yamane characterizes the funny comics as portraying middle-class consciousness. He feels even the graphic depiction is "bourgeois or neutral," adding, "The styles of drawing are not complex or abstruse, but simple and lacking in deviousness, soft in feeling, and simple without a great deal of shading. In short, they are uncomplicated and even naive, with no overwhelming feeling of either masculinity or femininity."[63]

A common feature of the humor offered in the comics is the gap between what the hero wants and what he can obtain and the impotence of his efforts at success. According to Yamane, "all of the comic cartoons give birth to laughter from the confusion and disorder caused by desire. This confusion, however, never reaches such ridiculous or impossible proportions that everyday life is torn loose from its moorings and thrown into chaos."[64] He added that no matter how farcical the strips become, the society portrayed is never completely turned upside down, thus making it safe, not black, humor.

One of the complaints sometimes levelled at Japanese comic art is the one offered by Theroux, that it can be vulgar and in poor taste. Especially since the 1960s, sex, violence, and scatology have found their way into the comic magazines, although the first examples were subdued compared with those of today. In the early 1960s, Fujio Akatsuka used irreverent parody—not really sex or violence dominated—that opened up new vistas for later artists who were more radical. Among the latter is Kazuyoshi Torii, who drew "Toiretto Hakase" [Professor Toilet] in *Shonen Jump*, a children's magazine. Schodt described Professor Toilet as

a scientist who specialized in scatology and worked in a toilet-shaped laboratory. The first episode set the tone for the rest: in a parody of the film "Fantastic Voyage," the professor and his assistant cured a beautiful girl of constipation by shrinking to microscopic size, entering her digestive system through the mouth, and attacking the problem in the rectum with shovels. When the assistant carelessly lights a cigarette there is an explosion and the pair are "blown" to freedom.[65]

Horn described the same strip: "In nearly every issue, the gang is involved in mischief that may consist of curing someone's constipation with a broomstick or diagnosing a friend's indigestion but always involves defecation and the toilet."[66] Torii claims he has broken a taboo and created a new genre—*unko* (shit) comics.

Other strips have introduced sado-masochism ("Dame Oyaji" [No good daddy]), overt eroticism ("Harenchi Gakuen," [Shameless school]), and realistically portrayed violence ("Ninja Bugeicho"). In both boys' and girls' comics, scenes of nudity, kissing, lovers in bed, homosexuality, and scatology are frequent. Restraint of comics artists has been attempted a few times over the years, but to little avail. The difficulty is that the Constitution prohibits censorship of any type, although Article 175 of the Penal Code does not allow for the distribution, sale, or display of obscene printed material. Under this code, pubic hair, adult genitalia, and sexual intercourse may not be shown, but children's genitalia can be depicted. Despite these restrictions, erotic comics have been very successful; there are about ninety erotic comic titles, including *Sexy Action, Gekiga Zipper*, and *Gekiga Butcher*. The police have been hard pressed to oversee the many magazines and to counter the artists' efforts at circumventing the law. Schodt said the most powerful restraint is the marketplace, and right now, the level of sex and violence tolerable in that market is rather liberal.[67]

Other comics offer religious and philosophical messages of a more serious nature. Among these are *Songoku*, the story of a Buddhist priest's pilgrimage, and *Kyojin no Hoshi*, a twenty-volume story of a father who raises his son to be a baseball star.

REFERENCE WORKS

During the last generation, comic art has attained a status in Japan that has nourished a coterie of critics and historians. Demanding readers have sought and obtained information about their favorite artists and heroes through dozens of biographies and autobiographies, magazines devoted to comics, newspaper columns, books, and television documentaries.

However, despite their importance, Japanese comics have not received much attention outside of Japan. Maurice Horn, in his worldwide encyclopedic treatments of cartoons and comics, has provided dozens of vignettes of Japanese artists and their creations. Biographical entries summarize the careers of cartoonists, editors, and producers. Horn writes "with emphasis on their cartoon work, their stylistic, thematic and sociological contributions, their influence on other artists and their cultural significance." The bibliographical entries deal with the works, including assessments of their histories, themes, plots, and adaptations to media. The volume on cartoons has at least seventy-five entries on Japanese cartoons and cartoonists, as well as a four-page section on cartoons and animation in Japan, written by Frederik Schodt. The companion work on comics has at least sixty entries. Both volumes include many illustrations of cartoon and comic art of Japan. Horn also wrote an article on Japanese comics in *Heavy Metal* in 1980.

The most definitive work in English on the topic is Frederik L. Schodt's *Manga! Manga! The World of Japanese Comics* (1983). Schodt knows Japanese comics intimately, having collected them and later translated some into English, including segments of Tezuka's "Phoenix," Matsumoto's "Ghost Warrior," Ikeda's "The Rose of Versailles," and Nakazawa's "Barefoot Gen," all appended to *Manga! Manga!* The book is beautifully produced, with numerous illustrations in color and black and white and anecdotal asides inserted into graphically appealing boxes. Schodt leaves very little uncovered, dealing with history, themes, genres, economics, regulation, artists, publishers, profits, and the future. This author agrees whole-heartedly with cartoonist Osamu Tezuka, who wrote in the foreword that Schodt's work has the "most-up-to-date information available . . . and is a true picture of comics culture in Japan."

In his pioneering collection on popular culture, Hidetoshi Kato includes chapters by Taihei Imamura on "Comparative Study of Comics: American and Japanese, Sazae-san and Blondie" and by Kanji Hatano on "Children's Comics in Japan." Both were written in the early 1950s. Still other shorter pieces on Japanese comics were written by Glenn Troelstrup, Kato, Jim Wheelock, and Cat Yronwode. Troelstrup's article is sketchy and impressionistic, while Kato's on "Sampei Shirato's Marxist Funnies" provides an analytical and descriptive overview of the works of one of Japan's most important *gekiga* artists. Wheelock's articles deal with Osamu Tezuka and appeared in *Comics Scene*, while Yronwode wrote about the Hiroshima bombing-inspired adventures of Gen. Leo Loveday and Satomi Chiba wrote an overview of Japanese comics for a volume entitled *Comics and Visual Culture*, edited by Alphons Silbermann and H.-D. Dyroff. Smaller journalistic articles have appeared in *Time*, *Asiaweek*, and *Asian Messenger*.

At least two works that are important for understanding the history of comic art are those by the editor of *Oriental Affairs* and by Taro Yashima. *Oriental Affairs* (1939) featured a detailed article on the development of *The Japan Punch*, using illustrations and excerpts from that pioneering Western influence. The author claimed to have seen all issues of the periodical. Yashima's *The New Sun* (1943) is an anthology of the cartoonist's wartime activity.

For readers interested in *ukiyoe*, woodblock prints, as examples of early caricature, there are dozens of books. Richard Lane's *Images from the Floating World* (1978) is an extensive history of *ukiyoe* that describes the artists as well as their techniques. In a few cases, Lane points out the caricature style of the artists. The oversized book is illustrated with more than 900 drawings in color and black and white, and is appended with a 151-page "Illustrated Dictionary of Ukiyo-e." James Michener (1954) included *ukiyoe* among his many interests and wrote a book called *The Floating World*; other books worth noting on the woodblock prints are those by Harada (1929), Munsterberg (1982), Takahashi (1965), Neuer (1978), and Whitford (1977).

Of the many Japanese-language sources, a few representative ones are given here. Historical works include those of Toshio Hasebe (1976), Jun Ishiko (1977, 1979), Junzo Ishiko (1975), Reiji Matsumoto and Satoshi Hidaka (1980), Masayuki Minejima (1975), Shigeo Miyao (1967), Isao Shimizu (1978, 1979, 1980), Keiichi Suyama (1968), Hiro Terada (1981), and Yoshihiro Yonezawa (1980, 1981). Special editions of periodicals abound with work on cartoons, including *Bungei Shunju Derakkusu* (1975), *Asahi Graph* (1974), *Kokubungaku: Kaishaku to Kyozai no Kenkyu* (1981), and *Eureka: Shi to Hihyo*. Studies critical of comic art are Mitsuo Matsuzawa's *The Comics That Have Ruined Japanese Minds* (1979) and Hotsuki Ozaki's *The Origin of the Modern Comic: An Attack on Laughter* (1972). Genres are covered in Yoshiya Soeda's *A Theory of Modern Comics* (1975), as well as in the works on eroticism in comics (Kusamori, 1971; "Ero Gekiga no Sekai," *Shimpyo*, 1979), girls' comics (Takemiya and Moto, 1980), and boys' comics (Fujio-Fujiko, 1977). Besides the latter, other books that deal with specific cartoonists include those on Osamu Tezuka by Mitsutoshi Ishigami (1977) and by Tezuka himself (1977, 1978, 1979, 1981), and on Ippei Okamoto (1930) and Reiji Matsumoto (*Shimpyo*, 1979).

RESEARCH COLLECTIONS

Research on Japanese comic art is difficult because some of the works were destroyed during World War II, while what remains is scattered in many private collections. It is probably safe to say that cartoon buffs and authors such as Maurice Horn, Frederik Schodt, and Dennis Gifford have extensive personal collections, as do the cartoonists themselves. Schodt in his *Manga! Manga!* mentions private collections in Japan held by Kazuhiko Suyama and Reiji Matsumoto, as well as those of institutions such as the Hiro Public Library, Omiya Manga Kaikan, Goto Museum, Mainichi Shimbunsha, Nakai Collection, and Tokyo National Museum.[68] He found other works in the Schumolowitz Collection of Wit and Humor in the San Francisco Public Library and the University of California at Berkeley Library.

Obviously, some of the best sources for comic art are the publications that featured it over the years. The Library of Congress and numerous other libraries, such as McKeldrin Library at the University of Maryland, have holdings of Japanese newspapers and periodicals that are useful in tracing the history and development of comics and cartoons. Publishing houses such as Kodansha and Shogakkan in Tokyo also have extensive collections.

The researcher looking into comic art must know from the outset that it is not an easy task because resources are scattered and fragmented, and because the field of study is relatively young. Although a few scholars from the 1930s and 1940s looked at the social impact of comic art in the United States, there has not been a concentrated effort at serious study of the genre until the last generation. The result has been the formation of groups (the most recent of which is in the genesis stage as a section of the International Association of Mass Communication Research, for which this author takes responsibility) dedicated to the study of comic art, the publication of books on comic art in many countries, and the establishment of journals and periodicals that treat comic art, like *Witty World*, *Journal of Popular Culture*, *International Popular Culture*, *Target*, *Comics Journal*, *Bedesup*, and *Cartoonist Profiles* among others.

NOTES

1. Paul Theroux, *The Great Railroad Bazaar* (Boston: Houghton Mifflin, 1975), pp. 277–78.

2. R. H. Blyth, *Oriental Humour* (Tokyo: Hokuseido Press, 1959), p. 286, and *Japanese Humour* (Tokyo: Japan Travel Bureau, 1963); Frederik L. Schodt, *Manga! Manga! The World of Japanese Comics* (Tokyo: Kodansha, 1983), p. 28.

3. Schodt, p. 29.

4. Ibid., p. 31.

5. Blyth, *Oriental Humour*, p. 286.

6. Schodt, p. 30.

7. Blyth, *Oriental Humour*, p. 29.

8. Schodt, p. 32.

9. Ibid.

10. Nathan Rogers, "Netsuke," *Franklin Mint Almanac*, March/April 1984, p. 18.

11. David Chibbett, *The History of Japanese Printing and Book Illustration* (Tokyo: Kodansha, 1977), p. 196.

12. Schodt, p. 33.

13. Ibid. pp. 33–34.

14. Seiichiro Takahashi, *The Japanese Wood-Block Prints Through Two Hundred and Fifty Years* (Tokyo: Chuokoren Bijutsu Shuppan, 1965), pp. 128–29.

15. Schodt, pp. 36–37.

16. James Michener, *The Floating World* (New York: Random House, 1954), pp. 202–3.

17. Ibid., pp. 211–12.

18. Richard Lane, *Images from the Floating World: The Japanese Print* (New York: Dorset Press, 1982), pp. 42, 146, 152.

19. Frank Whitford, *Japanese Prints and Western Painters* (New York: Macmillan, 1977), p. 41.

20. See Michener, *Floating World*; Hugo Munsterberg, *The Japanese Print: A Historical Guide* (New York: Weatherhill, 1982), p. 110; Roni Neuer, Herbert Libertson, and Susugu Yoshida, *Ukiyo-e: 250 Years of Japanese Art* (New York: Mayflower Books, 1978), p. 301; Jiro Harada, *Masters of the Colour Print: VI—Hiroshige* (London: "The Studio" Ltd., 1929), p. 4.

21. There are differences of opinion on the beginning date and longevity of the magazine. The editor of *Oriental Affairs* ("The Japanese Punch," *Oriental Affairs*, May 1939, p. 259), who claimed he looked at the only complete set of copies, said it was published between 1865 and 1867. Schodt (p. 39) said it was published from 1862 to 1887. Glenn C. Troelstrup ("Japanese Cartoons," *The East*, March/April 1969, p. 25) said it started in 1866, and Maurice Horn [*The World Encyclopedia of Cartoons* (New York: Chelsea House, 1976), p. 581] said it began in 1857. Schodt's figures are used in the text because his work represents the most systematic done on comics.

22. "The Japanese Punch," *Oriental Affairs*, p. 259.

23. Horn (*World Encyclopedia of Cartoons*, p. 407), who credited Nagahara Shisui with establishing *Tobae*, said the magazine was founded in 1893.

24. Schodt, p. 41.

25. The Japanese censored with little circles, thus the title *marumaru* (circles).

26. Horn, *World Encyclopedia of Cartoons*, p. 302.

27. Ibid., p. 541.

28. Ibid., p. 41.

29. Ibid., p. 42.

30. Ibid., p. 607.

31. Maurice Horn, *The World Encyclopedia of Comics* (New York: Chelsea House, 1976), p. 25.

32. Japanese cartoonists often banded together in the 1920s and 1930s in groups such as Nihon Mangaka Renmei and Shin Manga Shudan (New Cartoon School Group). Their purpose usually was to help artists find outlets for their work, although sometimes they became rather cliquish. Shin Manga Shudan was formed in 1932 to fight the conservatism of the Japanese cartoon world, but in 1939 the group became the Shin Nippon Mangaka Kyodai (New Japan Cartoonists Association).

33. Horn, *World Encyclopedia of Cartoons*, p. 341.

34. Schodt, p. 51.

35. Ibid., p. 56.

36. Anthony Rhodes, *Propaganda: The Art of Persuasion: World War II* (New York: Chelsea House, 1976), p. 253.

37. Taro Yashida, *The New Sun* (New York: Henry Holt, 1943).

38. Horn, *World Encyclopedia of Cartoons*, pp. 591–92.

39. Horn, *World Encyclopedia of Comics*, p. 28.

40. Taihei Imamura, "Comparative Study of Comics: American and Japanese, Sazaesan and Blondie," in *Japanese Popular Culture*, ed. Hidetoshi Kato (Westport, Conn.: Greenwood Press, 1959), p. 96.

41. Quoted in Schodt, p. 63.

42. Hidetoshi Kato, "Sampei Shirato's Marxist Funnies," *East-West Perspectives* (Fall 1980), 27.

43. Sadao Yamane, "Cartoons and Comics in Japan: Putting Laughter into Everyday Life," *Asian Culture* (January 1980), 6; Leo Loveday and Satomi Chiba, "Aspects of Development Toward a Visual Culture in Respect of Comics: Japan," in *Comics and Visual Culture*, eds. Alphons Silbermann and H.-D. Dyroff (New York: Saur, 1986), p. 163.

44. Kanji Hatano, "Children's Comics in Japan," in Kato, *Japanese Popular Culture*, pp. 103,104.

45. Ibid., pp. 104–8.

46. Schodt, p. 67.

47. Ibid., p. 138.

48. Ibid., p. 146.

49. "Appetite for Literature," *Time Magazine*, August 1, 1983, p. 86.

50. "Popular Comics," *Asian Messenger*, Autumn 1979/Spring 1980, p. 21.

51. Schodt, p. 25.

52. Ibid., p. 88.

53. Horn, *World Encyclopedia of Cartoons*, p. 559.

54. Schodt, pp. 73,75.

55. Horn, *World Encyclopedia of Cartoons*, p. 275.

56. Schodt, p. 79.

57. Ibid., p. 106.

58. Ian Buruma, "Kakusan, the Heroic Villain Who Betrayed His Roots," *Far Eastern Economic Review*, November 3, 1983, p. 58.

59. Schodt, p. 109.

60. Ibid., p. 112.

61. Yamane, p. 8.

62. Ibid., p. 9.

63. Ibid.

64. Ibid., pp. 11–12.

65. Schodt, p. 121.

66. Horn, *World Encyclopedia of Cartoons*, p. 554–55.

67. Schodt, p. 130.

68. Ibid., p. 260.

BIBLIOGRAPHY

"Ambassador of the New Japan." *Asiaweek*, September 9, 1983, p. 20.

"Appetite for Literature." *Time*, August 1, 1983, pp. 85–87.

Blyth, R. H. *Japanese Humour*. Tokyo: Japan Travel Bureau, 1963.

———. *Oriental Humour*. Tokyo: Hokkaido Press, 1959.

Buruma, Ian. "Kakusan, the Heroic Villain Who Betrayed His Roots." *Far Eastern Economic Review*, November 3, 1983, pp. 58–60.

Chibbett, David, *The History of Japanese Printing and Book Illustration*. Tokyo: Kodansha, 1977.

"Ero Gekiga no Sekai" [The world of erotic comics]. *Shimpyo*, supplement, Spring 1979.
新評 「エロ劇画の世界」 1 9 7 9 ・春

Fujio-Fujiko. *Futari de Shonen Manga Bakari Kaite Kita* [All we've ever done is draw boys' comics]. Tokyo: Mainichi Shimbunsha, 1977.

藤子不二雄　『ふたりで少年マンガばかり書いてきた』　毎日新聞社　１９７７

Harada, Jiro. *Masters of the Colour Print: VI—Hiroshige*. London: "The Studio" Ltd., 1929.

Hasebe, Toshio. *Shomin Manga no Gojunen* [Fifty years of the people's comics]. Tokyo: Nippon Joho Senta, 1976.

長谷部敏雄　『庶民マンガの50年』　日本情報センター　１９７６

Hatano, Kanji. "Children's Comics in Japan." In *Japanese Popular Culture*. Ed. Hidetoshi Kato. Westport, Conn.: Greenwood Press, 1959, pp. 103–8.

Horn, Maurice. "Comix International." *Heavy Metal*, November 1980, p. 7.

———. *The World Encyclopedia of Cartoons*. New York: Chelsea House, 1976.

———. *The World Encyclopedia of Comics*. New York: Chelsea House, 1976.

Imamura, Taihei. "Comparative Study of Comics: American and Japanese, Sazae-san and Blondie." In *Japanese Popular Culture*. Ed. Hidetoshi Kato. Westport, Conn.: Greenwood Press, 1959, pp. 87–102.

Ishigami, Mitsutoshi. *Tezuka Osamu no Kimyo na Sekai* [The strange world of Osamu Tezuka]. Tokyo: Kisotengaisha, 1977.

石上三登志　『手塚治虫の奇妙な世界』　奇想天外社　１９７７

Ishiko, Jun. *Manga Meisakuhan: Sengo Manga no Shujinkotachi* [A museum of comic classics: Heroes of postwar comics]. Tokyo: Tokuma Shoten, 1977.

石子順　　『漫画名作館：戦後マンガの主人公たち』　徳間書店　１９７７

———. *Nihon Mangashi* [A history of Japanese comics]. Vols. 1 and 2. Tokyo: Otsuki Shoten, 1979.

石子順　　『日本漫画史』（上・下）　大月書店　１９７９

Ishiko, Junzo. *Sengo Mangashi Noto* [Notes on the postwar history of comics]. Tokyo: Kunikuniya Shoten, 1975.

石子順造　『戦後マンガ史ノート』　紀ノ國屋書店　１９７５

"Japan Punch," *Oriental Affairs*, May 1939, pp. 259–70.

Kato, Hidetoshi, ed. *Japanese Popular Culture*. Westport, Conn.: Greenwood Press, 1959.

———. "Sampei Shirato's Marxist Funnies." *East-West Perspectives*, Fall 1980, pp. 26–31.

Kusamori, Shinichi. *Manga-Erochishizumko* [Comics and thoughts on eroticism]. Tokyo: Buren Bukkusu, 1971.

草森紳一　『漫画エロチシズム考』　ブレーンブックス　１９７１

Lane, Richard. *Images from the Floating World: The Japanese Print*. New York: Dorset Press, 1978.

Loveday, Leo, and Satomi Chiba. "Aspects of Development Toward a Visual Culture in Respect of Comics: Japan." In *Comics and Visual Culture*. Ed. Alphons Silbermann and H.-D. Dyroff. New York: Saur, 1986.

Matsumoto, Reiji, and Satoshi Hidaka, eds. *Manga Rikishi Dai Hakubutsukan* [A giant museum of comic history]. Tokyo: Buronzusha, 1980.

松本零士・日高敏編　『漫画歴史大博物館』　ブロンズ社　１９８０

"Matsumoto Reiji no Sekai" [The world of Reiji Matsumoto]. *Shimpyo*, supplement, Autumn 1979.

〝松本零士の世界〟　「新評」　１９７９．

Matsuzawa, Mitsuo. *Nihonjin no Atama o Dame ni Shita Manga-Gekiga* [The comics that have ruined Japanese minds]. Tokyo: Yamate Shobo, 1979.

松沢光雄　『日本人の頭をだめにした漫画劇画』　山手書房　　１９７９

Michener, James. *The Floating World*. New York: Random House, 1954.

Minejima, Masayuki. *Gendai Manga no Gojunen: Mangaka Puraibashi* [Fifty years of modern comics: A private history of comics artists]. Tokyo: Aoya Shoten, 1975.

峯島正行　『現代漫画の５０年：漫画家プライバ史』　青也書店　　１９７５

Miyao, Shigeo. *Nihon no Giga: Rekishi to Fuzoku* [Japanese cartoons: Their history and place in popular culture]. Tokyo: Daichi Hoki, 1967.

宮尾しげを編　『日本の戯画：歴史と風俗』　第一法規　　１９６７

Munsterberg, Hugo. *The Japanese Print: A Historical Guide*. New York: Weatherhill, 1982.

Neuer, Roni, Herbert Libertson, and Susugu Yoshida. *Ukiyo-e: 250 Years of Japanese Art*. New York: Mayflower Books, 1978.

"Nihon no Warai: Manga Sennenshi" [The humor of Japan: 1,000 years of comic art]. *Bungei Shunju Derakkusu*, September 1975.

『文藝春秋デラックス』　「日本の笑い：マンガ１０００年史」　　１９７５・９

Okamoto, Ippei. *Ippei Zenshu* [The collected works of Ippei]. Tokyo: Senshinsha, 1930.

岡本一平　『一平全集』　先進社　　１９３０

Ozaki, Hotsuki. *Gendai Manga no Genten: Warai Kotoba e no Attaku* [The origin of the modern comics: An attack on laughter]. Tokyo: Kodansha, 1972.

尾崎秀樹　『現代漫画の原点：笑い言語へのアタック』　講談社　　１９７２

"Popular Comics." *Asian Messenger*, Autumn 1979/Spring 1980, p. 21.

Rhodes, Anthony. *Propaganda: The Art of Persuasion, World War II*. New York: Chelsea House, 1976.

Rogers, Nathan. "Netsuke." *Franklin Mint Almanac*, March/April 1984, pp. 16–19.

"Sashi-e Manga ni Miru Showa no Gojunen: Kabashima Katsuichi kara *Dame Oyaji* Made" [Fifty years of the Showa period, as seen through illustrations and comic art: From Katsuichi Kabashima to *Dame Oyaji*]. *Asahi Graph*, special edition, October 30, 1974.

『アサヒグラフ』　「さしえマンガにみる昭和の５０年：樺島勝一からダメおやじまで」

１９７４・１０・３０

Schodt, Frederik L. *Manga! Manga! The World of Japanese Comics*. Tokyo: Kodansha, 1983.

Shimuzu, Isao. *Meiji Mangakan* [A museum of Meiji comic art]. Tokyo: Kodansha, 1979.

清水勲　『明治漫画館』　講談社　　１９７９

———. *Meiji no Fushi Gaka: Bigot* [Bigot: The Meiji period parody artist]. Tokyo: Shinchosha, 1978.

清水勲　『明治の諷刺画家：ビゴー』　新潮社　　１９７８

———. *Meiji Manga Yuransen* [An excursion into Meiji comic art]. Tokyo: Bungei Shunju, 1980.

清水勲　『明治漫画遊覧船』　文藝春秋　　１９８０

"Shojo Manga." *Eureka: Shi to Hihyo*, special edition, July 1981.

『ユリイカ』：詩と批評　「少女まんが」　　１９８１・７

Soeda, Yoshiya. "Gendai Manga no Techo" [A handbook of modern comics]. *Kokubungaku: Kaishaku to Kyozai no Kenkyu*, special edition, April 1981.

副田義也　〃現代漫画の手帳〃　「国文学：解釈と教材の研修」　４月、
１９８１．

————. *Gendai Mangaron* [A theory of modern comics]. Tokyo: Nihon Keizai Shim-
    bunsha, 1975.

副田義也 『現代マンガ論』 日本経済新聞社 １９７５

Suyama, Keiichi. *Nihon Manga Hyakunen* [One hundred years of Japanese comic art].
    Tokyo: Haga Shoten, 1968.

須山計一 『日本漫画１００年』 芳賀書店 １９６８

Takahashi, Seiichiro. *The Japanese Wood-Block Prints Through Two Hundred and Fifty
    Years*. Tokyo: Chuokoron Bijutsu Shuppen, 1965.

Takemiya, Keiko and Hagio Moto. *Shojo Mangaka ni Mareru Hon* [How to become a
    girls' comic artist]. Tokyo: Futami Shobo, 1980.

髙宮恵子・萩尾望都 『少女まんが家になれる本』 二見書房 １９８０

Terada, Hiro. *Manga Shonenshi* [A history of *shonen manga*]. Tokyo: Shonan Shuppan,
    1981.

寺田ヒロオ 『「漫画少年」史』 湘南出版社 １９８１

Tezuka, Osamu. *Boku wa Mangaka: Tezuka Osamu Jiden 1* [I am a cartoonist: Vol. 1
    of Osamu Tezuka's autobiography]. Tokyo: Yamato Shobo, 1979.

手塚治虫 『ぼくはマンガ家：手塚治虫自伝１』 大和書房 １９７９

————. *Manga no Kakikata: Nigao kara Chohen made* [How to draw comics: From
    portraits to story-comics]. Tokyo: Kobunsha, 1977.

手塚治虫 『マンガの書きかた：似顔から長編まで』 光文社 １９７７

————. *Tezuka Osamu Rando* [Osamu Tezuka-land]. Tokyo: Yamato Shobo, 1978.

手塚治虫 『手塚治虫ランド』 大和書房 １９７８．

————. *Tezuka Osamu Rando 2* [Osamu Tezuka-land, Vol. 2]. Tokyo: Yamato Shobo,
    1978.

手塚治虫 『手塚治虫ランド２』 大和書房 １９７８

————. *Tezuka Osamu no Subete* [Everything about Osamu Tezuka]. Tokyo: Daitosha,
    1981.

手塚治虫 『手塚治虫のすべて』 大都社 １９８１

Troelstrup, Glenn C. "Japanese Cartoons." *The East*, March/April 1969, pp. 23–25.

Wheelock, Jim. "The King of Japanese Cartoons." *Comics Scene* 3 (1982), 49–51.

————. "Osamu Tezuka's World." *Comics Scene* 4 (1982), 24–28.

Whitford, Frank. *Japanese Prints and Western Painters*. New York: Macmillan, 1977.

Yamane, Sadao. "Cartoons and Comics in Japan: Putting Laughter into Everyday Life."
    Asian Culture, January 1980, pp. 6–12.

Yashida, Taro. *The New Sun*. New York: Henry Holt, 1943.

Yonezawa, Yoshihiro. *Sengo Gyagu Mangashi* [A postwar history of gag comics]. Tokyo:
    Shimpyosha, 1981.

米沢嘉博 『戦後ギャグマンガ史』 新評社 １９８１

————. *Sengo SF Mangashi* [A postwar history of science fiction comics]. Tokyo:
    Shimpyosha, 1980.

米沢嘉博 『戦後ＳＦマンガ史』 新評社 １９８０

————. *Sengo Shojo Mangashi* [A postwar history of girls' comics]. Tokyo: Shimpyosha,
    1980.

米沢嘉博 『戦後少女マンガ史』 新評社 １９８０

Yronwode, Cat. "Gen of Hiroshima." *Comics Feature* 2 (1980), 30.

10

Science Fiction

ELIZABETH ANNE HULL AND MARK SIEGEL

Science fiction, both as a popular genre reflective of broadly felt social and cultural forces and as a specialized field of interest concerned with the nature of social and cultural change, can be an important basis for cultural analysis. Furthermore, the differences and similarities in the science fiction movements of different nations can help in assessing the similarities and differences of the two cultures at large.

The history and significance of science fiction as a cultural phenomenon depend on the definition of the genre. Different approaches fall into two groupings. One deals with all speculative fictions, including fantasies and utopias, that violate or transcend the physical laws or history of our world as we know it. A definition of this type, employed most notably by writers like Ursula K. Le Guin and scholars like Darko Suvin and Robert Scholes, focuses on science fiction as metaphor or as literature of "cognitive estrangement" or "cognitive dissonance." We are presented with a world different from our own that is a metaphor for some aspect of our world, intelligently illuminating that world through the unique perspective the work provides.[1]

Another approach is to define science fiction more narrowly as fiction extrapolating from known scientific principles into the unknown. This approach was epitomized by the early American science fiction pulp editors Hugo Gernsback and John W. Campbell, but is today often advanced in a more sophisticated form by writers such as Isaac Asimov and James Gunn.[2] There are different and more precise definitions,[3] but these polarized views are virtually all-inclusive.

The broader definition that includes all speculative works might, as James Gunn maintains, be founded on the human impulse to explain the inexplicable in the present and past and to foresee the future in order better to prepare for it. Scholars tracing this tradition in Western literature not infrequently find its roots in well-known utopias such as Plato's *Republic* and in fantastic allegories of human nature and origin such as Ovid's *Metamorphosis*. (National and religious mythologies are usually omitted from this list because they are not the work of any single author, though the omission is also a matter of convenience since it avoids the controversy of labeling works as "fiction" that some people believe to be literally true.) The potential social utility of such fiction is quite clear, though it may be used either to advocate change or to defend the status quo.

Science fiction allows us to reach a greater appreciation of the past and present through symbolic fictions, fictions that exaggerate or emphasize by displacement of some element of human life; they help us better plan for the future through hypothetically testing alternative courses of action. Whether or not much fantastical literature from *Gilgamesh* to *The Hobbit* actually originates from anything other than overactive imaginations and a desire to entertain is debatable. Science fiction stories describe men in conditions other than they are; they cannot help provide an index of concerns, fears, and desires relevant to evolving social and psychological situations.

The second definition of science fiction—extrapolation from known scientific fact—is easier to place in a cultural context, since it can arise only in a culture in which the idea of technological progress is commonly accepted. Historians working with this definition may locate occasional examples of the genre created by exceptional individuals during the Renaissance or earlier periods of scientific speculation. They agree, however, that science fiction appeared as a popular genre only after the industrial revolution was well under way. (Some earlier works like *Gulliver's Travels* and *The New Atlantis* are also sometimes admitted to the canon by this definition.)

Science fiction is the result of an interest in science itself and the way science and technology affect all phases of human life, including the individual's identity and relationships with family, society, and the physical world. James Gunn's definition of science fiction as "the branch of literature that deals with the effects of change on people in the real world as it can be projected into the past, the future, or to distant places"[4] seems particularly appropriate.

Exactly what "changes" become the concern for examination depends also on which variety of science fiction is examined. The Japanese monster films of the 1950s seemed to extrapolate from the sense of many postwar Japanese that the tragedy of their present lives was a disaster over which they had little control— perhaps they were being punished for past sins. Most contemporary science fiction television in Japan ("Ultraman," "Bioman," "Bluehawk," "Uchu Keiji Shiraiban") is derived from these films, but now it is infused with the confidence of contemporary Japanese in their ability to defend themselves from alien intrusions and to meet their own needs.[5]

Whatever definition is used, science fiction is a highly diverse literary movement that defies attempts to pin it down. Arthur C. Clarke, certainly one of the world's best-known science fiction writers, has defined it as the literature of change. We can learn a great deal about science fiction and, indirectly, about the cultures that produce it from the behavior it induces in the people who are most involved with the genre, the "fans."

HISTORICAL SURVEY

Western historians and social theorists tend to see the industrial revolution growing out of a number of gradual, perhaps inevitable trends in European history. It follows that science fiction developed even more naturally as a parallel and complementary movement. As Alan Berger pointed out in "Science-Fiction Fans in Socio-economic Perspective: Factors in the Social Consciousness of a Genre," American fans tend to perceive themselves as technologically oriented and upwardly mobile, the elite cadre of industrial society.[6] Whether or not science fiction enhances the possibilities for technological and social change, as many optimistic science fiction writers contend, or strengthens the hegemony of the ruling classes in technological societies, as Charles Elkins, Gerard Klein, and a number of Marxist critics maintain, that perception does seem to exist, despite the enormous influence of "Sword and Sorcery."[7]

Social history in Asia, on the other hand, stands in sharp contrast. The industrial revolution was not simply imported by the Orient; it was forced upon it, either through imperialistic exploitation or, in the case of Japan, as a defense against exploitation. When the Meiji government began to impose industrialization on its citizens in the second half of the nineteenth century, the outside social critic might have expected massive social upheavals. The resultant social problems were considerably less than in those Western nations that had chosen industrialization voluntarily (to the extent that such a thing is possible) and absorbed it over several hundred years. If science fiction is related to cultural adaption to technological and social change, then Japanese science fiction ought to tell something of how that remarkable adaption occurred.

Technological science fiction reflects the process of industrialization in Japan in that it was imported from the West at essentially the same time as industrialization itself. The earliest forms of fantastical science fiction also were imported as part of Chinese cultural and technological borrowings between the eighth and eleventh centuries. Japan has its own cosmogeny, collected 1,300 years ago in the *Kojiki* and the *Nihongi*, as well as a wealth of fairy tales (*mukashi-banashi*) and legendary tales (*densetsu*), but these have to be differentiated from the formal fantasy adventures and tales whose conventions were imported from other cultures. While the Chinese forms continued to dominate Japanese literature until the importation of Western models after the Meiji Restoration, some forms, such as Utopianism, never took root since they did not apply to the Japanese cultural identity.

The Japanese are perhaps the world's greatest cultural borrowers and adapters. The Japanese essayist Nyozekan Hasegawa has asserted that appropriating elements of other civilizations has been:

a shortcut toward the development by Japan of a civilization of its own. . . . While the Japanese, in ancient and modern times alike, have always been extremely susceptible to the influence of foreign culture, and extremely progressive in their willingness to adopt it themselves, another side of them has always clung obstinately to the traditional Japanese things. Not only do both sides exist at the same period in the same country, but they not infrequently exist simultaneously in the same individual as well.[8]

Shuichi Kato, a Japanese literary scholar, describes this process of cultural adoption as one in which

abstract, theoretical aspects [of foreign world views] are weeded out, the transcendental basic principle . . . excluded, the comprehensive system . . . dismantled and only the portion of it retained which had value in terms of practical application. What remained was a ''Japanized'' foreign world view.[9]

David Lewis (perhaps the most knowledgeable Westerner writing about Japanese science fiction) notes that ''clearly Japan has assimilated science fiction as it has assimilated so many other Western artifacts and is well on its way to molding it into a distinctly Japanese configuration.''[10]

The Japanese are profoundly traditional despite their cultural borrowing—they borrow that which is readily applicable, pragmatic elements that they can ''Japanize.'' Practical elements of a genre useful to Japanese culture are adopted, and elements of the foreign worldview that are incompatible with their own are excluded. Utopias and dystopias call into question the foundations of a society, and so are not particularly useful to the Japanese, who find their own culture quite well founded as it is. The most popular traditional fantasies, the *monogatari* (tales), despite their formal origins, always reflect Japanese social concerns. For instance, Japan's most famous novelistic fantasy, the 181-volume nineteenth-century *Satomi Hakkenden*, uses fantasy elements to expose the intergenerational conflict and psychological ambivalence toward massive cultural change in that turbulent period.[11] *Satomi* places these fantasy elements in a historical setting, and thus illustrates what Lewis notes about the thrust of Japanese science fiction in general: It is concerned with the way the Japanese past has produced the Japanese present, not the future.

Sociologists have often remarked on the extreme fascination of the Japanese with the question of their own identity. Japan is a remarkably homogeneous country. Perhaps more than any other nation, it has grown up free of invasion, of polyglot immigratation, of outside cultural influence except on its own terms. This may account for some of the national pastime of introspection. Certainly Japan's sf has inherited the trait, using its repertory of techniques to pose in ever more controlled settings the question ''Who are we now?'' rather than ''Who will we become?''[12]

The Japanese oral tradition in fantasy has always been distinct from that of other cultures in its combination of fantasy with extreme pragmatism. Folklorist Richard Dorson has noted that these tales ''belong not to a children's realm of fairyland but to a danger-laden adult world where *Kami* (deities) descend from the heavens and emerge from the mountains and swamps, whose essence they embody.... [However fantastic the adventure,] the sense of fiction and fantasy is much less pronounced'' that in Western folklore.[13] Because of the Japanese preoccupation with their past, ''there are very few well-realized futures that betray any difference in mores, social structure, and values from the present day.''[14]

There are a good many Western writers and theorists such as Le Guin who have argued that all science fiction concerns the present and not the future. David Lewis has provided an excellent bibliography that notes the works of Sakyo Komatsu, Ryu Mitsuse, and others who do employ elements of ''hard science'' extrapolation.[15] Japanese science fiction editor and writer Koichi Yamano has complained, to the contrary, that Japanese science fiction translations are overrun with technological stories and ''American-style'' futuristic extrapolation.[16] The mores, social structues, and values presented are no different from those of contemporary Japan. Their basic values are perceived as stable despite the adaption of pragmatic elements of technology to meet their changing needs. Nor is this attitude simpleminded ethnocentrism. A recent issue of *Omni* has pointed out that the Japanese have a history of cultural stability and social and economic success essentially unparalleled in the industrial world because their traditional culture does work remarkably well in a great variety of social and technological environments.[17]

One would also expect Japanese science fiction fandom to incorporate those elements of fandom worldwide that were compatible with Japanese culture, while simultaneously maintaining a distinctly Japanese fandom. The most distinct characteristic of fandom is its organization of individual enthusiasms and interests into group endeavors. Competition, game playing, and mutual reinforcement through award giving are all common elements of fandom, particularly of science fiction conventions that can exist only through fan groups. The rites and rituals, the publications, and the particular language of fandom are obviously designed to exclude outsiders and reinforce bonds between fan group members. Organization has given fans direct influence over the development of the genre that is generally exercised only by elites in the publishing community and literary establishment. Not only do fans enjoy access to many of their favorite authors through fanzines (fan magazines), prozines (professionals' magazines), columns, and conventions, but a fan award or criticism can play an important part in making or breaking a film or novel.

Japanese fandom does not yet seem to have acquired as much power as similar groups in the rest of the world, but given the group orientation of Japanese society, it seems likely that this is merely because of the relative youth of the movement.

Japanese Fandom

Some ''closet'' fans of science fiction in translation or written by Japanese writers existed before 1957. The most notable of the few, short-lived clubs was

Omega, which published two numbers of *Kagaku-Shosetsu* [Scientific novels]; its ten members were mostly semi-professionals or developing writers. The chairman was Keisuke Watanabe, an established mystery writer; Tetsu Yano and Allan Kiodomari were among the most active and able members. Organized fandom dates from May of that year when a high school mathematics teacher from Tokyo, Takumi Shibano, and about twenty other members founded the Kagaku-Sosaku Club (Science Fiction Club). *Kagaku* means science and *sosaku* means writing fiction or creating a fictitious story—fantasy as a euphemism for lie is perhaps the nearest word for *sosaku*. Shibano began publishing his own *Uchujin* [Cosmic dust], a mimeographed, fifty-page monthly, with an original circulation of more than one hundred. This preceded the initial publication of Japan's first commercially successful science fiction magazine (in December 1959), Hayakawa's *SF Magazine*. *SF Magazine* originally published mostly translations, but now it prints both foreign and Japanese science fiction. Although *Uchujin* printed mainly Japanese writers, it also contained translated fiction, criticism, and a letter column. Continuously publishing since then, it has printed contributions over the years from virtually all of Japan's most celebrated and popular writers, including Sakyo Komatsu, Tetsu Yano, Taku Mayumura, Shinichi Hoshi, Ryu Mitsuse, Kazumasa Hirai, Aritsune Toyota, Koji Tanaka, Masaki Yamada, Baku Yumemakura, Yoshio Aramaki, and many others. More than half of them became professional writers through *Uchujin*. Circulation today exceeds 1,000.

Like several American fanzine editors, Shibano has made fandom a way of life. He abandoned teaching in 1977 to devote all his time to writing and translating. He and his wife, Sachiko, have been frequent visitors to the worldcons (world science fiction conventions) since 1968, when he was the first TOFF (Trans Oceanic Fan Fund) winner (Baycon at Oakland, California). Upon his return to Japan after Baycon, Shibano introduced the lore of worldcons to Japan through slide presentations and reports in *Uchujin*. Shibano and the magazine were recently honored at two special events: the 1977 Tokyo Cosmicon—so named because Shibano publishes *Uchijin* [Cosmic dust] and has used the pen name Rei Kozumi (Cosmic Ray). It was followed by Yoitocon (named for the town Kusatsu, which is hailed in folk music as a "good place" or *yoitoko*) in 1982. Shibano has had a great influence on the development of science fiction in Japan. He regards it as a literary genre that has for a central subject something, technology, for example, that, although produced by human reason, begins to work alone automatically and gets out of control in the long run. This kind of automatism, Shibano asserts, can radically diverge from the domain of individual human reason to inhabit the domain of collective (racial or man/machine symbiotic) reason.

In June 1960 Yasutaka Tsutsui began publishing *Null* at Osaka, a quarterly that ran eleven issues, mainly concerned with fiction. Like Frederik Pohl (who began editing as a teenager in the United States), editor Tsutsui later made his own debut as a writer in Hayakawa's *SF Magazine* and then went on to become one of the most beloved science fiction writers, even developing a reputation as a mainstream writer over the years.

Five years after Shibano's original publication, a fan named Shiro Shima formed the SFM Society (for Hayakawa's *SF Magazine*) in Tokyo with one hundred members. They began publishing their own fanzine, *Uchu-Kiryu* [Space current] (based on a story by Isaac Asimov, *The Currents of Space*) in May 1962; this appeared monthly for four years. That same year in Nagoya, Den Yoshimitsu organized the first local fan group of about ten people as the Chubu-Nippon (middle Japan) SF Society. They also began publishing a fanzine, *Mutants*, which continues to be published with a circulation of about one hundred. Back in Tokyo the Society of SF Art was founded with Yasufusa Kaneko as president and published four issues of their fanzine, *SF Art* (a collection of artworks by their fifty or so members).

By November of 1965, fandom in Japan had grown to the point that it was time for coordination of their efforts. *Uchujin*, *Uchu-Kiryu*, the Society of SF Art, *Mutants*, *Paranoia* (Para-Club, Kobe), *Time Patrol* (Time Patrol Club), *Tentacles* (Kyushu SF Club), *Core* (Hokkaido SF Club), and SF Seminar all joined together to form the SF Fan Group Federation of Japan, also called simply the Federation. In 1966 the Silent Star Club (which published *Silent Star*, edited by Susumu Ishikawa in Tokyo) and Coacervate Club (publishing *Coacervate*, edited by Satoshi Ikeda in Osaka) also joined the Federation.

By this time fandom had matured enough to have its own "loyal opposition," and some of the youth fan groups—especially SF Company, Kukan Club, and Jigen (all in Tokyo)—constituted their own version of a fan group union, "Planets."

In 1966 Tsutsui also started *SF Times*, a quarterly newspaper that put out only three issues, but stimulated controversy concerning science fiction fan activity and science fiction itself by publishing debates and rebuttals. Of particular interest was the controversy between Koichi Yamano and Yoshio Aramaki over definitions of science fiction. This same year Masahiro Noda founded the SF Illustration Library in Tokyo, which distributed copies of his slides of old covers of American pulp magazines, especially space opera.

The next year fan groups in Shizuoka and Hiroshima joined the Federation as the number of fan groups began to increase. Two of the most important are the Institute of SF Research and the SF Fans Science Study Group, both headed by Dr. Fujio Ishihara of Kamakura. Ishihara, a university professor, later became a science fiction writer as well. Still another influential magazine appeared, *BEM* (Bug-Eyed Monster), edited by Masaya Okada in Nagoya, devoted mostly to the translation of classic Anglo-American science fiction. *BEM* focused on aliens, but without any particularly "trashy" connotations that a similar title might invoke in the United States. It also included speculative essays on the nature of extra-terrestrial life and further increased the influence of Western science fiction fandom. Okada's speculative essays categorized fictitious extra-terrestrials into "life with shape" and "life without shape." The latter was further categorized into "really no shape," for example, poltergeist, and "pseudo no shape," for example, ghosts or will-o'-the-wisps!

In 1968, four of the youth fan groups were combined into the Youth SF Terminal of Japan, chaired by Hiroyuki Namba of Tokyo, who later became a rock musician as well as a science fiction writer. He made four LPs, all dealing with science fiction—musical versions of such Western classics as *Ringworld*, *Solaris*, "Flowers for Algernon," and "Green Hills of Earth." The distinction between "young" and "adult" fandom was becoming sharper. Ironically, the "young" fans triggered a conflict between the fans and professionals by criticizing the literary defects of juvenile science fiction written by "adult" professional writers.

Takumi Shibano comments,

Planets was the first generation of youth fandom and SF Terminal was the second (three or four years younger). The first one was rather controversial youth[s] who fought against even pros. A part of the second as Vag-Shudan fought against everything, but the mainstream of the second youth [group] led by H. Namba and Y. Kato was constructive, and, as the result, they inherited adult groups. This reminds me of the American Immortal Storm era in the late 1930s. I feel *this* was the real beginning of our fandom, and we "adult" fans were just a sort of forerunner who lived in a pro-less world, fed by imported sf. . . .

[Today] there are conflicts between groups like the one between Iskateri and General Products about "Patriotic Command Dainippon," but this has nothing to do with generations. I think the first generation youth conflict was a very special case. Just when they started reading, there was a flood of translations of American sf of the golden age, and many bright boys (and few girls, not *a* few) believed that sf was everything. Then, when they got a little older, the bitterness of disillusion at the real sf (or its speciality) drove those who were not born sf fans to protest against those who were satisfied at the existing sf. The second generation, who were just three or four years younger, found sf as it is when they started reading, because there were many kinds of sf from fantasy to space operas (mainly translations) around them already. They [did not need to] have any illusions, and those who were not born sf fans could drop out from reading sf when they became disappointed with them. This was the special situation we had in those days.

I was at Baycon in 1968 and I planned to have an American style nationalcon in 1970 and announced it at the 8th nationalcon (Kyucon) in [the] summer [of19]69, and soon afterward, that controversy started. First, Vag-Shudan attacked Planets by issuing [their] inquisiting fanzine, which stimulated some first generation [fans] in Planets and they attacked adults . . . (Vag was rather playing games, but the first generation youth took it seriously). They declared their intention to sabotage the nationalcon of '70 and destroy our Federation. As the chairman of the Federation, I called them and had negotiations at the end of '69, but could not persuade them, and I declared my intention to give up chairing the nationalcon of the next year, predicting I would also quit as chairman of the Federation. They looked somewhat surprised because "the establishment" was so easily defeated. . . . As the result, Norio Itoh, who assisted me at the negotiations, [became] chair of the con, and the second generation youth group assisted him in the working committee which succeeded as Tokon–5 in '70.[18]

In 1969, as Shibano notes above, inspired by the student movement prevalent in those years, Vag Shudan, a youth group headed by Kosuke Hirai at Tokyo, started agitation by parody—seemingly serious but really fannish—which encouraged others to attempt to destroy the very backbone of fandom, the Fan Group Federation of Japan, which sets the dates for national conventions.

But the real destruction of "old-fashioned" Japanese fandom was virtually brought about by the growing number and variety of "fanacs," that is, fan activities not simply devoted to reading science fiction and writing letters to or talking with other fans. From 1965 on, high school and university students began to publish their own fanzines (such as Azabu High School's *Limit*, Kansai University's *Space*, and Kyoto University's *Chukanshi*). Since none of the high schools or universities taught science fiction—not even "units" devoted to science fiction within other courses—all of these activities were extracurricular fan activities.

Two more editors of fanzines that began at that time later both became science fiction writers themselves, following the U.S. model of the fan editor's transition to pro writer: Junya Yokoto of Tokyo, *SF Kurabu* (SF Club—its major interest is in classic Japanese science fiction), and Shozo Tokura of Kofu, *Micro SF* (the postcard fanzine that publishes superb short-short stories). The club Panpaka Shudan, headed by Mikikazu Mori (who later became a science fiction and fantasy translator) and others in Osaka, began seriously exploring the wide range of science fiction's possibilities. It studied Japanese classic science fiction, criticism of American comic strips, fiction writing, and even the organization of conventions.

In 1970, while interest in the United States was beginning to focus on the burgeoning number of female writers and feminist perspectives, three important semi-professional magazines began publishing in Japan. *NW-SF* is edited in Tokyo by Koichi Yamano, who is currently famous as a science fiction writer and critic and is the outstanding leader of the New Wave movement in Japan. *Kagaku-Makai*, also located in Tokyo, is edited by Takayuki Tatsumi, a science fiction critic and literary scholar. Tatsumi, an assistant professor at Keio University, recently completed his doctorate in English and American literature at Cornell University and hopes to introduce the first university-level science fiction course after he returns to Japan. *Iskateri* is edited in Sapporo by Hiroaki Hazu, a professional journalist.

Another important magazine is *Bamu* (edited by Yoshiaki Sekiguichi in Niigata). His group is well known not so much for its fanzine but for organizing one of the most famous local conventions, Gatacon). *Reimei*, a fanzine edited by Masakazu Kashiwaya, is coedited by Mineo Yoneyama, who writes best-selling violence and science fiction novels under the pen name of Baku Yumemakura. *Crystal* (the one and only science fiction art fanzine) is edited by Kenichi Matsuzaki and published in Tokyo by the club SF Crystal Art. In 1970 the Fan Group Federation started publishing the monthly *Fandom News* under the editorship of Yoshiyuki Kato, the powerful chairman of the Federation for so many years.

The Seiunsho, confusingly translated as Star Cloud or Nebula Award but in spirit—and even its physical shape (a rocket ship)—more comparable with the American Hugo, being voted by fans rather than writers, began in the same year. It is given for the best long and short Japanese and foreign science fiction stories, as well as for best media presentation. In 1984 a non-fiction category was added, which replaced the Fandom Award started in 1965. (See Appendix B for a complete list of winners of the Fandom Awards.) The Club Chojinrui, known in the 1960s as one of the youth groups, reorganized itself as Seigun. It began to publish a fanzine, edited by Masanori Takahashi, also called *Seigun*, mainly concerned with fiction writing. The Seigun Festival, its creative writing workshop, was started in 1975 and has been held every July since. It might be compared with the Clarion Workshops in the United States.

In 1973 a number of fan groups for individual Japanese authors were founded, including groups for Shinichi Hoshi, Sakyo Komatsu, and Yasutaka Tsutsui (the so-called big three), as well as for Ryo Hanmura and Ryu Mitsuse.

In 1974 three more big name fanzines or groups were organized or reorganized. *Null* (sometimes called *Neo-Null*), edited by Yoshihiro Yamamoto in Osaka, was revived after a pause of fourteen years. *SF Ronso*, edited by Masaaki Shindo in Fujisawa, is the only Japanese fanzine of academic science fiction criticism; it was published sporadically—five issues over the next eight years. In 1982 it gave birth to *The Book of Science Fiction*, a commercial science fiction criticism magazine. The Kaigai (overseas) SF Association published *Nova Express*, edited by well-known translator Hitoshi Yasuda, and *Orbit*, edited by Shinichiro Sumi. Sumi writes science fiction criticism under the pen name of Sukiyoshi (which means "water mirror" in Japanese, a play on the name of Walter Miller, Jr.). These two fanzines introduced to science fiction professionals a variety of critics and translators, including the editors themselves. Like science fiction editors in the United States, they became recognized by the fans, a rare circumstance in the publishing industry anywhere in the world. They also published the first *Japan SF Yearbook* in 1981. Perhaps because of the absence of any support from the prestigious and conservative Japanese university system, "ser-con" (serious and conscientious) projects have not yet attained much stability or long-term success.

In 1974 the second commercial science fiction magazine in Japan, Kiso-Tengaisha's monthly *Kiso-Tengai*, began publishing science fiction and mysteries, but lasted only ten issues. It resumed publication in 1976, this time devoted exclusively to science fiction, and continued until 1981, when it failed again. In 1979 the third and fourth commercial magazines appeared, Tokuma Shoten's *SF Adventure*, publishing Japanese authors exclusively, and the Japanese version of *Isaac Asimov's Science Fiction Magazine*, Kobunsha's *SF Hoseki* (now a real rival for *SF Magazine*). The latter also added some original Japanese stories, along with critical review columns and interviews with (mostly American) writers. It was financially successful but was eventually forced to suspend publication. Tsurumoto Room's *Starlog* appeared as the Japanese version of the American *Starlog*, which, in addition to translating the whole magazine, introduced Anglo-American movies to Japanese audiences. *SF-ISM*, a professional science fiction magazine, was also published. The golden age of commercial Japanese science fiction magazines had arrived.

While 1980 saw the "science fiction golden age boom" spread throughout Japan, in books as well as in magazines, some of the ser-con fanzines (*Kagaku-Makai*, *SF Ronso*, and *Iskateri*) began to apply more literary and academic standards of criticism. They helped to promote Space Fish's SF Seminar at Tokyo (chaired by Shinji Maki), a ser-con convention series initiated and held only once before this year.

In 1980 the first Japan SF Award, the equivalent of the Nebula, voted by the members of the Japan SF Writers Club (Nihon SF Sakka Kurabu), was given to Akira Hori's *Solar Wind Intersection*, a "hard science fiction" story. The Japan SF Award is sponsored by Tokuma Shoten, the publisher of *SF Adventure*, and carries a prize of 1 million yen (about 8,000 dollars). In 1981 the second Japan SF Award was won by Hisashi Inoue, a mainstream writer for *The Kirikiri People*. The story was a utopian extrapolation of the political situation in the north of Japan. Perversely, however, the ninth Kyoka Izumi Award, a relatively minor award given chiefly to mainstream fantasies, was bestowed on *Kyojin-Tachi* [The fictional people][19] by Yasutaka Tsutsui. The reversal of the two prizes might be seen as evidence of the Japanese culture's strong tendency to integrate subcultures into the mainstream.

Even in boom times for science fiction, in Japan as in America, not all publications prosper equally, and in 1981 both *SF Hoseki* and *Kiso-Tengai* semi-permanently suspended their publications. Science fiction in Japan had gotten so diverse that commercial magazines could not retain their initiative. The golden age of science fiction continued, but the magazine boom had undoubtedly ended. According to Takumi Shibano,

These two magazines were loved by the core fans better than others. *Kiso-Tengai* folded for their own economic reasons, defeated by [the] similar and bigger *SF Adventure*. *SF Hoseki* was killed by personnel changes in the publisher, Kobunsha, I hear. Fans in the core of our fandom all missed these two magazines.[20]

A revised version of the Fandom Awards of the 1960s was introduced in 1982, called the Fanac Awards, chosen by a committee headed by Takumi Shibano and the editorial board of the *Book of SF* and presented at the annual Japan Science Fiction Convention. These awards indicate what sorts of activities the Japanese appreciated most highly from June 1981 to June 1982:

Best Fanzine: *Seigun*. Fiji Murakami, ed. Kyoto.
Best Fan Fiction: Masaaki Shindo, "A Beachside City." *SF Ronso* 5 (1981), 95–143.

[Tokyo. Takao Shiga, ed.]. Yuji Miura, "The Orbit Intersection." *Isaktei* 19 (1981), 6–27. [Gumma. Hiroaki Hazu, ed.]

Best Fan Criticism: Takayuki Tatsumi, "An Introduction to Critical Methodologies of Science Fiction." *Kagaku Makai* 41 (1981), 66–85. [Tokyo. Takayuki Tatsumi, ed.]

Best Translational/Bibliographical Works: Kaigai SF Association, *The Japan SF Yearbook 1981* [As a special issue of *Nova Express*. Osaka. Toshiya Okamoto, ed.]

Takumi Shibano Award. Fujio Ishihara [for his publication of *Index*. Kanagawa: SF Shiryo Kenkyukai, 1980–81.]

The most active university group of 1982 may have been Kyoto University, which revived *Chukanshi*, edited by Mikuru Abo, and originated *Work Book*, a monthly edited by Tadahisa Hamaguchi and Tetsuya Kohama. Both of these publications were deeply involved in the introduction and translation of Anglo-American science fiction, and in starting another ser-con convention series, the Kyoto SF Festival. In 1982 the first Japanese critical science fiction magazine, *The Book of Science Fiction: Criterion and/or Deconstruction of Science Fiction*, was published by Studio Ambient, an editorial board composed of both men and women, and sponsored by the publisher Shin-Jidaisha.

In 1983, the second Fanac Awards were as follows:

Best Fanzine: Tohoku University's *Divergence*. [Sendai. Tohoku University's SF Association, ed.]

Best Fan Fiction: Yu Kyosho, "The Master's Planet." *Seigun Novels* 8 (1982). [Kyoto. Eiji Murakami, ed. This is especially noteworthy because the author is female]

Best Translational/Bibliographical Work: Ambivalence's *Index to Kiso-Tengai* (1981). [Kasugai. Hideki and Matsuo Watanabe, ed.]

Best Editorship: KSFA's *Nova Quarterly*. [Osaka. Toshiya Okamoto, ed.]

Best Illustration: No Award.[21]

Takumi Shibano Award: Yoshiaki Sekiguchi. For his *Bamu* (Niigata) as well as the continuous organization of Gatacon.

During 1983 a strong argument developed between *Iskateri* and General Products, a science fiction shop in Osaka whose animation film, "The Patriotic Commando Dainippon," despite its juvenile spirit, struck some people as politically aggressive. Through a Dutch fanzine, *The Shards of Babel*, the argument became internationally known. In addition, *Uchujin* published its twenty-fifth-anniversary issue, an event commemorated by Yoitocon, and Guincon (named for the protagonist of Kaoru Kurimoto's Guin saga) was held in Tokyo with an attendance of about sixty of her fans. Guincon followed the pattern of Rhocon, held the previous year for about one hundred fans of Perry Rhodan. It illustrates how quickly Japanese fans follow the principles established by American fans.

In 1984 the third Fanac Awards were as follows:

Best Fanzine: Keio University's *Horizm* (*Hora* means "tall-tale"and "*horizm*" is the "doctrine of tall-tale," making a pun on "horizon") [Tokyo. Keio University's SF Association, ed.]

Best Fan Fiction: Waku Ohba, "The Contact Game." *Uchujin* 185 (1984), 52–99. [Kanagawa. Takumi Shibano, ed.]

Best Fan Criticism: Toru Kakamura, "A Linguistic Approach to Chiaki Kawamata's Fiction." *Bagatelle* 2 (1983). [Tokyo. Chuo University's SF Association, ed.]

Best Translational/Bibliographical Work: *Divergence*. [Sendai: Tohoku University's SF Association, ed.]

Best Editorship: *Talking Heads*. [Tokyo. Kotaro Nagata and Shinji Maki, eds.]

Takumi Shibano Award: Takayuki Tatsumi (for his critical/ser-con/fannish activities) and Tetsu Yano (for his long translational/fictional/fannish activities)

This year Tetsu Yano was also feted at Yanocon, held by about fifty fans and pros who gathered from various parts of Japan at Niigata to celebrate his sixtieth birthday. Yano inspired pride in Japanese science fiction by winning a Hugo nomination for his short story, "The Legend of the Paper Spaceship."

The 1984 worldcon, held at Anaheim, California, received a large Japanese delegation (over one hundred). Translators Norio Itoh and Tetsu Yano have also gained world recognition for their work by winning Karel Awards, bestowed by the World SF, the International Association of Science Fiction Professionals (not to be confused with the American group of fans that sponsors the "worldcons").

The Fanac Awards for 1985 at Gatacon were as follows:

Best Fanzine: *Palantir* [Tokyo. Yoshio Kobayashi, ed.]

Best Fiction: Takumi Ishitobi, "The Myth of Minerva." *Seigun Novels* 9. (1984). [Fiji Murakami, ed.]

Best Criticism: Hideki Watanabe et al., "SF and Dream." *Perceptron* 4. 1984. [Nagoya. Nagoya University SF Society, ed.]

Best Research: *Palantir* 2 (special issue)

Editorial Sense: "SF File 1984." Nagoya: Chugakko—the Middle Japan SF Union of University Students, 1985.

Takumi Shibano Award: No Award

One interesting feature of both American and Japanese conventions is the room party. Such parties do not appear on the printed programs, but they are major social events, frequently considered far more important than the official agenda by fans in the know. In contrast to American meetings, Japanese room parties are rarer and seem more formal. They usually are not actually held in the host's room but in a special room rented for the occasion. Guests are typically seated on the floor around a table, Japanese style. More food is served than drink, and elaborate games with complicated rules may be played, with prizes awarded for the winners.

This sort of thing also happens as part of the program in America—for example, trivia contests or punning contests. These are usually scorned by true fans in the United States, whose approach to fandom is often far more serendipitous. Japanese partying is much more likely to be a meticulously planned part of the program, organized with specific group activities. The random circulation of convention goers as practiced in the United States would be considered rude behavior. Western fandom has also proven more likely to generate fan scandals and chicanery that are gossiped about for years, such as the fulfillment of Joe Haldeman's lime jello fantasy, which Robert A. Heinlein mentioned as an inside joke without explanation in his novel, *The Number of the Beast*, for the amusement of real fans.

In addition to the general outline above, several other influential conventions deserve mention. Noteworthy early conventions include the SF Festival of 1969, which was an alternative national-con in Tokyo when Kyukon, the eighth national-con, was held in Kyushu. The SF Christmas convention of 1969 featured games, quizzes, songs, and discussions. The SF Show of 1973, devoted to science fiction art and media, was more visual in its presentation than any other convention before or since.

Several ser-con conventions have sprung up and presumably will continue in the indefinite future. The Seigun Festival in Tokyo, begun in 1975, is a creative writing seminar and features educational panel discussions. The SF Seminar, started in 1977 in Tokyo, offers lectures on science fiction as well as a critical/academic symposium. The Kyoto SF Festival, instituted in 1982, has lectures on translation, publication, and fan activities, and is more journalistic than the SF Seminar. The Japan Fantasy Convention, first held in Tokyo in May 1982, presents lectures exclusively on fantasy and fantasy films.

Gatacon in Niigata in 1975 was memorable for its games, quizzes, discussions, and masquerade. Datecon in Sendai in 1977 had parties, quizzes, films, an art auction, and a discussion planned for one hour that continued eight hours, nearly overnight. Dontacon, a "one-shot" at Hakata in 1980, was especially for Kyushu citizens. Uracon at Kanazawa in 1982 was promoted by comics fans as well as science fiction fans. Its masquerade is always more attractive than any others.

A convention that combined ser-con and fannish activities was the Cry-Con Festival at Tokyo in 1978, which has been held bi-annually ever since for SF Crystal Art. Hamanacon in Hamamatsu in 1980 featured lectures, a quiz, and a video show. Some of the events at Dainacon in Nagoya in 1983 were discussions, quizzes, games, and the "entrance examination" for "SF University," which could be viewed as ser-con or trivia, depending on the observer.

One special event deserving particular attention was the International SF Symposium held in Tokyo, Nagoya, Osaka, and other cities in 1970, because it was the only international convention held in Japan. It was attended by, among others, Arthur C. Clarke from Sri Lanka, Judith Merrill from Canada, Frederik Pohl from the United States, Brian Aldiss from the United Kingdom, and a delegation of five people from the Soviet Union, including Eremey Parnov (writer) and

Julius Kagarlitski (university professor and H. G. Wells scholar). This meeting was a sort of League of Nations of science fiction—which led ultimately (by several intermediate steps) to the founding of World SF in Dublin in 1978. Writer Sakyo Komatsu is the World SF vice president for Asia, translator and writer Tetsu Yano is the national president, and Takumi Shibano is a national secretary.

Conclusions

In his excellent introduction to the entire field of science fiction, David Hartwell observes:

The people you play with are an essential facet of your social life. The sense of community within the sf field, especially among fans and professionals, is founded upon years of the social life of conventions and other fan gatherings, large and small. The fans and professionals eat together, drink together, play together (sleep together, exclude one another, criticize one another), act in some ways as an enormous extended family, complete with poor relations, rebellious children and dimwitted second cousins.

He adds that

the sf life-style may be the keystone holding the sf field in place and separating it from other genres of contemporary writing. . . . Fandom . . . is at the center of a discussion of sf, without which all else flies apart. Fandom is what makes for sf a world of difference.[22]

Japanese groups are distinguishable from groups and organizations in most Western societies by what sociologist Chie Nakane has called an emphasis on "frame," the particular social context of an interaction, over "attribute," the unchanging status or qualities of an individual. Nakane believes that this emphasis has allowed Japanese society to adapt easily to the various institutionalizations required by an industrial (or postindustrial) economy.

In American fandom, the fan organization serves to unite science fiction aficionados and to isolate them from the rest of society by reinforcing the particular tastes and behaviors of their preoccupation. The Japanese love to belong to a variety of groups: Family, work, and sporting or hobby groups are all common to a majority of Japanese. Many Japanese even report more than one religious affiliation. It seems possible that, in the future, the multiple memberships of science fiction fans in a variety of other groups will facilitate its growth in Japan. Clearly, the Japanese science fiction community would benefit from such activity. Most Japanese writers have traditionally belonged to cliques and exclusive groups, perhaps in compensation for being excluded from the corporate group structure common to most Japanese; and despite the pattern of progression from fan to writer, science fiction writers remain relatively isolated from the evolving fan organizations. Still, the influence of the fan/writer relationship has been notably stronger here than in other fields of writing.

Without question, science fiction in Japan has, in many ways, had a background, development, and growth cycle similar to those in the West. The emergence of modern science fiction in Japan was somewhat later in the twentieth century than in the United States, but the pattern has proven comparable in many important ways. And without question, American fandom has been the single most important outside influence on the development of Japanese science fiction. In fact, the literature is identified by the Japanese simply as ''sf,'' the short form fans prefer to ''sci-fi,'' even though sci-fi would actually be shorter to pronounce in Japanese.

Like the Americans, the Japanese have tried to seek legitimacy for Japanese science fiction by identifying literary antecedents. Literary critic Takashi Ishikawa traces its roots back through fantasy to the oldest book in Japan, *Kojiki* [Record of ancient matters] (A.D. 712), a chronicle of Japan's Imperial line. (Professor Ishikawa taught a science fiction course at the prestigious Tokyo University at the university's request on a one-time basis in 1978.) Japan has a long history of popular enjoyment of fantastic tales, especially for the amusement of children, but, as Kato suggests, also for adults, perhaps as a way of avoiding ''logic, the abstract, and systemization, in favor of emotion, the concrete and the unsystematic.''[23]

Despite its flirtation with mainstream literature in Japan, in the United States science fiction has been considered suitable only as a sedative for unruly young boys. It is generally scorned by the literary establishment and deemed unworthy of serious academic consideration. Like many Americans, thoughtful Japanese are not always sure, even today, that any literature that is ''popular'' with the young can be beneficial to their culture. Inevitably, science fiction is associated in the minds of the average Japanese with English and American translations, which, as Japanese editor, critic, and writer Koichi Yamano points out, are usually subsumed under the category of American popular fiction.[24]

Yamano is careful to distinguish simplistic, happy optimism, ''nuts-and-bolts spaceships and happy adventures'' stories by Americans such as Larry Niven and Frederik Pohl, from the ''more serious'' work of New Wave British writers like J. G. Ballard, Brian Aldiss, Michael Moorcock, John Brunner, Barrington Bayley, Christopher Priest, and the ''younger'' Americans influenced by them— Samuel R. Delany, Thomas Disch, and Harlan Ellison. Here the aesthetic seems to be based on the optimism or pessimism of the writers rather than their age or nationality or even writing style. In effect, this can be seen as a kind of selective Japanization of the American and English imports, by choosing to honor and sanction (as do other Japanese critics) those *gaijin* (foreign) influences who most conform to the traditional Japanese literary values of characterization, ambiance created by style, and preference for feeling and emotion over story line or tightly plotted sequence of events more prized by Western readers.

To be sure, there are some younger critics who are also trying to legitimize ''hardcore science fiction''—that is, serious, thought-provoking, interpretive speculation about changes, especially changes in technology, rather than escapist fantasy or mere nuts-and-bolts popularizing of science. A case in point is editor

Yoshio Kobayashi, the Japanese equivalent of Charles N. Brown, who, with his fanzine, *Palantir* (named for a character from Tolkien), has introduced recent American science fiction to Japanese audiences. He admits a preference for American fiction over Japanese, but says,

I do care about Japanese sf. Sf is the literature of change and change must come to Japanese sf. That's why I introduce recent foreign fiction. People are aware that something is happening but they don't know what that is, like Bob Dylan once sang, and sf must deal with that something. But most Japanese sf writers seem to care little about that. Some are content with traditional formulae like "What if?" while others are eagerly seeking commercial success. That is a natural case when a genre matures, except sf must not mature.[24]

Kobayashi also comments,

I notice that Japanese fans don't read sf anymore, which is why there are no winners in this year's [1985] Seiun Awards short fiction category. What they read are long series like "Guin Saga" and light entertainment. It reflects their love for serial animation and comics magazines. Today's youths like repetition and they don't quit their habits. [Bullying], called *ijime*, becomes a social problem when accidental killings and murders of revenge are common among junior high school. They don't judge or assess what they are doing. What is easy is natural and convenient. [Doing the] natural thing is a built-in function of human beings and convenience is the purpose of our civilization, so you can't help doing easy, repetitive things: That seems their logic to me. But I guess that might reflect their metamorphoses in the midst of the media and information revolution. When personal computers become popular, a myth is born that everything can be stored in the computer memories as data if enough storage capacity is available. Even one's self could be just another bit of information. Everything is bits and bytes. There's no meaning in judging values as long as every datum is available. People are happy in I/Oing [In-Outing] data. Repetitive formulae work fine in this regard. That's my personal . . . impression of the behavior of today's youth. And young fans seek just fun while young writers themselves just enjoy their status as professional writers who also seek fun and play music or draw comics or make videos. They are like television's favorite stars and feel very happy to entertain their audience. I have a very bitter feeling toward them.[25]

Takayuki Tatsumi of Keio University says that Japanese science fiction criticism is "certainly in the Childhood's beginning, not in the Childhood's end, with the result that it must be literally supported by children, just like me."[26] He considers himself to be the Japanese equivalent of Donald M. Hassler, because, like Hassler, his study of English literature, science fiction, and modern criticism is closely related to poststructuralist and deconstructive methods.

Another young critic, Kiyoshi Kasai, has written a book on selected Anglo-American science fiction writers, *Kikaijikake no Yume* [The clockwork dream], taking a post-Marxist and socialistic approach. He might be called the Japanese equivalent of Canada's Darko Suvin and was a politically active radical back in the age of the student movement. Tatsumi explains, "It is quite natural that, although [we] three are equally interested in 'hardcore sf,' [our] definitions of it differ strikingly—Kobayashi's might be 'sf as fantasy/commercial fiction,' Kasai's 'social/ideological fiction,' and Tatsumi's 'metaliterature/deconstructive fiction.' "[27]

Preparing the way for all these younger critics is Nobumitsu Omiya (who chaired the twenty-first national-con), grandmaster of Japanese science fiction criticism. His book, *The Critical Adventure of Science Fiction* (1984), is doubtless the greatest recent achievement in the field.

The closest Japanese counterpart to the American journal, *Extrapolation*, the Canadian *Science-Fiction Studies*, or the British *Foundation* is *The Book of SF*. *The Book of SF* even takes the title of its editorial, "The Launching Pad," from *Extrapolation*. It is edited by a team that includes several women, and they very proudly assert its particular interest in feminist criticism. This is unusual, considering Japan's cultural attitude toward women and the virtual non-existence of feminism. Nevertheless, it seems possible that within a few years the Japanese will be. at the forefront of feminist perspectives on science fiction.

At the opposite extreme of the academic and professional writers struggling for literary recognition are the Japanese science fiction comics, such as "Astro Boy," which has been animated and exported to China and the rest of the world. Katsuhiro Otomo, who won both the Seiunsho and the Japan SF Award for his cartoon "Domu" [Dreaming childhood], is serialized in the weekly *Young Magazine* and published in book form. These are clearly intended for juvenile consumption, and many writers in this field use pen names, such as the team of Fujimoto Hiroshi and Moto Abiko, who write as Fujio-Fujiko and who have collaborated for some thirty years.

In the field of the mass entertainment media, American imports are evident, at least as sources. 1984 saw the beginning of an animated serial television version of "Doc" Smith's *Lensman* stories as well as a feature-length film. However, this was seen by some fans as a debasement of the original.

This attitude of disappointment in adaptations is, of course, very similar to the reaction of a large number of print fans in America to the translation of their favorite tales into mass media forms. One could compare the reaction of mixed joy and disappointment over the filming of such classics as *Lord Greystoke* and the more recent *Dune*. On the other hand, such original productions as *Goodbye Spaceship Yamato* have been enormous successes, as have movies not made from print in the United States, like *Star Wars*. They do not have to meet comparisons with preconceived images in the minds of fans, and have been welcomed by the fan community as enthusiastically as by the general public.

Those Japanese animation films and television programs that have been sneered at by the Japanese literary establishment are getting serious study by American scholars, such as Mark Siegel at the University of Wyoming, as reflections of Japanese attitudes toward themselves and their relationship to the rest of the world. Siegel cites the "Ultraman" television series, which began in 1966 and over the years has produced "The Return of Ultraman," "Ultra Seven," "Ultraman Ace," "Ultraman Taro," "Ultraman Leo," "Astra: Ultraman King," "Ultra Brothers," "Ultraman '80," "Father of Ultra," "Mother of Ultra," "Zophy," "UGM (Utility Government Members)," "MAT (Monster Attacking Team)," "TAC (Terrible Monster Attacking Crew)," all of which have been exploited in fiction, film, toys, and *manga*. Siegel regards "Ultraman" as the synthesis of the Japanese attitude toward power: That is, power should be respected, even if it is alien, and, if possible, coopted for the benefit of Japan. This attitude may spring from different motivations, but it may be similar to the insular ethnocentrism of Americans, who are also willing to adopt foreign chic as long as it is sufficiently domesticated.

For those who may be interested in viewing Japanese animated science fiction films, there are serious collectors like Doug Rice (2064 N. Sheridan Road, #303, Chicago, Illinois 60626), who recently lent his personal film library to Capricon V (February 1985) for two days of continuous alternate film programing—which drew as many viewers as the traditional American film program track with which it competed. (One need not understand Japanese to follow the clear storytelling of the dramatic animation.)

Other Japanese science fiction films have also been inspired by native Japanese science fiction novels, ranging in complexity from Shigeru Kayama's *Gojira* [Godzilla] in 1954 to Sakyo Komatsu's *Japan Sinks* and his more recent *Bye, Bye, Jupiter*, based in his Seiunsho-winning novel, *Sayonara Jupiter*.

At the time of the rift between the "young" and "adult" fans, the younger generation were pejoratively dubbed the "galactic patrol." Fukushima said he did not want fanatic fans to buy his *SF Magazine*, that commercial success and popularity were more important. Instead of acting chastened, the youths responded by embracing their designation proudly, just as American fans had constituted themselves as the Dorsai (after the militant troops described in the fiction of Gordon Dickson). Some of the young fans so alienated the established Fan Federation (which determines the location of national-cons and generally represents fandom to the publishing industry) that they adversely affected their own careers in science fiction and had to seek success outside the field.

Kozo Miyakara (under the pseudonym of Minami) wrote *The Morning of Science Fiction* (about younger fans who wanted to be as strong as Astro Boy to defend science fiction against its commercial degradation), which severely criticized pro writers, parodying Fukushima's own story, *The Night of Science Fiction*. Young fans in Japan, like some of their Yippie counterparts in the United States, soon learned that fighting the establishment directly was less effective than working within the system to effect the changes they desired.

Rebellion against traditions seems as strong as or stronger than ever in some ways, sometimes manifested in bizarre convention behavior. At Ezocon 2, two fans got married—rather standard for American convention activity but hardly like the decorum usually associated with Japanese weddings. The editor-in-chief of Hayakawa's *SF Magazine*, Kiyoshi Imaoka, dressed in the costume of a woman, caused considerably tongue-wagging when he attempted to kiss another man!

Both technologically extrapolative and psycho-sociologically metaphorical science fiction are strongly represented in Japan today. The extrapolative tendency seems more oriented toward enthusiasm for the benefits or potential consequences of technology itself than for any social changes likely to be caused by that technology. (Japanese enthusiasm for fifth-generation computers, for instance, pervades Japanese youth to an extent even greater than enthusiasm for space exploration did American youth in the late 1960s.) The psychologically or sociologically oriented science fiction of Japan likewise seems less concerned with the idea of change than does its American equivalent. The two strains reinforce our image of Japan—and the Japanese self-image—as a traditionally stable culture where change occurs constantly, but change that concerns the pragmatic development of Japanese resources, leaving the essential Japanese personality and society unchanged.

More aware than ever that world fandom is everywhere, the Japanese, supported by their Fan Federation and especially by General Products of Osaka, a science fiction paraphernalia company, will try to organize a worldcon bid within the next ten years. It seems fair to say that Japanese science fiction is now "world class" and will be a force to be reckoned with in the future of the world literary movement called science fiction.

REFERENCE WORKS AND RESEARCH COLLECTIONS

The World SF Depository at the University of Kansas (Kenneth Spencer Library, Alexandra Mason, Director of Special Collections, Lawrence, Kansas) contains a fair number of Japanese science fiction works, both primary and secondary sources. An even better collection of Japanese science fiction (as well as American and other international science fiction) is the personal library and memorabilia of Forrest J. Ackerman, which is to be donated to Los Angeles as soon as the city establishes suitable housing for a museum. In the interim please contact him at 4e, 2495 Glendower Avenue, Hollywood, California 90027. Japanese members of the Science Fiction Research Association may also be helpful in further research: Phil Loux, Nishi 8-jo Minani 15–3, Obihiro, Hokkaido, Japan 080; Hitoshi Yasuda, 1–61, 4 Chome, Kagoike-dori, Chuo-ku, Japan 651; Nobuyuki Seki, 3–18–20 Yagumo Meguro-ku, Tokyo, Japan 152; Masaki Abe, P.O. Box 3, Hanawa P.O., Kazuno-shi, Akita, Japan 018–52; and Ken Yamaoka, Gohongi 1–9–9, Meguro-ku, Tokyo, Japan 153.

Works about Japanese Science Fiction Published in Japanese (Prepared by Takayuki Tatsumi)

Among the best bibliographical works are *Index to SFM* and *The Bibliography of SF Books Published in Japan* by the Institute of SF Research mentioned above. Another *Index to SFM* is published by a group of undergraduates at Ochanomizu Women's University. *Index to Uchujin* is published in Kanagawa by the Institute of SF Fanac Research (edited by Tosaku Mori). The checklists of Arthur C. Clarke, Yasutaka Tsutsui, and Sakyo Komatsu are published by Waseda University's Mystery Club. In 1974 *Seigun* saw some competition with the publication of a fanzine exclusively for fiction writing, *Hokusei Koro*, edited by Makoto Fujiki in Kyoto.

Other bibliographical works include:

Sekai no SF Bungaku Sokaisetsu [A detailed introduction to masterpieces of science fiction in the world], ed. Norio Itoh and Takashi Ishikawa. Tokyo: Jiyu-koku-miusha, 1978–. Revised twice. (Commercial publication.)

SF Tosho Kaisetsu Somokuroku [The complete catalogue of SF publications in Japan], ed. Fujio Ishihara. Kamakura: The Institute of SF Research, 1982. (Semi-commercial publication).

Nihon SF Nenkan [SF yearbook of Japan: 1981], ed. Toshiya Okamoto and Takeshi Shimada. Osaka: Kaigai SF Association, 1981. (Fan publication.)

Nihon SF Nenkan 1982 [The Japan SF yearbook: 1982], ed. Nobumitsu Omiya. Tokyo: Studio Ambient/Shin-Jidaisha, 1982. (Commercial publication.)

Kiso Tengai Index [Index to Kiso Tengai], ed. Hideki and Mutsuo Watanabe, et al. Nagoya: SF Fangroup "Ambivalence," 1982. (Fan publication.)

Selective List of Significant Japanese Science Fiction (Prepared by Takayuki Tatsumi)

Novels (in chronological order)

Kobo Abe, *Daiyon Kanpyo-ki* [Inter-ice age 4], Tokyo: Hayakawa, 1958. Future prediction computer, aquatic human being, and the end of the inter ice age 4—fusing these fascinating ideas, Abe, the mainstream writer, succeeded in creating an apocalyptic vision of the future, whose seriousness could easily be compared with that of Anglo-American writers in the 1950s. Japanese science fiction quite happily started with this unquestionably "hardcore" science fiction.

Ryu Mitsuse, *Hyakuoku no Hiru to Senoku no Yoru* [Ten billion days and one hundred billion nights], Tokyo: Hayakawa, 1966. The galactic- and spatiotemporal-level reinterpretation of Plato, Buddha, and Christ from the viewpoint of "Oriental nihilism" peculiar to this author. Undoubtedly represents Japanese science fiction in the 1960s.

Yoshio Aramaki, *Shinseidai* [The Planet of Bosch], Tokyo: Tokuma, 1978. The author's background of literature and art let him surrealistically create another world in which the fantastic vision of Hieronymous Bosch, the medieval Dutch artist, is actualized. Aramaki might be called the equivalent of J. G. Ballard. Note that this novel was written prior to Ian Watson's *The Gardens of Delight* (London: Gollancz, 1980), which is based on the same idea.

Taku Mayumura, *Shometsu no Korin* [Aureole of extinction], Tokyo: Hayakawa, 1978. This long novel, typically reflecting the author's sociohistorical interest, was

written as "an episode" in his "Governors of the Worlds" series, the equivalent
of Asimov's "Foundation" series. With this novel, Mayumura won the Kyoka
Izumi Award, which is annually given to the best mainstream fantasy.

Chohei Kanbayashi, *Teki wa Kaizoku—Kaizoku ban* [Enemies are the pirates—Pirate
edition], Tokyo: Hayakawa, 1983. While the above-mentioned novels by Aramaki and Mayumura signify the greatest achievement of Japanese science fiction in the 1970s, Kambayashi's works predict its course in the 1980s. This
Seiunsho-winning novel might be called a metaphysical space opera. Kambayashi is sometimes compared with P. K. Dick in his sense of entropy, but it
should not be forgotten that he by no means leaves out the "hardcore" essence
of science fiction.

Short Stories (in chronological order)

Shinichi Hoshi, "Bokko-Chan," 1957, in *Jinzo-Bijin* (Tokyo: Shinchosha, 1961). As
the original title, "Jinzo Bijin" [An artificial beauty], indicates, this is a tragi-
comedy that deals with the fate of an android maid, Bokko-chan. Hoshi is the
first full-time short-short story writer in Japan, whose works are sometimes
compared with those of Frederic Brown. Hoshi is also a one-time coeditor of
Uchijin.

Yasutaka Tsutsui, "Tatazumu Hito" [The standing woman], 1974, in *Tsutsui Yasutaka
Collection* (Tokyo: Shincho, 1985). Here the author, who is well known for his
absurd and slapstick technique, creates a Kafkaesque town whose streets are filled
with vegetableized people. Tsutsui, currently the president of SF Writers Club of
Japan, tends to deconstruct the boundary between science fiction and experimental
fiction, like the American New Writers or Latin American Writers.

Masaki Yamada, "Kamagari" [God hunt], 1974, in *Kamigari* (Tokyo: Hayakawa, 1975).
The author is a younger superstar of the 1970s, whose genuine "hardcore" science
fiction is capable of fusing quite a few physical/metaphysical systems, including
"meta-linguistics," in this novella into a coherent narrative. Now he is trying to
create the Japanese equivalent of "wide-screen baroque."

Sakyo Komatsu, "Gorudiasu no Musubime" [The Gordian knot], 1977. Describes an
extraordinary combination of medievalistic occult adventure and up-to-date
black hole theory, successfully done by the Japanese grandmaster of science
fiction.

Mariko Ohara, "Ginga Nettowaku de Uta o Utatta Kujira" [A portrait of a galactic whale
as a singer], 1982. Ohara is, for the time being, the only female "hardcore"
science fiction writer in Japan. Although this title itself reminds us of the work
of Robert F. Young, Ohara is generally considered a follower of Cordwainer
Smith in that she is also constructing a far-future history that comprises numerous
episodes.

Films (in chronological order)

Gojira [Godzilla], 1954. The director, Fiji Tsoburaya, is a genius of science fiction film
who triggered the boom of "monster" movies and the "Ultra" television series.

Nihon Chinbotsu [Japan sinks], 1973. Komatsu's original novel is closely followed.

Kurasha Jo [Joe the crasher], 1983. A superb animation space opera based on the original
story by Haruku Takachiho.

Toki o Kakeru Shoujo [A schoolgirl who travelled time], 1983. Tsutsui's original story, which the author himself does not very highly appreciate, is wonderfully revived by the director Nobuhiko Obayashi and the actress Tomoyo Harada.

Urusei Yatsura—The Beautiful Dreamer [Ram and her company—The beautiful dreamer], 1984. While Japanese science fiction film itself cannot be compared yet with the productions of George Lukas or Steven Spielberg, Japanese animated science fiction films are certainly the best in the world. Based upon Rumiko Takahashi's comedy, the director Mamoru Oshii succeeds in creating a pseudo-three-dimensional world by means of his incredible "magic realism."

Television (in chronological order)

"Tetsuwan Atomu" [Astro boy], 1963. Based on Asamu Tezuka's comic, the television version won a greater reputation. This is usually the case in the relationship between Japanese comics and television, and it is true of the following except for "Ultra Q."

"Urutora Q" [Ultra Q], 1966. With this Japanese equivalent of "Outer Limits," Tsuburaya's "Ultra Series" ("Ultraman," "Ultra Seven," etc.) started.

"Kamen Raida" [The masked rider], 1971. The original comedy was written by Shotaro Ishimori.

"Doraemon," 1979. Based on Fujio-Fujiko's wish fulfillment comic.

"Chojiku-Yosai Makurosu" [The super spatio-temporal fortress "Macros"], 1982. Unusual stress on science fiction gadgets in this kind of television encouraged the boom of science fiction toys.

Comics (in chronological order)

Jiro Kuwata, "Eitoman" [The eighth man]. Contrary to "Astro Boy," "The Eighth Man" is a completely android type. Based upon the original story of Kazumasa Hirai, who triggered the cult boom of Genma Taisen [The war with a devil king].

Moto Hagio, "Po no Ichizoku" [The family of Poe]. Romantic science fiction that treats a vampire family sympathetically. Hagio is, for the time being, the only female writer of "hardcore" science fiction comics.

Hideo Azuma, "SF Mechiru Metafiziku" [Science fiction methyl metaphysic]. A series of short "meta–science fiction" comics written by an absurd and slapstick writer, who also writes "Lolita Complex" comics.

Susumu Miyazaki, "Kaze no Tani No Naushika" [Nausica from the valley of wind]. A fantastic combination of the image of post–Third World War world, recalling Aldiss's *Hothouse* and the humanistic desire for survival/evolution.

Katsuhiro, Oyomo, "Akira." The most recent comic by the most promising writer of serious science fiction comics. Otomo has won the Japan SF Award, the Seiunsho Award, and Kodansha's Comic Award.

NOTES

1. Ursula K. Le Guin, "Introduction," *Left Hand of Darkness* (New York: Ace Books, 1976); Darko Suvin, *The Metamorphosis of Science Fiction* (New Haven: Yale University Press, 1979); Robert Scholes, *Structural Fabulation* (Notre Dame, Ind.: University of Notre Dame Press, 1975).

2. James Gunn and Stephen Goldman, *The Road to Science Fiction: From Gilgamesh to Wells* (New York: NAL, 1980), p. 1.

3. B[rian] S[tapleford] and P[eter] N[icholls], "Definitions of SF," in *The Science Fiction Encyclopedia*, ed. Peter Nichols (Garden City, N.Y.: Doubleday, 1979).

4. James Gunn, "Introduction," in Gunn and Goldman, p. 1.

5. Mark Siegel, "The Ritual Roots of Ultraman," *Channels of Communication*, July/ August 1985, pp. 18–19; and "Foreigner as Alien in Japanese Science Fantasy," *Science-Fiction Studies* 12 (November 1985), 252–63.

6. Alan Berger, "Science-Fiction Fans in Socio-economic Perspective: Factors in the Social Consciousness of a Genre," *Science-Fiction Studies* 4 (1977), 237.

7. Charles Elkins, "An Approach to the Social Functions of American SF," *Science-Fiction Studies* 4 (1977), 228–32; Gerard Klein, "Discontent in American Science Fiction," *Science-Fiction Studies* 4 (1977), 3–13.

8. Nyozekan Hasegawa, *The Japanese Character: A Cultural Profile* (Tokyo: Kodansha International, 1982), p. 70.

9. Shuichi Kato, *A History of Japanese Literature: The First Thousand Years*, trans. David Chibbett (Tokyo: Kodansha International, 1979), p. 21.

10. David Lewis, "Japanese SF," in *Anatomy of Wonder*, ed. Neil Barron (New York: Bowker, 1981), p. 473.

11. Takizawa Bakin's *Satomi Hakkenden* [Satomi and the eight dog warriors] was published between 1814 and 1842 and has been republished in original and condensed forms numerous times over the last 140 years. It was also the source for several films and popular television programs. The first English translation (of a condensed version) was published in 1986 by Charles E. Tuttle and Company.

12. Lewis, "Japanese SF," p. 474.

13. Richard Dorson, "Foreword," in *Folktales of Japan*, ed. Keigo Seki (Chicago: University of Chicago Press, 1969), pp. xiii-xiv.

14. Lewis, "Japanese SF," p. 474.

15. Ibid., pp. 475, 477–94.

16. Koichi Yamano, "English Literature and British Science Fiction," trans. David Lewis, *Foundation* 30 (1984), 28.

17. Hisako Matsubara, "First Word," *Omni Special Edition: Japan 2000*, June 1985, p. 6.

18. Takumi Shibano, letter to Hull, August 1, 1985.

19. Translated by Edward Lipsett as "Empty Giants."

20. Takumi Shibano, letter to Hull, August 1, 1985.

21. The "No Award" vote is unmistakable evidence that the balloting is patterned after the Hugos and Nebulas. This appears far more frequently than in the United States, an indication of the seriousness of the Japanese about the quality of the recipients of their awards.

22. David Hartwell, *Age of Wonders: Exploring the World of Science Fiction* (New York: Walker, 1984), pp. 174, 175.

23. Kato, pp. 1–2.

24. Yamano, p. 27.

25. Yoshio Kobayashi, letter to Hull, August 5, 1985.

26. Takayuki Tatsumi, letter to Hull, September 17, 1984.

27. Takayuki Tatsumi, letter to Hull, August 3, 1985.

APPENDIX A: The Japan National Science Fiction Conventions
(information supplied by Takayuki Tatsumi)

Date	Con Name	City	Attendance	Con Chair
1962 May	Meg-Con	Tokyo	180	Takumi Shibano
1963 October	Tokon 1	Tokyo	300	Takumi Shibano
1964 July	Daicon 1	Osaka	150	Yasutaka Tsutsui
1965 August	Tokon 2	Tokyo	400	Takumi Shibano
1966 August	Meicon 1	Nagoya	130	Den Yoshimitsu
1967 August	Tokon 3	Tokyo	180	Takumi Shibano
1968 August	Tokon 4	Tokyo	250	Masahiro Noda
1969 August	Kyukon	Kumamoto	100	Shinji Matsuzaki
1970 August	Tokon 5	Tokyo	250	Norio Itoh
1971 August	Daicon 2	Osaka	250	Masanori Takahashi
1972 August	Meicon 2	Nagoya	250	Junko Koda
1973 August	Ezocon 1	Hokkaido	80	Yuji Miura
1974 August	Miyacon	Kyoto	320	Akira Odane
1975 August	Shincon	Kobe	1,000	Koji Shimizu
1976 August	Tokon 6	Tokyo	700	Masahiro Noda
1977 August	Hincon	Yokohama	300	Junichi Kadokura
1978 August	Ashinocon	Hakone	400	Masami Kato
1979 August	Meicon 3	Nagoya	700	Hirohisa Suzuki
1980 August	Tokon 7	Tokyo	1,300	Hiroshi Sasaki
1981 August	Daicon 3	Osaka	1,500	Yasuhiro Takeda
1982 August	Tokon 8	Tokyo	1,500	Nobumitsu Omiya
1983 August	Daicon 4	Osaka	4,000	Toshihiko Nishigaki
1984 August	Ezocon 2	Jozankei	1,000	Masayuki Mikami
1985 August	Gatacon	Yahiko	1,250	Kazuyoshi Kakizaki
1986 August	Daicon 5	Osaka	2,000	Hiroshi Yamane
1987 August	Uracon '87	Yamanaka	1,200	Yumiko Ura

APPENDIX B: Winners of the Fandom Awards of the 1960s
(supplied by Takumi Shibano)

1965   Shinichi Hoshi, Tetsu Yano, Masami Fukushima, Ray Tackett, and Takumi Shibano

1966   Sakyo Komatsu, Ryu Mitsuse, Asamu Tezuka, Masahiro Noda, and Norio Itoh

1967   Yasutaka Tsutsui, Fiji Tsuburaya, Mitsuo Makimura, and Forrest J. Ackerman

1968   Taku Mayumura, Kazumasa Hirai, Aritsune Toyota, Den Yoshimitsu, Shinji Mat-
       suzaki, and Fujio Ishihara

1969   Takashi Ishikawa, Hiroshi Sasaki, and Shin Watanabe

1970   Masaru Mori, Yoshio Aramaki, and Hisako Negi

APPENDIX C: Winners of the Seiunshos (supplied by Yoshio Kobayashi)

JN: Japanese novel; FN: foreign novel; JS: Japanese short story; FS: foreign short story;
TP: theatrical presentation; C: comics; A: art.

1970   JN: *Reicho-rui Minami e*, Yasutaka Tsutsui
       「霊長類南え」　筒井康隆
       FN: *The Crystal World*, J. G. Ballard
       JS: ''Furu Neruson,'' Yasutaka Tsutsui
       ″フル・ネルソン″　筒井康隆
       FS: ''The Squirrel Cage,'' Thomas M. Disch
       TP: *The Prisoner, Charly* (tie)

1971   JN: *Tsugi no wa Dare ka*, Sakyo Komatsu
       「次のは誰か？」　小松左京
       FN: *The Andromeda Strain*, Michael Crichton
       JS: ''Bitamin,'' Yasutaka Tsutsui
       ″ビタミン″　筒井康隆
       FS: ''The Poem,'' Ray Bradbury
       TP: *UFO*

1972   JN: *Ishi no Ketsumyaku*, Ryo Hanmura
       「石の血脈」　半村良
       FN: *Nightwings*, Robert Silverberg
       JS: ''Shirakabe no Moji wa Yuhi ni Haeru,'' Yoshio Aramaki
       ″白壁の文字は夕陽に映える″　荒巻義雄
       FS: ''The Blue Bottle,'' Ray Bradbury
       TP: *The Andromeda Strain*

1973   JN: *Kagami no Kuni no Arisu*, Tadashi Hirose
       「鏡の国のアリス」　広瀬正
       FN: *The Sirens of Titan*, Kurt Vonnegut, Jr.
       JS: ''Kessho Seidan,'' Sakyo Komatsu
       ″結晶星団″　小松左京
       FS: ''The Black Ferris,'' Ray Bradbury
       TP: *A Clockwork Orange*

1974   JN: *Japan Sinks*, Sakyo Komatsu
       「日本沈没」　小松左京
       FN: *Dune*, Frank Herbert
       JS: ''Nippon Igai Zenbu Chinbotsu,'' Yasutaka Tsutsui
       ″日本以外全部沈没″　筒井康隆
       FS: ''A Meeting with Medusa,'' Arthur C. Clarke
       TP: *Soylent Green*

1975   JN: *Ore no Chi wa Tanin no Chi*, Yasutaka Tsutsui
       「俺の血は他人の血」　筒井康隆
       FN: *Up the Line*, Robert Silverberg
       JS: ''Kamigari,'' Masaki Yamada
       ″神我り″　山田正紀
       FS: ''Eurema's Dam, F,'' R. A. Lafferty
       TP: *Space Cruiser Yamato*
       「宇宙船ヤマト」

1976 JN: *Nanase Futababi*, Yasutaka Tsutsui
「七瀬ふたたび」　筒井康隆
FN: *This Immortal*, Roger Zelazny
JS: ''Vomisa,'' Sakyo Komatsu
〝ヴォミーサ〞　小松左京
FS: ''Wet Paint,'' A. Bertram Chandler
TP: *Sutaa*
「スタア」　筒井康隆

1977 JN: *Saikoro Tokkotai*, Musashi Kanbe
「サイコロ特攻隊」　かんべむさし
FN: *The Dragon Masters*, Jack Vance
JS: ''Metamorufosesu Gunto,'' Yasutaka Tsutsui
〝メタモルフォセス群島〞　筒井康隆
FS: ''Rosprawa,'' Stanislaw Lem
TP: No Award
Special Award: Yoshiyuki Kato (for his devotion to science fiction fandom)

1978 JN: *Chikyu; Seishin Bunseki Kiroku*, Masaki Yamada
「地球・精神分析記録」　山田正紀
FN: *I Will Fear No Evil*, Robert A. Heinlein
JS: ''Gorudiasu no Musubime,'' Sakyo Komatsu
〝ゴルダイスの結び目〞　小松左京
FS: No Award
TP: *Solaris*
C: ''Tera e,'' Keiko Takemiya
「地球へ．．．」　竹宮恵子

1979 JN: *Shometsu no Korin*, Taku Mayumura
「消滅の光輪」　眉村卓
FN: *Ring World*, Larry Niven
JS: ''Chiku wa Purein Yoguruto,'' Shinji Kajio
〝地球はプレイン・ヨーグルト〞　梶尾真治
FS: ''Inconstant Moon,'' Larry Niven
C: ''Fujori Nikki,'' Hideo Azuma
〝不条理日記〞　吾真ひでお
A: Naoyuki Kato
加藤直尤

1980 JN: *Hoseki Dorobo*, Masaki Yamada
「宝石泥棒」　山田正紀
FN: *Rendevous with Rama*, Arthur C. Clarke
JS: ''Daatii Pea no Daiboken,'' Haruka Takachiho
〝ダーティペアの大冒険〞　高千穂逢
FS: No Award
TP: *Alien*
C: ''Sutaa Reddo,'' Moto Hagio
「スター・レッド」　萩尾望都
A: Noriyoshi Curai
生頬範義
Special Award: Motoichiro Takebe (for life achievement)
武部本一郎

1981   JN: *Kaseijin Senshi*, Chiaki Kawamata

「火星人先史」　川又千秋

FN: *Inherit the Stars*, James P. Hogan

JS: "A Green Requiem," Motoko Arai

〝グリーン・リクイエム〟　新井素子

FS: "A Relic of the Empire," Larry Niven

TP: *The Empire Strikes Back*

C: "Densetsu," Waka Mizuki

〝伝説〟　水樹和佳

A: Yoshikazu Yasuhiko

義和安彦

1982   JN: *Kirikirijin*, Hisashi Inoue

「吉里吉里人」　井上ひさし

FN: *The Genesis Machine*, James P. Hogan

JS: "Nepuchun," Motoko Arai

〝ネプチューン〟　新井素子

FS: "The Brave Little Toaster," Thomas M. Disch

TP: No Award

C: "Kibun wa mo Senso," Katsuhiro Otomo

〝気分はもう戦争〟　大友克洋

A: Shusei Nagaoka

長岡秀星

Special Award: *Uchujin*

「宇宙塵」

1983   JN: *Sayonara Jupitaa*, Sakyo Komatsu

「さよならジュピター」　小松左京

FN: *Dragon's Egg*, Robert E. Forward

JS: "Kotobazukaishi," Chohei Kanbayashi

言葉使い師〟　神林長平

FS: "Nightflyers," George R. R. Martin

TP: *Bladerunner*

C: "Gin no Sankaku," Moto Hagio

銀の三角〟　萩尾望都

A: Yoshitaka Amano

天野善孝

1984   JN: *Teki wa Kaizoku, Kaizoku ban*, Chohei Kanbayashi

「敵は海賊・海賊版」　神林長平

FN: *The Garments of Caean*, Barrington Bayley

JS: "Suupaa Fenikkusu," Chohei Kanbayashi

〝スーパー・フェニックス〟　神林長平

FS: "Unicorn Variation," Roger Zelazny

TP: *The Dark Crystal*

C: "Domu" [Dreaming Childhood] Katsuhiro Otomo

〝童夢〟　大友克洋

A: Yoshitaka Amano

天野善孝

1985   JN: *Sento Yosei Yukikaze*, Chohei Kanbayashi

「戦闘妖精・雪風」　神林長平

FN: *Zen Gun*, Barrington J. Bayley
JS: No Award
FS: No Award
TP: Kaze no Tani no Naushika

「風の谷のナウシカ」

C: "X-Y," Moto Hagio

〝 Ｘ－Ｙ〟　萩尾望都

A: Yoshitaka Amano

天野善孝

APPENDIX D: Winners of the Taisho
(Japan Science Fiction Award) (supplied by Takumi Shibano)

1980   *Solar Wind Intersection (Taiyofu koten)* by Akida Hori (a collection of nearly ten
       years' worth of short stories, ''hard science fiction'')

「太陽風交点」　堀晃

1981   *Kirikiri People* by Hisashi Inoue

「吉里吉里人」　井上ひさし

1982   *The Last Enemy* by Masaki Yamada

「最後の敵」　山田正紀

1983   ''Domu'' [Dreaming Childhood] by Katsuhiro Otomo

「童夢」　大友克洋

1984   *Genshi Gari* [Pursuit of the dream poem] by Chiaki Kawamata, which deals with
       surrealism and time warping, the premise being built around a poem that ''is said
       to create time itself through words'' (Kobayashi, Maki, and Lipsett, *Locus*, January
       1985: 31), and inevitably leads those who read it to die shortly thereafter.

「幻詩狩り」　川又千秋

Note: This is certainly too small a sampling to suggest a pattern, but suffice it to say that
the Japanese authors have already established an eclectic attitude toward their own work
in science fiction.

SELECTED BIBLIOGRAPHY

This list includes not only works cited in this essay, but also reference works valuable
for an overview of science fiction fandom throughout the world.
The editors gratefully acknowledge the expert assistance of Professor Tatsumi in preparing
this essay for publication.

Apostolou, John L. ''Japanese Science Fiction in English Translation.'' *Extrapolation*
       25 (Spring 1984), 83–86. Valuable bibliography with an introductory overview.
Asimov, Isaac. *In Memory Yet Green: The Autobiography of Isaac Asimov, 1920–1954*.
       New York: Avon, 1979.

Bailey, J.[ames] O.[sler]. *Pilgrims Through Space and Time*. 1947; rpt. Westport, Conn.: Greenwood Press, 1972. Inspired the name of the award for criticism and scholarship bestowed annually by the Science Fiction Research Association; Bailey was the first Pilgrim winner.

Bakin, Takizawa. *Satomi Hakkenden*. Tokyo: Charles E. Tuttle, 1986.

Berger, Alan. "Science-Fiction Fans in Socio-economic Perspective: Factors in the Social Consciousness of a Genre." Science-Fiction Studies 4 (1977), 236–45. *The Book of Science-Fiction: Criterion and/or Deconstruction of Science Fiction*. Tokyo: Studio Ambient/Shin-Jidaisha, 1982.

Budrys, Algis. *Benchmarks: Galaxy Bookshelf by Algis Budrys*. Carbondale: Southern Illinois University Press, 1985.

Dorson, Richard. "Foreword." In *Folktales of Japan*. Ed. Keigo Seki. Chicago: University of Chicago Press, 1969, iii-xxix.

Elkins, Charles. "An Approach to the Social Functions of American SF." *Science-Fiction Studies* 4 (1977), 226–35.

Gunn, James. *Alternate Worlds: The Illustrated History of Science Fiction*. Introd. Isaac Asimov. Englewood Cliffs, N.J.: Prentice-Hall, 1975.

Gunn, James and Stephen Goldman. *The Road to Science Fiction: From Gilgamesh to Wells*, 4 vols. New York: NAL, 1980.

Hartwell, David. *Age of Wonders: Exploring the World of Science Fiction*. New York: Walker, 1984.

Hasegawa, Nyozekan. *The Japanese Character: A Cultural Profile*. Tokyo: Kodansha, 1982.

Hull, Elizabeth Anne. "DaiCon IV Convention Report." *Locus* 16 (December 1983), 24–25. With pictures.

―――. "Japanese SF Criticism." *Locus* 17 (January 1984), 37. [News report on *The Book of SF*]

Ishihara, Fujio, ed. *The Bibliography of SF Books Published in Japan*. Kamakura: The Institute of SF Research, 1982.

―――. *Index to SFM*. Kanagawa: SF Shiryo Kenkyukai, 1980–81.

Itoh, Norio, and Takashi Ishikawa, eds. *Sekai no SF Bungaku Sokaisetsu*. Tokyo: Jiyu-kokuminsha, 1978.

伊藤規夫　石川孝、編　「世界のＳＦ文学総解説」　東京　自由国民社　１９７８．

Kato, Shuichi. *A History of Japanese Literature: The First Thousand Years*. Trans. David Chibbett. Tokyo: Kodansha, 1979.

Klein, Gerard. "Discontent in American Science-Fiction." *Science-Fiction Studies* 4 (1977), 3–15.

Knight, Damon. *The Futurians: The Story of the Science Fiction "Family" of the 30's That Produced Today's Top SF Writers and Editors*. New York: John Day, 1977.

Kobayashi, Yoshio, and Edward Lipsett. "SF in Japan: An Overview." *Locus* 17 (March 1984), 21.

Kobayashi, Y.[oshio], S.[hinji] Maki, and E. [dward] Lipsett. "Science Fiction in Japan." *Locus* 18 (January 1985), 31–32.

Le Guin, Ursula K. "Introduction." In *Left hand of Darkness*. New York: Ace Books, 1976.

Lerner, Frederick Andrew. *Modern Science Fiction and the American Literary Community*. Metuchen, N.J.: Scarecrow, 1985. A historical perspective; optimistic about science fiction's academic respectability.

Lester, Colin, ed. *The International Science Fiction Yearbook, 1979*. New York: Pierrot, 1978; in Japan: Music Sales Corporation, 4–26–22 Jinguame, Shibuya-ku, Tokyo 150, Japan. Reveals fan linkage from the 1970s.

Lewis, David. "Ezocon II." *Locus* 17 (October 1984), 29–30.

———. "Japanese SF." In *Anatomy of Wonder*. Ed. Neil Barron. New York: Bowker, 1981, 467–92. Write Lewis at 303 Coop Masa-shino, 3–3–5, Kyonancho, Musashino-shi, Tokyo 180, Japan.

———. "SF in Japan." *Locus* 14 (November 1981), 14.

Lundwall, Sam. *Science Fiction: An Illustrated History*. New York: Grosset & Dunlap, 1977.

Maki, Shinji, and Yoshio Kobayashi. "Japanese National Convention." *Locus* 18 (December 1985), 26, 31.

Matsubara, Hisako. "First Word." *Omni Special Edition: Japan 2000* (June 1985), 6.

Mori, Tosaku, ed. *Index to Uchujin*. Kanagawa: Institute of SF Research.

Moskowitz, Sam. *The Immortal Storm: A History of Science Fiction Fandom*. Westport, Conn.: Hyperion, 1954.

Nakane, Chie. "Criteria of Group Formation." In *Japanese Culture and Behavior*. Ed. Takie Lebra and William Lebra. Honolulu: University of Hawaii Press, 1979, 156–79.

Nicholls, Peter. *The Science Fiction Encyclopedia*. Garden City, N.Y.: Dolphin Books, 1979.

Okamoto, Toshiya, and Takeshi Shimada, eds. *Nihon SF Nenkan*. Osaka: Kaigai SF Association, 1981.

岡本としや・島田たけし編　『日本ＳＦ年鑑』大阪　海外ＳＦ研究会　　1 9 8 1

Omiya, Nobumitsu. *The Critical Adventures of Science Fiction*. Tokyo: Shin-Jidaisha, 1984.

———, ed. *Nihon SF Nenkan 1982*. Tokyo: Studio Ambient/Shin Jidaisha, 1982.

日本ＳＦ年鑑編集委員会編　『日本ＳＦ年鑑』東京　新時代社　　1 9 8 2

Pohl, Frederik. *The Way the Future Was: A Memoir*. New York: Ballantine, 1978.

Reamy, Tom, ed. *Midamericon Program Book*. Five thousand copies privately printed for the 1976 Worldcon. Any worldcon program book will serve to introduce the "neo" to fandom; this (hardcover) one is particularly helpful and complete.

Scholes, Robert. *Structural Fabulation*. Notre Dame: University of Notre Dame Press, 1975.

Siegel, Mark. "Foreigner as Alien in Japanese Science Fantasy." *Science-Fiction Studies* 12 (November 1985), 252–63.

Stephan, John J. *Hawaii Under the Rising Sun: Japan's Plans for Conquest After Pearl Harbor*. Honolulu: University of Hawaii Press, 1984. See pp. 151 and 168–69 on the use of speculative literature as propaganda.

Suvin, Darko. *The Metamorphosis of Science Fiction*. New Haven: Yale University Press, 1979.

Tanaka, Yoshiyuki. "Foreign Science Fiction in Japan." *REM:3* (January 1986), 7–8. See Charles Platt, 1955 S. Beverly Glen, Los Angeles, CA 90025.

Tucker, Wilson. "Neofan's Guide" (pamphlet). N.p.: Dean Grennell, 1955; 2nd ed., n.p.: Robert and Juanita Coulson, 1966.

Van Troyer, Gene. "Uru no Haka" [The grave of U!] (review of the Japanese poem). *Star Line: A Newsletter of the Science Fiction Poetry Association* 5 (January/February 1982), 28–29. Refutes the notion that Japanese science fiction poetry is nonexistent; many otherwise knowledgeable American fans might make the same claim in the United States, but science fiction poetry exists in both languages. Gene Van Troyer reads Japanese.

Watanabe, Hideki and Mutsuo, et al., eds. *Kiso Tengai Index*. Nagoya: SF Fangroup Ambivalence, 1982.

渡辺英樹編　『奇想天外インデックス』　ＳＦファングループアンビバレンス

１９８２

Yamano, Koichi. "English Literature and British Science Fiction." Trans. David Lewis. *Foundation* 30 (1984), 26–31.

11

Japanese Mystery Literature

KAZUO YOSHIDA

This survey is an introduction to Japanese mystery literature. Since this essay must inevitably cover detective stories, adventure stories, and occult erotic-grotesque stories, all of which may feature riddles, fear, or suspense, the term "mystery literature" is used here in a most general sense, as are the terms "detective story" and "mystery."

Mystery literature has not been a favored subject of academic research, but this kind of literature has been popular with the Japanese people for more than a century and now seems to be enjoying a boom, aided by movies and television. Almost every best-selling mystery has been turned into a movie or a television program, which has then drawn more people to the story itself. Rampo Edogawa, a modern master of the Japanese detective story, explains how the elements of plot, setting, and character are put together to make a good detective story:

The basic purpose of the detective story lies in the logic of solving a complex puzzle. Therefore, it almost never describes the mentality of the murderer in detail. A good detective story is expected to surprise the reader without telling him much about the culprit; an unexpected turnabout is an important element. . . . In other words, the detective story is a novel in which a murder case is written from the point of view of a detective.[1]

Mystery literature seems concerned with problem solving. Murders that take place where they would appear impossible are one problem, and detection is the solution. A pair of men are usually introduced, a detective and his assistant, who become the major characters and the problem-solvers. Solving the case despite a complex set of events and possible solutions is the main concern of the story. The reader's curiosity is maintained through suspense and surprise, but the plot must also remain logical. From the writer's point of view, logic determines whether or not the details of the killing can be put together in a believable manner. The reader is left to follow the preconceived process of the killing by reading the story. The reader of mystery literature thus is treated as the apostle of reason.

Mystery literature is usually concerned with murder and the detection of the murder, so the genre seems to be politically conservative. Indeed, that may be one of the reasons for its popularity.

HISTORICAL SURVEY

The turning point in the development of the Japanese mystery is 1868, the year of the Meiji Restoration and the beginning of modern Japan.

As early as 1649, the first substantial book on crime was introduced to the people of Japan—a collection of Chinese criminal cases. The original book, Kuei Wan-Jung's *Tang Yin Bi Shi* [Toinhiji] (1207), was meant to be consulted by lawyers and police officers, but the Japanese version found a good number of general readers. Some forty years later, Saikaku Ihara (1642–1693), a famous novelist of the time, wrote a book in 1689 that was a collection of criminal cases in Japan. More than one hundred years later, the next Chinese book of crime was introduced to Japan when a book of forensic pathology, Dr. Zong Ci's *The Cases of the Acquitted* [Muen rokujitsu] (1247), was translated by Shokyu Kawai in 1768.

The first Western detective story translated into Japanese was Jan Christemeijer's *Belangrikke tafereelen uit de Geshiedenis der liifstraffelijke regtsplegling* [Yongeru kidan] (1820). Kohei Kanda translated two stories out of the eleven in Christemeijer's collection in 1887. In the following year, George McWatter's *Detectives of Europe and America* [Kigoku] (1877) was translated by Inokichi Chihara (1888). S. M. Phillips's *Famous Cases of Circumstantial Evidences* [Jokyoshoko gohan roku] (1873) was translated by Kenzo Takahashi in 1881.

Victor Hugo, Arthur Conan Doyle, R. Austin Freeman, Maurice Leblanc, and other early Western mystery writers were gradually introduced to Japanese detective story readers. A good example of how Western stories were adapted and introduced to the Japanese audience is a tale written by Encho Sanyutei (1839–1900), a storyteller who was popular partly because of his originality in introducing new stories from foreign sources.

The following story was told by Encho who had heard it from a friend who had read the original story in English. A girl called Ran was the daughter of a *samurai*, but later worked at a tea house. Yamasaburo Ishii, the Lord of Uraga, was impressed by her hard work and by her dedication toward her parents. The lord pitied her and gave her some money, but forget his wallet at the tea house. Ran found it and returned it to him. On the way home she was attacked by a gang, but was rescued by a man who fell in love with her and married her.

While her husband was away for some months on a business trip, Ran went to see her friend, a *geisha* in Kamakura. There Ran found out that her husband was the boss of notorious robbers who also kidnapped girls and sold them into slavery. As soon as the husband learned that Ran now knew what he was, he caught her and buried her alive.

Meanwhile, Lord Ishii, who had been fishing, drifted to the shore of Kamakura and heard about the buried woman. He sent men to check the incident and they found the woman alive in a coffin. The lord was chivalrous enough to confront the boss of the robbers to try to reform the gang, but the angry criminals planned to take revenge against Lord Ishii. Having heard the gang's plan, Lord Ishii contrived a plan to round them up. In the end, Ran became a nun.

Another interesting figure who contributed greatly to the development of mysteries in Japan was Black Kairakutei (?—1923). This Englishman came to Japan in the 1860s with his father, a journalist. They published a newspaper, and Black became involved in giving speeches and telling stories. He joined a group of storytellers called Sanyusha (a group of storytellers headed by Encho Sanyutei, 1839–1900); he became a storyteller himself, and introduced a number of detective stories that he had adapted from originals in English. One of Black's stories, published in 1902, made fingerprints the clue that identified the murderer. At that time, the real police department was not prepared to use fingerprints to differentiate the innocent from the guilty; only ten years later, in 1912, did the police department open a fingerprint bureau.

After the Meiji Restoration, Japan opened its doors to countries outside Japan. Culturally the opening of the country meant the opening of people's eyes to Western writing, including mysteries. In the transitional period right after the restoration, as crime stories in translation were being read by the Japanese, a number of mysteries were also written by Japanese writers. One of the most outstanding among them was a true story of a woman-criminal, Oden Takahashi. Robun Kanagaki's *Oden Takahashi, the Devil* [Takahashi oden yashamonogatari] (1879) became a classic of its kind. The story was about a woman who had murdered her husband, among other serious crimes, and was hanged for it.

While these storytellers were popularizing detective stories, the time was ripening for the appearance of a real professional translator and writer of detective stories.

Ruiko Kuroiwa (1862–1913) was one of the most influential writers in the early history of detective stories in Japan. Ruiko Kuroiwa translated plot-oriented stories by Emile Gaboriau and Fortune Du Boisgobey. In 1888 Ruiko Kuroiwa published his first translation from an English version (*Widow Lerouge*) of Emile Gaboriau's *L'Affaire Lerouge* under the title *Man or Devil* [Hito ya oni ya]. In the same year he began writing a series entitled *The Beauty in the Court* [Hotei no bijin] for the *Konnichi Press* (1889).

Koson Aeba's translation of Edgar Allan Poe's *The Black Cat* (1845) had been published in the *Yomiuri Daily Press* in 1887. Gaishi Nanyo's version of *The*

Adventures of Sherlock Homes (1892) was printed in a daily paper, the *Chuo Press*, in 1899. The daily papers played an important role in bringing Western detective stories to the Japanese.

Nansui Sudo's *The Sword in the Flaming Field* [Shoen kenbo] (1888) and Ruiko Kuroiwa's *The Miserable* [Muzan] (1888), whose title was later changed to *Three Strands of Hair* [Misuji no kami], are among the first original stories. Rohan Koda (1807–1947), a scholar and a novelist, had a more complex type of mystery story. His *Surprise* [Ayashiyana] (1889) introduced a device of his own origin having to do with the fact that when mercurious chloride and hydrochloric acid are mixed in the stomach, they become a corrosive poison.

After the turn of the century, readers were ready to enjoy the original works of the second generation of writers after Ruiko Kuroiwa, among them Junichiro Tanizaki (1886–1965), Ryunosuke Akutagawa (1892–1927), and Haruo Sato (1892–1964). Although all of them were later recognized as mainstream writers rather than mystery writers, they were apparently interested enough in crimes and mysteries to produce some excellent stories.

Tanizaki liked things mysterious and exotic; his earlier stories such as *The Magic of Hassan Khan* [Hassan khan no yojitsu] (1917), *The Scabbed Face* [Jinmen so] (1918), and *The Ghost in Broad Daylight* [Hakuchu kigo] (1918), are full of strange and unnatural things, and they influenced Rampo Edogawa and Seishi Yokomizo who became the two incomparable giants of Japanese mystery literature. Akutagawa wrote a few crime stories, but no mysteries. *The Robbers* [Chuto] (1917) and *The Bamboo Bush* [Yabu no naka] (1918) are his major stories. Sato, who is recognized as a poet rather than a detective story writer, wrote a story called *The Finger Print* [Shimon] (1919). He also wrote an essay in 1924 in which he defined the detective story as a product of romanticism, the fruit of eroticism and curiosity. His essay had a great impact on later mystery writers.

The golden age of Japanese mystery literature dawned in 1920 with the publication of a new magazine for mysteries, *The New Youth* [Shin seinen], which provided promising mystery writers with a stable market. A number of precursors had been issued, but none of them lasted long. A market for *The New Youth* had been created by mysteries in translation and true stories of criminals. Western mysteries especially whetted the reader's appetite for original mysteries by the Japanese writers. *The New Youth* became one of the few magazines in which both overseas detective stories and Japanese original stories were included. From its first issue it sponsored a prize contest for short mystery stories. Many modern giants in mystery literature, including Rampo Edogawa and Yokomizo, made their debut by winning the contest.

The name of Rampo Edogawa (1894–1965) may not mean anything to Western readers, but if it is put in the Japanese order, family name first and given name last, and if it is syllabicated according to phonetic symbols, it would be pronounced in the following way: "Edogawa aram po," or Edgar Allan Poe. This deduction itself may serve as a clue as to how the mysteries in Japan developed.

Mystery literature would not have developed in Japan unless a man like Rampo Edogawa had read many of the great Western mysteries.

The Edogawa Rampo Prize for mystery literature was founded by Kodansha in 1955 in honor of his dedication to the development of mystery literature in Japan. Every year since, the prize has been given to an original mystery or two and has become the young writer's gateway to success. (A list of the prize winners is provided in the Appendix.)

At the turn of the century, factual crime stories and true stories in general were very popular and widely read. In addition to the popularity of adventure stories, the importance of writing style should also be mentioned. There was a literary movement at the time to promote writing in the style of speech. In Japanese, the literary and the colloquial styles were different. The literary style of the day and the spoken language were very dissimilar. To this movement and to the development of detective stories, a popular storyteller of the time, Encho Sanyutei (1839–1900), contributed greatly.

Ruiko Kuroiwa came out of this kind of social milieu. His rhythmical colloquialism and exciting stories were full of surprises taken from French writers and inevitably were a great success. Ruiko Kuroiwa's *Man or Devil* was published by the *Konnichi Press* in March (or April) of 1888. It was an adaptation of an English translation (*Widow Lerouge*) of Emile Gaboriau's *L'Affaire Lerouge* (1866). It can hardly be called a translation since it was freely reconstructed to fit a Japanese audience. The main characters have Japanese names, although they sound like the original French names. The most important aspects of the story are preserved, including the private detective's problem-solving process and the scene where the crime took place. Ruiko Kuroiwa's adaptation was so cleverly done that his version sounded natural to Japanese readers.

Beginning with *Man or Devil*, Ruiko Kuroiwa published a series of adapted mystery stories in various daily newspapers over the following five years. Most of the stories he translated were works by Emile Gaboriau and Fortune Du Boisgobey.

Ruiko Kuroiwa, however, should not be remembered only as the best translator of mystery literature. He should also be remembered for his original stories like *Three Strands of Hair* (1889). As has been described previously, the analysis of the young detective in this story was scientific and logical, and Ruiko Kuroiwa showed himself to be an apostle of reason.

Ruiko Kuroiwa's originality was not quite appreciated by the readers of the time, but Rampo Edogawa found the story quite creative and wrote an essay to defend Ruiko Kuroiwa's originality. In his essay, Rampo regrets that Ruiko could have been a first-class original writer rather than the best translator, had audiences of the time been mature enough to appreciate Ruiko's story.

Although slow to develop, enthusiasm for original mysteries was never extinguished. Rohan Koda's *Anxiety* [Fuan] (1897) used an original trick. Two persons shared an apple; one person died, but not the other. Poison on the fingernail of one person affected only the part of the apple to be given to the person who was to be killed. The originality of the story, however, was not fully appreciated by the writers of Koda's generation.

Rampo Edogawa appeared as the leader of the following generation and emerged as the father of Japanese mystery literature. His memoirs, *Forty Years of Writing Detective Stories*, tell in detail about his stories, writer-friends, criticism, and daily living.

Rampo Edogawa was constantly exposed to Japanese and foreign mysteries as a child because his mother had been a great fan of Ruiko Kuroiwa. Rampo Edogawa himself confessed in his memoirs that he was really indulged in reading mysteries when he was in his early teens. A little later in life, he found Poe and Doyle and was fascinated with the charm of their detective stories. Problem solving set his imagination on fire—one more indication that there would have been no mysteries in Japan unless there had been a great influence from the West.

It was not too surprising that Rampo Edogawa's first successful story, "Tuppence Coin" [Nisen doka], centered on decoding an original cipher of Chinese characters. An earlier story, *The Murder on D Street* [D-saka no satsujin jiken] (1925), shows his interest in psychological tricks. The murdered housewife in the story turned out to be a masochist who had been a lover of her neighbor, who was a sadist. The murder took place when the sadist lover squeezed the masochist woman's throat too hard.

Rampo Edogawa's interests, after producing his great original detective stories, turned to the grotesque. *A Disabled Soldier* [Imomushi] (1929) is a good example of the type. This is a story of a married couple in which the man comes home from the war in the form of a mass of flesh. His four limbs are severed; he cannot speak; he is a strange creature with only desires for food and sex. In the end he kills himself by throwing himself into an old well. Rampo Edogawa wrote a number of stories of this kind.

As Rampo Edogawa's interest turned to the grotesque and erotic, the stage was prepared for another genius of the genre—Seishi Yokomizo (b. 1902). Yokomizo is great in that he is a writer who knows much about domestic and foreign detective stories, has translated detective novels and short stories, has been an editor for a mystery magazine, and writes mystery literature.

The stories he wrote before 1940 were mainly fantastic—mysterious and unrealistic Gothic stories, with the exception of *The Secret of Crimson* (1921).

Yokomizo's postwar creative period began with receiving the first Detective Story Writers Club of Japan Prize for *The Murders at the Inn, Honjin* in 1947. In this story Yokomizo introduced his fictitious investigator, Kyosuke Kindaichi. Kyosuke Kindaichi became so famous that some young students believed that he was a real man. As in *The Murders at the Inn, Honjin*, Yokomizo included many observations and speculations on the Japanese character as he developed complex stories. Another great success, *The Village of Eight Tombs* [Yatsu haka mura] (1950), is a story of a vicious feud over generations between two wealthy families in a village cursed by the spirits of eight *samurai* murdered some hundred years before. Given the fact that the spirits of the dead are still faithfully worshiped in Japanese culture, the impending mood of the story gives it a definitely Japanese flavor.

Among the contemporaries of Edogawa and Yokomizo who have become popular through the magazine, *The New Youth*, are Saburo Koga (1893–1945), Fuboku Kozakai (1890–1929), Udaru Oshita (1896–1966), Masayuki Jo (b. 1904), Jun Mizutani (b. 1904), Kyusaku Yumeno (1889–1936), Juu Uno (1897–1949), Shiro Hamano (1896–1935), Mushitaro Oguri (1901–1946), and Kotaro Kiga (1897–1969). Collections of the works of all the above writers are available.

While *The New Youth* provided a constant market for mystery writers in prewar Japan, the postwar period saw the end of *The New Youth* and the birth of a new mystery magazine. *The Jewel* was first published by Iwatani in March 1946 and began serving as a gateway to success for young writers of mysteries. *The Jewel* lasted as a magazine for mysteries until October 1946 when all rights to the magazine were taken over by Kobunsha, which keeps publishing the magazine under the same title, but not as a mystery magazine.

During the American occupation, *The Jewel* got a ration of paper for 8,000 copies, but the editors had accumulated a much greater amount on the black market. Fifty thousand copies of the first issue were sold as soon as it was out. People were hungry not only for food but also for reading pleasure.

The magazine sold well, but the greatest war in which Japan was ever involved seriously affected the creation of new mysteries. *The Jewel* tried to find young writers by offering cash prizes for original stories, but only a few applied. The editors were not discouraged with this reaction, however. Being highly motivated, they kept going, even though there were times when they could not pay the prize money because of their debts.

One of the greatest mystery writers in postwar Japan has been Seicho Matsumoto. The secret of his success as a literary artist lies in his views on motives; his themes involve men entangled in conflicts with their social backgrounds or organizations rather than their personal relations. There are many other mystery writers who consider motive as important in developing stories, but Matsumoto emphasizes realistic characterization while simultaneously introducing plausible plot gimmicks. The reality of his characterization is presented in the following scene:

Detective Jutaro Torigai sat at a dinner table with his face streaming, just having come out of a bath. His great pleasure at dinner was to pass a few hours cherishing two small bottles of sake with his favorite foods such as bits of fresh sea urchin, squid and herring.[2]

The dinner menu may not be realistic to Americans who have never had raw fish, but the scene rings very true to millions of Japanese.

Matsumoto is also aware that the setting of the story should be realistic. In *The Ceremony of Sea Vegetable Hunting* (1972), for example, a group of *haiku* lovers go to see the ceremony at the Mekari Shrine in Kyushu. The ceremony is an annual event; many tourists go to see it every year. This practice of a group of *haiku* lovers visiting these ceremonies and festivals to write their *haiku* is as common as Americans going to see a football game. The murderer in the story uses the occasion to prove his alibi.

The situation is plausible, and the detective who solves the problems is not necessarily a genius, but simply an ordinary police officer who uses trial and error. The writer often deals with so-called social evils, evils that may be necessary to maintain business or political organizations.

Seishi Yokomizo (b. 1902) is another giant of the genre. Yokomizo stands out as an all-around mystery writer in that he is well-informed concerning mysteries both domestic and foreign, has translated both novels and short stories, is experienced in editorial work, and has succeeded in publishing his own stories. As already mentioned, Yokomizo made his debut as a mystery writer for *The New Youth*, which later invited him to be an editor.

Yokomizo wrote quite a few stories before the last war, but they were essentially gothic novels. Right after the war, in April 1946, he began writing a true detective novel, *The Murders at the Inn, Honjin* [Honjin satsujin jiken], for the new magazine, *The Jewel* [Hoseki]. The first Detective Story Writers Club of Japan Prize was given to the novel in 1947.

Seicho Matsumoto (b. 1909) is another contemporary superstar in mystery literature. He did not start his career as a mystery writer, but established himself as a newspaper reporter by the time of his first novel, *Bills Called Saigo* [Saigo fuda] (1951). It was only after receiving the Akutagawa Prize for literature for his *A Note on the Ogura Diary* [Aru Ogura nikki den] (1953) that he began writing full time. He was forty-four years old.

Originally Matsumoto's interest in literature had been in mainstream novels, but soon after receiving the prize he switched to mysteries. In 1957 he was honored with the tenth prize of the Association of Mystery Writers of Japan for his story, *The Face* [Kao] (1956). Then followed *Points and Lines* [Ten to sen] (1958), *Walls of Eyes* [Me no kabe] (1957), *Focus Zero* [Zero no shoten] (1958), *The Blue Sketch* [Aoi byoten] (1959), and *The Ceremony of Sea Vegetable Hunting* [Jikan no shuzoku] (1961). Practically all of them were best sellers.

Of the postwar mystery writers who are considered to be of major importance, Shigeru Kayama (1905–1975) made his debut by winning a contest sponsored by *The Jewel*. In the following year he published in the same magazine a story called *The Curious Stories from the House of Eel* [Kaimanso kidan] (1947), which won the first prize of the Detective Story Writers Club of Japan in 1948.

Futaro Yamada (b. 1922) appeared before the public through *The Jewel*. *The Devil in the Eyes* [Ganchu no akuma] (1948) won the Detective Story Writers Club of Japan Prize in 1949. He later developed the art of expressing fantastic eroticism in a series of *samurai* stories that were constructed using a combination of magic and disguise. His collected works total thirty-one volumes.

Akimitsu Takagi (b. 1920) considers himself lucky to have survived the war.

Afterward he devoured Yokomizo's *The Murders at the Inn, Honjin* (1946) and other Japanese works and, just to raise money, wrote a story, *The Tattoo Murder* [Shisei satsujin jiken], which he sent to Edogawa who recommended it to a publisher. The story was published in 1948 and proved to be a great success.

The story revolves around three great effects: a person with two roles, a dead man without a face, and a murder in a locked room. These effects give the story its strength, not its style. His style was criticized as being too simplistic, especially in characterization. The writer created a detective, Kyosuke Kamizu, and ten volumes of Kamizu stories were published by Wado-shuppan in 1957. It should be noted that he based his mysteries on actual cases that had been brought to court. A sixteen-volume set of his works was published by Kobunsha from 1971 to 1974.

Kazuo Shimada (b. 1909) won the Detective Story Writers Club of Japan Prize in 1951 for his short story, *Reporter in the Social Department* [Shakai bu kisha] (1950). He originally tried to write so-called puzzlers, but it was not until he wrote stories involving a newspaper reporter who solved problems that he became popular and established himself as a mystery writer. His most notable work, *Jiken Kisha*, is the collection of scripts he did for *Police Reports*, a program that ran for over 400 stories in eight years from 1955 through 1962. His collected works are available.

Tsutomu Minakami (b. 1919) received the fourteenth prize of the Detective Story Writers Club of Japan for his story, *The Fangs of the Sea* [Umi no kiba] (1960). One of his earlier stories, *Fog and Shadow* [Kiri to kage] (1959), which had been well received by critics, was published after seven rewritings. He also received the prestigious literary prize, the Naoki Prize, in 1961 for his novel, *The Wild Goose Temple* [Kari no tera] (1961), which is believed to have been written from the experiences he had gone through as a disciple in a temple in Kyoto, where he was sent by his father to reduce the number of dependents in the family. After *The Wild Goose Temple*, he turned to mainstream writing and human interest stories.

Shoji Yuki (b. 1927) debuted as a mystery writer by winning a contest sponsored by the Japanese *Ellery Queen's Mystery Magazine* in 1959 for his *Swimming in the Winter* [Kanchu suiei] (1959). Five years later in 1964, he earned the Association of Mystery Writers of Japan Award (formerly the Detective Story Writers Club of Japan Prize) for *When Night Is Over* [Yoru no owaru toki] (1963). He also received the Naoki Prize for *Under the Ensign* [Gunki hatameku shitade] in 1970.

Seiichi Morimura (b. 1933) is probably the most important mystery writer after Seicho Matsumoto. Morimura began working at the Hotel Otani after graduating from college in 1964 and stayed there for the next ten years. He used the position to support writing novels that dealt with various social issues, but the novels were unsuccessful. In 1969 his fortunes changed when his mystery, *Death in the High-Rise*, was honored with the fifteenth Rampo Prize. In 1973 he received the Association of Mystery Writers of Japan Prize. His stories have continued to be best sellers and have established him as one of the most popular mystery writers of the time.

Morimura is careful to make his works realistic. He does field work that results in provocative documentaries like *The Feast of Devils* [Akuma no hoshoku] (1981), a realistic account of Bio-chemical Unit 731 of the Japanese Army, which operated in Manchuria during the last war. This unit was involved in experimenting with new chemicals on Chinese and Russian prisoners.

The role of the movies in the present popularity of mystery literature should also be mentioned. Rampo Edogawa's fictitious detective, Kogoro Akechi, made his first appearance before the reading public in the film, *The Murder on D Street*, in 1925. He appeared in a wrinkled kimono with his hair unkempt, his appearance far from that of a dandyish investigator. According to the stories written since, he spent about three years in China and India. He reappeared in *The Spiderman* [Kumo otoko] in 1928 as a different man. He was no longer dirty and miserable looking; instead he was presented in a white suit wearing white shoes, looking as if he were a prince.

Kogoro Akechi first appeared in a movie when *The Dwarf* [Issunboshi] was made into a film in 1927, but this film turned out to be a disaster. For the next twenty years, Edogawa's stories were not adapted into films. After the last war, *The Psychological Test* (published in 1925) was made into a film. The following ten years saw a number of movies based on Edogawa's stories.

Kyosuke Kindaichi is another well-known fictitious detective created by Seishi Yokomizo. The detective first appeared in *The Murders in the Inn, Honjin*. He stands about five feet, ten inches. His disheveled hair, wrinkled kimono, and well-worn hat suggest a Japanese version of Lieutenant Colombo. Like Colombo, Kindaichi's insight and detection are surprisingly sharp. Movie versions of Yokomizo's stories were produced from the 1950s through the 1970s. A great revival of his mysteries began in 1975. A popular fictitious detective like Kyosuke Kindaichi may appear with his hair sticking out every which way and his kimono looking wrinkled and disheveled, but still amazingly shrewd as he searches for clues in contemporary situations.

Popular mysteries, however, may deal with conflicts in an older time setting, say, in the Edo period (1603–1867). The detective hero as a *samurai* detective projects an image somewhat like a sheriff appearing on a horse with a six-shooter in his gun belt. The *samurai* detective stories in Japan are as popular as westerns in America.

The *samurai* versions of detective stories are another popular pastime for mystery readers. The following five collections are best known: *The Memoirs of Hanshichi* [Hanhichi torimonocho] (1917) by Kido Okamoto, *The Memoirs of Umon Kondo* [Umon torimonocho] (1928) by Mitsuzo Sasaki, *The Memoirs of Heiji Zenigata* [Zenigata Heiji torimonocho] (1931) by Kodo Nomura, *The Memoirs of Sahichi Ningyo* [Ningyo Sahichi torimonocho] (1938) by Seishi

Yokomizo, and Masayuki Jo's *The Memoirs of Prince Samurai* [Wakasama samurai torimono hikae] (1939).

Series of *samurai* detective stories have been very popular. *The Memoirs of Umon* became a series of thirty-five movies in 1929. Another series based on *The Memories of Heiji Zenigata* was first turned into film in 1932 and was followed by eighteen more.

Mystery literature should continue to be enjoyed as long as it concerns itself with man and his way of living, even though the literary genre emphasizes murder and the processes of finding the murderer. A wealth of good Japanese mystery stories are still waiting to be appreciated. Mystery literature is a significant addition to the great literary tradition of Japanese culture that has been enriched by such works as *The Manyoshu Anthology* (the eighth century), *The Tale of Genji* [Genji monogatari] (the eleventh century), and *samurai* sagas like *The Rise and Fall of the Heike Clan* [Heike monogatari] (the thirteenth century).

Criticism

One of the most difficult things for researchers is that there are very few critical works on Japanese mystery literature. There seem to be two major reasons for the scarcity of criticism: There is a very small market for serious critical writing on the genre, and no courses on mystery literature are offered at the university level. This situation offers virgin territory to researchers, but it also makes the research itself a much more difficult task.

The Association of Mystery Writers of Japan has published a series of studies of mystery literature called *Studies of Mystery Literature* [Suirishosetsu kenkyu] (1977). The thirteenth number was compiled as a special issue to include all mystery literature published since 1946. The fifteenth issue of the journal (1980) features an article on the thirty years of the Association of Mystery Literature of Japan, and the sixteenth (1980) is an inclusive catalog of science fiction.

Issues 14 (1978) and 17 (1983) are devoted to discussions by leading critics of the genre. The points of the discussions may be summarized as follows: (1) Mystery literature was read by only a few before 1940, but the genre has been enjoying a boom since the mid–1950s. (2) While mystery writers have approached star status, no full-time critics of the genre exist as no publisher is interested in publishing such criticism.

The only market for critics of mystery literature seems to be a few pages of comments that are attached to the ends of books. The comments are only platitudes and promote sales of the books. These sale-oriented postscripts are inevitably biased and therefore not valid criticism.

Owing to the closed market for genuine criticism, critics of mystery literature complain that they cannot make a regular living, but there *are* a number of full-time literary critics. In 1976 one major mystery literature publisher, Hayakawa Publishing Co, sponsored a series of lectures on mystery literature by Jinichi

Uekusa. He collected his lectures into a book called *Let's Write Mystery Through the Night* [Mystery no genko wa yonakani tetsuya de kako] (1979), which won the Association of Mystery Writers of Japan Prize in 1979.

The book itself is basically an outline of Western mystery literature. The author organized his lectures using works such as Thomas Narcejac's *Le Roman Policier* (1958) and Julian Symons's *Bloody Murder* (1972) as references. It does, however, contain anecdotal information that explains to a certain extent how significantly the Japanese mystery writers were influenced by Western writers of the genre. One example is that of Rampo Edogawa's discovery of Gaston Leroux's *Le Mystere De La Chambre Jaune* (1907) through reading Dickson Carr's analysis of it. The author also reveals that he locates new stories through the Sunday edition of the *New York Times*.

REFERENCE WORKS

Unfortunately, there is a lack of scholarly research on mystery literature in Japan. This scarcity of serious studies is in direct contrast to the richness of the works. There are, however, a few studies to which researchers can refer.

Kawataro Nakajima, in his work, *The History of Japanese Mystery Literature* [Nippon suirishosetsushi] (1964), deals with writers and their works written in the 1880s, the earlier history of Japanese mystery literature. The book covers the major aspects of the genre: influences from the West, translations, major writers, and their works during the period.

Nakajima's book also deals with other important aspects such as the development of *The New Youth*, Junichiro Tanizaki's crime novels (1886–1965), and Ruiko Kuroiwa's mystery novels and brilliant translations (1862–1920).

Much critical work has been done on Ruiko Kuroiwa. Ito's *The Study of Ruiko Kuroiwa* [Kuroiwa Ruiko] (1979) and Rampo Edogawa's essay, "On Ruiko's *The Miserable*" [Ruiko no sosaku *Muzan* nitsuite] (1947), are especially notable. The latter is included in a collection of Rampo Edogawa's critical essays, *The Illusory Castle* [Geneijo] (1951; rpt. 1979). Rampo Edogawa contends Ruiko's *Three Strands of Hair* (1889) is a logically structured piece taken from a theme of Poe's. The story is about two detectives. The skill of the first is dependent on his experience, and that of the other, younger, detective on scientific analysis. The story revolves around these two detectives and an unidentified dead man. The only clue to the murderer is three strands of hair in the dead man's hand and a deep cut in his head. The young detective solves the case by a surprising deduction. Rampo Edogawa claims that Ruiko might have left more original stories and not just good translations, had *Three Strands of Hair* been accepted by the readers of the time.

The Illusory Castle is one of the earliest and most important collections of critical essays on mystery literature by Rampo Edogawa himself. The collection reflects his serious thought about the nature of mystery literature. The book comes in two volumes: the first one published in 1951 and the other in 1954.

The first book contains a number of interesting articles such as an essay on the nature and types of mystery literature and an essay in *The New Youth* [Shin seinen]. In *The New Youth*, Rampo Edogawa talks about the great editor Uson Morishita who actually helped the magazine come into being, introduced Western detective stories, and encouraged Japanese writers to produce good stories. Uson Morishita liked Rampo Edogawa's first story, "A Tuppence Coin" [Nisen doka] and published it in the magazine.

The second volume of *The Illusory Castle* was published in 1954. It includes, among others, an article written in 1953 about categories of tricks. It is the first attempt of its kind to classify tricks used in the detective stories by British and American writers. When the article became available, it was most appreciated by the writers themselves who could avoid repeating an old trick somebody else had already used. It is the kind of work an academic should have written. *The Illusory Castle* is a reference work that cannot be overlooked by anyone who is interested in mystery literature in Japan.

Rampo's memoirs, *Forty Years of Writing Detective Stories* [Tanteishosetsu yonjunen] (1979) in two volumes, also served as a personal history of modern Japanese mystery literature. Another collection of Rampo's essays, *The Riddles of Detective Stories* [Tanteishosetsu no nazo] (1956), includes an article, "Meiji Novels That Feature Fingerprints" [Meiji no shimon shosetsu[(1950).

Shiro Kuki's *The Detective Story and All That* [Tanteishosetsu hyakka] (1975) is a rather ambitious attempt to cover all aspects of mystery literature and contains an outline of the history of Japanese detective stories, an introduction to major Western and Japanese writers, a review of magazines, and lists of plot devices. The researcher on Japanese mystery literature may find Kuki's book valuable for its encyclopedic coverage of genre.

Seishi Yokomizo's *Fifty Years of Writing Mysteries* [Tanteishosetsu gojunen] (1977) is a collection of essays. He started his career as a detective story writer by publishing a short story, "Horrible April-fool" [Osoroshiki shigatsu baka], in the April 1921 issue of *The New Youth* when he was nineteen years old. Soon he began associating with Rampo Edogawa who recommended him to be an editor of *The New Youth*. The book includes information and analysis, noting, for example, that his story, "The Secret of Crimson," was the first to use color blindness as a plot twist. Yokomizo was a devoted fan of such writers as Freemen W. Crofts (1897–1957). John Dickson Carr (b. 1906), and Agatha Christie (1891–1976). His book is a personal history of modern Japanese mystery literature.

Yotaro Hazama's *An Encyclopedia of Mystery* [Mystery hyakkajiten] (1981) consists of four major chapters: human anatomy; plants and animals; customs and manners; and common items in the environment (telephones, clocks, dolls, wax, letters). An extra chapter on jewels, tobacco, and gambling is also provided. If one wants to find a work in which a certain item was used as an important clue or device, it may be found in this book. The book is better used as a compilation of information than as a critical reference. It also contains many errors of omission. For example, Tetsuya Ayukawa's *The Murder at the House of Rose* [Baraso satsujin jiken] (1958) is entered under "color blindness," and Seishi Yokomizo's *The Secret of Crimson* [Shinko no himitsu] (1921) is not mentioned at all.

Even before the 1880s, collections of criminal cases or non-fiction reports of actual murders were in print and, like Shokyu Kawai's *The Cases of the Acquitted* (1768), offered some practical information to prosecutors and lawyers. *The Cases of the Acquitted* [Muen rokujitsu] comes in two volumes. Although the first volume includes charts that illustrate the parts of the body from the front and the back, it devotes most of its pages to methods of investigating the dead body. The author lists a number of points an investigator should be careful to note. For example, "When you check the body, you must look at the back of the head. You may find a nail buried in the hair, in a wound that had been cauterized so that it would not bleed." Volume 2 includes a list of various manners of death, such as strangling, drowning, clubbing, blows, cutting by knife, self-inflicted knife wounds, burning, freezing, getting hit by a horse or bull, acupuncturing while making love, and so forth.

The paragraphs on death by poisoning are summarized by Shiro Kuki in his book, *The Detective Story and All That* [Tanteishosetsu hyakka] (pp. 17–18). As an illustrative example, the section on death by strangling may be paraphrased as follows: The person who was strangled to death keeps his (or her) mouth and angry eyes open. The part of the skin of the neck where he was strangled will remain dark all around the neck. The neck will be broken and the Adam's apple will be caved in. Then, the person may be judged as strangled to death. If the person had strangled himself (or herself) to death, his (or her) tongue will have been hanging out. And the mark on the neck will not go around the neck all the way. The eyes will be closed and so will the fists. The back of the ears will be dark purple. The author also points out in detail how to differentiate suicide from murder on various deaths from one another by paying attention to all parts of the body from eyes to anus.

Some of the early books on crime that were available to Japanese readers were apparently more for practical purposes than for enjoyment. Readers had to wait for Japanese writers to encounter Western mysteries before they produced good mystery literature.

RESEARCH COLLECTIONS

Researchers may find most mystery writers' works in the National Diet Library in Tokyo. The library was built in the manner of the Library of Congress in the United States, and holds most books published in Japan. Some translations published in the 1880s that had a great influence on the development of Japanese mystery literature are also kept at the National Diet Library. Those are Kenzo Takahashi's translation (1881) of S. M. Phillips's *Famous Cases of Circumstantial Evidences* (1877), Inokichi Chihara's translation (1888) of George

McWatters's *Detectives of Europe and America* (1877), Ruiko Kuroiwa's *Man or Evil* (1888), a translation of an English version *Widow Lerouge*, of the French original, Emile Gaboriau's *L'Affaire Lerouge* (1886), and many others.

The works of the major Japanese writers who left some significant mark in helping to develop mystery literature in Japan, such as Ruiko Kuroiwa, Rampo Edogawa, Seishi Yokomizo, and Seicho Matsumoto, can also be found at the National Diet Library.

The works kept at the National Diet Library can be found both in collections and in individual works. Collections published some years after the writer's death include not only all the works by the writer but perhaps also the writer's correspondence, diary (if he kept one), and essays or memoirs of various kinds. These collections are most useful for researchers.

Works by such writers as Ruiko Kuroiwa, Kodo Nomura, Rampo Edogawa, Seishi Yokomizo, and Seicho Matsumoto are a very basic reference in mystery literature. While most university libraries shun such literature, major university libraries in the Tokyo area hold some of the works by those writers mentioned above. The Tokyo University Library has works by Ruiko Kuroiwa, Rampo Edogawa, and Seicho Matsumoto. The Waseda University Library keeps only Rampo Edogawa and Seicho Matsumoto. That of the Keio University has some works by Ruiko Kuroiwa, Rampo Edogawa, and Seicho Matsumoto. The Chuo University Library holds only Rampo Edogawa's works. The Meiji University Library maintains only those of Seishi Yokomizo. Hosei University keeps a part of Ruiko Kuroiwa's and Rampo Edogawa's stories. The Aoyamagakuin University Library has those of Ruiko Kuroiwa, Rampo Edagawa, Seishi Yokomizo, and Seicho Matsumoto. Hitotsubashi University keeps none of them.

There are a number of magazines that publish mainly mystery literature and can sometimes be found in libraries, but the situation is not good. Even such an important magazine as *The New Youth* cannot be found in its entirety. Volumes 1 to 10 and 28 to 31 are kept at the Narita Library (Chiba Prefecture). Showa Women's University Library has Volumes 1 through 17 and 25 to 28, and the Waseda University Library keeps most volumes of the magazine. Kagawa University (Kagawa Prefecture) holds only one volume. *The Jewel* was published from March 1946 until October 1964. Most issues of the magazine can be located at the National Diet Library and some at the Tokyo Public Library.

Researchers may also find it a great help to contact the publishers of mystery literature, such as Sogensha, Hayakawa, and Kodansha. Hayakawa has been publishing a Japanese version of *Ellery Queen's Mystery Magazine* since July 1956, the only one of its kind. The name of the magazine was changed to *Mystery Magazine* in January 1966, probably because the former name was too long in Japanese. Researchers who are interested in stories imported to Japan are encouraged to contact the editorial staffs of the above publishers. They are generally friendly and happy to answer inquiries.

Another important magazine the researcher of Japanese mystery literature should not overlook is called *Studies on Mystery Literature*, which has been published once a year since 1965 by the Association of Mystery Writers of Japan in Tokyo. Researchers may find the reference information collected in the magazine rather limited, but the office is willing to provide information upon request.

Foreign researchers affiliated with a Japanese institution where the holdings of mystery literature or reference books are limited may find an interlibrary service useful. Services of this kind may be costly or time consuming, but they are available.

The most important aspect of conducting research on mystery literature, however, is an understanding of Japan and its culture. It is impossible to understand a master work like Seicho Matsumoto's *Points and Lines* (1957–1958) unless the researcher is well acquainted with the public transportation system and aware of the fact that Japanese use the trains every day. It is not easy to imagine tens of thousands of people streaming over the platforms during rush hour (roughly 400,000 commuters daily at Tokyo Station, and trains on the twenty-two tracks coming and leaving one after another), but without an understanding of the situation at Tokyo Station, the plot is meaningless.

Finally, it should be noted that researchers will be frustrated unless they are well equipped with a knowledge of the Japanese language.

APPENDIX: THE WINNERS OF THE EDOGAWA RAMPO PRIZE

1955 Kawataro Nakajima. *The Dictionary of Detective Stories* [Tanteishosetsu jiten]. Series in *The Jewel* magazine, 1952–1957.
中島河太郎　　探偵小説事典

1956 Hayakawashobo. *The Pocket Mystery* Series. [Pocket mystery]. Tokyo: Hayakawashobo, 1953–.
早川書房　　ポケット・ミステリー

1957 Etsuko Niki. *The Cat Knew It* [Neko wa shitteita]
仁木悦子　　猫は知っている

1958 Kyo Takikawa. *The Tears* [Nureta kokoro]
多木川恭　　濡れた心

1959 Ayako Shijo. *The Dangerous Relation* [Kikenna kankei]
新章文子　　危険な関係

1960 No prize winner.

1961 Chen Shuen Ch'en. *The Roots of the Dried Weeds* [Karekusa no ne]
陳舜臣　　枯草の根

1962 Masako Togawa. *The Great Dream* [Oinaru genei]
Hisomu Saga. *The Glorious Corpse* [Hanayakana shitai]
戸川昌子　　大いなる幻影　　　　佐賀潜　　華やかな死体

1963 Shota Hujimura. *The Lonely Street* [Kodokuna asphalt]
藤村正太　　孤独なアスファルト

1964 Noboru Saito. *Under the Ant Tree* [Ari no ki no shita de]
西東登　　蟻の木の下で

1965 Kyotaro Nishimura. *The Angel with a Scar* [Tenshi no kizuato]
西村京太郎　　天使の傷跡

1966 Sakae Saito. *The Death Match of the Chess Players* [Satsujin no kifu]
斎藤栄　　殺人の棋譜

1967 Hidesuke Kaito. *Berlin 1888*
海渡英祐　　伯林―１８８８

1968 No prize winner

1969 Seiichi Morimura. *Death in the High-Rise* [Koso no shikaku]
森村誠一　　高層の死角

1970 Yotaro Otani. *Murderous Music* [Satsui no enso]
大谷羊太郎　　殺意の演奏

1971 No prize winner

1972 Shunzo Waku. *A Fancy Ball in the Court* [Kamenhotei]
和久俊三　　仮面法廷

1973 Gen Komine. *Archimedes Never Gets His Hands Dirty* [Archimedes wa te o yogosanai]
古峰元　　アルキメデスは手を汚さない

1974 Kyozo Kobayashi. *A Dark Notice* [Ankoku kokuchi]
小林久三　　暗黒告知

1975 Keisuke Kusaka. *The Butterflies Are Now* . . . [Chotachi wa ima . . .]
日下圭介　　蝶たちは今・・・

1976 Akira Tomono. *Death in Half a Million Years* [Go jumanen no shikaku]
伴野朗　　五十万年の死角

1977 Tatsuo Kaji. *A Clear Season* [Tomei na kisetsu]
Izumi Fujimoto. *The Tide* [Toki o kizamu shio]
梶龍雄　　透明な季節　　藤本泉　　時をきざむ潮

1978 Kaoru Kurimoto. *Our Times* [Bokura no jidai]
栗本薫　　ぼくらの時代

1979 Yoshio Takayanagi. *The Clowns from Praha* [Praha kara no doketachi]
高柳芳夫　　プラハからの道化たち

1980 Motohiko Izawa. *The Dream Trip of Sarumaru* [Sarumaru genshiko]
伊沢元彦　　猿丸幻視行

1981 Akira Nagai. *Crabs in a Nuclear Reactor* [Genshiro no kani]
長井あきら　　原子炉の蟹

1982 Fumihiko Nakatsu. *Golden Quicksand* [Ogon ryusa]
Fuhito Okajima. *Dark Brown Pastel* [Kogechairo no pastel]
中津文彦　　黄金の砂　　岡島二人　　焦茶色のパステル

1983 Katsuhiko Takahashi. *The Murder of Sharaku* [Sharaku satsujin jiken]
高橋克彦　　写楽殺人事件

Note: All books were published by Kodansha, which founded the Edogawa Rampo Prize (except as noted).

NOTES

1. Rampo Edogawa, ''Criminal Psychology in Detective Stories,'' *Science for the Intellectuals* [Bunkajin no kagaku] (1947), in Rampo Edogawa's *The Riddles of Detective Stories* [Tanteishosetsu no nazo] (Tokyo: Shakaishisosha, 1956), p. 127.
江戸川乱歩　　″文化人の科学″　　「探偵小説の謎」　　東京　社会思想社 １９５６、　p.１２７.

2. Seicho Matsumoto, *Points and Lines* [Ten to sen] (Tokyo: Kobunsha, 1960), p. 40.
松本清張　「点と線」　東京　講談社　１９６０．

BIBLIOGRAPHY

Reference Works

Edogawa, Rampo. *Forty Years of Writing Detective Stories* [Tanteishosetsu yonjunen]. Tokyo: Kodansha, 1979.
江戸川乱歩　「探偵小説四十年」　東京　講談社　１９７９．
―――. *The Illusory Castle* [Geneijo]. 2 vols. 1951; rpt. Tokyo: Kodansha, 1979.
江戸川乱歩　「幻影城」　２巻　東京　講談社　１９７９．
―――. *The Riddles of Detective Stories* [Tanteishosetsu no nazo]. Tokyo: Shakaishi-sosha, 1956.
江戸川乱歩　「探偵小説の謎」　東京　社会思想社　１９５６．
Hazama, Yotaro. *An Encyclopedia of Mystery* [Mystery hyakkajiten]. Tokyo: Shakaishi-sosha, 1981.
間羊太郎　「ミステリー百科事典」　東京　社会思想社　１９８１．
Ito, Hideo. *The Study of Ruiko Kuroiwa* [Kuroiwa Ruiko]. Tokyo: Togensha, 1979.
伊藤秀男　「黒岩涙香」　東京　桃源社　１９７９．
Kuki, Shiro. *The Detective Story and All That* [Tanteishosetsu hyakka]. Tokyo: Kinensha, 1975.
九鬼紫郎　「探偵小説百科」　東京　金園社　１９７５．
Nakajima, Kawataro. *Contemporary Mystery Writers* [Suirishosetsu tenbo]. Tokyo: To-toshobo, 1965.
中島河太郎　「推理小説展望」　東京　東都書房　１９６５．
―――. *The History of Japanese Mystery Literature* [Nippon suirishosetsushi]. Tokyo: Togensha, 1964.
中島河太郎　「日本推理小説史」　東京　桃源社　１９６４．
Narcejac, Thomas, and Pierre Boileau. *Le Roman Policier*. Paris: Payot, 1958.
Symons, Julian. *Bloody Murder*. London: Faber and Faber, 1972.
Tamura, Sakae. *Matsumoto Seicho*. Tokyo: Keiryuikakushinsha, 1976.
田村栄　「松本清張」　東京　啓隆閣新社　１９７６．
Uekusa, Jinichi. *Let's Write Mysteries Through the Night* [Mystery no genko wa yonakani tetsuya de kako]. Tokyo: Hayakawashobo, 1979.
植草甚一　ミステリーの原稿は夜中に徹夜で書こう」東京　早川書房　１９７９．
Yokomizo, Seishi. *Fifty Years of Writing Mysteries* [Tanteishosetsu gojunen]. Tokyo: Kodansha, 1977.
横溝正史　「探偵小説五十年」　東京　講談社　１９７７．

Articles

Edogawa, Rampo. "On Ruiko's *The Miserable*." *The Illusory Castle* [Geneijo]. 1951; rpt. in *The Collection of Edogawa Rampo*. Vol. 1. Tokyo: Shunyodo, 1979. pp. 125–27.
江戸川乱歩　「幻影城」　２巻　東京　講談社　１９７９，
　　ｐｐ．　１２５－１２７．

Gonda, Manji. ''On Japanese Detective Story Writers'' [Nippon tanteisakka ron]. *Geneijo*
    (1976), n.p.
権田　治　″日本探偵作家論″　「幻影城」　１９７６．
Yamamura, Masso. ''Some Thoughts on the Detective Story Writers'' [Waga kaikyuteki
    tanteisakka ron]. *Geneijo* (1977), n.p.
山村正夫　″我が階級的探偵作家論″　「幻影城」　１９７７．

Journals

Ellery Queen's Mystery Magazine, Tokyo, 1956–1966; also known as *Mystery Magazine*,
    Tokyo, 1966–.
The Jewel [Hoseki], Tokyo, 1946–1964.
「宝石」　東京　１９４６－１９６４
The New Youth [Shinseinen], Tokyo, 1920–1950.
「新青年」　東京　１９２０－１９５０
Studies on Mystery Literature [Suirishosetsu kenkyu], Tokyo, 1965–.
「推理小説研究」　東京　１９６５－

Books

Aeba, Koson. *The Black Cat*. Serialized in *Yomiura Shinbun*, November 3–9, 1887, n.p.
Akutagawa, Ryunosuke. *The Robbers* [Chuto]. *The Bamboo Bush* [Yabu no naka]. In
    The Collection of Modern Japanese Literature [Gendai Nippon bungaku zenshu].
    Vol. 56. Tokyo: Kodansha, 1960.
芥川龍之介　「偸盗」、「藪の中」、「日本現代文化全集」　第５６巻
　　東京　講談社　１９６０．

Ayukawa, Tetsuya. *The Murder at the House of Rose* [Baraso satsujin jiken]. Tokyo:
    Kodansha, 1960.
鮎川哲也　「バラ荘殺人事件」　東京　講談社　１９６０．

Chihara, Inokichi, trans. *Detectives of Europe and America* [Kigoku]. Kyoto: Nippon
    Domei Hogakkai, 1888. Translation of George McWatters, ed. *Detectives of
    Europe and America*. Chicago: Laird & Lee, 1877.
千原猪吉、訳　「きごく」京都　日本度明法学会　１８８８（翻訳）
Edogawa, Rampo. *A Disabled Soldier* [Imomushi]. In *The Collection of Showa Popular
    Literature* [Showa kokumin bugaku zenshu]. Vol. 18. Tokyo: Chikuma Shobo,
    1977.
江戸川乱歩　「いも虫」、「昭和国民文学全集」　第１８巻　東京　筑摩書房１９７７．

———. *The Dwarf* [Issunboshi]. In *The Collection of Edogawa Rampo* [Edogawa Rampo
    zenshu]. Vol. 3. Tokyo: Kodansha, 1979.
江戸川乱歩　「一寸法師」、「江戸川乱歩全集」　第３巻　東京　講談社
　　１９７９．

———. *The Murder on D Street* [D-saka no satsujin jiken]. In *The Great Collection of
    Popular Literature* [Taishu bugaku taikei]. Vol. 21. Tokyo: Kodansha, 1973.
江戸川乱歩　「Ｄ坂殺人事件」、「大衆文学大系」　第２１巻　東京　講談社１９７３．

———. *The Psychological Test* [Shinri shiken]. In *The Great Collection of Popular
    Literature* [Taishu bungaku taikei]. Vol. 21. Tokyo: Kodansha, 1973.
江戸川乱歩　「心理試験」、「大衆文学大系」　第２１巻　東京　講談社
　　１９７３．

————. *The Spiderman* [Kumo otoko]. In *The Collection of Masterpiece Novels* [Cho-henshosetsu meisaku zenshu]. Vol. 4. Tokyo: Kodansha, 1950.
江戸川乱歩　「蜘男」、「長編小説名作全集」　第４巻　東京　講談社 1 9 5 0 。
————. "A Tuppence Coin" [Nisen doka]. In *The Collection of Modern Japanese Literature* [Nippon gendai bungaku zenshu]. Vol. 73. Tokyo: Kodansha, 1964.
江戸川乱歩　「二銭銅貨」　「日本現代文学全集」第７３巻　東京　講談社 1 9 6 4 。
Gaboriau, Emile. *L'Affaire Lerouge*. Paris: E. Dentu, 1866.
Hamano, Shiro. "Did He Do It?" [Kara ga koroshitaka]. In *The New Youth*, January–February, 1929.
Jo, Masayuki. *The Memoirs of Prince Samurai* [Wakasama samurai torimonotcho]. 12 vols. Tokyo: Kozaishuppan, 1958.
城昌幸　「若様侍捕物帖」　東京　コザイ出版　1 9 5 8 。
Kanagaki, Robun. *Oden Takahashi, the Devil* [Takahashi oden yashamonogatari]. Tokyo: Kinshodo, 1879.
仮名垣魯文　「高橋阿伝夜叉だん」　東京　金松堂　1 8 7 9 。
Kanda, Kohei, trans. Ryuhoku Narishima, ed. *Jonger's Curious Stories* [Yongeru kidan]. N.c.: Tetsujiro Nakajima, 1887, trans. Jan Christemeijer. *Belangrikke tafereelen uit de Geshiedenis der lijfstraffelijke regtsplegling* [Interesting portraits in the administration of criminal justice]. Amsterdam: n.p., 1821.
神田孝平訳　「楊牙児奇談」　中川　鉄太郎　東京　　1 8 8 7 。
Kawai, Shokyu, trans. Dr. Zong Ci. *The Cases of the Acquitted* [Muen rokujitsu]. 2 vols. trans. 1247; N.c.: n.p., 1768.
Kayama, Shigeru. *The Curious Stories from the House of Eel* [Kaimanso kidan]. In *The Great Collection of Modern Mystery Literature* [Gendai no suirishosetsu taikei]. Vol 7. Tokyo: Kodansha, 1973.
香山滋　「海鰻荘奇談」、「現代の推理小説大系」　第７巻　東京　講談社 1 9 7 3 。
Koda, Rohan. *Anxiety* [Fuan]. In *The Collection of Modern Japanese Literature* [Gendai nippon bungaku zenshu]. Vol. 8. Tokyo: Kaizosha, 1927.
幸田露伴　「不安」、「現代日本文学全集」　第８巻　東京　改造社 1 9 2 7 。
————. *Surprise* [Ayashiyana]. 1889. In *The Great Collection of Japanese Mystery Literature*. [Nippon suirishosetsu taikei] Vol. 1. Tokyo: Toto Shobo, 1960.
幸田露伴　「あやしな」（1 8 8 9）、「日本推理小説大系」　第１巻　東京　トト書房　1 9 6 0 。
Kuei, Wang-Jung. *Tang Yin Bi Shi*. 1207. In *Toinhiji*. N.c.: n.p., 1649.
Kuroiwa, Ruiko. *The Beauty in the Court* [Hotei no bijin]. 1889. In *The Collection of Kuroiwa Ruiko* [Kuroiwa Ruiko zenshu]. Vol. 1. Tokyo: Takara Shuppan, 1981.
黒岩涙香　「法廷の美人」（1 9 8 9）、「黒岩涙香全集」　第１巻　東京　宝出版　1 9 8 1 。
————. *Man or Devil* [Hito ya oni ya]. In *The Collection of Kuroiwa Ruiko* [Kuroiwa Ruiko zenshu]. 1888. Vol. 2. Tokyo: Takara Shuppan, 1981.
黒岩涙香　「人耶鬼耶」（1 8 8 8）、「黒岩涙香全集」　第２巻　東京　宝出版　1 9 8 1 。
————. *The Miserable* [Muzan]. 1890. In *The Collection of Kuroiwa Ruiko* [Kuroiwa Ruiko zenshu]. Vol. 9. Tokyo: Takara Shuppan, 1981.
黒岩涙香　「無惨」　（1 8 9 0）、「黒岩涙香全集」　第９巻　東京　宝出版　1 9 8 1 。
————. *Three Strands of Hair* [Misuji no kami]. Formerly published as *The Miserable*. 1893. In *The Collection of Kuroiwa Ruiko* [Kuroiwa Ruiko zenshu]. Vol. 31. Tokyo: Takara Shuppan, 1981.
黒岩涙香　「三筋の髪」、「黒岩涙香全集」　第３１巻　東京　宝出版　1 9 8 1 。

Leroux, Gaston. *Le Mystere De La Chambre Jaune*. Paris: Lafitte, 1908.

Matsumoto, Seicho. *Bills Called Saigo* [Saigo fuda]. In *Shincho Collection of Japanese Literature* [Shincho nippon bungaku]. Vol. 50. Tokyo: Shinchosha, 1970.

松本清張　「西郷札」、「新潮日本文学」　第５０巻　東京　新潮社　１９７０。

―――. *The Black Cover Sketchbook* [Kuroi gashu]. 1960. In *The Collection of Matsumoto Seicho* [Matsumoto Seicho zenshu]. Vol. 4. Tokyo: Bungeishunju, 1971–1974, 1981.

松本清張　「黒い画集」（１９６０）、「松本清張全集」　第４巻　東京　文芸春秋　１９７１－１９７４、１９８１。

―――. *The Blue Sketch* [Aoi byoten]. Tokyo: Kobunsha, 1960.

松本清張　「青い描点」　東京　弘文社　１９６０。

―――. *The Ceremony of Sea Vegetable Hunting* [Jikan no shuzoku]. 1962. In *The Collection of Matsumoto Seicho* [Matsumoto Seicho zenshu]. Vol. 1. Tokyo: Bungeishunju, 1971–1974, 1981.

松本清張　「時間の習俗」（１９６２）、「松本清張全集」　第１巻　東京　文芸春秋　１９７１－１９７４、１９８１。

―――. *The Face* [Kao]. In *The Collection of Modern Novels* [Gendai chohen shosetsu zenshu]. Vol. 46. Tokyo: Kodansha, 1959.

松本清張　「顔」、「現代長編小説全集」　第４６巻　東京　講談社　１９５９。

―――. *Focus Zero* [Zero no shoten]. 1979. In *The Collection of Matsumoto Seicho* [Matsumoto Seicho zenshu]. Vol. 3. Tokyo: Bungeishunju, 1971–1974, 1981.

松本清張　「ゼロの焦点」（１９７９）、「松本清張全集」　第３巻　東京　文芸春秋　１９７１－１９７４、１９８１。

―――. *A Note on the Ogura Diary* [Aru Ogura nikki den]. In *Shincho Collection of Japanese Literature* [Shincho Nippon bungaku]. Vol. 50. Tokyo: Shinchosha, 1970.

松本清張　「ある小倉日記伝」、「新潮日本文学」　第５０巻　東京　新潮社　１９７０。

―――. *Points and Lines* [Ten to sen]. 1957–1958; rpt. Tokyo: Kobunsha, 1968.

松本清張　「点と線」（１９５７－１９５８）　東京　弘文社　１９６８。

―――. *Wall of Eyes* [Me no kabe]. In *The Collection of Matsumoto Seicho* [Matsumoto Seicho zenshu]. Vol. 2. Tokyo: Bungeishunju, 1971.

松本清張　「眼の壁」、「松本清張全集」　第２巻　東京　文芸春秋　１９７１。

Minakami, Tsutomu. *The Fangs of the Sea* [Umi no kiba]. In *The Great Collection of Japanese Mystery Literature* [Nippon suirishosetsu taikei]. Vol. 15. Tokyo: Toto Shobo, 1961.

水上勉　「海の牙」、「日本推理小説大系」　第１５巻　東京　トト書房　１９６１。

―――. *Fog and Shadow* [Kiri to kage]. 1959. In *The Great Collection of Japanese Mystery Literature* [Nippon suirishosetsu taikei]. Vol. 13. Tokyo: Toto Shobo, 1961.

水上勉　「霧と影」（１９５９）、「日本推理小説大系」　第１３巻　東京　トト書房　１９６１。

―――. *The Wild Goose Temple* [Kari no tera]. 1960. In *Shincho Collection of Japanese Literature* [Shincho nippon bungaku]. Vol. 59. Tokyo: Shinchosha, 1970.

水上勉　「雁の寺」（１９６０）、「新潮日本文学」　第５９巻　東京　新潮社　１９７０。

Mizutani, Jun. ''The Pale Faced Guard of the Kochoen Garden'' [Kochoen no aojiroki bannin]. *The New Youth*, Special Spring Issue, 1930.

Morimura, Seiichi. *Death in the High-Rise* [Koso no shikaku]. 1969; rpt. Tokyo: Kadokawa Shoten, 1977.

森村誠一　「高層の死角」（１９６９）、　東京　角川書店　１９７７。

————. *The Feast of Devils* [Akuma no hoshoku]. Tokyo: Kobunsha, 1981.

森村誠一 「悪魔の飽食」 東京 弘文社 1981.

Nanyo, Gaishi. *The Adventures of Sherlock Holmes* [Fushigi no tantei]. Serialized in *Chuo Shinbun* (July 1899), n.p.

Oshita, Udaru. "The Kite" [Tako]. Serialized in *The New Youth* (August 1936), n.p.

————. *The Notebook Under the Rock* [Ishi no shita no kiroku]. In *The Great Collection of Modern Mysteries* [Gendai suirishosetsu taikei]. Vol. 2. Tokyo: Kodansha, 1973.

Sato, Haruo. *The Finger Print* [Shimon]. In *The Collection of Modern Popular Literature*. Vol. 27. Tokyo: Kadokawa Shoten, 1958.

佐藤春夫 「指紋」 東京 角川書店 1958.

Shimada, Kazuo. *Police Reporter* [Jiken kisha]. Tokyo: Seijusha, 1977.

島田一男 「事件記者」 東京 セイジュ社 1977.

————. *Reporter in the Social Department* [Shakai bu kisha]. In *The Collection of Modern Popular Literature*. Vol. 27. Tokyo: Kadokawa Shoten, 1958.

島田一男 「社会部記者」 東京 角川書店 1958.

Sudo, Nansui. *The Sword in the Flaming Field* [Shoen kenbo]. Ehime Prefecture: Hanko Meirinkan, 1888.

Takagi, Akimitsu. *The Tattoo Murder* [Shisei satsujin jiken]. Tokyo: Kadokawa Shoten, 1973.

高木アキミツ 「刺青殺人事件」東京 角川書店 1973.

Takahashi, Kenzo, trans. S. M. Phillips. *Famous Cases of Circumstantial Evidences* [Jokyoshoko gohan roku]. 1873. Tokyo: Department of Justice, 1881.

高橋ケンゾ訳、S.M.フィリップス 「情供証拠誤判録」（1873） 東京 法務省 1881.

Tanizaki, Junichiro. *The Ghost in Broad Daylight* [Hakuchu kigo]. 1918. In *The Collection of Tanizaki Junichiro* [Tanizaki Junichiro zenshu]. Vol. 5. Tokyo: Chuokoronsha, 1967–1969.

谷崎潤一郎 「白昼鬼語」（1918）、「谷崎潤一郎全集」 第5巻 東京 中央公論社1967−1969.

————. *The Magic of Hassan Khan* [Hassan Khan no yojitsu]. 1917. In *The Collection of Tanizaki Junichiro* [Tanizaki Junichiro zenshu]. Vol. 5. Tokyo: Chuokoronsha, 1967–1969.

谷崎潤一郎 「ハッサン・カーンの妖術」（1917）、「谷崎潤一郎全集」 第5巻 東京 中央公論社 1967−1969.

————. *The Scabbed Face* [Jimmen so]. 1918. In *The Collection of Japanese Detective Stories*. [Nippon tanteishosetsu zenshu]. Vol. 5. Tokyo: Kaizosha, 1929.

谷崎潤一郎 「人面そ」（1918）、「日本探偵小説全集」 第5巻 東京 改造社 1929.

Uno, Ju. *Stealing the Earth* [Chikyu tonan]. Tokyo: Radio Kagakusha, 1937.

Yokomizo, Seishi. *Horrible April Fool* [Osoroshiki shigatsubaka]. In *Horrible April Fool*. Tokyo: Kadokawa Shoten, 1983.

横溝正史 「恐ろしき四月馬鹿」 東京 角川文庫 1983.

————. *The Murders at the Inn, Honjin* [Honjin satsujin jiken]. In *The Great Collection of Modern Mystery Literature* [Gendai suirishosetsu taikei]. Vol. 4. Tokyo: Kodansha, 1972.

横溝正史 「本陣殺人事件」、「現代推理小説大系」 第4巻 東京 講談社1972.

————. *The Secret of Crimson* [Shinko no himitsu]. In *Horrible April Fool*. Tokyo: Kadokawa Shoten, 1983.

横溝正史 「信仰の秘密」、「恐ろしき四月馬鹿」 東京 角川文庫 1983.

————. *The Village of Eight Tombs* [Yatsu haka mura]. Tokyo: Kadokawa Shoten, 1971.

横溝正史 「八墓村」 東京 角川書店 1971.

Yuki, Shoji. *Swimming in the Winter* [Kanchu suiei]. In *The Warm-hearted Judge* [Onjo hanji]. Tokyo: Kadokawa Shoten, 1981.

結城昌治 「寒中水泳」．「恩情判事」 東京 角川書店 1981．

―――. *Under the Ensign* [Gunki hatameku shitadi]. Tokyo: Chuokoronsha, 1970.

結城昌治 「軍旗はためく下に」 東京 中央公論社 1970．

―――. *When Night Is Over* [Yoru no owaru toki]. Tokyo: Kadokawa Shoten, 1970.

結城昌治 「夜の終わるとき」 東京 角川書店 1970．

Collections

Akutagawa, Ryunosuke. *The Collection of Akutagawa Ryunosuke* [Akutagawa Ryunosuke zenshu]. Ed. Seiichi Yoshida, et al. Tokyo: Iwanamishoten, 1977–1978.

芥川龍之介 「芥川龍之介全集」 吉田精一他編 東京 岩波書店 1977－1978．

Ayukawa, Tetsuya. *The Murder at the House of Rose* [Baraso satsujinhiken]. Tokyo: Kodansha, 1960.

鮎川哲也 「バラ荘殺人事件」 東京 講談社 1960．

Chihara, Inokchi, trans. *Jyokyoshoko Gohan Roku*. Tokyo: Shihosho, 1881.

千原猪吉、訳 「情供証拠誤判録」 東京 司法省 1881．

Edogawa, Rampo. *The Collection of Edogawa Rampo* [Edogawa Rampo zenshu]. 16 vols. Tokyo: Shunyodo, 1979–1980.

江戸川乱歩 「江戸川乱歩全集」 16巻 東京 春陽堂 1979－1980．

The Great Collection of Japanese Mystery Literature [Nippon suirishosetsu taikei]. 16 vols. Tokyo: Toto Shobo, 1960–1961.

「日本推理小説大系」 1巻 東京 トト書房 1960－1961．

Kanagaki, Robun. *Oden Takahashi, the Devil* [Takahashi oden yashamonogatari]. Tokyo: Kinshodo, 1879.

仮名垣魯文 「高橋阿伝夜叉だん」 東京 金松堂 1879．

Kanda, Kohei, trans. *Yongeru Kidan*. Tokyo: Kunshido, 1887.

神田孝平，訳 「楊牙児奇談」 中川鉄太郎 東京 クンシド 1887．

Kigi, Takataro. *The Collection of Takataro Kigi* [Kigi Takataro zenshu]. Tokyo: Asa-hishinbunsha, 1971.

木々高太郎 「木々高太郎全集」 東京 朝日新聞社 1971．

Koda, Rohan. *The Collection of Koda Rohan* [Koda Rohan zenshu]. 43 vols. Tokyo: Iwanamishoten, 1978–1980.

幸田露判 「幸田露判全集」 43巻 カキュウ会編 東京 岩波書店 1978－1980．

Koga, Saburo. *The Collection of Koga Saburo* [Koga Saburo zenshu]. Ed. Shiro Kuki. 10 vols. Tokyo: Minatoshobo, 1947–1948.

甲賀三郎 「甲賀三郎全集」 シロクキ編 10巻 東京 港書房 1947－1948．

Kozaki, Fukoku. *The Collection of Fukoku Kozaki* [Kozaki Fukoku zenshu]. Ed. Rampo Edogawa. Tokyo: Kaizosha, 1929.

古坂フコク 「古坂フコク全集」 江戸川乱歩編 東京 カイゾ社 1929．

Kuroiwa, Ruiko. *The Collection of Kuroiwa Ruiko* [Kuroiwa Ruiko zenshu]. 69 vols. Tokyo: Takara Shuppan, 1981–.

黒岩涙香 「黒岩涙香全集」 69巻 東京 宝出版 1981－．

Matsumoto, Seicho. *The Collection of Matsumoto Seicho* [Matsumoto Seicho zenshu]. 56 vols. Tokyo: Bungeishunju, 1971–1974, 1981–.

松本清張 「松本清張全集」 56巻 東京 文芸春秋 1971－1974 1981－．

Minakami, Tsutomu. *The Collection of Minakami Tsutomu* [Minakami Tsutomu zenshu]. 7 vols. Tokyo: Chuokoronsha, 1979.

水上勉　「水上勉全集」　7巻　東京　中央公論社　１９７９．

Morimura, Seiichi. *The Best of Morimura Seiichi's Mystery Novels* [Morimura Seiichi chohen suiri zenshu]. 15 vols. Tokyo: Kodansha, 1976–1978.

森村誠一　「森村誠一長編推理全集」　１５巻　東京　講談社　１９７８．

———. *The Best of Morimura Seiichi's Short Mystery Stories* [Morimura Seiichi tanpen suiri zenshu]. 10 vols. Tokyo: Kodansha, 1978.

森村誠一　「森村誠一短編推理全集」　１０巻　東京　講談社　１９７８．

Nomura, Kodo. *The Collection of Zenigata Heiji Torimonocho* [Zenigata Heiji Torimonocho zenshu]. 50 vols. Tokyo: Dokosha, 1951–1955.

野村胡堂　「銭形平次捕物帳全集」　５０巻　東京　同光社　１９５１－１９５５．

Oguri, Mushitaro. *The Collection of Mushitaro Oguri* [Oguri Mushitaro zenshu]. Tokyo: Togensha, 1979.

小栗虫太郎　「小栗虫太郎全集」　東京　桃源社　１９７９．

Okamoto, Kido. *The Collection of Okamoto Kido's Plays* [Okamoto Kido gikyokushu]. 14 vols. Tokyo: Shunyodo, 1924–1930.

岡本キド　「岡本キド戯曲集」　１４巻　東京　春陽堂　１９２４－１９３０．

Sasaki, Mitsuzo. *The Collection of Umon* [Umon torimonocho zenshu]. 5 vols. Tokyo: Dokosha, 1956.

佐々木味津三　「右門捕物帖全集」　５巻　東京　同光社　１９５６．

Sato, Haruo. *The Collection of Sato Haruo* [Sato Haruo zenshu]. 12 vols. Ed. Shimada Kinji, et al. Tokyo: Kodansha, 1965–1970.

佐藤晴夫　「佐藤春夫全集」　島田謹二他編　１２巻　東京　講談社　１９６５－１９７０．

Takagi, Akimitsu. *The Collection of Takagi Akimitsu's Mystery Novels* [Takagi Akimitsu chohen suiri shosetsu zenshu]. 16 vols. Tokyo: Kobunsha, 1971–1974.

髙木アキミツ　「髙木アキミツ長編推理小説全集」　１６巻　東京　光文社１９７１－１９７４．

Tanizaki, Junichiro. *The Collection of Tanizaki Junichiro* [Tanizaki Junichiro zenshu]. 30 vols. Tokyo: Chuokoronsha, 1981–1983.

谷崎潤一郎　「谷崎潤一郎全集」　３０巻　東京　中央公論社　１９８１－１９８３．

Yamada, Futaro. *The Collection of Yamada Futaro* [Yamada Futaro zenshu]. 16 vols. Tokyo: Kodansha, 1971–1972.

山田風太郎　「山田風太郎全集」　１６巻　東京　講談社　１９７１－１９７２．

———. *The Collection of Yamada Futaro's Samurai Stories* [Yamada Futaro ninpo zenshu]. 15 vols. Tokyo: Kodansha, 1963–1964.

山田風太郎　「山田風太郎忍法全集」　１５巻　東京　講談社　１９６３－１９６４．

Yokomizo, Seishi. *The Collection of Nigyo Shaichi* [Nigyo Shaichi torimonoho]. 8 vols. Tokyo: Kodansha, 1971.

横溝正史　「人形佐七捕物帳」　8巻　東京　講談社　１９７１．

———. *The Collection of Yokomizo Seishi* [Yokomizo Seishi zenshu]. 10 vols. Tokyo: Kodansha, 1970.

横溝正史　「横溝正史全集」　１０巻　東京　講談社　１９７０．

Yuki, Shoji. *The Collection of Yuki Shoji* [Yuki Shoji sakuhinshu]. 8 vols. Tokyo: Asahishinbunsha, 1973–1974.

結城昌治　「結城昌治作品集」　8巻　弘文社　朝日新聞社　１９７３－１９７４．

Yumeno, Kyusaku. *The Collection of Yumeno Kyusaku* [Yumeno Kyusaku zenshu]. Ed. Kawataro Nakajima, et al. Tokyo: Sanichishobo, 1970.

夢野久作 「夢野久作全集」 中島カワタロ編 東京 三一書房 １９７０．

12

Japanese Popular Culture Reconsidered

HIDETOSHI KATO

One of the best-known festivals of Japan is the Gionmatsuri of Kyoto, which has been held every year on July 14 since the seventeenth century. Hundreds of thousands of spectators from various parts of the country and abroad are excited by the splendid parade of floats, decorated with exotic materials. The hot and humid air of that season in Kyoto makes the people damp, even wet, but they still dare to watch the festival in mid-day with joy and fascination.

Though Gionmatsuri is typical of the traditional-popular culture of Japan, very few people are aware of the origin and significance of the event. In order to clarify a major point of this essay, a modest reminder of its historical background is necessary.

As many historians have proved, Gionmatsuri was inaugurated by wealthy merchants of Kyoto late in the seventeenth century to commemorate the golden days of international trade before the Tokugawa government decided to adopt an isolationist policy in 1612. The merchant-traders who had been active in foreign trade with the countries of Southeast Asia before the enforcement of the new policy were obliged to confine their commercial activities solely to the domestic market. The huge merchant ships, which used to make regular voyages to Thailand, the Philippines, and Indonesia, where adventurous Japanese had already established colonies with populations of thousands, became useless. Out of frustration and disappointment, they decided to cut down the masts of their boats and to install them as the center poles of parade floats, called *hoko*, which they decorated with foreign imports like Persian carpets and European tapestries obtained in the heyday of foreign trade. In other words, Gionmatsuri was invented partly as a humble resistance against a new foreign (or anti-foreign) policy, and partly as nostalgic sentimentalism on the part of the merchants.

This story of Gionmatsuri is indicative not only of the nature of Japanese society but also of modern and contemporary Japanese popular culture in the sense that Japan during her period of isolation achieved a unique cultural maturity. Indeed, as Arnold Toynbee aptly remarked, from 1612 through 1868, approximately two and a half centuries, there existed in Japan the only period in the whole of human history where absolute peace prevailed and society devoted its efforts to cultural enterprises. Of course, there were minor internal conflicts, but after the Tokugawa government firmly established its power, Japan's economic surplus, which otherwise would have been used for foreign investment and external expansion, found its outlet in the area of domestic cultural development, particularly popular culture in the strict sense of the term.

As is known by most Japanologists, this social stability and cultural development started with the famous *katanagari* or "sword hunting" of 1588, which was executed by Toyotomi Hideyoshi* (1536–1598), the predecessor of the Tokugawa government. Under this policy and regulation, Japanese common people were totally disarmed. Every sword owned by commoners was confiscated by the government, permitting only the *samurai* class to possess swords. Moreover, even the *samurai* class was discouraged from being rude and militant, and it was not allowed to use its swords except in case of danger and emergency. These historical facts are quite contrary to the popular image depicted in such contemporary popular fiction as *Shogun*. As a matter of fact, *daimyo* (feudal lords) were prohibited from building military castles and forts, as well as from having forces with firearms. The policy was to minimize armed forces and to maximize socioeconomic and cultural development, and the *samurai* class was very adaptive to this new policy.

Actually, it may be safe to say that there had been a literary tradition among Japanese *samurai* even before the isolation policy was adopted. For instance, since the medieval period, it was customary among *samurai* to exchange poetry with their opponents before fighting on the battlefield. A *samurai* who was illiterate or had little learning and poor literary taste was despised by his peers. It was natural, therefore, that the *samurai* after the seventeenth century became essentially civilian bureaucrats rather than brutal fighters. In this connection, as early as the late seventeenth century, each *daimyo* started to inaugurate schools, called *hanko*, for the higher education of his retainers. *Daimyo* were eager to invite eminent scholars, and they were very competitive in recruiting good instructors in order to raise the cultural level of the elites of their territories. It is interesting to note here that many of these *hanko* have continued until today as local universities and high schools. The *samurai* of this period, especially after the mid-eighteenth century, were required to be literate on a sophisticated level. They also had to be competent in calculation and computation since they had to deal with professional merchants when selling local products or borrowing money. Both were necessary if their local economy was to enjoy stability and

---

*Proper names in this essay are in the Japanese style of family name, given name.

prosperity. It was also often necessary for them to be knowledgeable about technological innovations in textiles, ceramics, and other products.

In a word, *samurai* were expected not only to be sharp bureaucrats but also forward-looking technocrats. In their spare time, they indulged themselves in such artistic activity as the tea ceremony (which, incidentally, was one of the most important arts for their social interaction), music, and sometimes *noh* drama. Even though they carried swords, these were simply symbols to indicate their privileged status, and, as mentioned before, swords were never used as weapons. Indeed, the martial arts of modern Japan were simply physical exercises and the object of artistic appreciation for *samurai*.

The same was true with merchants. By definition, their major concern was moneymaking, but in their value system leisure activities had great importance. According to Miyamoto Mataji (b. 1907), an authority on the local history of Osaka, the center of commercial transactions of the day, the ideal of the Osaka merchant was to retire from business at the earliest possible age (after successful capital accumulation) and to delegate routine business to a trusted chief clerk. Retired merchants could then enjoy music, dance, book reading, or the tea ceremony. It may be worthwhile to note here that this tradition has been continued in contemporary Japan. As has been often noted, at social gatherings such as banquets, all Japanese, especially men, are supposed to give a performance— usually singing. Nowadays it is often accompanied and amplified by an electronic gadget known as a *karaoke*. This amateurism in the arts can be traced back to the days of the Tokugawa period.

The merchants of the Tokugawa era were also patrons of great artists. As is known by most art connoisseurs, such artists as Koetetsu, Korin, and Sotatsu were not only appreciated and encouraged by wealthy merchants of the Kyoto-Osaka area but also financially supported by them.

The implication of the social history of the period of the isolation policy is that, in spite of literary class distinctions, both the *samurai* class and the merchant class had to have a common arena where they could (often had to) mix and socialize with each other. As mentioned in preceding paragraphs, the *samurai* had to deal and work with merchants, and for down-to-earth business negotiations a "neutral zone" was needed to erase class distinctions. In order to meet this new need, the *chaya* (teahouse) came into business, which later turned into what is usually known as the *geisha* house in the West. As a matter of fact, the *chaya* later in its evolution became an establishment with female entertainers. An absolute rule in such establishments was to have the *samurai* deposit their swords at the entrance gate. In short, as far as the *chaya* was concerned, as Kato has pointed out in his *Toshi to Goraku*, its time and space were regarded as not only neutral but also classless.

Farmers, who were between the *samurai* and the merchants in caste system but who were actually the poorest of all, also made an effort to be highly literate because they were supposed to keep the records of the village. In addition, whatever surplus they could save was often used for intellectual betterment. They were unable to be the patrons of artists, but they were willing to offer hospitality to travelling men of letters. As is well known, when Matsuo Basho (1644–1694), one of the greatest *haiku* poets, wrote his famous "Oku-no-hosomichi," he was hosted by both wealthy merchants and rich farmers during his extensive journeys. Wherever he stayed, he was asked to give instruction in *haiku* to those who were interested in this form of short poetry. Painters also did not have much difficulty finding host families wherever they went. They were usually solicited to do their paintings on sliding doors or on scrolls to pay for their room and board, and they often stayed in a village for several months. It is no wonder that Western missionaries who visited Japan in the eighteenth century noted with amazement that "in Japan, even a peasant is a poet."

Popular education also penetrated the farming class. There were no regulations or laws regarding elementary education, but the farmers, even the poorest peasants, were willing to send their children to local private *terakoya* (literally "temple school" because the classes were usually held in Buddhist temples where monks and/or priests gave lessons in reading, writing, and arithmetic) in the hope, as R. P. Dore argues, that the children might succeed in their upward mobility. According to a historical survey, at the end of the eighteenth century, each rural community throughout the nation had at least one *terakoya* (the total number of rural communities of the period was something like 70,000). As a result, Japan became the country with the highest literacy rate early in the nineteenth century. (The literacy rate of the nation at that time is estimated at between 45 and 50 percent.)

The implication of the high literacy of the Japanese population is extremely important in understanding modern and contemporary Japanese popular culture. First, it should be noted that Japan was the first country that succeeded in forming a "mass audience" in the field of popular fiction. The publication of the popular fiction usually known as *Kibyoshi* or *Ninjobon* began to flourish in the mid-eighteenth century, and the "reading public" came into existence at that time. Such best-selling authors as Takizawa Bakin (1767–1848) sold thousands of copies, and historians claim that Bakin was the first author in the world to succeed in establishing himself as a perfectly independent writer in the sense that he earned his living solely by his royalties and honoraria from his writing activities. *Kibyoshi* and *Ninjobon* were numerous, and many people, including women, read these publications with enthusiasm, especially in urban areas.

Rapid secularization took place along with developments in literacy and artistic taste. Borrowing the dichotomy of Eliade, what had been regarded as "sacred" was transformed into something "profane." A good and typical example is *kabuki*. This theatrical form was invented by Izumo-no-Okuni (1572-?), a shaman of the Izumo Shrine, and in 1603 she gave her first secular performance in Kyoto. Furukawa Miki has shown how since then *kabuki* gradually became a popular theater. The term *kabuki* is the noun form of the verb *kabuku*, meaning "to deviate from the norm," and in its usage in the seventeenth century, *kabukimono* meant people who dressed and behaved with extreme eccentricity. In other words, *kabukimono* were the punks of the seventeenth century, and Izumo-no-Okuni was the leading figure of this eccentric group. At any rate, her performance attracted huge audiences, and the number of theatergoers increased almost explosively in the eighteenth century. Here again, an important aspect of the performing arts as represented by *kabuki* was that the theater was not monopolized by any particular social class. The majority of audiences were urban commoners, but quite a few *samurai* and wealthy farmers were also found among theatergoers.

Another example of secularization may be found in the development of *sumo*, the well-known form of Japanese wrestling. Etymologically speaking, *sumo* originally meant "simple (undressed) dance" dedicated to holy deities, and the sport used to be performed only in sacred shrines. Sometime in the fifteenth century, however, *sumo* transformed itself into a secular game where wrestlers competed in power and technique. A careful observer of *sumo* today will find the remains of the original religious ritual in the ceremonial parts of the sport, for example, the process of purification of the arena by salt and the Shintoist shrine roof hung over the arena.

The art of storytelling, as Yasutaka Teruoka (1898–   ), and others (Kazuo Sekiyama, for example) have shown, also had a sacred origin. That is to say, storytelling in Japan originated in the preaching of Buddhist missionaries. In order to make their appeal more popular, the preachers invented more attractive methods of speech. Thus, storytelling, both serious and comic, became a new form of popular entertainment. With the development of urbanization, especially in Edo (Tokyo), Osaka, and Kyoto (incidentally, these three cities were called *santo*, meaning three cities, and became one of the favorite subjects of the writers of the day), smaller theaters specializing in storytelling and vaudeville appeared as new entertainment facilities. These places were originally called *yoseba*, or "temporary gathering places," but later evolved into permanent establishments, and the original name was abbreviated as *yose*. According to historical records cited by Geinoshi Kenkyukai, there were more than 800 *yose* in Edo alone toward the end of the eighteenth century. Furthermore, as media researchers have learned in their studies, television's versions of *yose* have been constantly gaining extremely high ratings. *Yose* alone is a unique audio service that can be found only in the international flights of Japan Air Lines. Jetsetters and tourists alike enjoy this traditional popular art during their long and boring flights. It is interesting and important to note that the vaudeville performances that originated in the eighteenth century can be heard aboard one of the world's largest fleets of 747s.

Reference to 747s and package tours should remind one of the development of mass tourism in Japan, which also started in the middle of the eighteenth century. During this period, the government strictly prohibited commoners from travelling, because free physical mobility might have brought the migration of farmers from relatively poor regions to more affluent areas. However, an exception was made for those who wanted to travel for religious purposes. For example, if a merchant or a farmer submitted an application for a private tour to the Ise Shrine or a pilgrimage to the famous eighty-eight temples of Shikoku Island, such a petition was almost automatically approved since religious trips were thought to be admirable, desirable, and, at least, harmless behavior. Therefore, major shrines and temples became interested in organizing groups of people who were supposed to be devoted believers of these sacred places. In order to attract more people, secularized quasi-priests organized groups called *ko* in each community, and *ko* members travelled together to shrines and temples. Even though poor farmers could not afford the cost of travel, *ko* were organized on a mutual aid system, and people were able to join such organized trips on a rotation basis. As a result, Ise Shrine or Koyasan Temple became the equivalent of Mecca among Moslems, and people thought that they had to visit at least one of these places once in their lifetime.

Good accommodations were prepared to entertain these groups of tourists. As represented in Hiroshige's famous series of *ukiyoe* depicting the fifty-three stations of Tokaido, the major trunk road connecting Edo and Kyoto, small towns emerged along the roads of pilgrims. Of course, for many, shrine or temple worship was simply an excuse to justify their holiday trip. As is familiar to most students of popular culture and modern Japanese history, such great humorous fiction as *Tokaidochu Hizakurige* (1802–1809) by Juppensha Ikku (1765–1831) was the product of the mass tourism of the era. As a matter of fact, it is worthwhile to note that Yasumi Roan (1760-?), another popular writer and traveller, wrote *Ryoko Yojinshu* [The art of traveling] in 1810, which turned out to be one of the best-selling books at the turn of the nineteenth century. The Japanese group tour of today is world famous, sometimes even notorious, and that popular image of Japanese tourists is quite correct in many occasions; but at the same time it should be understood that such group tours have been a part of traditional popular culture and that the 747s are part of a continuity from the day of Ikku to the contemporary technological age.

These historical reflections show, in summary, three important characteristics of Japanese popular culture: (1) Japanese popular culture came into maturity during Japan's period of isolation when the nation's surplus energy found its outlet in the field of cultural activities and developments. (2) In spite of nominal class distinctions, Japan became an egalitarian society where everybody could enjoy popular culture ranging from tea ceremony to *kabuki*. (3) Popular culture in contemporary Japan should be studied as a continuous tradition dating from the Tokugawa period.

Research: The Early Years

As was mentioned in the preceding section, with the rise of the reading public, the publication business gradually developed as a pioneer of the Japanese information industry, and many authors tried to sell their books; at the very least, there were many people who liked to write. Thus, we have excellent access to the writings of the eighteenth and early nineteenth century. In the field of essays alone, for instance, there are such voluminous collections of works as *Nihon Zuihitsu Shusei* (1979) in roughly one hundred volumes of 300 pages each. Interestingly enough, quite a few authors liked to keep records of urban popular culture, and this includes *Kiyu Shouran* (1830) by Kitamura Takaniwa (1783–1856). This book was an encyclopedia of the everyday life of that era, and the author made his best efforts to clarify the origin and function of very trivial yet important objects, events, manners, and customs, ranging from housing to cosmetics, language to food habits. In the preface of this great encyclopedia, Kitamura said,

From my childhood, my only hobby has been reading books, and knowing that my ancestors left a huge library, I thought that it might be worthwhile to organize trivia. I know that ants make their nest by accumulating small bits of soil. What I am trying to do in this volume is something similar to their enterprise.

With this philosophy in mind, Kitamura started his data gathering. His style of writing was genuinely secular, yet scholarly and academic, in the sense that he was quite familiar with Japanese as well as Chinese classics; he attempted to give the definition, common usage, and etymology of each word he used. For instance, under the heading of *utage* (banquet), the author traced the usage of the word in ancient Japan as well as Korea; according to his theory, this term originated in the gathering of newlyweds with their parents. This kind of study of individual items in popular culture is a treasure trove for those who are interested in the everyday life of common people, not only of his day but also of today. It is no wonder that *Kiyu Shouran* is used as the classic and basic source book by students of popular culture research, even today.

Another important characteristic of Japanese popular culture research has been the fact that folklore in its broadest sense was fully explored by researchers, and that folklorists in this country, as represented by Yanagita Kunio (1875–1962), have worked vigorously in the field of popular culture. In his celebrated book, *Meiji Taisho Seso Shi* [A social history of the Meiji-Taisho era], Yanagita looked at the changes that took place after the Meiji Revolution (usually referred to as the "Meiji Restoration") in such everyday life areas as drinking, courtship, family life, entertainment, and so forth. Indeed, it seems that one of the features of Japanese academia was, and is, a genuine scholarly interest in everyday trivia. Thus, popular culture research in this country gained "citizenship" in intellectual circles several centuries ago.

Yanagita stated in the preface of this widely read book that "this . . . is not a history book quoting the actions and words of heroes and bigshots. I am simply concerned with the ideas and attitudes upon which common people in the country can agree, if they think a little bit about their own personal experience" (pp. 13–14). Yanagita and his students in the last few decades concentrated their efforts on studying popular practices in food habits, religion, festivals, special local occasions, changes in the consumption of alcoholic beverages, and many other miscellaneous facts by means of extensive field research. Yanagita himself, being a folklorist according to his own style, left voluminous writings about the popular belief system and finally his grand theory of cultural diffusion in East Asia. His most frequently used word was *jomin* (common people), and he never forgot the importance of the everyday life of *jomin*. In this sense, it may be safe to say that Yanagita and his group were the pioneering researchers of popular culture. As a matter of fact, Miyamoto Tsuneichi (1907–1982), one of Yanagita's students and colleagues, left an excellent study of *sarushibai*, or street entertainment performed by tamed monkeys.

As is obvious from the preceding paragraphs, folklore, or *minzokugaku*, in Japan has been slightly different from the common usage of the term in English. It is true that Yanagita borrowed, or at least hinted at, the works of Frazer and other European folklorists when they became interested in the daily lives of the *jomin*. However, their concern was not the archaic, historical, or primitive aspects of society. Their basic belief was that in order to understand Japanese society, as well as other societies, the facts of life of the *jomin* living in contemporary society were the key issue. Yanagita emphasized repeatedly the importance of this discipline by saying that the shortcoming of historians and social observers was their focus only on the elite circle. According to him, most social records in both the past and the present were more or less those of political, economic, or administrative figures; very few records of *jomin* were kept. But Yanagita claimed that throughout history it was the *jomin* who shaped and led the society at work. He says, in this connection, that to listen to "the voices of the voiceless" is the most urgent task for *minzokugaku*. In order to realize this task, he and his colleagues made extensive trips all over the country, collecting oral histories and observing the manners and customs of various parts of Japan. This group of folklorists finally compiled a handbook of field research titled *Minzokugaku Nyumon* [An introduction to folklore research] (1947), which consists of some 2,000 questions to be asked of *jomin*, rural and urban alike. Indeed, the writings of Yanagita in thirty-one volumes are a great resource book for the understanding of popular culture. Those interested in the historical roots of Japanese rituals, games, sports, and entertainments cannot afford to neglect Yanagita's work. In other works, *minzokugaku* was and still is the discipline from which modern popular culture research emerged.

Another name that should be introduced as a pioneer in the field of popular culture research is Kon Wajiro (1888–1973). Trained as a graphic designer in his youth, Kon became interested in recording miscellaneous yet important aspects of the lives of his Japanese contemporaries in visual form. For example, he was the first artist who kept records of the floor plans of farm houses as well as slum areas of Tokyo. He also made detailed studies of the possessions of these people. He counted the kinds and numbers of clothes, kitchenware, furniture, and other household materials by direct observation, and made wonderful drawings of these items. He was fascinated by the way people lived, and coined a new word, "modernology." According to him, just as archaeologists dig archaic remains from underground, "modernologists" follow their discipline by digging into the everyday life of their contemporaries, in both their material culture and their behavior patterns.

In order to prove the importance of modernology, Kon explored many new innovative methodologies, and his most famous work was done in the Ginza, the busiest shopping street of Tokyo in the early 1930s. In this study, for example, he spent all day in a coffeeshop watching the attire of the people passing by: the number of men wearing hats, the number of women in kimonos, the number of umbrellas, handbags, and their combinations. All were counted and each percentage was calculated. Being an artist, he did not use a camera. Instead he used his sketchbook, and left huge numbers of quick and yet precise sketches of what he saw. His most interesting study, however, was what is known as the "private eye" method of social observation. He picked up a person on the street at random, and chased after this person for hours to see what one did in the Ginza. A middle-aged lady, for example, started her rambling by window shopping at a jewelry store, stopping there for three minutes. Then she crossed the street to pay a visit to a department store, first in the kimono section, then in the houseware section where she purchased three tea cups. After the department store, she went to the ticketing office of a theater just to take a look at the posters and the price of tickets. Kon followed her until she took a bus, probably to go back home. For each stop of his "silent informant," he carefully and accurately took memos on her use of time and space as well as the amount of money she spent. Kon also conducted time and space research vis-à-vis crowd behavior in the Ginza by counting the number of people in each street intersection by the time of the day and the days of the week, in the hope that he might be able to find regularities in the street life of urban populations.

These direct observational records in themselves did not have any immediate sociological significance, but Kon had a firm belief that the behavior of people is indicative of the day and that observational records could be good historical data. His data, partially used by William Whyte in the late 1970s for comparative research (in Kato's *A Comparative Study of Street Life*), were another milestone in the history of popular culture study in Japan.

Quite apart from Yanagita's *minzokugaku* and Kon's "modernology," another classic of popular culture research appeared in the 1920s, by a scholar whose original discipline was the German language. His name was Gonda Yasunosuke (1887-1951), and his works are still quoted by most scholars in popular culture research as well as mass media studies. As a matter of fact, Gonda was the first scholar who paid proper and serious attention to the effects of movies.

In his representative work, *Minshu Goraku Mondai* [The problems of popular entertainment], published in 1920, he studied the number of people attending theaters in Tokyo from 1902 through 1918 and discovered that the number of the annual total audience increased from 8 to 21 million in these seventeen years. He was struck by the fact that attendance at live theaters had declined as the overwhelming part of the audience by the late 1910s were movie fans. Indeed, according to the statistics, it was clear that the absolute numbers of the audience in live theaters, including *yose*, declined drastically despite the increase in the total number of theatergoers. In other words, theaters in the late 1910s meant almost automatically "movie theaters" rather than traditional "live theaters."

Gonda further found that, in contrast to traditional theaters, movie theaters were full of young people, including elementary school children. These facts made Gonda very much concerned with the sociocultural effects of this new audiovisual medium of mass communications. With this problem in mind, he conducted the first audience survey in 1917 by the questionnaire method, soliciting the cooperation of thirty-one elementary school principals. Altogether, he obtained responses from some 12,000 children and found that, without a single exception, the children were familiar with movies and that they were exposed to the media as early as the age of six. The frequency of moviegoing, on average, was found to be approximately once a month, but Gonda discovered that, though the number was small, there were "heavy viewers" who attended movie theaters more than three times a week. In order to find a possible correlation between movies and juvenile delinquency, he further studied major juvenile detention homes in Tokyo and its vicinity and found that considerable numbers of the young people in these facilities were heavy viewers of movies. In extreme cases, there were a few who told him that they indulged themselves in movie theaters all day every day, skipping their schoolwork. At the same time, when he interviewed the children in the detention homes, Gonda learned that 27 percent of them said that they were influenced by movies before they committed minor crimes such as stealing or shoplifting. Thus, Gonda concluded that, in spite of the great potential of movies for educational purpose, this new form of entertainment might pose a new social problem, especially among the youth.

It is true that modern methodologies of social research were not introduced when Gonda conducted his survey, and a sociologist today might argue about the validity of his data, but it is surprising that such large-scale audience research was done at the turn of the century, and that it was done by a scholar whose major interest was the German language, and not popular culture research.

Gonda, however, was extremely sympathetic toward popular culture phenomena, partly because of a populist attitude derived from his interest in Marxism (while studying the German language and linguistics, he encountered Marxian economists who were reading the works of Marx and Engels in German) and partly because of his own urban background. He repeatedly remarked in his writings that, with the rise of movies and other modern entertainment, the arts were liberated from the monopoly of the rich and that a new era of popular culture, which was shared by the masses, was coming. Essentially, he believed in the great potential of this emerging new cultural trend supported by the common sense of the people. With the money, which was not a great fortune, that he earned from his renowned *Gonda's German Japanese Dictionary*, he performed extensive field work. He interviewed various popular entertainers, visited movie districts of major cities, and observed the menus of inexpensive restaurants to learn the details of the "eating out" habits of lower-class people. His energetic studies were compiled in the four volumes of the *Selected Works of Yasunosuke Gonda* by his admirers in 1974 with annotations so that popular culture students today can appreciate Gonda's pioneering and extraordinarily suggestive work.

Another important contribution to popular culture studies was made by Ohya Souchi (1900–1970), a freelance journalist and social critic who was also interested in observing the everyday life of the people. As a graduate of Tokyo University, where he majored in sociology, Ohya was interested in various aspects of the lives of the common people. Among his numerous writings, a reader will easily locate many essays written from the 1930s to the 1960s related to popular culture at large. He did, for example, a study of historical changes in the lyrics of popular songs as the reflection of the sociocultural environments of each period. Ohya also was a very talented participant-observer and a great investigative reporter who utilized imaginative journalistic techniques. One of his earlier works included a collection of the records of taxicab passengers at midnight. In order to learn what middle-class men talk about in taxicabs, he disguised himself as an assistant to the driver (thanks to an earlier model of the Ford, which required extra hands) and listened to what passengers in the back seat said to each other, or sometimes what they talked about to Ohya, who pretended to be an honest young assistant to the driver. By doing so, he did marvelous work on "the topics of the town." In the postwar period, he continued to work in the same style. Through his connections with underground organizations, he succeeded in sneaking into one of the illegal gambling spots in Tokyo and published his findings. When striptease became a new genre of popular entertainment, he went to those theaters and, without hesitation, rushed backstage to interview the performers, asking about their backgrounds as well as their observations of the audience from the stage. He sometimes claimed that he was the John Gunther of Japan and said that most of his works were the pieces of his own *Inside Japan*.

In 1953, when television was introduced to Japan, Ohya took a very critical and serious attitude toward the media, and published his well-known "peanuts theory of TV." According to his observations as well as his own experience, television watching is similar to having a bowl of peanuts on the table. A person usually continues almost unconsciously to pick up peanuts and eat until the bowl becomes empty. Likewise, once the switch is on, a person usually continues to watch television, and scarcely turns it off regardless of what is on the screen. Ohya said that television was an addictive information machine, and since many of the programs were, in his judgment, sheer nonsense, he predicted that if the Japanese people became television addicts, they might be in danger of becoming a collection of fools. Thus, he coined the phrase "one-hundred-million-fool-making effect" (100 million meant the whole population of the country), which was borrowed by hundreds of journalists, critics, and scholars, either supportively or negatively, for years. Ohya sometimes defined his ideological position as "an

irresponsible social observer,'' but his keen insights and interpretations stimulated a concern about popular culture phenomena in contemporary Japan.

These reflections lead to the following summarized statements: (1) Intellectual
interest in popular culture in Japan can be traced back as far as the late nineteenth
century, when scholars and writers had an enthusiastic interest in the everyday
affairs of common people. Such a trend was accelerated by urbanization, especially in the three cities of Edo (Tokyo), Kyoto, and Osaka. (2) Popular culture
studies and research were conducted by scholars with diverse backgrounds. They
were, more or less, detached from orthodox academia, but their contributions
have been properly appreciated and evaluated in academic circles. (3) The facts
and data related to popular culture recorded by these pioneers are still valuable
sources in popular culture studies, and, for those who are interested in Japanese
popular culture research, their works should not be neglected. Popular culture
researchers in Japan today are well aware of the importance of the intellectual
tradition in this field in the last two centuries.

Research: Today

As was indicated in the preceding paragraphs, Japanese culture, especially
urban culture, came into maturity during the period of isolation, a time when
Japan also developed its high literacy and experienced a notable growth of the
arts. Contemporary Japanese popular culture can be seen as a continuation of
developments that began in the eighteenth century. Indeed, *kabuki* theaters still
attract millions of people every year. *Yose*, in spite of Gonda's warning, also
still survive, though the number has declined with the diffusion of radio and
television. Artistic practice among amateurs, *haiku*, for instance, is more popular
than ever. Millions of Japanese who enjoy *haiku* write to sections of newspapers
devoted totally to this poetic contest every week. Or one may argue that photography, a world-famous pastime of the Japanese people, is a contemporary
version of *haiku* in the sense that each snapshot is a visual presentation of the
photographer's sentiment and feeling at a particular time and place. Though the
forms of presentation are different, both *haiku* and a photographic snapshot are
aesthetic expressions of a person, and, most important, such expressive behavior
is shared by the whole population of the country. In the nightspots where the
geisha entertained their guests in the past, today one will find charming hostesses
in bars and nightclubs as their replacement, though their contemporary counterparts are not as talented in the arts of music or poetry. The point here is that,
though seemingly new, Japanese popular culture today is a historical product
and that a student in this field must look into the continuities of popular culture
in their historical context.

As a matter of fact, Japan is a country of popular culture in the sense that the
society has been essentially not only homogeneous but also egalitarian for at
least the past two centuries. In his well-known popular fiction, *Ukiyoburo* [A
story of a public bath] (1809), Shikitei Samba (1776–1822) stressed the fact that

in a public bath, where people enjoy the hot air and water totally naked, a man is simply a man regardless of his social status. He says, "A public bath makes everybody equal. Nobody can discern a *samurai* from a garbage collector, a wealthy merchant from a poor peasant," and Samba's philosophy has been well accepted by the public in both past and present. Though the concept of "equality" in the sense of Western intellectual history was alien when the idea was introduced after the Meiji Revolution, Japan developed its own unique view on "equality" as represented by *Ukiyoburo*.

Egalitarianism in Japan has been dramatically accelerated in the last forty years in the process of "democratization." In the first place, through radical land reform, without a single exception, the agrarian population in Japan became independent farmers, even though the size of the average land holding is very small. In other words, the traditional landlord-tenant relationship in rural communities has totally disappeared. With the rise of small independent farmers, middle-class consciousness came to prevail even in small local villages.

In addition to the emergence of millions of independent farmers, the development of the mass media coupled with the improvement of the transportation infrastructure made existing urban-rural cultural gaps disappear. In Japan today, one cannot find much difference between a central metropolitan area and a small island several hundred miles away from any major island of the Japanese archipelago. Various commodities are distributed nationwide, and the broadcast media cover every corner of the country. In the past, those who lived deep in the mountains, which cover 70 percent of the total land surface of Japan, were handicapped and underprivileged, sometimes even deprived, economically, socially, and culturally. Now, thanks to technological innovations, they can enjoy the same conveniences and advantages as city people.

Another equalizing effect came from the diffusion of higher education, as Kato demonstrates in *Education and Youth Employment in Japan*. In the past, major universities were concentrated in large urban areas. For instance, the old Imperial universities were found only in seven cities, namely, Sapporo, Sendai, Tokyo, Nagoya, Kyoto, Osaka, and Fukuoka. However, under the new educational reform, national universities were established in each prefecture, so that young high school graduates everywhere could have the opportunity of a university education. It should also be noted here that in Japan today senior high school education is almost compulsory (98 percent of junior high graduates go to senior high, and the dropout ratio is almost negligible). As was mentioned before, the Japanese population was quite literate by the eighteenth century, and the new education reform of 1946 raised its literacy raised its literacy to one of the highest levels in the world. If popular culture is the product of mass society in which the traditional dichotomy between elite and mass does not have much significance, then Japan probably can be defined as a country of popular culture.

In addition to the "equalization" brought by agrarian and educational reforms, there is another important factor that makes the society more egalitarian—an extremely progressive income tax. In Japan today, personal income is classified into twenty-two brackets, probably the most differentiated system of categorization in the world, and those whose income is in the top bracket have more than 70 percent of their income taken by the internal revenue agency. For example, a business executive whose annual salary is 15 million yen (approximately 120,000 dollars) takes home only 50 percent of his nominal income. On the other hand, a young secretary-typist who earns 2.5 million yen (20,000 dollars) pays some 10 percent of her income as tax. In other words, an executive in his fifties earns only three or, at best, four times more than a young employee in her twenties (or even late teens) if personal income is considered in substantial terms. Democratization of income distribution in Japan, in this sense, is extraordinary, and its result is obvious. In short, what happened in Japan in the last twenty years resulted in the dominance of middle class consciousness.

According to annual public opinion surveys conducted by the Prime Minister's Office, the number of those Japanese who think of themselves as belonging to the middle class has increased every year, and in 1984 more than 90 percent of the Japanese responded that they were the members of the middle-class. Needless to say, responses to this type of public opinion research are essentially subjective, but it is worthwhile to note here that a small farmer as well as a business executive, a service station attendant along with a college professor, feel equally that they belong to the middle class.

There are reasons on their part to justify their middle-class consciousness or awareness. Their income level is close to the national average, which is made public by the Economic Planning Board or other government agencies, though the amount a person earns could be a little more or less than average. Without exception they have at least a senior high school diploma, which assures them that they are average Japanese. They have a standard set of durable goods, another token of middle class–ness, which includes a refrigerator, a vacuum cleaner, a stereo, a television, a small automobile, and more recently a videotape deck. The material possessions of a factory foreman are essentially the same as those of the prime minister. Therefore, the Japanese declare without doubt or hesitation that they *are* middle-class people.

Of course, there are a few who are slightly skeptical about their identification with the middle class. Some think that they cannot be middle class until they become independent homeowners rather than tenants in a housing project. Others may feel that the real middle class comprises university graduates, while others may think that their cars are too old and that such automobiles are not becoming to the middle class. On the other hand, there may be a relatively wealthy group of people who are afraid that they may not be middle class simply because they have bigger houses or better cars than the average. But, generally speaking, the majority of the Japanese people today feel that they are middle class.

Of course, either implicitly or explicitly, class distinctions in terms of behavior patterns, artistic taste, kinds of magazines read, wardrobe, or use of language can be discovered if the public is carefully examined. However, everybody in Japan today is the recipient of and audience for popular culture. For instance, baseball, *sumo*, and other sports are enjoyed and appreciated by millions of people regardless of their social status or educational background. It is not strange to see, for instance, a senior vice president of a large firm enjoy his conversation on the scores of professional baseball games of the previous day with the driver of his limousine on his way to his office. Indeed, Paul Fussell's hypothetical figures called "X People," introduced in his witty book, *Class*, also seem to exist among upper-class Japanese today.

A good example of such trends, or even efforts, can be observed in group pleasure trips to hot springs, a common practice among business firms in Japan. The major purpose of this kind of trip, usually for one or two nights, under the name of "workshop" or "employees' welfare," is to make sure that everybody in the organization feels equal. In a huge banquet room, top management consciously mixes with newly recruited junior clerks, drinking together, singing together, and sometimes even sharing a room. On these occasions juniors are allowed to tease seniors, and vice versa, so that they can reconfirm their equality and solidarity as human beings. Not only on these special occasions, but also in daily office life, the egalitarian philosophy is at work. The same company cafeteria is used by both the president of the firm and by factory workers, and their topic of conversation, again, is *sumo* or favorite popular singers. In this sense, Japanese popular culture today may have the function of a social cement that closes the gaps between upper class and lower middle class, between highly educated and high school graduates, and sometimes even between male and female.

Interestingly enough, in Japanese society intellectual snobbery is almost nil. Of course, there are the minority who have high artistic taste, that is, are "highbrow." But "high-brows" in this country are also very knowledgeable about popular culture. It is a commonplace scene, at a bar at midnight, for a university professor or a high court judge to sing a popular song with a carpenter or taxicab driver. Such snobbery as "conspicuous non-ownership of television," which Reuel Denney brilliantly interpreted years ago, is totally alien in Japanese society. It is quite probable the spirit and philosophy of *Ukiyoburo* is still in action in contemporary Japan. Popular culture in this country is *the* culture that is shared by every single individual. In this sense, a new scope and perspective are needed to study not only the popular culture phenomena of Japan but also popular culture research methodology.

A new wave in popular culture research in Japan seems to be emerging, partly inheriting the tradition established by Yanagita, Kon, Gonda, Kitamura, and others and partly stimulated by mass media research that was introduced from the United States in the postwar period. At the same time, the populism that Gonda expressed in his work is another factor encouraging "progressive" scholars from such disciplines as sociology, psychology, political science, and literature to work on popular culture issues. Indeed, there was a group called the "Science of Thought" (see Shunsuke Tsurumi) that devoted much of its energy in the 1950s to popular culture study. This group consisted of intellectuals, mostly university professors, who felt that they were obliged to understand the everyday interests of the common people, or *jomin*, in order to establish real democracy in Japan. In this sense, popular culture research in Japan in the earlier postwar period, had, more or less, a political tone. As a matter of fact, left-wing political parties in the 1950s, while criticizing money-making capitalist popular culture as possibly another form of the suppression and exploitation of the proletariat, encouraged "productive" and "democratic" popular culture so that the lives of working-class people could be improved and that the proletariat could be prepared to fight with the capitalist system.

At the same time, scholars in academia also began to show interest in popular culture, especially when mass communications and journalism became part of the social science curriculum in colleges and universities. A few sociologists and anthropologists started ambitious and unique projects such as the sociology of bars (Kouri Takada), the sociology of *bonsai* (Nozomu Ikei), and the anthropology of housing (Naoki Sugimoto). In the initial phase, there was criticism from conservative and traditional social scientists, but by the 1980s these seemingly deviant research projects had been accorded recognition in academia.

Summarizing the results of the previous discussion, it may be safe to say that: (1) Japan has been an egalitarian country, though the origin and nature of the philosophy are somewhat different from those of Western countries. Japanese egalitarianism was accelerated by the reforms of the postwar period. (2) The Japanese population is extremely homogeneous, and the gaps between social classes are probably much narrower than in other societies. (3) On the part of the elite in Japan, there seems to be less class consciousness and anxiety. They usually do not have much psychological and ideological resistance to popular culture. (4) In conclusion, Japanese popular culture is unique, and its research methodology requires that special consideration be given to this singularity.

BIBLIOGRAPHY

Craig, Albert M., and Donald H. Shively. *Personality in Japanese History*. Berkeley: University of California Press, 1970.

Denney, Reuel. *The Astonished Muse*. Rev. ed. Chicago: University of Chicago Press, 1975.

Dore, R. P. *Aspects of Social Change in Modern Japan*. Princeton: Princeton University Press, 1967.

———. *City Life in Japan*. Berkeley: University of California Press, 1958.

Furukawa, Miki. *Misemono no Rekishi* [A history of street shows]. Tokyo: Yusankaku Shuppan, 1970.

古河三樹　「見世物の歴史」　東京　雄山閣出版社　１９７０．

Fussell, Paul. *Class*. New York: Summit, 1983.

Geinoshi Kenkyukai. *Yose* [Vaudeville]. Tokyo: Heibonsha, 1971.

藝能史研究会　「寄席」　東京　平凡社　１９７１．

Gonda, Yasunosuke. *Gonda Yasunosuke Chosakushu* [Selected works of Yasunosuke Gonda]. Tokyo: Bunwa Shobo, 1974–1975.

権田保之助　「権田保之助著作集」　東京　文和書房
　１９７４−１９７５．

Ikei, Nozomu. *Bonsai no Shakaigaku* [Sociology of bonsai]. Kyoto: Seikai Shisosha, 1978.

池井望 「盆栽の社会学」 東京 世界思想社 １９７８．

Japan Culture Institute. *Great Historical Figures of Japan*. Tokyo: Japan Culture Institute, 1978.

Juppensha, Ikku. *Tokkaidochu Hizakurige* [Two men's travel on the Tokkaido]. 1802–1899; rpt. Tokyo: Kodansha International, 1978.

十返舎一九 「東海道中膝栗毛」 東京 講談社 １９７８．

Kato, Hidetoshi. *A Comparative Study of Street Life*. Tokyo: Gakushuin Daigaku Toyo Bunka Kenkyusho, 1978.

———. *Education and Youth Employment in Japan*. Berkeley: University of California Press, 1978.

———. *Toshi to Goraku* [Cities and entertainment]. Tokyo: Kashima Kenkyujo Shuppankai, 1967.

加藤秀俊 「都市と娯楽」 東京 鹿島研究所出版会 １９６９．

Kitamura, Takaniwa. *Kiyu Shouran* [An encyclopedia of miscellany]. 1830; rpt. Tokyo: Yoshikawa Kobunkan, 1958.

喜多村タカニワ 「嬉遊笑覧」 東京 古川弘文館 １９５８．

Kon, Wajirou. *Kon Wajirou Shu* [Selected writings of Wajirou Kon]. Tokyo: Domesu Shuppan, 1971–1972.

今和次部 「今和次部集」 東京 ドメス出版 １９７１－１９７２．

Kotaka, Yoshisaburo. *Nihon no Yugi* [Games of Japan]. Tokyo: Haneda Shoten, 1943.

小高吉三郎 「日本の遊戯」 東京 羽田書店 １９４３．

Matsuo, Basho. *Oku no Hosomichi* [A travelogue in the Tohoku area]. 1694; rpt. Tokyo: Iwanami Shoten, 1959.

松尾芭蕉 「奥の細道」 東京 岩波書店 １９５９

Miyamoto, Mataji. *Kansai to Kanto* [Japan: East and West]. Tokyo: Aogaeru Shobo, 1966.

宮本又次 「関西と関東」 東京 青蛙房 １９６６．

Miyamoto, Tsuneichi. *Miyamoto Tsuneichi Chosakushu* [Writings of Tsuneichi Miyamoto]. Tokyo: Miraisha, 1968–1977.

宮本常一 「宮本常一著作集」 東京 未来社 １９６８－１９７７．

Nihon Zuihitsu Taisei Henshu-Bu, ed. *Nihon Zuihitsu Taisei* [Collection of Japanese essays]. Tokyo: Yoshikawa Kobunkan, 1973–1979.

「日本随筆大成」 東京 吉川古文館 １９７３－１９７９・

Ohya, Souichi. *Ohya Souichi Zenshu* [Writings of Souichi Ohya]. Tokyo: Soyosho, 1980–1982.

大宅壮一 「大宅壮一全集」 東京 蒼洋社 １９８０－１９８２．

Plath, David W. *Long Engagements*. Stanford: Stanford University Press, 1980.

Shikitei, Samba. *Ukiyoburo* [A Story of public bath]. 1809; rpt. Tokyo: 1957.

式亭三馬 「浮世風呂」 東京 岩波書店 １９５７．

Sourifu, Kouhoshitsu. *Gekkan Yoron Chousa* [Monthly public opinion surveys]. Tokyo: Sourifu Kouhoshitsu, May 1984.

総理府公報室 「月刊世論調査」 東京 総理府公報室 ５月、１９８４

Sugimoto, Naoji. *Nihon no Sumai no Genryu* [The origins of Japanese housing]. Tokyo, 1984.

杉本尚次編 「日本のすまいの原流」 東京 文化出版局 １９８４．

Takada, Kouri. *Sakaba no Shakaigaku* [Sociology of drinking establishments. Kyoto, 1983.
高田公理 「酒場の社会学」 京都 ＰＨＰ研究所 １９８３．

Teruoka, Yasutaka. *Rakugo no Nenrin* [A history of comic arts]. Tokyo, 1973.
暉峻康隆 「落語の年輪」 東京 講談社 １９７３．

Tsurumi, Shunsuke. *Dojidai* [The common age]. Tokyo, 1971.
鶴見俊輔 「同時代」 東京 １９７１．

―――. *Gendai Nihon no Shiso* [Modern ideas of Japan]. Tokyo: 1967.
鶴見俊輔 「現代日本の思想」 東京 １９６７．

―――. *Genkai Geizyutsuron* [Theory of marginal arts]. Tokyo: 1967.
鶴見俊輔 「限界芸術論」 東京 １９６７．

―――. *Hokubei Taiken Saikou* [Memories of North American experiences]. Tokyo, 1971.
鶴見俊輔 「北米体験再考」 東京 １９７１．

―――. *Manga no Sengo Shiso* [Post-war ideas in comics]. Tokyo, 1973.
鶴見俊輔 「漫画の戦後思想」 東京 １９７３．

―――. *Ryu Souetsu* [Ryu Souetsu]. Tokyo, 1976.
鶴見俊輔 「柳宗悦」 東京 １９７６．

―――. *Sengo Nihon no Taishu Bunkashi* [A history of post-war popular culture]. Tokyo, 1984.
鶴見俊輔 「戦後日本の大衆文化」 東京 岩波書店 １９８４．

―――. *Takano Choei* [Takano Choei]. Tokyo: 1975.
鶴見俊輔 「高野長英」 東京 １９７５．

―――. *Tsurumi Shunsuke Chosaku Shu* [The collection of Shunsuke Tsurumi]. Tokyo, 1975–1976.
鶴見俊輔 「鶴見俊輔著作集」 東京 １９７５－１９７６．

―――. *Watashi no Chiheisen no Ue ni* [My viewpoint]. Tokyo, 1956.
鶴見俊輔 「私の地平線の上に」 東京 １９５６．

Yanagita, Kunio. *Meiji Taisho* [A social history of the Meiji-Taisho era]. Tokyo, 1931.
柳田国男 「明治大正史（世相篇）」 東京 朝日新聞社 １９３１．

Yanagita, Kunio, and Seki Keigo, eds. *Minzokugaku Nyumon* [An introduction to folklore research]. Tokyo: Toyodo, 1947.
柳田国男、 関敬吾共著 「日本民俗学入門」 東京 東洋堂
　　１９４７．

Yasumi, Roan. *Ryoko Yojinshu* [The art of traveling]. Ed. Kato Hidetoshi. Tokyo: Chuo Kouronsha, 1972.
八隅庵ロアン 「旅行用心集」 東京 八坂書房 １９７２．

Index

About the Contributors

THEODORE C. BESTOR is an Assistant Professor of Anthropology and East Asian Studies at Columbia University. From 1983 through 1985, he served as Program Director for Japanese and Korean Studies at the Social Science Research Council. He has spent five years in Japan conducting research on contemporary urban life. He received his doctorate in anthropology and a master's in Asian studies from Stanford University, and did his undergraduate work at Fairhaven College. His book *Neighborhood Tokyo* was published in 1988.

H. BYRON EARHART is Professor of Religion at Western Michigan University, where he was named a Distinguished Faculty Scholar. He studied at the University of Chicago under Mircea Eliade, Joseph Kitagawa, and Charles Long, and completed his dissertation on Haguro Shugendo, which was published by Sophia University (*Monumenta Nipponica*) and translated into Japanese and published by Kobundo. He has written two widely used texts on Japanese religion and is editor of a nine-volume series, *Religious Traditions of the World*. His earlier research on Japanese New Religions resulted in a bibliography published by Sophia University (*Monumenta Nipponica*) and in a second edition by Michigan's Center of Japanese Studies. A joint study of the Japanese New Religion Gedatsu-kai with Hitoshi Miyake was the basis for a volume of essays (in Japanese) edited by Miyake and Earhart, published by Meicho. Earhart's monograph on Gedatsu-kai (in English) is in preparation.

LINDA FUJIE received the Ph.D. degree in ethnomusicology from Columbia University, specializing in the music of Japan and music in the urban context. Her publications include articles appearing in the *Yearbook for Traditional Music* and in Japanese journals that concern Shinto festival music as it is performed in modern-day urban settings. She has conducted field work primarily in New York City and in Japan. In addition to her interest in Japanese popular music in relation to present-day Japanese society, Fujie's current research interests include the folk performing arts of Japan, the music of Asian-Americans, and the traditional music of Maine. She currently teaches ethnomusicology and East Asian studies as an Assistant Professor at Colby College in Waterville, Maine.

ELIZABETH ANNE HULL has for the last fifteen years taught science fiction at William Rainey Harper College in Palatine, Illinois. With her husband, Frederik Pohl, she recently coedited *Tales from the Planet Earth*, an anthology of science fiction stories from seventeen countries. Editor of the *SFRA Newsletter* from 1981 to 1984, she is currently Secretary of SFRA and has been active in World SF (Editor of the *World SF Newsletter*, 1980 to present) and the International Conference on the Fantastic in the Arts. She cochaired the science fiction/fantasy sessions for the Popular Culture Association (1975–1977) and helped establish the Science Fiction section of the Midwest MLA. A frequent contributor to *Locus*, *Science Fiction Chronicle*, *Extrapolation*, and *Fantasy Review*, her latest fiction is "Second Best Friend" in *Aboriginal SF* (December 1986).

HIDETOSHI KATO, who has published twenty-six books in the fields of communications, popular culture, social issues, and literature, is currently Professor of Sociology at the University of the Air in Chiba, Japan. He has taught in the Faculty of Law, Gakushin University, as well as at Stanford, Grinnell, Kent (England), Kyoto, Doshisha, and the Chinese University at Hong Kong. He is the Director of the Research Institute for Oriental Cultures, and a fellow or member of the board of the Central Education Board of the Japanese Ministry of Education, the Japan Association, the East-West Center, and the Rockefeller and Ford Foundations. Kato has represented the Japanese government at many international conferences, and has conducted field work in Japan, Canada, England, the United States, New Zealand, and the South Pacific Islands. His collected works in twelve volumes were published in 1981.

JOHN A. LENT has studied and written about Asian mass communications since 1964. He is the author or editor of twenty-eight books and monographs and hundreds of journal articles concerning Third World (Asian and Caribbean, more specifically) media. His latest works are *Comic Art: An International Bibliography* and *Global Guide to Media and Communications*. Professor Lent, who is a Third World media consultant living in Drexel Hill, Pennsylvania, teaches at Temple University, and was the first Coordinator of the Mass Communications Program in Malaysia in 1972–1974 and a Fulbright scholar to the Philippines.

WILLIAM R. MAY is a candidate for the doctor of philosophy degree at the University of Illinois Institute of Communications Research and a sports writer for the Kyodo News Agency in Tokyo. His dissertation, a cultural history of Japan's English-language press, will be an examination of the system of values and meanings that have guided Japanese English-language journalism for 120 years. Away from the dissertation, he is currently pursuing a critical re-evaluation of the social and cultural aspects of sports in Japan and an interest in the relationship between international sport and international communication. He, along with Japanese sport sociologist Mamoru Suzuki, collaborated on a chapter for *Global Ritual: Olympic Media Coverage and International Understanding*, a research report submitted to UNESCO by Michael Real in July 1985.

KEIKO I. MCDONALD was born in Nara, Japan, and received her graduate education in the United States. She is Associate Professor of Japanese/Comparative Literature and Cinema at the University of Pittsburgh. Her publications include *Cinema East: A Critical Study of Major Japanese Films* (1983), *Mizuguchi* (1984), and numerous articles on both Japanese cinema and literature. Her current project is a book entitled *Japanese Classical Theater in Films*.

RENATO A. PIROTTA resides in Tokyo where he is an architect and architectural consultant for Japanese companies. He is a member of the boards of the German East Asiatic Society and the International Christian Youth Exchange Programme. He has studied architecture at the Tokyo National University of Fine Arts and Music and has lectured at the city of Luzern in Switzerland on design and materials. He is now doing research on historical and modern heating systems in Japan.

RICHARD GID POWERS was a Fulbright Professor at the University of Hiroshima in 1976–1977 and 1987–1988. A Professor of History and American Studies at the City University of New York's College of Staten Island, he is the editor of the *Journal of International Popular Culture* and has edited many publications in the fields of American and international popular culture. He is the author of *G-Men: Hoover's FBI in American Popular Culture* and *Secrecy and Power: The Life of J. Edgar Hoover*.

MARK SIEGEL, formerly an Associate Professor of English at the University of Wyoming, has specialized in popular culture, popular fiction, film, and contemporary American fiction, publishing seven books and over sixty articles in those areas and others. He spent two years as Distinguished Visiting Professor of American Culture at Osaka University in Japan. Shortly after being elected Acting Head of the English Department at the University of Wyoming in 1985, he left academia.

BRUCE STRONACH is an Assistant Professor of Political Science at Merrimack College. His research and teaching interests are in Japanese-American political and cultural relations, Japanese politics, and Japanese modern culture. Current work in progress includes a paper on the problems of Japanese-American university relations and a book on the effect of cultural differences on Japanese-American economic and political relations. Dr. Stronach received his Ph.D. from the Fletcher School of Law and Diplomacy and served as a Visiting Researcher and Visiting Lecturer at Keio University.

KAZUO YOSHIDA is Professor of Comparative Culture at Kyoto Sango University. His principal fields are American and Japanese popular culture. He has travelled extensively in Europe, Asia, and North America, and has lived and gathered data in the United States for seven years. He is the author of *Ibunka Sesshoku Saizensen* [On two cultures: American and Japanese]. He is now working on the American cowboy myth and Japanese popular culture.

MUNEO JAY YOSHIKAWA is Associate Professor of Japanese Language and Culture at the University of Hawaii. His research has focused on Japanese and American modes of communication, Japanese language and culture learning, and the development of a theoretical model for intercultural communication. He is coauthor of *Japanese Language and Culture for Business*, and has published articles in *International and Intercultural Annals, Vol. 2, Communication Theory: Eastern and Western Perspectives, Modern Language Journal*, and *Communication and Cognition*, among others.